THE AEGEAN FROM BRONZE AGE
TO IRON AGE

Following Oliver Dickinson's successful *The Aegean Bronze Age*, *The Aegean from Bronze Age to Iron Age* is an up-to-date synthesis of the period between the collapse of the Bronze Age civilisation in the thirteenth and twelfth centuries BC, and the great advances towards Greek civilisation in the eighth century BC.

Breaking away from outmoded theories which give undue credit to Athens for Greek development, Dickinson offers a fresh examination of the latest material and archaeological evidence and forms the compelling argument that many characteristics of Ancient Greece developed in the Dark Ages.

In accessible thematic chapters, this highly informative text considers the structure and economy of the early Iron Age communities, their crafts, burial customs, external contact, trade and religion, with a separate chapter on the Postpalatial period, and comments on the relevance of Homer, revealing:

- the reasons for the Bronze Age collapse, bringing about the Dark Ages
- the processes that enabled Greece to emerge from the Dark Ages
- the degree of continuity from the Dark Ages to later times.

Including chapter bibliographies, distribution maps and new illustrations, this book will prove to be essential reading for students and specialists alike, as well as an illuminating read for the interested general reader. This is an authoritative survey of the period from a leader in the field.

Dr Oliver Dickinson recently retired as Reader Emeritus from the Department of Classics and Ancient History, University of Durham, where he taught from 1976–2005. He is a specialist in Greek prehistory.

THE AEGEAN FROM BRONZE AGE TO IRON AGE

Continuity and change between the
twelfth and eighth centuries BC

Oliver Dickinson

Routledge
Taylor & Francis Group

LONDON AND NEW YORK

First published 2006
by Routledge
2 Park Square, Milton Park, Abingdon, Oxon, OX14 4RN

Simultaneously published in the USA and Canada
by Routledge
270 Madison Ave, New York NY 10016

Routledge is an imprint of the Taylor & Francis Group, an informa business

Transferred to Digital Printing 2011

© 2006 Oliver Dickinson

Typeset in Garamond 3 by
RefineCatch Limited, Bungay, Suffolk

British Library Cataloguing in Publication Data
A catalogue record for this book is available from the British Library

Library of Congress Cataloging in Publication Data
A catalog record for this book has been requested

ISBN10: 0–415–13589–3 (hbk)
ISBN10: 0–415–13590–7 (pbk)
ISBN10: 0–203–96836–0 (ebk)

ISBN13: 978–0–415–13589–4 (hbk)
ISBN13: 978–0–415–13590–0 (pbk)
ISBN13: 978–0–203–96836–9 (ebk)

Dedicated to the memory of Dorothea Gray and Vincent Desborough, my mentors in Homeric and Early Iron Age archaeology; Mervyn Popham, who encouraged me to study the Protogeometric material from Lefkandi; Bill McDonald, who offered me the opportunity to participate in the excavations at Nichoria; and Willy Coulson and Cindy Martin, valued colleagues at Nichoria.

CONTENTS

ILLUSTRATIONS

Figures

Tables

PREFACE

This book essentially shares the purpose of *The Aegean Bronze Age* (hereafter Dickinson 1994a), to provide a short introductory survey, as up to date as possible, of a period in Greek prehistory, in this case that commonly termed the Dark Age. This is generally considered to take in most or all of the five centuries 1200–700 BC (all subsequent dating references will be BC unless otherwise specified), a period that has increasingly been perceived to play a pivotal role in the long-term processes of Greek development, since it represents the transition between two very different forms of civilisation. The collapse of the Bronze Age civilisations at the beginning of the period meant the end of a sophisticated system of social organisation that had dominated the leading regions of the Aegean for centuries, and it has generally been taken to involve a good deal more, the uprooting and dispersal of whole populations and the reduction of surviving communities throughout the Aegean to small and impoverished villages, which at best had only intermittent contact with a wider world. How these communities were able to rebuild themselves and establish the very different civilisation of later Greece, and how much this owed to developments in the intervening period, have been scholarly preoccupations for a long time.

Since the 1970s, when three seminal studies were written (Snodgrass 1971; Desborough 1972; Coldstream 1977), the period has attracted an increasing amount of attention. This has focused particularly on the Geometric period (900–700), for which much more material has become available, but there has also been some important work on the earlier phases. However, the need for a new general survey that takes account both of all the new material and of the increasingly critical approach to traditional viewpoints and methods of interpreting archaeological data has not yet been met. Snodgrass (1971) was reissued in 2000, but contains only a new foreword. Thomas and Conant (1999) covers the whole period, but is unsatisfactory at the basic level of its methodology, in using single sites (and not always the most obvious) to illuminate the successive centuries, and contains many questionable statements. Lemos (2002) is a useful if rather traditional account of the material, but focuses solely on the Protogeometric period and on a limited part of

Greece. A reissue of Coldstream (1977) with a supplementary chapter in 2003 is very useful, as are various shorter discussions of the 'Dark Age' that are part of more extensive studies (Morris, I. 1987, 1997, and 1999: chs 3 and 6; Snodgrass 1987: ch. 6; Whitley 1991a, and 2001: ch. 5), but though valuable these do give some prominence to debatable hypotheses.

I hope, rather rashly, to improve on all these, but must stress that this book cannot be expected to do more than give an introduction to the period and its problems. Responding to the strictures of some reviewers of Dickinson (1994a), I emphasise that this does not mean that it can be easily understood by someone who knows nothing whatever about Greece or Aegean archaeology. Rather, it means that it is of limited length, so that topics cannot be discussed exhaustively, and major sites and collections of data must be referred to rather than described at length.

I trust that I will be forgiven for frequent references to Dickinson (1994a), but where I have discussed a topic in some detail there and have not altered my views significantly, this seems the best way to make use of limited space. Among the references that I have chosen to cite are unpublished conference papers, when I think that their content is sufficiently important to merit this; I hope that I have conveyed their content correctly. It is almost inevitable, given the amount now being published, that I will have overlooked some discussions, and I may well not have paid sufficient attention to some that oppose or update views that I have chosen to follow, especially on such topics as 'Homeric society'. But this study has been delayed long enough already; I now commit myself to publication.

Oliver Dickinson
September 2005

ACKNOWLEDGEMENTS

I would like to cite, in the place of honour, Sue Sherratt, who has been good enough to read draft chapters twice, at a five-year interval, and whose extremely valuable comments have made this a far more consistent and, I hope, coherently argued book than it would have been without them. I am also especially indebted to Cathy Morgan for valuable comments on several chapters; to Fanouria Dakoronia, Sigrid Deger-Jalkotzy, Birgitta Eder, Maria Kayafa, and Mary Voyatzis for generously sharing significant information and for sending unpublished texts about important material; to John Bintliff for providing copies of his own and others' articles at a crucial moment; and to Zofia Stos and Ellis Jones for providing much help on the topic of metal sources and their exploitation. Many others have also provided books, offprints, information, original illustrations, and comments: I would like to mention Claire Adams, Vasiliki Adrymi-Sismani, Bob Arnott, Paul Åström, Clarissa Belardelli, Elisabetta Borgna, Helen Hughes Brock, Cyprian Broodbank, Gerald Cadogan, Jill Carington-Smith, Hector Catling, Richard Catling, Nicolas Coldstream, Anna Lucia D'Agata, Jack Davis, Katie Demakopoulou, Søren Dietz, Nicoletta Divari-Valakou, Robert Drews, Lisa French, Barbro Santillo Frizell, Ioannis Georganas, Kevin Glowacki, Robin Hägg, Donald Haggis, Jonathan Hall, Anthony Harding, Georgia Hatzi, Reinhard Jung, Vassos Karageorghis, Imma Kilian-Dirlmeier, Irene Lemos, Yannos Lolos, Joseph Maran, Holly Martlew, Hartmut Matthäus, Jennifer Moody, Sarah Morris, Penelope Mountjoy, Jim Muhly, Richard Nicholls, Krzysztof Nowicki, Robin Osborne, Mani Papakonstantinou, John Papadopoulos, Michaelis Petropoulos, Peter Rhodes, David Ridgway, Jerry Rutter, Hugh Sackett, Elizabeth Schofield†, Cynthia Shelmerdine, Anthony Snodgrass, Christiane Sourvinou-Inwood, Andreas Vlachopoulos, Leonidas Vokotopoulos, Gisela Walberg, Saro Wallace, Ken Wardle, Todd Whitelaw, James Whitley, Malcolm Wiener, Jim Wright, Assaf Yasur-Landau, and Marika Zeimbekis. I would also like to thank my Ph.D. student Guy Middleton for his astute comments on some ideas of mine.

I am extremely grateful to Sven Schroeder and Hayley Saul of the

ACKNOWLEDGEMENTS

Department of Archaeology, University of York, for their help with the figures, almost all of which Miss Saul has prepared.

I am indebted to the University of Durham for the grant of terms of research leave in 1996, 1998 and 2003, and to the Department of Classics and Ancient History for its cooperation in allowing me to follow the 1998 term with a term of unpaid leave in 1999, funded by a generous grant from the Institute for Aegean Prehistory. This largely freed me from academic responsibilities for most of a year, which was invaluable in the writing of this book, and I am deeply grateful to all the institutions concerned.

Thanks are also due to the following for providing photographs or line drawings and for giving permission to publish them: Mrs V. Adrymi-Sismani (the original of Figure 2.3); Prof. D. Haggis (Figure 4.4); the Department of Classics, University of Cincinnati, and Prof. T. Palaima (Figure 2.2); the Department of Classics, University of Cincinnati and Dr S. Stocker (Figure 3.2); The National Archaeological Museum, Athens, and Dr Papazoglou-Maniati (Figure 3.3); the American School of Classical Studies at Athens: Agora Excavations (Figure 5.2); the British School of Archaeology at Athens (Figures 2.5, 5.1, 5.11, 5.12, 5.23, 7.2, 7.3, 8.5); the Deutsches Archäologisches Institut, Athens (Figures 5.9, 5.15, 5.16, 6.4).

ABBREVIATIONS

Periodicals

AA	Archäologischer Anzeiger
AAA	Athens Annals of Archaeology (Αρχαιολογικά Ανάλεκτα εξ Αθηνών)
AD	Αρχαιολογικόν Δελτίον
AJA	American Journal of Archaeology
AR	Archaeological Reports (supplement to *JHS*)
AS	Anatolian Studies
AthMitt	Mitteilungen des Deutschen Archäologischen Instituts: Athenische Abteilung
BCH	Bulletin de correspondance hellénique
BICS	Bulletin of the Institute of Classical Studies, University of London
BSA	Annual of the British School at Athens
CAJ	Cambridge Archaeological Journal
CQ	Classical Quarterly
CR	Classical Review
IJNA	International Journal of Nautical Archaeology
JDAI	Jahrbuch des Deutschen Archäologisches Instituts
JFA	Journal of Field Archaeology
JHS	Journal of Hellenic Studies
JMA	Journal of Mediterranean Archaeology
OJA	Oxford Journal of Archaeology
OpAth	Opuscula Atheniensia
PAE	Πρακτικά τής εν Αθήναις Αρχαιολογικής Εταιρείας
ProcCamPhilSoc	Proceedings of the Cambridge Philological Society
PZ	Praehistorische Zeitschrift
RDAC	Report of the Department of Antiquities of Cyprus
SMEA	Studi micenei ed egeo-anatolici

Others

CAH I–III	Cambridge Ancient History (third edition)
CAH I–III, pl . . .	Cambridge Ancient History, Plates to Volumes I–III (third edition)
BA	Bronze Age
cm	centimetres
D.	diameter
DA	Dark Age
EB(A), MB(A), LB(A)	Early, Middle, Late Bronze (Age)
(EG, MG, L)G	Early, (Middle, Late) Geometric
EH, MH, LH	Early, Middle, Late Helladic
(E)IA	(Early) Iron Age
EPG, MPG, LPG	Early, Middle, Late Protogeometric
H.	height
ha	hectare(s)
Herod.	Herodotus
HMB	handmade burnished
L.	length
LM	Late Minoan
m	metres
pers. comm.	personal communication
SM	Subminoan
SPG	Sub-Protogeometric
Submyc	Submycenaean
Thuc.	Thucydides

A NOTE ON USAGE AND NOMENCLATURE

I shall be citing Greek place-names and terms for pottery types and other artefacts in the most familiar and commonly used forms, without strict adherence to any system of orthography. The names for provinces and regions in and around Greece will reflect ancient rather than modern usage, and the ancient territorial designations Mesopotamia, Anatolia/Asia Minor, Syria, Phoenicia, and Palestine will be used in preference to the names of the modern countries which include them. The term 'Near East' will be used to refer generally to the whole region of the ancient eastern civilisations, including Egypt.

INTRODUCTION

'The Dark Age of Greece is our conception.' This crisp statement of Whitley's
(1991a: 5) cannot be faulted. Although Greek tradition generally spoke of an
age of heroes in the past, most vividly described in the Homeric epics, when
kings ruled wide lands from palaces full of fabulous treasures, and great
deeds were performed, it recognised no period of catastrophic decline intervening between this and more recent times. Rather, it presented the age of
heroes as shading, after the Trojan War, into a period of less striking deeds
that ended with the migrations by which, supposedly, the later map of mainland and Aegean Greece was largely created. There followed an ill-defined
period about which virtually nothing was reported, which blended, around
what we would term the second half of the eighth century, into the period
about which some information was preserved, although even this may largely
reflect fifth- and fourth-century reworking of semi-legendary traditions about
the past. Although the genealogies of some great families, which derived
them from prominent heroes like Herakles and Ajax, supposedly bridged the
whole span of time from the age of heroes to Classical times, no information
was preserved about the majority of the persons named in them. It is symptomatic of the general lack of information that Thucydides, in his famous
account of the past of Greece, found it easiest to calculate the dates when the
Boeotians and Dorians supposedly moved into southern Greece by reckoning
downwards from the Trojan War (I.12), rather than backwards from his own
day as he did for some later events.

Thucydides was not impressed by the age of heroes (I.2–12), but like his
fellow-Greeks he believed that the traditions about their remote past contained truth; he simply tried to interpret them rationally. He evidently did
not find in them any hint that major centres of the Classical world like Argos,
Athens and Thebes, which figure so largely in the legends, had declined
greatly from their first flourishing before rising again. Rather, in the only
systematic attempt at recounting the past of Greece that did not involve
retelling the legends, he presented the whole past of Greece as a period of
fitful progress from small beginnings, always liable to be interrupted by
migrations and other disturbances until relatively recent times. This was a

1

legitimate reading of the only sources of information available to him, the traditional legends and especially the epic poems, which concentrated, in a way typical of such material in any culture, on monster-slayings, wars and cattle-raids, the movements of peoples, and the foundation or capture of famous sites, in all of which the legendary heroes naturally figured prominently. The only possible counter-indication to this picture of progress was Hesiod's account in *Works and Days* of a sequence of races from golden to iron, but this was surely not intended to contain any kind of historically useful tradition. It is a moral myth, of a kind which has various parallels in ancient Asiatic religious thought, that represents human history as a series of stages of decline from perfection. Into this Hesiod, for his own reasons, subtly blended the race of heroes, who represent an improvement on the bronze race (see most recently West 1997: 312–19, and Rosen in Morris and Powell 1997: 485–7).

It was probably not too difficult for the Classical Greeks to see their past as a continuous if only vaguely conceived process of development from the age of heroes, because they did not really imagine the age of heroes as fundamentally different in character from their own. In the epic poems and other traditional material, the heroes were presented as moving in a world in which many of the later *poleis* and great religious sites were already established (cf. Snodgrass 1986: 48). They worshipped the same gods as the later Greeks with much the same rituals, and in the Homeric poems accepted standards of behaviour that were still considered in some ways exemplary for the elite in historical times. If some practices of the heroic age, like weapon-carrying and piracy, were no longer considered respectable in the most civilised parts of Greece, they were known to have been quite common in the recent past, and stated by Thucydides to be prevalent in the less-developed parts of Greece in his own day.

When archaeology began to reveal the reality of the Aegean Bronze Age (hereafter BA) in modern times, the reliability of the Greek traditions was widely considered to have been demonstrated by the discoveries at Troy, Mycenae, Tiryns, and other sites famous in legend, and essentially Thucydides' lead was followed in accepting that the traditions incorporated real historical information about Greece's remoter past. Despite some significant discrepancies between the material remains of what quickly became called the Mycenaean civilisation and important cultural features described in the Homeric poems (e.g. in burial customs), many scholars found it possible to envisage the Mycenaean ruling class as rather warlike and predatory, like Homer's heroes, and their world as rather unstable. In consequence, although the end of Mycenaean civilisation was accepted to involve violent destruction, the displacement of populations, and a decline in the level of material culture, it was still possible to see it in rather Thucydidean terms as a continuation or revival of previous instability. Also, the destroyers, Dorians and kindred groups, could be made responsible for introducing significant innovations, such as the use of iron, the decoration of pottery with purely

2

geometric motifs, the cremation burial rite, and new developments in religion, particularly the cult of Apollo.

How then did the idea of a Dark Age arise? In part, it seems to derive from the establishing of a more accurate chronology of the LBA and the succeeding period. This made it clear that Mycenaean civilisation, now perceived to have superseded the older Minoan civilisation as the dominant force in the Aegean, reached its height in the fourteenth and thirteenth centuries, while the most striking material of the EIA belonged in the ninth and eighth centuries. Very little material could be placed in the intervening period, and what there was seemed notably unimpressive. The bulk of it was provided by the Kerameikos cemeteries at Athens, in which the graves, themselves of simple form, contained few goods, mainly pots and unremarkable metal items. The pottery which belonged to the Athenian Protogeometric style could at least be admired for its well-defined shapes and carefully arranged decoration in a good-quality dark paint, and the Athenian potters could be argued to have influenced pottery production over a wide area of Greece with this superior style, which they supposedly developed, as they certainly did the even more influential succeeding Geometric style. Largely on this basis, Athens was often considered the most important Greek settlement of the period (e.g. Desborough 1972: 341, 346; Kirk 1975: 843). But the relative rarity and limited range of other grave-goods at Athens, the even more limited quality of the material found in the few though widely distributed graves of the period known from other parts of Greece, and the total lack of evidence for decent architecture all contributed to an impression of poverty, while the very local character of the pottery in many parts of Greece suggested that contacts within the Greek world were sporadic at best, especially away from the south Aegean coasts and islands.

More accurate chronology also made it clear that the Dorians and their 'West Greek' relatives could have brought no substantial material innovations with them. On the contrary, since the destruction of the major Mycenaean centres was attributed to them, emphasis was increasingly laid on their responsibility for a catastrophic drop in the level of material culture, as encapsulated in this quotation:

> The important fact, however, is that after their second invasion the Dorians conquered virtually the entire Ionian–Mycenaean world, from the Peloponnese to Rhodes, with the exception of Miletus in Asia Minor, Athens, and Aeolian Iolkos. The civilization thus built up over many centuries by the Mycenaeans, with the help of the Minoans, was destroyed. Although they spoke the same language, the Dorians came as invaders and destroyers, culturally half a millennium behind the people whom they vanquished. It was a catastrophic, unprecedented disaster . . .
>
> (Schweitzer 1971: 10–11)

It even came to be commonly suggested, as Schweitzer does in a preceding passage, that the movement of the Ionian and Aeolian Greeks from the mainland to Asia Minor reflected the flight of refugees from the Dorian terror, although there is little warrant for this in the traditions. These certainly describe royal families and whole population groups as being displaced by Dorian and other conquerors and moving elsewhere, but they place the 'Ionian Migration' two full generations after the period of Dorian conquests in the Peloponnese, and present the 'Aeolian' movement into Lesbos and north-west Asia Minor as a totally separate affair.

Another theory that quickly became well established is that, since they supposedly overthrew the Mycenaean civilisation, the Dorians must have come from outside its territory, although this was hard to square with the tradition that their latest homeland before entering the Peloponnese was the territory of Doris in central Greece. The tendency to associate them specifically with Epirus can be traced to a time before anything much was understood about prehistoric Greece, and seems to be associated with an idea that the people of north-west Greece and Albania preserved the supposedly pastoral way of life of the ancient Dorians (e.g. Reclus 1875: 185). Those who accepted that the Dorians were apparently undetectable archaeologically made much use of the belief that they were semi-nomadic pastoralists, whose material culture would barely survive in the archaeological record, therefore (the classic statement is Hammond 1932).

Although these theories were only interpretations of the traditions in the light of what was believed about the archaeology, they have become embedded in discussion of these traditions and are still commonly encountered. The belief that the Homeric poems gave a fairly reliable picture of Mycenaean civilisation also continued to prevail, and this may have had an insidious effect. For if it could be argued from the poems that some of the most characteristic features of later Greece in the fields of religion and social structure were already established before the end of the Mycenaean period, the Dark Age might seem to be a period in which there was virtually no significant development.

Perhaps the strongest contribution to the image of the Dark Age was made by the decipherment of the Linear B script as Greek in 1952. This quickly revealed that in the leading Mycenaean centres, where the script was used, the level of social organisation showed notable similarities with the great Near Eastern civilisations. Thus the catastrophic effects of their destruction were enhanced still further. Ironically, it was in the introduction to *Documents in Mycenaean Greek* that Wace chose to argue against the whole concept of a Dark Age, suggesting that the Dorian invasion should be seen as bringing about 'not a cultural but only a political change in Greece', and that the history of the Greeks and Greek art should now be seen to begin in the MBA (Ventris and Chadwick [1956] 1973: xxxi–xxxiv). But the contrast between the society that the tablets revealed and what could be surmised about society in the succeeding period was too great. It was generally accepted that the collapse of Mycenaean civilisation involved a major break in continuity, which was detectable archaeologically not merely in the destruction and non-replacement of palaces and other major buildings, and the loss of luxury crafts, but in the widely attested abandonment of ordinary settlement sites.

Attention was thus focused on the characteristics of the Dark Age and the problem of how Greece had been able to recover from it. Three British scholars, V.R. Desborough, A.M. Snodgrass, and J.N. Coldstream, wrote extremely valuable studies (Desborough 1964, 1972; Snodgrass 1971; Coldstream 1977), which may be considered to have shaped the modern picture of the 'Dark Age' to a great extent. Desborough (1972) and Snodgrass (1971), which focused on the 'Dark Age' proper, had several features in common. Both paid considerable attention to the Greek traditions of population movement, especially the 'Ionian migration', though sceptical of the details. Desborough, indeed, saw population movements as responsible for most developments, good and bad, over the period that he covered (see his summary ch. 24 throughout). Both laid emphasis on the concentration of evidence at settlements based on or near the coasts of the Aegean, especially Athens, which they identified as 'progressive'. Both laid some stress on the breakdown and later revival of communications, both within the Aegean world and between the Aegean and the Near East, in which these 'progressive' communities played a major part.

But while Desborough felt that the 'Dark Ages' were over by c. 900, Snodgrass saw the evidence for increasing levels of communication and links with the Near East in the late tenth century as something of a 'false dawn' (1971: 402), while in his seminal study of Geometric Greece Coldstream described his 'Awakening' phase of c. 855–30, marked by strong evidence for Near Eastern contacts at certain communities, in similar terms (1977: 71), and like Snodgrass placed the final revival of Greece no earlier than the mid-eighth century. In searching for explanations for this, Snodgrass was most concerned with internal developments, placing some emphasis on what he perceived as a return to agriculture from a Dark Age concentration on pastoralism (1971: 378–80, cf. 1980a: 35–6 and 1987: 209), while Coldstream laid particular emphasis on a major rise in population (1977: 367–8), a point already referred to by Snodgrass (1971: 367, 417) and later elaborated in a discussion that has had great influence (1980a: 23–5).

Since the 1970s there have been no comparable surveys, although Snodgrass has revisited the period (1987: ch. 6, and the introduction to the 2000 reissue of Snodgrass 1971), making use of the great increase in our knowledge. Morris's brief survey (1997) gives an overview of this. In particular, knowledge of settlement sites has increased substantially, especially through the excavations at Nichoria in Messenia (whose publication includes, exceptionally, studies of the animal bones and plant remains), Asine in the

5

Argolid, Koukounaries on Paros, and many sites in Crete, especially Knossos and Kavousi, as well as the essentially ritual sites at Isthmia in the Corinthia and Kalapodi in Phocis. The discoveries at Lefkandi in Euboea, particularly the great structure known as the 'Heroön', its contents, and the associated Toumba cemetery, have been such as to virtually overshadow everything else known for the pre-900 period. Survey work, chance discoveries of small cemeteries and single graves, and occasional finds in excavations have allowed the identification of many new sites that must have been occupied at some point in the period. Although a great part of the new material falls in the eighth century, these discoveries have filled out the map of Greece considerably for other parts of the period, and new evidence is continually coming in.

Yet it cannot be denied that, in comparison with the range, quantity, and quality of the data that can be mobilised in the study of both the preceding LBA and the succeeding Archaic period, the material available for evaluating the period remains scanty. In particular, a great deal still derives from graves and their contents, and, as will become clear in ensuing chapters, the discussion of crucial areas like the settlement pattern, farming economy, trade, and ritual behaviour must depend to a great extent on hypothesis and reasoned speculation. An inevitable consequence of the lack of data has been a tendency to base very important and wide-ranging conclusions upon what evidence there is (cf. the use made of the original report on the animal bones from Nichoria, Sloan and Duncan 1978, in various publications). Often this involves placing more weight upon this evidence than it will bear. Also, written material of often questionable relevance or value has been used to bulk out the archaeological data, in a continuation of the respect for textual evidence that has been characteristic not only of ancient historians but of many archaeologists. But such material deserves the kind of rigorous analysis applied in Hall (1997) to the origin legends of population groups. It certainly should not be taken at face value or even treated as a coherent body of information.

Discussion of the period involves other difficulties. As Papadopoulos has well remarked, 'Because this "Dark Age" does not readily belong . . . in the intellectual realm of the prehistorian nor is it firmly in that of the classical archaeologist, it floats rather uncomfortably in between' (1994: 438). The term 'Dark Age' itself involves a basic conceptual problem. In their 1970s' surveys Snodgrass and Desborough argued strongly for its appropriateness, but it is abandoned in Snodgrass (1987) (however, see Snodgrass [1971] 2000: xxiv). Its potential to mislead has become increasingly apparent. For it has generally been understood to indicate not only a period of which very little is known, but one which can be described in terms such as those used by Tandy:

> On mainland Greece and the Aegean islands, the human condition
> and the number of persons experiencing it had not changed very

6

much for several hundred years when, in the latter part of the ninth century, the population began rather suddenly to grow.

(Tandy 1997: 19)

and

During the Dark Age, the Greeks had little archaeologically measurable contact with the outside world . . . in the main, the Greeks of the Dark Age appear to have kept to themselves and to have attracted little attention.

(Tandy 1997: 59)

These comments represent a very emphatic version of a viewpoint that is probably still widespread but has, in my view, become impossible to sustain. Although there are difficulties in his basic approach, I feel that Papadopoulos's comment, 'Too much was happening in Early Iron Age Greece for it to warrant the term "dark age" ' (1996a: 254–5, cf. 1993: 194–7), is a closer approximation to the truth. It is highly desirable that the period should have a name with less highly charged overtones.

The obvious alternative is the Early Iron Age, which is succinct in comparison with the more accurate but clumsy 'transitional Bronze Age – Iron Age period', is probably more meaningful to students of European prehistory, and in Snodgrass's view reflects one very significant feature of the period ([1971] 2000: xxiv). But it also has potential to mislead, since for at least the first quarter of the period covered iron items were very rare in the Aegean, and it remains questionable when local manufacture began (see Chapter 5). I have found it preferable to confine this term (hereafter EIA) to the shorter period from *c.* 1050 until *c.* 700, and to apply the term Postpalatial Period to the final phases of the Bronze Age, as in Dickinson (1994a). Thus the change of terms fits the conventional break between the Mycenaean system of pottery nomenclature and the Protogeometric–Geometric system (see Figure 1.1), although neither of these systems has universal application in the Aegean and no clear-cut line can be drawn between them, because the pottery develops in different ways and at different rates in the various regions (see further Chapter 1). This use of two terms may seem an unnecessary complication, but it models the actual processes of development better. The usage 'Dark Age' cannot be avoided altogether, however, because of its prominence in previous discussion.

A beneficial feature of the lack of knowledge has been that it has encouraged attempts to produce general hypotheses of development that offer an escape from the image of the 'Dark Age' encapsulated in the quotations from Tandy (1997) cited above. Until recently, such attempts at explaining what was happening and at imagining how society worked in this period have been of a rather old-fashioned kind, influenced, whether consciously or not, by long-established but increasingly questionable ideas (including that of the wholly redistributive economy, deriving ultimately from Polanyi, which permeates Tandy 1997). But in recent years there has been less concern with the economy than with attempts to use the archaeological material to throw light on social development, within and beyond the period (e.g. Morris I. 1987, 1997, and 1999: chs 3 and 6; Morgan 1990; Whitley 1991a, and 2001: ch. 5; de Polignac 1995). These have often encountered considerable criticism, but they have encouraged general reconsideration of the period's problems. It seems appropriate to comment, though, that several show a tendency to treat the 'Dark Age' as a completely new beginning, and to argue for the prevalence of forms of social organisation and exchange directly analogous to those described by modern anthropologists studying regions where, to our knowledge, more sophisticated forms of organisation had never existed, unlike the EIA Aegean. Such analogies are useful in stimulating thought, but the BA background of the EIA cannot simply be ignored. It has become increasingly clear that society in the Aegean did not have to be re-created from scratch. There were significant continuities, and it is highly unlikely that the Aegean was ever completely cut off from the contacts with a wider world that were so much a feature of the LBA.

Because of its limited length this book can only make a beginning on offering a coherent new approach. But, whereas I have decided to depart from my predecessors' example by abandoning the term 'Dark Age', I believe, with them (and *contra* Papadopoulos 1993: 194–7, 1996a: 254, and the general tenor of Muhly 1999), that many of the features which have been considered characteristic of this period are indeed genuine and significant. It is not my intention to give equal coverage to every part of the period *c.* 1200–700. What is often called the Geometric period, equivalent to the ninth and eighth centuries, stands on the verge of Greek history. In particular, so much archaeological material relevant to the eighth century is now known, and it has been so much discussed, that to give it space proportionate to its quantity would completely unbalance the book. My intention is to focus primarily on the collapse of the Bronze Age palace societies, which will receive extensive consideration in Chapter 2, and on the period which still remains 'dark' in terms of the extent of our knowledge, equating more or less to the twelfth, eleventh and tenth centuries.

Thus, I will be aiming to concentrate on the period covered by Desborough (1964, 1972), but, as the subtitle of this book indicates, I will be concerned throughout with questions of continuity between the Bronze Age and the emerging Greek world of the eighth century, and with analysing the processes of change which made that world different in many important respects from that of the Mycenaean palaces. It will be the purpose of this book to argue that, while there undoubtedly were continuities from the BA, there were also considerable dislocations, from which Greece took a considerable time to recover, and that the period of recovery saw the making of positive choices, which laid many of the foundations of 'classical' Greek culture.

The geographical horizons will be somewhat wider than in Dickinson (1994a). While the BA civilisations remained focused on the southern Aegean islands and southern Greek mainland for almost their entire history, this study must give some attention to the western Anatolian coast, the islands of the north Aegean, and parts of northern Greece, as they became part of or more closely linked to the developing Greek world. But Cyprus will not receive detailed treatment, for, while it had become a largely Greek-speaking island (at least at elite level) by the end of the period, and shows many cultural links with the Aegean, historically and culturally it belongs more with the Near East. Nevertheless, it will frequently be mentioned, for its links with the Aegean were often of importance to developments there.

Bibliography

The most extensive discussions of the concept of the Dark Age in ancient Greek and modern thought are Snodgrass (1971: ch. 1) (his ideas are updated in Snodgrass 1987, ch. 6, and his latest views are to be found in the new introduction to the 2000 reissue of his book) and Morris (1999: ch. 3). For very succinct summaries see Whitley (1991a: 5–8 and 2001: 55–7).

For detailed accounts of the finds at particular sites Desborough (1964, 1972), Snodgrass (1971) and Coldstream (1977) remain invaluable up to the date of their publication; they also include site gazetteers and provide more copious illustrations than this book can do (see also Lemos 2002 for Proto-geometric). The reader is urged to consult these and other sources cited in the chapter bibliographies for further information (see Morris, I. 1997 and Whitley 2001: ch. 5, for useful summaries with recent references).

1

TERMINOLOGY AND
CHRONOLOGY

In this chapter, for clarity, classificatory terms will be spelled out in full; in later chapters the abbreviations listed on p. xv will be used. As set out in the Introduction, the period to be covered will be divided between the Postpalatial Period, equivalent to Late Helladic/Minoan IIIC and Submycenaean/earlier Subminoan, and the Early Iron Age, equivalent to Protogeometric and Geometric.

Establishing a terminology

The outer limits of the period covered in this book take in a half-millennium, the twelfth to eighth centuries (the proposal in P. James *et al.*, *Centuries of Darkness* (London: Jonathan Cape, 1991) to reduce this period to a century at most will not be discussed here, since it has been universally rejected; see Dickinson 1994a: 17 for references, also Snodgrass [1971] 2000: xxvi). If only because of its situation between periods for which some kind of historical chronology can be established, this long period cannot be treated as a unit. In fact, as noted in the Preface, it is becoming customary to separate the eighth century from the rest as a period on the threshold of true Greek history. But the severe problems of establishing a reliable absolute chronology that can be applied throughout the Aegean region make it impossible to discuss developments for the whole period purely in terms of centuries or fractions of them, let alone to date individual events within it.

The period has a reasonably clear-cut beginning in the series of destructions that marks the end of what, following the usage of Dickinson (1994a), will be termed the Third Palace Period (which in Dickinson 1994a incorporates what is often called the Mycenaean Palace Period of the fourteenth and thirteenth centuries). Although such destructions cannot be identified at every significant Aegean site, they must reflect an important series of events that effectively represents the collapse of the Aegean palace societies within a relatively short period of time (see further, p. 44). But thereafter all is uncertainty, for further 'destruction horizons' of the kind which so conveniently divide important stages of the Aegean Bronze Age are lacking, and it is quite uncertain whether the site destructions that have been identified

10

within the Postpalatial Period can be grouped to form a comparable horizon. It is even less clear whether any destructions can be related to the severe climatic event represented in tree-ring evidence found in Turkey, now sited between *c.* 1174 and 1162 (Kuniholm, cited by M.H. Wiener in *BSA* 98 (2003) 244) and often attributed to an eruption of Mt Hekla in Iceland which fell in the first half of the twelfth century (Kuniholm 1990: 653–4; but Buckland *et al.* 1997: 588 question whether this eruption had widespread climatic effects). After the Postpalatial Period, destructions of major sites are hard to identify at all, except in Crete, until the eighth century, when they may sometimes be given a historical setting (e.g. the destruction of Asine in the Late Geometric pottery phase have been linked to the tradition of conquest by Argos, supposedly datable near 700).

Thus, the archaeological record offers no natural breaks to facilitate a subdivision of the period that is not based on pottery phases. Nevertheless, it is the only source that can provide a framework for such subdivision. Sometimes, the 'Dorian invasion', 'Ionian migration' and related population movements reported in the Greek traditions have been treated as historical events that can be approximately dated and used as chronological signposts in the earlier part of the period. But, even if these traditions could be accepted as containing genuine information, the basis for dating them is shaky indeed. As noted in the Introduction, such movements were essentially dated by reckoning downwards from the Trojan War, but this was not fixed; very varied dates were calculated for it by ancient scholars, all of whom must have based their work on varying interpretations of the genealogies that linked historical persons with famous heroes. But it has long been recognised that these genealogies, among which those of the Spartan royal families are the best known, are too short to fit any possible chronology, if the 'age of heroes' is assumed – though this is a very questionable assumption – to have a historical basis in the world of the Mycenaean palaces (see Snodgrass 1971: 10–13; Desborough 1972: 323–5).

Snodgrass has nevertheless argued that several sources suggest a comparable number of generations going back to an ancestor figure or god, and if one allows some thirty years to a generation and reckons backward from the time that these genealogies were recorded, in the fifth century, all seem to begin around the tenth century, which could be considered to represent a horizon of historical significance, even perhaps reflecting the date of the 'Ionian migration'. But such genealogies cannot be assumed to be trustworthy, even in their 'human' generations, without external checks. As is demonstrated in Thomas (1989: ch. 3, especially 180–6), there is good reason to suppose that such 'full' genealogies were effectively created from family traditions by the first systematic genealogists in the fifth century, and that this process of creation involved many misinterpretations and distortions, in addition to anything that may have happened during the transmission of the material previously (cf. Davies 1984: 90–1). It would be unwise to believe

11

that even as accounts of descent such genealogies represent information transmitted intact from the past, and this must discredit any dating system based on them.

The archaeological material, then, must be the only basis for establishing some kind of framework for the period. This has principally been done on the basis of pottery phases (cf. most recently Whitley 1991: 83–6, primarily concerned with Athens, and Morris I. 1997, where slightly differing sequences are proposed for central, western and northern Greece and for Crete). But it is undeniable that historical processes do not necessarily fit themselves neatly into phases defined stylistically, and other attempts have been made to suggest a sequence which, although taking its chronology from dates estimated for the pottery phases, is based on more general perceptions of observable processes. But such perceptions are subject to change as new material is discovered. Thus, Snodgrass argued that after the end of the Bronze Age there was continuing decline, which reached a nadir in a phase of 'bronze shortage', for which he suggested outer limits of *c.* 1025 and 950, and which he saw as the time of maximum isolation and poverty. This was followed by recovery, with the revival of communication, in the later tenth century, and culminating in a final 'renaissance' in the eighth century (1971: ch. 7; see also Snodgrass 1987: ch. 6). However attractive this might once have appeared as a model of development, more recent finds have called it into question (see Muhly 2003: 23). In particular, the rich burials that the Lefkandi 'Heroön' contained are agreed to date to the local Middle Protogeometric phase, which has close links with Attic Middle Protogeometric and should fall chronologically within Snodgrass's period of maximum isolation and poverty (see now Snodgrass [1971] 2000: xxvii–xxix, in which many of Snodgrass's older views are substantially qualified if not totally withdrawn).

Similarly, Coldstream has withdrawn the original subdivisions of 'Isolation', 'Awakening' and 'Consolidation' which he saw in the period *c.* 900–770, termed 'the passing of the Dark Ages', accepting that this reflected a largely Athenocentric viewpoint (1977: ch. 1; see now 2003: 371).

The lesson to be drawn from these cases is that the evidence of one or a few sites cannot provide a universal pattern of historical development for the whole Aegean region. The local histories of regions and sites may have been very different for much of the period, so that no general system of historical phases can be devised for the whole Aegean until the eighth century, when it does become possible to speak of processes that seem to have been at work over much of Greece. For want of anything better, the material will have to be discussed in terms of pottery sequences, of which something must now be said.

Relative chronology

The difficulty with using decorated pottery as the primary basis for relative chronology in the period is that, with certain notable exceptions, the pottery produced for the greater part of the Early Iron Age in most parts of Greece has little distinctive character, being extremely limited in its range of shapes, motifs, and styles of decoration (see further, pp. 128–9). There are enough variations in details between regions for it to be clear that at first there were no centres whose stylistic lead was closely followed over a very wide area. Even when Athens achieved something like a leading position in this respect, its example was never followed completely faithfully, and sometimes seems to have been positively resisted, even in neighbouring regions. Much of the time, the simplicity of the motifs and of the manner in which they were deployed makes it difficult to identify connections between the local styles with any certainty: occurrences of the same motifs, deployed in similar ways, could often be attributed as plausibly to inheritance of a common stock derived from the Late Helladic IIIC styles, as to the exertion of influence by one region on another. Similarly, a generally limited range of shapes makes resemblances between those of one region and another unsurprising.

Also, the deficiencies in the database cannot be stressed too often. Although the situation is improving, large stratified deposits of settlement material are still rare and most of our evidence comes from graves. These generally contain complete vases, in contrast with settlement deposits which consist mostly of sherds, but such vases are seldom numerous and tend to differ considerably from those used in settlements, both in preferences for particular shapes and in the quality of their decoration. Hence it is difficult to compare styles defined from grave-associated material and those defined from settlement deposits with complete confidence.

Enough common features can nevertheless be identified in the archaeological material of the Postpalatial Period to make it possible to suggest a very general sequence of Late Helladic IIIC phases, that applies through much of the Aegean, although precisely how the phases of Cretan Late Minoan IIIC, which are less well defined, should be correlated with this sequence remains a subject of debate. There was a quite substantial Late Helladic IIIC Early phase, marked by competent but unexciting pottery that has many similarities over a wide region, to which at least two building levels can be attributed at Mycenae, Tiryns and Lefkandi. This was followed by a comparably substantial Middle phase, during which several sites and regions produced some extremely individual fine wares that can be seen to interact in complex patterns of cross-influences. Finally, there was a Late phase, generally reckoned to be shorter, of abrupt-seeming decline in quality and range. Even at the beginning of this sequence, although there is a good deal of homogeneity over a wide area, local features can be observed. In the course of it, the local sequences tend to diverge increasingly, retaining a

13

family resemblance but becoming more and more distant towards the end, so that placing individual pieces within the sequence is often a matter for prolonged discussion of parallels.

A Submycenaean stage following Late Helladic IIIC Late has often been identified, but the use of this term has become fraught with difficulties. Morgan has commented (1990: 235) that the term's originators intended it to indicate whatever falls between Late Helladic IIIC and Protogeometric in any region, without any implication of a strictly defined style, culture, or chronological period. The tendency has nevertheless been to use it as a pottery term, but, as is pointed out in accounts of its use (most recently Whitley 1991a: 81–2; Papadopoulos 1993: 176–81; Morgan 1999: 254–6; Mountjoy 1999: 56), it has been given very varied meanings. Sometimes it has been interpreted as simply the local west Attic variant of Late Helladic IIIC Late (Desborough's original view) or as the style found on vases buried in graves contemporary with Late Helladic IIIC Late settlements (Rutter 1978), sometimes as the style that succeeded Late Helladic IIIC over a substantial area of the central mainland (Desborough's later view, but see Mountjoy 1999: 56–7).

The difficulty of producing an agreed definition arises partly because the increasingly marked regionalism that appeared in Late Helladic IIIC pottery entails that whatever followed is hardly likely to show any marked stylistic coherence between different regions. More fundamentally, despite attempts at definition by Desborough and Mountjoy, Submycenaean does not have a very distinctive character; as Desborough comments, 'even the word "style" is hardly appropriate' (1972: 41). It is often unclear what distinguishes it from Late Helladic IIIC Late, let alone what is so distinctive about it that it deserves a separate term (Frizell 1986 uses 'Final Mycenaean'). It is symptomatic that Mountjoy has felt able to reclassify as Late Helladic IIIC Late some of the material from Salamis and the Kerameikos that was originally used by Furumark to define Submycenaean (Myc. IIIC:2 in his terminology, 1972: 77–8), and that levels 13–23 at Kalapodi, originally defined as covering the end of Late Helladic IIIC and Submycenaean, have now been reassigned to Submycenaean, Transition to Protogeometric and Early Protogeometric (compare Felsch 1987: 3 n. 8 with 1996: xvi). All this emphasises how the material of this obscure period, which is known much better from grave-groups than settlement deposits, is typified by gradual transitions rather than marked changes of direction, allowing different scholars to interpret the material in different ways (cf. Lemos 2002: 7–8 on Submycenaean, and Catling in *NorthCem*: 295–6 on Subminoan).

In fact, the most distinctive types are those of the stage which has been defined as late Submycenaean in the Athens and Lefkandi cemeteries, in which the lekythos has become very prominent, largely replacing the stirrup jar, and Cypriot-derived forms (the bird or duck vase, ring vase, bottle, and flask) are found (Desborough 1972: 43–4, 54; Lemos 2002: 79–80, 81–3).

The bird vase has a long and complex history, and probably originated earlier in the Aegean and came back there from Cyprus in two forms, one found in various parts of the Greek mainland, especially Achaea, and on Skyros, the other on Crete and Cos (Lemos 1994, 2002: 82–3). Examples of the flask and bottle also come from Early Protogeometric tombs at Lefkandi and settlement contexts at Asine, and from a tomb at Karphi (Desborough 1972: 61) (see Figure 7.1 for distribution). Although the closest parallels for these types are Late Cypriot IIIB (but they continue later in Cyprus), occurrences in the Aegean need not represent a very tight chronological link with this phase. Some certainly occur in Protogeometric contexts, while the earliest bird vases of the later forms may well be of later Late Helladic IIIC/Late Minoan IIIC date (all examples from Achaea and Palaiokastro in Arcadia are classified as Late Helladic IIIC Late in Mountjoy 1999: 299, 441). Only at Athens and Lefkandi does it seem legitimate to suggest a close chronological link, although a more generalised overlap between Submycenaean, earlier Subminoan, and the latest Achaean Late Helladic IIIC may be supposed (see Desborough 1972: 61–2, 93). This 'late Submycenaean' stage merges with the beginnings of Protogeometric, although the Cypriot types largely disappear from the ceramic repertoire. In fact, Attic Early Protogeometric really seems a transitional phase, in which types that might separately be classified as Submycenaean and Protogeometric are found in the same grave.

The difficulties of definition must lead to the question whether Submycenaean is a useful term. At best, it can be taken to identify the last, not in itself especially significant, stage of the Mycenaean pottery style in some central regions of the mainland, which was probably not very long-lived and can hardly be taken to represent a major phase of historical development (*contra* Lemos 2002: 26, which allows it two generations, with a third covering the transition to Protogeometric). There seem to have been comparable but different survivals of Mycenaean types elsewhere, as at Kalapodi, already mentioned, and in western Greece, especially the 'Submycenaean' material of the graves at Elis (Morgan 1990: 235–7, considers this probably later than Attic Submycenaean) and the Dark Age I of Nichoria (see p. 18). But whether the chamber tomb cemeteries of Achaea and Cephallenia continued in use into the eleventh or even tenth century (see most recently Morris, I. 1997: 549) is quite uncertain; Mountjoy (1999) classifies nothing from them as Submycenaean, although she identified Submycenaean and a transition to Protogeometric on Ithaca (1999: 475–8). In Crete, the current styles (the classification of Subminoan, well defined in the Knossos region, may not be appropriate everywhere; cf. the discussion of the Kavousi sequence in Hallager and Hallager 1997: 366–9) clearly derived from Late Minoan IIIC traditions, and certainly continued well past the point when Protogeometric styles, had become established in central mainland regions. In other regions there is either a still unbridgeable gap between the latest Mycenaean and the next well-represented style (as in Laconia), or a sequence that has no very obvious links with anything Aegean, as in Thasos, Epirus and to a great extent Macedonia, although here a painted style inspired by Mycenaean was popular for a considerable time.

With the establishment of the full Attic Protogeometric style the position becomes much more clear-cut. Knowledge of the Attic sequence is based almost entirely on the evidence of graves at present, particularly those of the Kerameikos and Agora, although considerable deposits, mainly from wells, have been found in the Agora region and some details have been published concerning them (Papadopoulos 2003: 5 and ch. 2). But despite the resulting rather limited amount of material for detailed analysis, the phases of the Attic Protogeometric and Geometric styles as defined in Desborough (1952) and Coldstream (1968) (Early, Middle and Late Protogeometric, Early Geometric I and II, Middle Geometric I and II, Late Geometric Ia, Ib, IIa and IIb) have been generally accepted as valid. Desborough argued that Early and Middle Protogeometric were short phases, no more than a generation each, but Late Protogeometric was long (Desborough 1972: 134–5), a view followed by Lemos (2002: 26). Smithson developed a four-part classification on the basis of the Agora material (Papadopoulos 2003: 5 n. 11). But this material remains unpublished at present, and it seems best to continue with the conventional terminology for now.

Once fully established, examples of the Attic Protogeometric style were evidently exported to, and had some influence over, an increasingly wide region of Greece, while the sequence of changes in the Attic Geometric style has been shown in Coldstream (1968) to be followed with varying degrees of closeness in many other regions. Examples of imported Attic pottery and close local imitations are sufficiently numerous to make establishing the relative position of most material a fairly easy matter in neighbouring parts of Greece from Late Protogeometric onwards, but of these only the Argolid and Euboea have produced good evidence for earlier stages in the sequence.

The Argolid sequence has largely been established on the basis of graves, with some support from settlement deposits not yet fully published, from Argos, Tiryns (Papadimitriou 1998) and Asine. The Asine deposits run without break from 'Final Mycenaean' into Protogeometric and are overlaid by Middle and Late Geometric deposits. They include numerous Attic Middle and Late Protogeometric imports, though nothing that looks like the very latest Attic Protogeometric, but unfortunately their value is limited. Although there is a stratigraphical and architectural sequence, there are Attic Late Protogeometric pieces even in the first Protogeometric phase distinguished by Wells (I am grateful to Dr I. Lemos for confirming this; see Lemos 2002: 5–6 for critical comments on Wells's analysis of the Asine material). The deposits must, therefore, be mixed, which explains why there is little discernible development. Nevertheless, there is local Early Protogeometric at Asine, which can be paralleled in other Argive material, and although Middle Protogeometric is poorly represented, Late Protogeometric

16

is well documented here and elsewhere (Lemos 2002: 13–14, 17, 21–2). Later, the Argive potters can be seen to follow the changes in Attic Geometric style so closely that they even imitated Early Geometric I, uniquely (on present evidence) in Greece. There are indications that Argive Geometric pottery was influential in other areas of the Peloponnese, but earlier links are very few and often speculative.

The Euboean style is best represented by the material from Lefkandi, though an increasing amount is being published from other sites, particularly, for the later Geometric phases, from Eretria. At Lefkandi a sequence of increasingly rich graves runs continuously from late Submycenaean into the period of Attic Middle Geometric I. Their evidence is complemented by that of an extremely large deposit of settlement material, datable to Middle Protogeometric, from the 'Heroön' building at Toumba, which may derive from Xeropolis, and a sequence of settlement deposits on Xeropolis running from Late Protogeometric to Late Geometric. Numerous Attic imports from Middle Protogeometric onwards allow tying the successive phases of the Euboean sequence very closely to Attic. Its special character is particularly noticeable in the phases equivalent to Attic Early Geometric to Middle Geometric I, when a Sub-Protogeometric style continued dominant. The Euboean sequence is particularly significant, not only because material very similar in style to its Late Protogeometric and Sub-Protogeometric was produced over a wide area, at its most extensive taking in eastern central Greece, eastern Thessaly, coastal central Macedonia, and many Aegean islands, but because most of the earliest Greek pottery found in the east Mediterranean is of these styles rather than Attic.

The situation in other parts of mainland Greece is more complex, and much of the material is not fully published. At Kalapodi in Phocis, there is a continuous series of stratified deposits of varying richness, stretching from Late Helladic IIIC Early through into historical times. Although links with Euboea are particularly strong, there are also plausible points of contact with the Peloponnese, including likely imports, in the Protogeometric and Geometric phases. But other material from central Greece that may be related to this sequence is still scanty. Some Protogeometric to Sub-Protogeometric settlement material has been published from Iolkos (Sipsie-Eschbach 1991), but the stratigraphical support for the suggested sequence, in which Protogeometric types are slowly adopted alongside a strongly surviving Late Helladic IIIC tradition, is not very strong, and, as at Asine, types that one would attribute elsewhere to widely differing phases are found together, leading to the suspicion that much of the material is mixed (see Lemos 2002: 6, citing critical analysis by M. Jacob-Felsch).

In western Greece there is a major stratified sequence at Nichoria in Messenia, for which a sequence of Dark Age I–III phases was devised by Coulson (*Nichoria III*: ch. 3), applied by him in later studies to all the material from Messenia and to that from Polis in Ithaca (Coulson 1986,

1991). But there are difficulties, in particular that Nichorian Dark Age I is not defined on the basis of any substantial and distinct deposits, and could include material covering a wide range from later Late Helladic IIIC downwards (*Nichoria II*: 767, cf. 519 on the links with advanced Late Helladic IIIC; it should be noted that Mountjoy 1999: 363, 475–7 classifies 'Dark Age I' material from Nichoria and Polis as Submycenaean), that Dark Age II/III is local to Nichoria and represented only by material from the second floor of Unit IV–1 (and so could be interpreted as a variant style, as in Morgan 1990), and that Dark Age III almost certainly overlaps with Late Geometric (Morgan 1990: 77, 268–9; cf. Catling in *Nichoria III*: 281–2 on the parallels of a bronze figurine from a Dark Age III context). Also, as has been pointed out by Snodgrass (1984), the absolute chronology proposed for the sequence is weakly based, since the most plausible stylistic links are with the sequences of Ithaca and Achaea, which themselves have no basis for an absolute chronology, and the dates accepted for some of the parallels are questionably high. All that can be said for certain is that the clearly continuous Nichoria sequence seems to begin with a style which has strong Mycenaean elements, so may be thought unlikely to have started much later than *c.* 1000. The presence of early (Submycenaean–Early Protogeometric) bronze types on the site (Catling, in *Nichoria III*: 276–8 on nos. 1, 5, 8), though none are in context, suggests a beginning within the eleventh century. The long and important Dark Age II phase (incorporating Dark Age II/III) may well have fallen largely in the ninth century, though starting in the tenth, and could even overlap into the eighth (Catling, in *Nichoria III*: 277 on no. 6; Coulson 1991: 45, in fact suggests this for Dark Age II at Polis).

The Ithacan material, as represented by the deposits at Polis (which consist almost exclusively of open shapes and so are probably of special character) and Aëtos, appears to run continuously from Late Helladic IIIC Late through the Early Iron Age. But the material is very distinctive and can only be linked to the standard Aegean sequence at the very end of the period, through the presence in quantity of Corinthian Geometric, mainly Late Geometric, imports and imitations, and there is no real stratigraphical support for any system of phases. The Achaean Protogeometric material comes entirely from tombs and has no demonstrable link to Late Helladic IIIC, but pots from tombs in and around Elis and newly found material from deposits at Olympia provide a skeleton sequence from Submycenaean into Geometric (Eder 1999, 2001). Occasional pieces that seem to be Protogeometric imports from further east, found in both Messenia and Ithaca, and the occurrence of what may be an Ithacan import at Medeon in Phocis, closely paralleled at Derveni in Achaea (Morgan 1990: 248–9, there dated *c.* 840–790), help to suggest general parallels between these west Greek sequences and the Aegean.

The situation is similar for Laconia, in that what was evidently quite a long-lived style can only at present be subdivided through stylistic analysis

(Coulson 1985; see Lemos 2002: 194 n. 33 for scepticism about the supposed chronological linking of Laconian Protogeometric with the earliest Proto-geometric phase at Asine). Comparable material, but showing some signifi-cant differences from Laconian proper, has been found at Tegea, associated with local types and some that resemble standard Attic or Argive Late Protogeometric, Early and Middle Geometric, including possible imports. But the stratification is complex and it is not easy to isolate clear evidence of development (Voyatzis 1997; I am very grateful to Prof. Voyatzis for valuable information on this material).

It has to be said that Coulson's identification of a 'west Greek koinē', taking in the western Peloponnese, Ithaca, and Aetolia, to which he relates 'Laconian Protogeometric', seems a misuse of the term. There is no common style in these regions, as there is to a great extent in the 'Thessalo-Euboean koinē' identified by Desborough. Rather, there is a group of regional styles which have elements in common, such as the ridge-stemmed kylix, but also strong local features. The kantharoi, which are a common shape in Ithaca, Achaea, Elis and Aetolia, are the nearest thing to a koinē type comparable to the Thessalo-Euboean skyphoi, but their decoration varies between regions and the shape has not been identified in Messenia or Laconia. Stylistically, the Ithacan and Elean material also seems to have developed from the local and rather different Late Helladic IIIC styles represented in the Cephal-lenian and north-west Peloponnesian chamber tomb cemeteries respectively (Desborough 1972: 88, 243–7); there may have been a degree of convergence between these styles at a time equivalent to Protogeometric. But it is not possible, for lack of material, to trace such a development for Messenia or Laconia, and most Messenian material is conspicuously lacking in close links with the most distinctive features of any other style – the resemblances cited by Coulson are generally rather vague, involving simple and widespread motifs.

On Crete the sequence is quite distinct, and clearly developed at a differ-ent pace and under different stimuli from the major mainland areas. Until recently the best-known sequence was that of Knossos, known largely from the cemetery evidence and scattered settlement deposits, which form no useful stratified sequences. Recent excavations at Knossos have provided a clear sequence from Late Minoan IIIC to Subminoan (Warren 1983: 69–83), but excavations at Kavousi have been even more fruitful, providing, mainly from the Kastro site, an apparently continuous sequence of settlement deposits from Late Minoan IIIC to the seventh century. Relatively little of this material has been published as yet, but it will provide an important check on Knossos. For the later part of the period, from the later tenth century onwards, the deposits of Kommos will also be important. But Knossos still provides much the best evidence for links with the Greek mainland: Attic, Euboean and other pottery appears there from some time in Late Protogeometric onwards. The site's often idiosyncratic products evidently had some influence elsewhere in Crete, in the ninth century particularly, in whose later part a precocious 'orientalising' style known as Protogeometric B was developed at Knossos. The influences of this style survived alongside those from successive phases of mainland Geometric, but during the eighth century north Crete came more and more into line with the mainland sequences. The dating of these developments is still largely a matter of reasoned guesswork (cf. *NorthCem* 410–12).

Absolute chronology

(*Note*: This chapter was in final form when, through the kindness of Dr K. Wardle, I was made aware of remarkable new evidence from Assiros, bearing on the beginning of Protogeometric (Newton *et al.* 2003, published in 2005) and the dating of Late Helladic IIIB (Wardle *et al.* 2004). On the basis of a combination of dendrochronology and radiocarbon 'wiggle-match' dating it is argued that Protogeometric started before 1070, and Late Helladic IIIB ended before 1270/1250. But the case for the former date does rest on an assumption which is not beyond question, that the Group I amphorae represent an influence from Attic Protogeometric. Since their distribution shows little overlap with that of earlier Attic Protogeometric (they coincide only at Lefkandi: see Figure 7.1), it seems quite possible that this type was developed quite independently. At any rate, given that there are no reliable chronological fixes for this period, as Newton *et al.* point out, this could be accommodated, if with difficulty. But the date for the end of Late Helladic IIIB seems impossible to reconcile with the range that has been thought acceptable on the basis of contextual evidence and ceramic cross-connections (I am grateful to Dr E.S. Sherratt for advice and comment here). It seems best to await the reactions of other experts, and in what follows I have kept to the 'standard' chronology. If either of these suggestions was accepted, it would raise all dates suggested below for Late Helladic IIIC and/or Protogeometric phases by 25–50 years.)

Evidence for absolute chronology is still remarkably scanty, so that all previous references to centuries in this chapter are estimated guesses and deliberately vague. Arguments which combine radiocarbon dates and mainly Egyptian synchronisms for putting the end of Late Helladic IIIB, equivalent to the end of the Third Palace Period, within and perhaps near the end of a 1200–1180 range were set out by Warren and Hankey (1989: 159–62). Scientific forms of dating have rarely been used for succeeding phases, and have generally been unhelpful, as is the case with two radiocarbon dates from the Lefkandi Late Helladic IIIC Early destruction, which seem too high and have a very wide range when calibrated (*c.* 1410–1230), and a series of radiocarbon dates from Nichoria for Dark Age I–III contexts, which are inconsistent, where not obviously contaminated. A radiocarbon date from

Asine Structure IO falls in the right range for the conventional dating for Protogeometric (976 ± 73, according to Manning and Weninger 1992: 639), but again the calibrated range is too wide to be very helpful.

The discovery of stirrup jars of Late Helladic IIIC style at Beth Shan in Palestine used to be thought to provide a good chronological link for Late Helladic IIIC (Warren and Hankey 1989: 164–5). But there are several problems, notably that the Beth Shan material is certainly Cypriot (as reported in D'Agata *et al.* 2005, where Yasur-Landau links the strata in which it is found with the reigns of Ramesses III and IV, *c.* 1185–1147). How its dating should be applied to the Aegean sequence is open to debate, although stylistically it should fall within or close to Late Helladic IIIC Middle. More worrying are Yasur-Landau's criticisms of how this material is combined with a separate item from Megiddo dating to the reign of Ramesses VI (*c.* 1143–1136) to suggest a date of 1150/1140 for the *beginning* of LH IIIC Middle (2003: 238–9). He contrasts this with the perception that pictorial kraters from Ugarit, probably destroyed before *c.* 1185, have close links with east Aegean material which Mountjoy assigns to LH IIIC Middle (2003: 236). If the end of Late Helladic IIIB is to be raised well into the thirteenth century, then higher dates for the Late Helladic IIIC Middle phase might well be acceptable, but at present there seems no easy solution to these problems.

It has been argued that both Late Helladic IIIC Early and Middle were long phases, because of the number of building phases identifiable, especially at Mycenae and Tiryns, and Late Helladic IIIC Late was short (Warren and Hankey 1989: 167–8; cf. Mountjoy's detailed chart in 1988: 27). This argument has weaknesses, in that there is no agreed way to turn building phases into periods of years or generations, but it does seem reasonable to suppose that Late Helladic IIIC Early and Middle were both several decades long. However, there is no comparable basis for allowing two full generations for Submycenaean (as in Lemos 2002: 26); Mountjoy's two generations for the Pompeion cemetery, referred to by Warren and Hankey, actually begin in Late Helladic IIIC Late. It seems safest to suggest that taken together the Late Helladic IIIC phases and Submycenaean covered from near the start of the twelfth century until at least the middle of the eleventh, on the conventional chronology. But the survival of 'Mycenaean' types in various ways in different parts of Greece makes it impossible to give a universally applicable end-date for Late Helladic IIIC.

A beginning date of *c.* 1050 for Attic Protogeometric was suggested in Desborough (1972: especially p. 55), in preference to the *c.* 1025 of Desborough (1952), on the basis of the links with Late Cypriot IIIB mentioned above. This would clash with the low dates suggested for Submycenaean by Warren and Hankey (1989: 167–8), but Hankey has argued for lowering the beginning of Protogeometric in Mountjoy (1988: 35–6), by redating the links with Cyprus. However, as Bikai notes (1978: 66), the chronology of Cypriot pottery is itself dependent on Syro-Palestinian links, and the chronology of this region is no more secure between the twelfth and ninth centuries than that of the Aegean. Thus, the stratified sequence of Late Bronze Age and Early Iron Age levels at Tyre published by Bikai (1978: especially ch. III), and commented on by Coldstream (1988), has produced relatively many Greek imports. But the series of likely Euboean and Attic pieces from later strata in the sequence (Coldstream 1988: 38–41) is used to support the suggested absolute chronology of the Tyrian phases, which otherwise depends almost entirely on Cypriot imports (cf. comments in Warren and Hankey 1989: 167; also Hannestad 1996: 47). These finds cannot, then, provide any independent support for the standard Protogeometric-Geometric sequence thought to cover the tenth, ninth and eighth centuries. Nor can the discovery of a fragment of a probably Euboean Middle or very early Late Protogeometric dinos at Tel Hadar in Galilee (Coldstream 1998b: 357–8; Snodgrass [1971] 2000: xxvi; Lemos 2002: 25) be very helpful, when the basis for an absolute context date estimated by the excavators as no later than *c.* 980 remains unclear. To sum up, the best that can be said is that it seems reasonable to suggest that Protogeometric began no later than *c.* 1025 and that the transition from Middle to Late Protogeometric was no later than *c.* 950, quite possibly earlier. The Lefkandi 'Heroön' and its massive Middle Protogeometric deposit fall close to but before this transition, so could well date a decade or two before *c.* 950.

Effectively, then, there are no links that might be helpful for absolute chronology until the later Geometric pottery phases, if then. The dividing line between Attic Protogeometric and Geometric at *c.* 900 is convenient but purely conventional, and the estimated lengths of the Protogeometric and Geometric pottery phases remain based essentially on their perceived significance in stylistic development, and to some extent on the quantity of material that is assigned to them, which is not necessarily a sound basis. Coldstream's discussion of the absolute chronology of the Geometric phases (1968: ch. 13) provided what has become accepted as a standard dating system, but several of its foundations have become insecure. Forsberg has recently demonstrated the fallacies involved in accepting supposedly fixed historical dates for the destructions of Samaria and Tarsus (1995). Also, the claimed foundation dates of the Greek colonies in Italy and Sicily, which at the earliest relate to the later eighth century, should be excluded from the argument, although on the conventional chronology they are compatible with the available archaeological material (Morris 1996). Not only do they derive from foundation myths whose relationship to genuine historical data is strongly open to question (Osborne 1997), but there may well be good reason to reassess the lengths calculated for the later Geometric phases. Suggested changes in the central Italian chronology, on the basis of well-stratified radiocarbon samples (Nijboer *et al.* 2001), may yet require an earlier beginning of Middle Geometric and later end of Late Geometric.

Date BC	Historical phases used in this book	Finally Mycenaean pottery phases		Central Cretan pottery phases
1200/1190		LH IIIC Early		
	Postpalatial	—		LM IIIC
1150/1140		LH IIIC Middle		
1100/1090		—		—
		LH IIIC Late and Submycenaean		
		Central regions' pottery phases, especially Attic	Suggested extent of Coulson's western Greek pottery phases	Subminoan
1050/1025				
950	Early	EPG	↑?	
		MPG	Dark Age I	
900	Iron	LPG	↓	
			↑	
850	Age	EG I and II		MPG and LPG
			Dark Age II	
800		MG I		PG B
			↓?	
750		MGII and LG Ia		MG
			Dark Age III and LG	
700		LG Ib, IIa, IIb		LG

Figure 1.1 Terminological system, with relative and absolute chronological phases.

Thus, while a chronology close to the standard one is suggested in Figure 1.1, it should not be pressed in terms of years (see the useful comments in Boardman 1998: 9–10).

Bibliography

Warren and Hankey (1989: 162–9) is the most extensive treatment of the absolute chronology of Late Helladic IIIC and Submycenaean; see also Hankey in Mountjoy (1988: 33–7). Manning and Weninger (1992) survey radio-carbon dates from the Aegean relevant to the last stages of the Bronze Age published to that date, but could not take account of Wardle *et al.* (2004).

Snodgrass (1971: ch. 2) is a detailed attempt to establish a relative chronology covering the entire Early Iron Age, incorporating the results of Coldstream (1968: ch. 13). Lemos (2002: 24–6) usefully surveys the material with special reference to Protogeometric, but could not take account of Kromer *et al.* (2004).

Hannestad (1996) is the latest discussion of Early Iron Age chronological links with the Near East consulted.

2

THE COLLAPSE OF THE BRONZE AGE CIVILISATION

The background

One of the most interesting problems of Greek history, which this book is bound to address, is what brought about the collapse of BA civilisation in the Aegean (hereafter to be referred to simply as 'the Collapse'). First, some discussion of this civilisation's development and nature is needed. The Minoan culture of Crete may be considered to have flowered into a full civilisation in the early centuries of the second millennium, when the major building complexes termed 'palaces' were established in Crete and Minoan influence began to make itself felt in other parts of the Aegean. But after reaching a peak around 1600–1450 it went into decline, and by the thirteenth century had long been supplanted as the major source of cultural influence in the Aegean by the Mycenaean civilisation. This civilisation's greatest centres were on the mainland, in the Peloponnese and central Greece, but it may be considered to have spread its influence through most of the Aegean, forming a zone which showed more cultural homogeneity than ever before in Greek prehistory, although there were still significant regional and local variations. Crete, in particular, retained several distinctive traditions.

Quite how much of the mainland should be included within the Mycenaean cultural region remains an interesting question (cf. Feuer 1983). But Snodgrass's view that in areas in central Greece such as Phocis, Locris and Aetolia

> the reflections of Mycenaean culture were faint and fleeting at best;
> and where as a result the material features of Middle Helladic times
> appear to merge directly and uninterruptedly into those of the post-
> Mycenaean period . . .
>
> (Snodgrass [1971] 2000: xxvi)

is unacceptable. Chamber-tomb cemeteries, one of the commonest Mycenaean features, are widespread in Phocis and Locris; Mycenaean pottery seems to be

24

common in both decorated and plain forms, rather than occurring only as a rare import; and many other forms of Mycenaean artefact, including seal-stones (which clearly have considerable cultural significance), are widely found. The situation is not so clear in Aetolia (Thermon, where many typical plain Mycenaean forms are missing, is considered unlikely to be 'Mycenaean', see Wardle and Wardle 2003: 150), or in western Thessaly, and there may well have been a Mycenaean/non-Mycenaean interface in these regions. But overall the impression given by the material is that the boundaries of the Mycenaean culture on the southern mainland coincided fairly closely with the area considered Greek in Classical times (Figure 2.1).

The leading settlements of the Mycenaean civilisation were substantial. Their populations probably reached several thousands, comparable in size to the smaller cities of the Near East, and the most important centred upon the major ceremonial and administrative structures that we call palaces. The palaces are generally regarded as the nerve centres of Mycenaean civilisation, giving their name to the system of organisation known as the palace society, which made use of the Linear B script for administrative purposes (Figure 2.2). Such societies are most unlikely to have existed in every part of the Aegean, but they seem typical of the leading regions, although there were evidently flourishing areas that have not yet produced evidence of them (Deger-Jalkotzy 1995: 373–4), and it is likely that the general prosperity of the Aegean depended upon them to a large extent.

Unlike Near Eastern cities, major Mycenaean settlements did not have a secondary focus in a large temple complex, nor did they normally have encircling walls, although some, like Thebes and Pylos, may have had walls that enclosed a significant proportion of the settled area (on Pylos, see Shelmerdine 2001: 337–9; convincing evidence for a Theban circuit of non-'Cyclopean' type was presented in an unpublished paper given by Dr V. Aravantinos at the POLEMOS conference, see Laffineur 1999). More common, though still relatively rare, were the massive walls in 'Cyclopean' style that encircled citadels only, as at Mycenae, Tiryns and Athens. But some settlements of considerable importance have not yet produced any evidence of fortifications at all, such as Orchomenos, the Menelaion site, and the extensive town at Dhimini plausibly identified as Mycenaean Iolkos (Adrymi-Sismani 1994; a large complex of palatial character, apparently con-structed in LH IIIB2, was described in Lemos and Deger-Jalkotzy 2003 by Mrs V. Adrymi-Sismani – see Figure 2.3). Nevertheless, Orchomenos evi-dently commanded very considerable resources, for it was surely the centre responsible for the construction of the enormous fortified site at Gla and a whole network of associated dykes, artificial levees or polders and subsidiary fortifications in the Lake Copais region (Iakovidis 1998: 197–204, 275–8). There also exist extensive fortified sites on low hills, such as Krisa and Teikhos Dymaion, which do not seem to enclose a palace or other major building, but may nevertheless represent centres of major local importance.

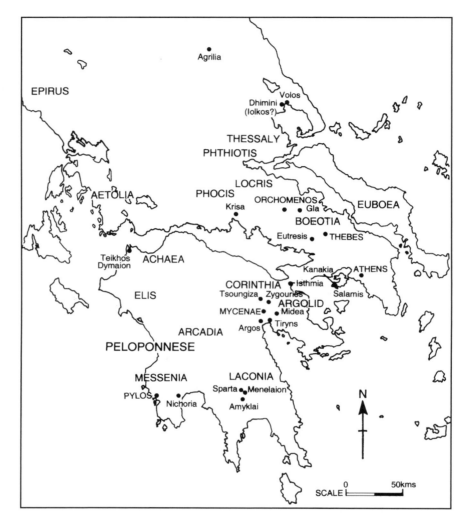

Figure 2.1 Significant Third Palace Period sites on the mainland and nearest islands.

International relations

It is sometimes suggested that the Mycenaean world was largely or wholly organised into a single political system or state under the rule of Mycenae, which might then be equated with the kingdom of Ahhiyawa frequently mentioned in the Hittite texts. An interesting argument presented by Postgate (in Voutsaki and Killen 2001: 160) is that the remarkable level of homogeneity in the format of tablets written in Linear B over a long period would suggest, to a Near Eastern specialist, that at least the centres which

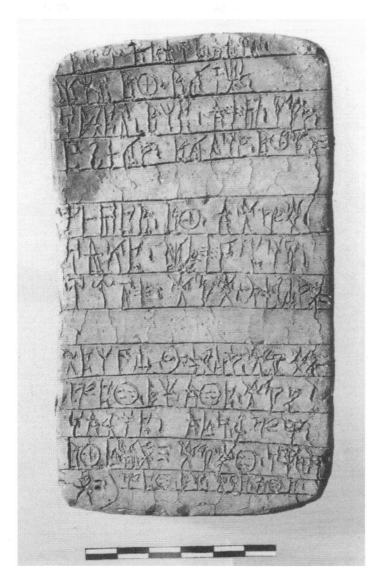

Figure 2.2 Linear B tablet An 657, first of the *o-ka* series, from the palace at Pylos. Courtesy of the Department of Classics, University of Cincinnati, and Prof. T. Palaima.

have produced them all fell under a single authority. But none of the material so far recovered gives any hint of subordination to a superior, and the areas concerned (central and western Crete, the central Argolid, much of Messenia, eastern Boeotia) seem too remote from each other to be easily

27

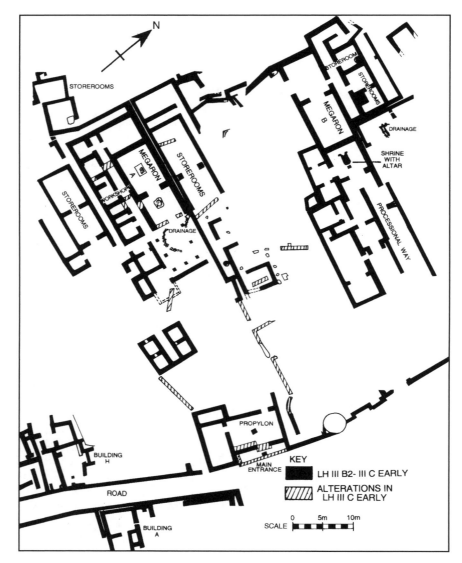

Figure 2.3 Plan of Dhimini palace. Courtesy of Mrs V. Adrymi-Sismani.

controllable from a single centre, and have never until modern times been part of a single state, unless it was much more extensive. Other arguments traditionally presented for a unified Mycenaean political system are weak. There is no reason why the considerable degree of cultural homogeneity should imply political unity, and, while the relevance of the *Iliad* to any sort of Bronze Age reality is highly debatable, it does not in any case represent the other rulers and commanders as Agamemnon's vassals, duty bound to follow him. Rather, the Achaean confederacy is clearly temporary, if formed under both temporal and divine pressure (for Hera's involvement in raising the army see *Iliad* 4.26–8).

It is likely that there were many major and minor principalities in the Aegean in the Third Palace Period, which were linked in networks of alliance and dependency (in a paper presented at Laffineur *et al.* 2005, Eder offered arguments that regions of central and northern Greece may have been formally dependent on the palace centres), and may have been ruled by inter-related families. The possible existence of an 'international' ruling aristocracy in the Aegean has been argued for by Killen, on the grounds that some of the apparently high-status personages identified as 'collectors' at Knossos and Pylos have identical names. This view has been supported by Olivier (Voutsaki and Killen 2001: 151–6), but various features of the argument are reasonably questioned by Rougemont (in Voutsaki and Killen 2001: 129–38). If the 'collectors' should prove to belong to such an aristocracy, it is noteworthy that virtually none of their names occur in the mythical geneal-ogies of the heroic age. But, even if this were accepted, it remains quite undemonstrable that the Aegean region was largely united within a single political framework.

The topic of Ahhiyawa deserves further comment. The latest work on the geography of western Anatolia in Hittite times leaves no room for doubt that the mainland territories of Ahhiyawa can only have been situated in the archaeologically Mycenaean or strongly Mycenaeanised south-west, although the core of this state was evidently situated overseas (Hawkins 1998: 30–1). The possibility that the name represents *Akhaiwia*, 'land of the Achaeans', is thereby strengthened (*contra* Dickinson 1994a: 253). The evidence for the rela-tively swift exchange of letters between the Hittite and Ahhiyawan kings and the indications that there could be personal relationships between the respect-ive ruling elites of these states (Gurney 1990: 40) would make best sense if Ahhiyawa's centre was situated close to the Anatolian coast, e.g. on Rhodes, as argued by Mountjoy (1998: 49–51; see Sherratt 2001: 218 n. 9). But it is hard to find on Rhodes convincing evidence for the existence of a powerful state, whose kings would be treated with the respect shown to the kings of Ahhiyawa by several Hittite kings, and it may yet prove that Mycenae or Thebes (the two most obvious candidates) was the capital of Ahhiyawa, and therefore controlled not only territory on the Greek mainland but some of the Aegean islands and parts of south-west Anatolia, especially the region of Miletus.

However, there is no mention of Ahhiyawa outside the Hittite documents, which makes it hard to estimate just how important this state really was in the power politics of the time. Perhaps the Hittite kings, who had to deal with potential and actual enemies on several fronts, were forced to show more respect to the kings of Ahhiyawa than they would have wanted to do, because, being based outside the Anatolian mainland, these could not be easily reached by punitive expeditions and were in a position to cause serious trouble in western Anatolia. Certainly, there is not much other evidence to suggest that rulers in the Aegean might have had diplomatic ties with rulers in the Near East. Cline (1995: 146–7) assembles some references, especially regarding links with Egypt, but nothing later than the mid-fourteenth century, and there is no Nineteenth Dynasty material in thirteenth-century Aegean contexts (J. Phillips, pers. comm.). Sandars' comment 'There was a rich man's club, and it looks as though the Aegean rulers were not full members' ([1978] 1985: 184) rings true (see also Voutsaki 2001: 212; Sherratt 2001: 217–18).

The nature of overseas exchange

The position of the rulers of Aegean principalities in the eyes of their contemporaries in the Near East (see Figure 2.4) has significance for more than political history. It does not seem exaggerated to suggest that the standard of living of the Aegean ruling elite, and to some extent of the population as a whole, was dependent on exchange, particularly with the Near East, which must have been the major source of several valuable materials: gold, ivory, tin, glass, even probably copper. Although Laurion in south Attica seems to have been a significant copper source, it and other sources in the Aegean are unlikely to have produced enough to provide for all Aegean needs, and Cypriot copper has been identified increasingly in thirteenth-century contexts (these comments assume that the results of lead-isotope analysis have been correctly interpreted, but see Chapter 4, p. 83). How this exchange was conducted must therefore be a matter of considerable importance.

In the absence of written documentation (the Linear B tablets provide very little help in this respect), much use has been made of analogy with the Near East and modern anthropological data. It has been argued, notably by Snodgrass (1991), that Aegean relations with the Near East were conducted almost entirely by the palace centres, which on this interpretation completely dominated the mobilisation and distribution of commodities within their territories. It has further been suggested that, where precious and exotic materials were involved, these relations took place very much in the context of (probably infrequent) exchanges of ceremonial gifts, such as are well documented in the Near East (Cline 1995). Ships of any size would have been owned by the palaces or at least the elite, and those who captained them would have been acting as their agents. Thus, there would have been virtually no scope for 'commercial' trade, particularly not by Aegean 'merchants', although the possibility of 'merchants' entering the Aegean from the Near East, which was more developed economically, could not be excluded.

But this analysis raises many questions, quite apart from its questionable emphasis on the palaces' central redistributive role (see further, pp. 37–8). Not least of these is how far the practice of ceremonial gift exchange actually

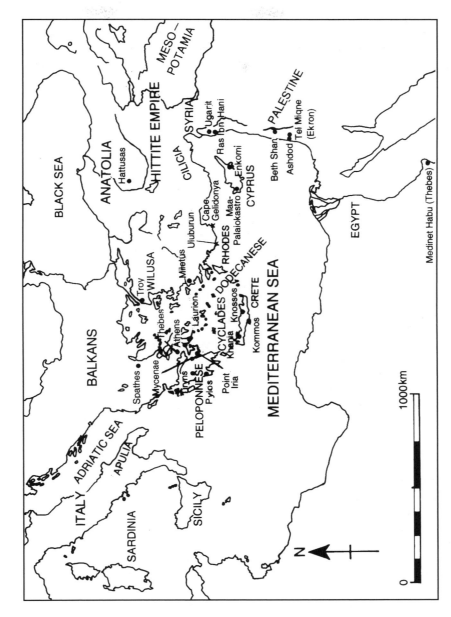

Figure 2.4 The international setting of the Aegean in the Third Palace Period.

dominated the distribution of commodities in the Near East; Cline (1995: 149) describes it as only the 'tip of the iceberg'. In fact, Aegean products which would be suitable for ceremonial gifts, especially the typical luxury items of the Third Palace Period, jewellery, precious vessels, and inlaid furniture, to which the numerous fine ivory works in relief must belong (Figure 2.5), are found extremely rarely in the Near East. Also, it remains only a

Figure 2.5 Ivory inlay from the House of Sphinxes, Mycenae. H. *c.* 4.5 cm. Courtesy of the British School at Athens.

plausible surmise that the high-quality textiles produced by palace-supervised work teams were used in long-distance exchange, although there is good Near Eastern evidence for a comparable use of textiles. However, in Cyprus finely decorated Mycenaean pottery seems to have had prestige value at more than one social level (Steel 1998), and both here and elsewhere the containers that form a large proportion of this pottery may have held the perfumed oil known to have been produced on a large scale under palace supervision, which could well have been used in gift exchange or served as an exchange commodity.

One is bound to wonder how, on Snodgrass's view, large-scale exchange is supposed to have operated before there were palaces, as apparently on the mainland before the fourteenth century, or in regions not controlled by palaces. It is noteworthy that Kommos, which looks most like an international port of all Aegean centres (Cline 1994: 87; but increasing quantities of 'foreign' material are being found at Tiryns), was not demonstrably under such control, though it could have acted as the port of a principality based at Ayia Triada. Further, palace-organised states seem totally lacking from the parts of Europe with which the Mycenaean civilisation was apparently in contact, including the north Aegean and more northern parts of the Balkans, the Adriatic, southern Italy and the central Mediterranean as far as Sardinia. This wide spread of exchange activity (Figure 2.4) was arguably very important to the Aegean world, especially the link with the central Mediterranean, which may well have been a source of metals, especially copper and silver, and with which Cypriot centres also seem to have been establishing an important relationship by the thirteenth century. Exchange relations here must surely have been carried on in a rather different manner from Snodgrass's model.

Consideration of the evidence from shipwrecks also demonstrates how complex the picture could have been, for each of those now known, from Uluburun, Cape Gelidonya, and Point Iria, may be interpreted to represent a different type of exchange, although types of stone anchor that have good Near Eastern parallels, but are rarely reported from Aegean contexts (Pulak 1998: 216), are associated with all three. The natural deduction, that the ships came from the Near East, is strengthened in the case of the Uluburun and Cape Gelidonya wrecks by the dominant Near Eastern element in their cargoes and among the items likely to have been ship's gear or the possessions of crew and passengers (see especially Pulak 1998: 216–18 on Uluburun). These include sets of pan-balance weights of Near Eastern types, such as would be used in commercial transactions, whereas Aegean types of weight are wholly missing.

The Uluburun wreck, which dates close to 1300, certainly held high-status goods that would be suitable for ceremonial exchange, and such enormous quantities of valuable raw materials, especially copper, tin, glass, terebinth resin, and African blackwood (the ancient ebony), as to seem far in excess of what any private individual could accumulate for use in trade. Nevertheless, many other items among the very heterogeneous range of items found, which include precious metal items that seem likely to be scrap, storage amphorae whose contents include olives, yellow arsenic, and glass beads, and ordinary clay bowls, wall brackets and lamps, hardly seem appropriate to a ceremonial context. The many pan-balance weights also constitute a strong indication of commercial activity (Pulak 1998: 209–10 estimates that there are enough for at least three persons to have separate sets, both for accurate small measurements and for heavier weights). It may therefore be best to imagine this as the ship of some high-status trader like Sinaranu of Ugarit (on whom see Heltzer 1988), who acted as a royal agent but also traded on his own account. There may have been important passengers aboard (Pulak 1998: 218 argues for two high-status 'Mycenaeans'). Sherratt suggests that, if intended for a single Mycenaean ruler, the material would have been trans-shipped on the edge of the Aegean, at somewhere like Rhodes or Kommos (2000: 89 n. 3). But the sheer quantities of materials and the heterogeneity of the cargo make it possible that the ship was not heading for a single destination, but intending to visit a number of ports (Dickinson 1994a: 238), which need not all have been in the Mycenaean Aegean. Several major kingdoms extended to the coast in western Anatolia, including Wilusa, which should be placed in the Troad and of which Troy itself may well have been the capital (see recently Hawkins 1998).

In contrast, the owner of the Cape Gelidonya ship, datable close to 1200, seems to have been mainly a dealer in metal, in that the cargo consists largely of metal ingots, totalling far less in quantity of metal than was found in the Uluburun ship, and a mass of fragmentary items that are probably scrap; there were also at least two Aegean storage stirrup jars (Bass 1991: 69–71) and other items. The thin bars of low-alloy tin-bronze, large quantities of probable scrap, and various tools that would suit a smithy have been inter-preted as evidence that the ship carried a smith who could offer tinkering work while in port, although other explanations are possible. The apparently non-Cypriot copper of these bars and the presence of Aegean stirrup jars again provide indications that this ship could have had a complex itinerary that involved calls at several ports, while the absence of elite items argues against any direct connection with ceremonial gift exchange.

Finally, it seems impossible to interpret the Point Iria wreck, the only one found within the Mycenaean region, in the context of ceremonial gift exchange or even of the large-scale movement of staples which in Snodgrass's view was the palaces' main method of overseas trade. The pottery consists very largely of storage vessels, including, in almost equal quantities, Cypriot pithoi, storage stirrup jars from southern central Crete, so alike that they probably belong to a single shipment (Haskell 2003), and Helladic storage jars and amphorae. There are a few smaller vessels, among them part of a decorated deep bowl that should date the whole group to LH IIIB2. This looks most like the ship of a trader in local produce, carried in 'recycled' storage vessels of various origins; but more details are needed.

Ultimately, then, we must admit that we still know very little about the context of Aegean long-distance exchange. The evidence for it certainly cannot be used, in the absence of written documentation, to argue for high-level ceremonial exchanges of the kind that would indicate diplomatic contacts between rulers in the Aegean and Near East. Nor does it seem likely that relations were close enough and the Aegean dependent enough for it to be, in World Systems Theory, a 'periphery' to the Near East's 'core'.

In this connection, it is important to mention Sherratt's interesting hypothesis that the Mycenaean palace states essentially depended on their involvement in trade routes (2001). But this is bound up with discussion of the nature of the Mycenaean palace states, to which we must now turn.

The nature of Mycenaean palace society

A palace was evidently at one and the same time the residence for a monarch-like figure, the *wanax*, the administrative centre for the territory over which he presided, and the place where important public cult activities took place, perhaps even focused on the *wanax* himself (see recently Maran 2001: 116–17 and Albers 2001: especially 132–5). It was effectively common ground until recently that a palace's administrative system could be described as 'an elaborate bureaucratic organization relying on intense centralization of resources and elaborate mechanisms of control' (Voutsaki and Killen 2001: 6). But the degree to which agricultural and craft production and the movement of resources were centrally controlled and organised has been the subject of increasing discussion recently (see further, pp. 37–8), and Sherratt has offered a very different analysis. This lays stress on what she perceives as the uniformity and lack of innovation in many features of the palace societies, including the way that Linear B was used, and interprets the palace society as 'a client-based warrior society onto which the outward trappings of a derivative, and essentially symbolic, idea of "palatial" civilisation were rather clumsily grafted' (2001: 238). In her view, the palaces did not necessarily even control solid blocks of territory, but rather sections or nodes of trade routes.

Sherratt's arguments are interesting and deserve more detailed consideration than can be offered here, but they reflect a very individual presentation of data which are usually interpreted otherwise. At least one palace, at Pylos, does seem to have controlled a substantial block of territory which contained many settlements of varying size, from townships to villages and hamlets; *c.* 240 place-names have been recognised (Whitelaw 2001: 63), far more than one would expect if trade routes through territory were all that was being controlled. Thebes also seems, to judge from the place-names in Linear B documents found there, to control substantial parts of eastern Boeotia and even of south Euboea. In fact, the administrative systems identified through analysis of the Linear B tablets and of the sealings found in many major centres seem much too sophisticated to be simply 'outward trappings', and there is evidence for development and improvement even within Linear B (e.g. Palaima 1988: 341). There may even have been significant differences in the administrative systems between sites. Thus, the 'archive' at Pylos, which contains about 80 per cent of all tablets found there, has no obvious parallel at Thebes, where substantial groups of tablets have appeared in several separate locations, as is also the case in the 'Linear B palace' at Knossos, and probably, to judge from the more scanty remains, at Mycenae and Tiryns. The failure to develop the use of writing itself beyond very narrow limits, emphasised by Sherratt, is equally applicable to the Second Palace Period Minoan civilisation, which lasted for a comparable time to Mycenaean palace civilisation.

Further, the sample on which Sherratt's analysis is based is very small, and there is more evidence for variation than she allows. Essentially, only three Mycenaean palace plans have been uncovered more or less completely: at Mycenae (the least well known), Tiryns and Pylos. We do not know whether the plan at Thebes, arguably a more important site than Pylos, was closely comparable, although it seems unlikely (Dakouri-Hild 2001: especially 105). The complex recently uncovered at Dhimini (Figure 2.3), which may well be the nearest thing to a palace that will ever be found in Thessaly, has a much less integrated plan than the Peloponnesian examples and has produced no frescoes. Where found, frescoes do indeed include repeated themes, but these cannot always be shown to have Minoan antecedents, especially those depicting hunting and the (very rare) war scenes, and there are notable variations in other themes between the major sites. Finally, it is hard to find evidence for the kind of atmosphere that would be appropriate to a 'warrior society', particularly in the areas where the palace societies were clearly established (Dickinson 1994a: 81, 306–7). The distribution of the massive 'Cyclopean' fortifications, whose function is surely as much to display wealth and power as to defend, does not match that of palaces at all well, for neither Pylos nor Thebes has one, while several sites without palaces do, as noted above. The society may well have had militaristic overtones, but no more so then the Near Eastern civilisations.

It seems best, then, to adhere to some version of the standard interpretation of the palace societies. To accept this is to envisage that they provided security and organised government for the population of their territories and that they exploited the resources of these territories through forms of taxation, that not only produced raw materials for the craft specialists working for and supervised by the palaces but also food rations and other supplies for the personnel that the palaces partly or wholly maintained, who will have included a wide range of administrative and religious functionaries, craft specialists and skilled workers. They surely also supplied and maintained the workforces that would have been needed for major building and engineering projects, while these were being built. Further, they are likely to have played a major role in the acquisition of raw materials that were not available locally, principally metals, through external exchange. Plausibly, the palaces also acted as the organising centres for public religion, from which offerings were distributed to shrines within their territories, as Linear B texts from Pylos and Thebes demonstrate. But there is scope for considerable debate about the degree of palatial control in all these areas, which has an important bearing on the extent to which they were dynamic or static, even stagnant, as Sherratt's analysis would have it, and therefore on the likelihood of their collapse.

The Linear B documents have often been interpreted, following the influential account of Renfrew (1972: 296–7, 464; cf. 1989: 134–5), which ultimately reflects Finley's analysis (de Fidio 2001: 15–16), to suggest that the palaces' influence was omnipresent in the economy of the territories that they controlled, and that they stood at the centre of redistributive economies in which the products of their territories were all sent to the centre and redistributed from there. Renfrew even suggested that they fostered regional specialisations in certain crops and so created a dependence on the palace organisation to provide basic commodities that were not produced locally, and it has been argued that this led to overspecialised economies with a dangerously limited base (e.g. Betancourt 1976).

But more recently it has been pointed out that the documents themselves provide no warrant for theories of local specialisation. Halstead (1999b) has argued persuasively that, although there was considerable interaction between the palaces and ordinary settlements, concentration on wheat, wool and olive oil was characteristic only of the sector of the economy concerned with bulk production for palace purposes, while the economy of most ordinary settlements remained unspecialised, concerned with a wide variety of crops and livestock (see also Halstead 1992 and Dickinson 1994a: 81–4). Further, he has suggested that both wheat and wool were produced for the palaces through share-cropping arrangements with local communities or individuals, in which the palace may have owned neither the land nor the sheep (Halstead 1999a, 1999c, 2001). Foxhall has also pointed out that the palaces cannot have offered the kind of support for subsistence farmers that is documented in Mesopotamia (1995: 240–1). In other respects too the palaces' control may have been less tight than has frequently been suggested: both Whitelaw and Knappett argue in Voutsaki and Killen (2001) against direct palatial control of pottery production, and Gillis has concluded that bronzesmiths were independent of the palace (1997).

Indeed, there is no evidence that the palace acted as a central clearing house for all goods and commodities manufactured in its territory. At most, it distributed certain specific commodities on occasion, and exercised close control over craftwork and perfumed oil production performed specifically for it, with careful oversight of the materials provided for the work if this was performed through the *ta-ra-si-ja* system, even when, as often, this work was carried out in locations outside the palace itself (Killen 2001). However, it can be accepted that by its demands for labour and commodities, the palace could have had a considerable general effect on the economy, not only within the territory it controlled but over whole regions. In this respect, at least, it might well seem likely that the palaces were central to the economy of the whole southern Aegean, and that the collapse of the palace societies, identifiable in a major series of destructions and abandonments of important sites at the end of LH IIIB, would ultimately lead to the collapse of Aegean civilisation generally. But all theories which rely on the central redistributive role of the palaces must be considered open to question, and it should be recognised that the specialists are emphasising more and more that the Linear B records cover only a fairly narrow range of topics that was of concern to the palace administrators, not the total economic activity of the territory controlled.

Any suggestion that in palace societies a narrow aristocratic class lorded it over a serflike mass, from which it was quite distinct (e.g. Drews 1988: 195, and 1993: 156), is surely undermined by the wide distribution and large numbers of chamber tombs and related grave-types, whose construction must have required skilled labour. It is implausible that the occupants of these should have been 'serfs'. The human bone material that has been argued to show evidence of undernourishment (see Dickinson 1994a: 88–9) in fact comes largely from chamber tombs, and thus may reflect not widespread poverty but the effects of normal fluctuations in food supply in societies where it was not always abundant, or perhaps of particularly prevalent diseases. The Linear B texts of Pylos also seem to indicate that craft specialists, herdsmen, and other fairly ordinary-seeming persons could exercise considerable freedom of action in the area of land tenure (Dickinson 1994a: 84–5). It might be argued that access to fine craft products and the prosperity that this is generally taken to symbolise were limited to the upper levels of the population, but the finely made pottery has been found at all known types of site, down to the smallest.

The comprehensive survey by Cavanagh and Mee (1998) has demonstrated the variability in burial customs within, as well as between, Mycenaean regions (see also Cavanagh 1998), and regional peculiarities can also be observed in Crete. Yet there are very prevalent patterns in the Third Palace Period, particularly the almost universal practice of inhumation on the grave floor or in a pit or niche constructed within the grave, and the tendency to use tombs on several successive occasions. Only in the Dodecanese is use for only one to three burials normal, although use of a tomb for a very few burials is also a common feature in Crete (Dickinson 1983: 65). Also typical is the grouping of tombs in cemeteries; quite often different types of tomb are found together, but always one, usually the chamber tomb, is dominant. The provision of grave-goods of some kind, particularly pottery, is common, but Lewartowski has calculated that *c.* 20 per cent of chamber tomb burials did not receive them (1995: 106, and cf. 2000: 47, 49), and there is considerable variation in the quantities and types provided, not only between 'rich' and 'poor' graves but also between different burials in the same grave. In the course of repeated use, and perhaps also as a result of ritual practices, the goods of burials often became confused and damaged, and sometimes seem to have been largely removed, so that it is very difficult to establish patterns of provision (cf. Dickinson 1994a: 228; Cavanagh and Mee 1998: 78–9).

All the indications are that the group entitled to burial in chamber tombs and related types in the Third Palace Period represents a considerable proportion of the population (Dickinson 1983: 63; Mee and Cavanagh 1984: 56; Cavanagh and Mee 1998: 78), although women may be under-represented (Mee 1998) and infant and child burials are rare, so that to speak of these as 'family tombs' may be giving a false impression. The precise proportion of the population represented remains unclear. Features of the Linear B texts like the strikingly small number of persons listed as involved in land tenure at any level in *Pa-ki-ja-ne*, one of the sub-provinces of the Pylian state (eighty plus, Dickinson 1994a: 84), could be interpreted to suggest that a large part of the population goes unmentioned in the Linear B texts, because it was dependent on those who are mentioned, although such persons include ordinary-seeming persons like shepherds as well as what appear to be major landholders and religious functionaries. But the difficulties of interpreting the only other identifiable burials, in cists and pits, as those of a clearly lower social stratum than chamber-tomb users have been well brought out by Lewartowski (1995, and 2000: especially 47–51). He shows that there is a considerable overlap between burial practices in the different types of tomb, although a higher proportion of cist and pit burials lacked grave-goods and there are other potentially significant differences. Such burials are also rarer in the Third Palace Period than before or afterwards, especially those in cists, which is not what one would expect if they represented a major social stratum at that time (cf. Dickinson 1983: 62–3; Lewartowski 2000: 13–14, 18). It may rather be that, as hypothesised by Morris for Archaic Attica and Greece more generally (1987: 94), there was a basic social distinction between a fairly large 'elite', which included but was not limited to the 'aristocracy' and might make up as much as 50 per cent of the population, and the rest, and that the burials of the latter are rarely if ever recognisable, though they might include some of the poorest pit and cist burials.

The identification through archaeological survey in many parts of the Aegean region of a multitude of small undefended settlements, probably ranging in nature from quite substantial villages to farmsteads, could allow the presumption that the palaces' control promoted stability and a growth in population, but the interpretation of this evidence is not straightforward. The material recovered in such surveys, particularly that from the smallest sites, is normally classifiable only within broad limits. It should not be assumed that all sites shown as occupied in LH IIIA2-B (Dickinson 1994a, fig. 4.24) or in LH IIIB (Popham 1994a: 282) were occupied simultaneously or throughout those phases, and it could be suggested that quite a number of them were short-lived, and had been abandoned before the Collapse. Excavation can define a site's apparent period of occupation more precisely than survey, but, because of the partial nature of most excavations and the degree to which evidence of earlier phases can be effaced by later activity on a site, findings always have to be regarded as provisional, and subject to revision in the light of later study or new finds. Thus, evidence of LH IIIC activity as late as the Middle phase is reported from Zygouries (Morgan 1999: 245), often thought to have been abandoned before the Collapse, and from Tsoungiza (Morgan 1999: 365–6; Shelmerdine 2001: 341 n. 57). Other indications, such as the large number of sites identified within the likely territory controlled from Pylos and the even larger number of toponyms in the tablets (Whitelaw 2001: 63) suggest that small sites remained common to the end of the Third Palace Period.

There are many pitfalls involved in turning the number of recorded sites into population figures, but it can at least be considered likely that for much of the Third Palace Period the Aegean, especially the Mycenaean heartland, was well populated. But the claim, based largely on tendentious interpretations of the Minnesota Messenia Expedition's findings and the Linear B documents of Pylos, that the Greek mainland was becoming overpopulated, inducing a movement into marginal land and even a movement away from farming to craftwork as a means of subsistence (most explicitly, Sandars [1978] 1985: 77), cannot be accepted. The most recent estimate of the population of the state of Pylos is about fifty thousand (Whitelaw 2001: 64), which seems well within the carrying capacity of the land. Only a very few sites, which cannot even be certainly identified as agricultural settlements, have been found on land that can be defined as marginal (Dickinson 1994a: 50–1, where 'ten' reflects a misreading of McDonald and Rapp 1972, table 11–1; the correct figure is six). It must also be considered inherently implausible, given the likely position of the crafts and craft specialists, that a substantial proportion of the population could have derived its subsistence solely from full-time craftwork (Dickinson 1994a: 95–7).

In general, the evidence suggests to me, in opposition to some interpretations (especially Deger-Jalkotzy 1996: 717–18, and 1998: 122), that a mild degree of prosperity was spread through much of Mycenaean society, and that it was not, by the standards of the ancient world, unduly rigid or oppressive. Many of the great construction projects, like the palaces themselves, the tholos tombs, and fortifications, served to enhance the prestige of the ruling elite. But others, like dams (and an artificial harbour at Pylos: Shelmerdine 2001: 339), could have been more generally beneficial (Wardle 1994: 230–2), though roads are more likely to have had military or ceremonial than economic purposes. Similarly, while much that was acquired by exchange was probably reserved for the use of the highest social classes, simple items of bronze are frequently found in more ordinary contexts.

The view that the palaces' tax demands and forced labour on their construction projects bore heavily on their subjects requires better demonstration than has so far been offered. The most extensive Linear B documentation, from Pylos, has produced no evidence for general taxation at all, except in a group of products that does not include any agricultural staples apart from wool; it is hard, therefore, to argue that there was an excessive and impoverishing tax burden. The large construction projects were not exclusive to the palace societies (e.g. the fortification walls at Krisa and Teikhos Dymaion), were probably spread over many years, and need not have involved very large labour forces (Loader 1998: ch. 3.3, especially 71–2; see also her Appendix 3 on the time needed to construct the 'Cyclopean' walls). Their potential role in severely undermining the economic basis of the palace societies is considerably lessened by the point that they may have been completed as much as thirty years before the Collapse, at least in the Argolid (E.B. French, in discussion after Loader 1995); major work at Gla was finished even earlier, within LH IIIB1 (Iakovidis 1998: 189). The deterioration of the natural environment for which Deger-Jalkotzy cites evidence could as easily reflect the needs of the expanded population, which the palace societies had fostered, as the demands of the palaces themselves.

Indications of trouble?

It is possible to advance arguments that the impression of stability and prosperity given by general overviews of the evidence, even if appropriate for much of the Third Palace Period, may be misleading for its final stages. Cavanagh and Mee have made the point (1998: 79) that the popularity of chamber tombs, generally intended for use over several generations, indicates widespread confidence in the stability of society. But it remains unclear how many were newly constructed in LH IIIB, and it has been argued that there was a decline in the number of tombs in use and the number of grave-goods placed in them during the period. However, the evidence is hardly clear-cut: the decline between LH IIIA and IIIB in the number of tombs in use is not very marked, while the decline in the provision of grave-goods might be interpreted to reflect greater stability and so less need for display (Cavanagh and Mee 1984: 57, 62).

It has also been suggested that the almost obsessive recording of minor details in the Linear B documents and the expenditure of so much wealth on building programmes at the major centres might be interpreted as signs of 'insecurity and impending crisis' (Voutsaki and Killen 2001: 7). Indications of economic decline have been detected in the very marked diminution in the quantity of Mycenaean pottery being traded to the east Mediterranean in the later thirteenth century and the evidence that much of the palace at Pylos was converted into a factory for producing perfumed olive oil in the same period (Shelmerdine 1985). Such a decline could be interpreted to indicate that the palace societies were having to make increasingly desperate efforts to maintain their position in the international exchange systems (cf. Shelmerdine 1987; Sherratt 2001). It has also been suggested that the palace societies' economies were breaking down for internal structural reasons, but all such arguments are based on reasoned hypothesis rather than proof. A more tangible indication that all was not well might be seen in the apparent abandonment of the major international port of Kommos in mid-LM IIIB (Shaw 1998: 17).

Evidence that the Mycenaean world was facing a military threat of some kind in the later thirteenth century has been deduced from the construction or extension of fortifications at several major sites and the construction of water supply systems accessible from within the citadels at Mycenae, Tiryns and Athens (incidentally, such works indicate how considerable were the resources that the major centres could command even at this late stage). But there is a basic difficulty in the view that fortifications were built or extended to face an immediate threat, for the time and resources required to build them make it extremely unlikely that they could have been built fast (Loader 1995, and 1998: 65 n. 16, 72–3). They might better be seen, like their predecessors earlier in the period, as primarily expressions of power and wealth, designed to impress subjects and rivals and to strengthen control over territories. Certainly, their construction could indicate that the more significant Mycenaean states were becoming increasingly competitive at this period, which should surely be considered a destabilising factor (cf. Tainter 1988: 202). In this connection, it should be stressed that the supposed wall across the Isthmus of Corinth, so often given a prominent place in historical analyses, is best omitted from the discussion altogether. The data available are inadequate to demonstrate its date and purpose, whether it was completed, or even whether all uncovered sections belong to the same structure (Morgan 1999: 362–5, 437–8; although in a forthcoming work Prof. R. Hope Simpson provides a strong defence of the original interpretation, I believe that too many uncertainties remain for it to be usable in historical reconstruction).

Destructions datable within the thirteenth century, which often affect palaces or other important buildings, as at Mycenae, Zygouries, Thebes and Gla, have been interpreted as evidence of warfare. The evidence for repeated destruction of buildings thought to be part of the palace at Thebes seems particularly striking, although the possibility that at least some destruction may reflect local accident, or deliberate destruction prior to rebuilding (a suggestion I owe to Dr E.S. Sherratt) cannot be ruled out. It has further been considered significant that at Mycenae various impressive structures, including the 'Ivory Houses' group of buildings which had important administrative functions, were not rebuilt after the LH IIIB1 destruction, although there is evidence for continued occupation in other areas outside the citadel. However, claims once made that substantial sites like Zygouries were abandoned before the end of LH IIIB cannot be substantiated, although they may have dwindled considerably (see p. 40).

Finally, it has been argued that the Linear B documents of Pylos provide evidence that a crisis involving an external threat had arisen just before the palace's destruction. This interpretation has been seriously questioned (Palaima 1995; Shelmerdine 1999: 405, and 2001: 375), but some of the cited documents give plausible indications of internal trouble, if not a crisis, that may have been developing over some time (Sacconi 1999). Shelmerdine also detects an atmosphere of increased wariness, reflected in defensive measures, at many major palace centres, including Mycenae and Tiryns (2001: 372–3). But there is no reason to suppose that any threat came exclusively, or at all, from outside the Aegean world. The arguments for this seem tendentious, and the most plausible indications of destruction by hostile action and concern with security could equally be interpreted as the results of warfare between Mycenaean states. This might be taken as another sign that competitiveness between the states was reaching dangerous levels, and might be connected with the indications that economic conditions were deteriorating, which could be a source of increasing inter-state tensions. Nevertheless, it must be admitted that all this rests on suggestive indications rather than solid evidence, and there is no unassailable basis for supposing that the Collapse was inevitable.

The destructions and attempts to explain them

It has long been recognised that a whole series of major Mycenaean sites on the mainland underwent destructions by fire, often if not always devastating – the evidence is particularly clear in the Citadel House area at Mycenae (Taylour 1981: 10) and the Pylos palace – at or near the end of the LH IIIB pottery phase. The relative dating of the various destructions has provided much scope for argument, but although, as noted above, evidence for earlier destructions can be identified at several important sites, some of which like Gla were abandoned or dwindled subsequently, the main destructions of Mycenae, Tiryns, and many lesser sites have always been given this dating. The most recent refinement is that of Mountjoy (1997), who argues, in opposition to Popham's proposal to place the destruction deposit of the palace at Pylos in early LH IIIB, that the material belongs to a transitional phase between LH IIIB2 and LH IIIC Early (see also Shelmerdine 2001: 373 n. 277). She has identified diagnostic pottery types of the same transitional phase in well-defined destruction or abandonment deposits at Midea, the Menelaion, Nichoria, Thebes and Eutresis, as well as in less clear-cut contexts at various other Peloponnesian, Attic and Boeotian sites. But such types

43

appear at Mycenae, and perhaps Tiryns also, in both destruction and post-destruction deposits (on Mycenae, French 1999; on Tiryns, Mountjoy 1997: 117), and Demakopoulou has strongly resisted the classification of the Midea deposits as anything but late LH IIIB2 (2003: especially 91), while other finds could come from contexts postdating the Collapse. The identification of this separate intervening phase remains a matter for debate, then, and the discussion serves as a reminder that pottery style is always in a process of change, which can be frozen at different stages on different sites, or even different deposits on the same site. The evidence can at least be taken to suggest that the destructions fall relatively close together, but as Popham has pointed out (1994a: 281) they could still have taken place over a quarter century or more, and have had various and unrelated causes. For example, the great destruction level at Mycenae shows no signs of having been caused by an earthquake (French 1999), in contrast to that at Midea.

For some time, as noted in the Introduction, this series of destructions and the widespread abandonment of small sites that has often been associated with them were seen as caused by invading Dorians and related groups. Schweitzer encapsulated the traditional view in suggesting that Greek-speaking tribes moved out of the north-west in two waves; in his vivid words, 'These Dorians must have advanced with the irresistible force of an avalanche as they spread across the country and changed the map of Greece' (1971: 10). The idea of an invasion from north-west Greece still seemed the best explanation to Desborough, but he argued that it was followed by retreat rather than settlement, for which he could see no archaeological evidence. He placed a second invasion from the same region, this time involving settlement, considerably later, suggesting that its archaeological correlate was his 'Sub-Mycenaean culture' and finding backing for this too in the traditions (1972: 22–3, 111). Snodgrass (1971: 311–12) also considered the Dorian hypothesis tenable if 'the Dorians and other immigrants were essentially indistinguishable in their material culture from Mycenaean survivors', as he thought likely. But he pointed out that accepting this view would mean substantial modifications of the traditions where they did not fit the archaeology, as in Laconia, which showed no sign of new settlement after LH IIIB. Alternatively, Hooker (1976: 173, 179) and Chadwick (1976b) have argued that the 'Dorians' and other speakers of West Greek dialects were the lower classes of the Mycenaean population, who revolted to throw off their masters.

The apparent absence of archaeological evidence that could indicate the Dorians' arrival has led many to place the 'Dorian invasion' later and to explain the Collapse by other means, often involving some other kind of population movement. Thus, Bouzek (1994) favours an influx of warlike invaders from central Europe, but sees them as settling down as a ruling class and quickly becoming 'Hellenised' in the Aegean, though retaining a separate identity elsewhere in the Balkans and in Anatolia. Such a movement has been seen as part of a 'wholesale migration of peoples throughout the eastern Mediterranean' (Hood, reviewing Sandars 1978 in *JHS* 99 (1979) 201), and identified as part of the reported activities of the 'Sea Peoples'. Hood further supplied a rationale, in arguing that what caused these migrations was 'force: other and stronger peoples wanting their lands – a commonplace of history'. In contrast, Kilian (1988: 134) gave the 'Sea Peoples' only an offstage part, arguing that by blocking access to the east Mediterranean they prevented the Mycenaean states from recovering from the economic loss caused by catastrophic earthquakes, which he saw as causing the final collapse of already over-extended if not near-bankrupt palace economies.

Many others have laid stress on the effects caused by either economic deterioration or simply the inherent nature of the palace economies, widely seen as overcentralised and overspecialised, and therefore unable to cope effectively with the effects of a major natural disaster such as drought or earthquake, as Betancourt (1976) was one of the first to argue. Indeed, it has been plausibly argued that a series of earthquakes could have struck the Aegean over a relatively short period of time (Nur and Cline 2000), producing a cumulative effect. Some authors have argued for a period of widespread and devastating drought as the main cause of the Collapse (Carpenter 1966; Bryson *et al.* 1974; Stiebing 1980). Hooker preferred to lay emphasis on a breakdown of overcentralised control caused by internal and perhaps also external pressures (1982: 216), presumably seeing the 'peasant revolt' which he believed to lie behind the traditions of the Dorians as one of these pressures or as the natural result of the breakdown. A similar emphasis on the failure of an overcentralised administrative system is basic to Renfrew's theory of 'systems collapse', applied to the Mycenaean civilisation among others (1989: 133–4), and to Muhly's interpretation of the collapse as the culmination of a crisis that had been developing since the mid-thirteenth century (1992: 11–12), while Tainter (1988: 202) argued that a spiral of competitiveness between the Mycenaean states brought about mutual exhaustion and virtually simultaneous collapse.

The most notable attempt at combining elements of these approaches is that of Sandars (1964), who originally favoured the idea that the destructions were caused by a great overland raid from the north. More recently she has argued that the Aegean palace societies, which were already suffering from overpopulation and land-exhaustion, collapsed under the pressure of adverse trading conditions, that the Mycenaean ruling class then resorted to large-scale raiding by land and sea to support themselves, and that their activity around the Anatolian coasts may in turn have dislodged many of the participants in the 'Sea Peoples' movement ([1978] 1985: 184, 187).

Links to the 'Sea Peoples' are also features of some very recent attempts at explanation. Drews (1993), after providing a useful discussion of all the types of theory previously put forward, has offered an effectively military explanation for what he terms the 'Catastrophe' in the Aegean and Near East, that a change in equipment and tactics allowed warlike 'barbarians' to combat the civilised states' armies successfully and initiate a prolonged and exceptionally successful period of raiding, which resulted in the destruction of a great many major centres, especially in the Aegean. Popham (1994a) offered a circumstantial account of the progressive collapse of Mycenaean civilisation, involving an unexpected early thirteenth-century attack on Pylos that stimulated an increased concern with defence at the greater Mycenaean centres, then mid-thirteenth-century trouble in the Argolid, followed by further extension and strengthening of defences at Mycenae and elsewhere, and finally the major series of destructions around the end of the thirteenth century. Although he allowed some scope for the effects of interstate warfare, internal dissension, and 'systems collapse', Popham argued that 'The success of the attacks against such well-protected centres . . . points to an efficient military force', which he saw as a branch of the 'Sea Peoples' and linked to the central Mediterranean (1994a: 287–8).

Most recently Sherratt has returned to an economic explanation, in which the palaces' position, argued by her to be dependent on the control of trade route segments, was undermined by a proliferation of direct trade from east to west in the Mediterranean, 'which either bypassed them entirely or subverted their surrounding populations into the (probably willing) belief that they could do better without them' (2001: 238).

Discussion of the Collapse

The problems of traditional forms of explanation

It will be evident from the account of the Mycenaean palace societies given above that any theories that depend on the idea that they were dangerously overcentralised and overspecialised must be considered questionable because of their basic premise. Centralised control and inter-state competitiveness may have had deleterious effects, but they do not seem to have been the prime forces behind the Collapse. The idea that the palace societies effectively bankrupted their economies by expenditure on major building projects is questionable, because, as noted on p. 41, the Collapse probably took place well after these were completed. Theories postulating a major natural catastrophe fail in other basic premises. In the case of drought, the settlement pattern following the Collapse simply does not fit the postulated changes in weather pattern which it is supposed to demonstrate (for detailed comments and criticisms see Shrimpton 1987 and Drews 1993: ch. 6, especially 79–80). Proponents of devastating earthquakes must explain why earthquakes had such a deleterious effect at this particular time, when in earlier periods they were followed by substantial recovery. Finally, any suggestion that a plague or other epidemic disease, such as afflicted the Hittite Empire somewhat earlier (Bryce 1998: 223), had a major disruptive effect, perhaps dramatically reducing the population, might seem superficially attractive as a possible explanation for the abandonment of sites and of whole regions (Walloe 1999), but faces the difficulty that, following the destructions phase, population coalesced at many of the previous central sites, where disease would surely be most likely to linger.

Should we then look to an external factor? The view that the period around 1200 was characterised in both the Aegean and the Near East by large-scale raiding, often associated with population movements, which caused the destruction or grave weakening of most centres of civilisation, has in one form or another dominated most historical reconstructions of the period until recently, and deconstructing it is not easy because so many assumptions have become embedded in the discussion (Silberman 1998 gives an excellent account of the modern climate of opinion within which such ideas were formulated and the changing approaches to the 'Sea Peoples' and other 'invaders').

Long ago Schaeffer and Hooker expressed considerable scepticism about the supremely efficient destructiveness attributed to the 'Sea Peoples' (Hooker 1976: 156–60), and at the conference whose proceedings are published in Ward and Joukowsky (1992) some widespread beliefs about the supposed course of events involving them in the Near East were questioned with good reason. In particular, it must be emphasised that almost everything that we think we know about the 'Sea Peoples' derives from sources written to glorify Egyptian pharaohs, which, as a considerable body of evidence demonstrates, can be exaggerated, even wholly fabricated (see recently Drews 2000). That there are historical elements in the inscriptions of Ramesses III in the Medinet Habu temple is likely enough, but the true setting and course of events that these purport to describe remain open to debate. Redford (2000: 12–13) defends the texts' reliability in some crucial areas, but his claim that the archaeological record from Anatolia, Cyprus and north Syria is consonant with the Medinet Habu accounts is surely far too sweeping. In particular, it seems extremely unlikely that the Hittite Empire was destroyed by an invading horde. When so much depends on the interpretation of texts that are either fragmentary, unclear, or of questionable reliability, and of archaeological evidence from a series of sites whose relative and absolute chronology is debatable, it is necessary to resist the seductively plausible accounts like that of Nowicki (2000: ch. VII). These tie together supposedly historical events in the Near East and archaeological phenomena in the Aegean, but beg enormous questions in their assumptions and assertions about the 'historical evidence'.

More generally, we should reject the image so often associated with the term 'Sea Peoples', of large bands of 'aggressive, well-armed, efficient and ruthless raiders' (Popham 1994a: 287), mobile 'sea warriors' (Nowicki 2000: 263–5), if only on common-sense grounds. I know of no historical analogy for a situation in which such large bands could live entirely by raiding, as in

Nowicki's and Drews's historical reconstructions they are suggested to do, let alone that this might continue for decades. When large pirate fleets ravaged the Aegean or more generally the Mediterranean in historical times, they did so from fixed bases, and in the fifteenth and sixteenth centuries AD, often cited in analogy, with the support of a major power, the Ottoman Empire. Land-raiders and pirates in the Aegean and elsewhere have historically tended to operate in relatively small groups, whose basic tactic would be fast sweeps to gather up what could be easily taken, whether human captives, livestock, or portable loot. The words of the king of Alashiya (now generally agreed to be located in Cyprus) in Amarna letter 38, 'Men of Lukki, year by year, seize villages in my own country' (Moran 1992: 111), surely reflect the reality of such raiding.

It seems most unlikely that such groups would be prepared to settle down to besiege well-fortified centres, allowing an opportunity for forces to be mobilised against them (as the Cicones are mobilised against Odysseus' forces in *Odyssey* 9.47–50), unless they could feel reasonably sure of a quick, successful and profitable outcome. Yet it may be questioned whether the Mycenaean centres offered a very tempting prospect, for they were not rich cities like Ugarit, and probably did not contain much readily portable, high-value loot. The stores that the palaces controlled more probably consisted mainly of the bulky products of agriculture and stock-rearing. Such considerations would surely not encourage large-scale raids, such as the 'Sea Peoples' are supposed to have mounted, at a considerable distance from their usual areas of operation. Admittedly, more local raiding from the rougher and poorer parts of the Greek mainland or further north in the Balkan peninsula cannot be excluded, but it is difficult to believe that this could be on a scale sufficient to destroy large fortified centres and cause the collapse of major states.

In fact, there were always difficulties in accepting that the 'Sea Peoples', as traditionally imagined, were responsible for the destruction of major sites on the Greek mainland, which has produced much the best evidence for such destruction. There is little archaeological trace of the damage that they would surely have caused in the Aegean islands, which they must pass through on their way to or from the Near East. Indeed, if the Medinet Habu statement that they were based in 'islands' (an interpretation defended in Redford 2000: 12) has any validity, the Aegean might seem their most likely source, as Nowicki (2000: 264) and Drews (2000: 181–2) have suggested for some elements, and is commonly suggested for the ancestors of the Philistines (most recently Yasur-Landau 2003; more caution is shown in Sandars [1978] 1985: compare 188 with 201).

But casting doubt on any potential impact of the 'Sea Peoples' in the Aegean or elsewhere need not invalidate Drews's (1993) theory previously referred to, since he ascribes the adoption of new tactics not only to the 'Sea Peoples' but also to 'north Greeks' who were neighbours of the palace societies and, in his view, were responsible for the destructions in the Aegean world (see further Drews 2000: 181). Essentially, he argues that the armies of civilised states in the LBA, including the Aegean palace societies, were dominated by chariots, used as mobile platforms for archers, and that infantry forces played a minor role in warfare until 'barbarian' peoples developed new tactics. These defeated chariot-dominated armies by combining the use of the javelin, small round shield, and long cut-and-thrust sword, especially the European Type II, thus initiating an era in which massed infantry forces dominated the battlefield.

This is not the place to discuss all aspects of the theory (for more detailed comment see Dickinson 1999). Here I will simply state that this surely undervalues the role of infantry in the Near East considerably, and that since such infantry frequently included archers and other missile-users, it is very hard to accept that the idea of using them to disable chariotry had not occurred to anyone before this time. Drews also fails to demonstrate that the 'barbarian' peoples were first to adopt the 'new' weapons. In fact, the earliest examples of Type II swords and short javelin heads in the Aegean and Near East come not from supposedly 'barbarian' regions but from centres of civilisation like Mycenae and Enkomi, to which they were most plausibly brought via the Mediterranean sea routes (cf. the example associated with the Cape Gelidonya wreck, Bass 1991: 69). Furthermore, Drews never indicates what advantage the supposed new tactics could confer in attacking walled towns and citadels, a point of considerable importance since it is the destruction of these that provides the most striking evidence of his 'Catastrophe'. He seems to be relying on a belief that the 'barbarians' came in overwhelming numbers, for which he can offer no very convincing evidence. Finally, in treating all the destructions as evidence of a single 'Catastrophe', and dismissing all other explanations, he is ignoring the very strong possibility that they may represent quite unrelated sequences of events, and that in specific instances these other explanations may be plausible, even if they cannot be applied generally.

Turning to the Aegean specifically, it can be commented that, whatever the likelihood of Drews's theories regarding chariot use in the Near East, the terrain in most parts of the mainland and Crete is simply not suited to the kind of massed charges and wheeling movements that he envisages. Moreover, in scenes representing warfare or warriors, infantrymen carrying long thrusting spears and/or swords are prominent, as are spearheads and sword blades in the archaeological record throughout the Aegean LBA to the time of the Collapse. The natural interpretation of this is that the best-armed Aegean warriors fought on foot with these weapons, although archers and other missile-users could also have played a significant role. Already by the thirteenth century there were changes in equipment, in that shields and weapons were being made smaller, which would tend to greater mobility. Thus, the supposed superiority of the 'barbarian' warriors over the armies of civilised Aegean states may be largely illusory.

49

Drews's view that a more warlike population of 'north Greeks', including the ancestors of the Dorians, occupied most of mainland Greece west and north of Boeotia (which seems to depend largely on another theory, that the exploits of Achaeans and Argives in the Greek legends originally related to the historical activities of 'north Greeks'; see Drews 1979, and 1988: 223) is hard to reconcile with the archaeological evidence, which gives no indication that the people of Phocis, Locris, Phthiotis and much of Thessaly were any less Mycenaean, or more warlike, than those of the palace societies (see p. 24). But, even supposing that there existed populations of warlike 'north Greeks' and that, as Drews further suggests, the palaces recruited mercenary infantry from among them, surely these would not only familiarise the commanders of the palace societies' armies with the new weapons and tactics but also provide the first line of defence against them. Further, as noted above, any superiority in field tactics or fighting ability that 'north Greeks' might have had would be largely nullified in the sieges that Drews must imagine his raiders to have undertaken to capture and destroy the walled Mycenaean centres. It is most unlikely that they could have come in sufficient force to overwhelm these centres by sheer weight of numbers, for the archaeological evidence does not suggest that there were especially large populations in the northern provinces of Greece and immediately beyond. It must be suspected that this suggestion is made, as it used to be for the Dorians, simply because it is not evident how the great Mycenaean citadels could have been taken otherwise. To sum up, I would suggest that any historical interpretation that relies on a picture of massive forces of raiders scouring the Aegean, whether by land or sea, owes more to romance than reality.

Despite these criticisms, Drews does make an important point. Explanations couched in terms of processes such as 'systems collapse' or economic decline, whether linked to loss of control over trade or some other cause, require further subsidiary hypotheses to cope convincingly with the fact that so many palaces, citadels and major settlements suffered serious destruction involving fire. Natural disasters such as earthquakes could have caused some of the destructions, but it remains hard to believe that in every case they should have caused severe fires. It seems far more plausible that the destructions most often reflect some kind of violence. So, if this did not take the form of major attacks by external forces, what was it?

New people?

Here it is necessary to return to theories already mentioned above which depend on the notion that the traditions of invasion by Dorians and other groups encapsulate historical fact, and that the Mycenaean centres were in fact destroyed and their territories conquered by other Greek-speaking peoples. Often their source has been suggested to be Epirus, particularly by Hammond (1932, 1975), although there is no warrant for this in the

50

ancient traditions, which do not derive any of the supposedly incoming peoples from outside the boundaries of Classical Greece. As noted above, it has often been thought a difficulty that no major archaeological change can be associated with such an invasion, but this is much less of a problem if the Dorians and allied groups in fact came from within the area of Mycenaean culture.

A common-sense objection to seeing the destructions as the work of invading peoples is that there is no sense in destroying what you wish to rule, but the real difficulty lies in the belief that these traditions offer reliable evidence, when in fact they are internally inconsistent, logically incoherent, and sometimes demonstrably at odds with the archaeological evidence. Hall's analysis shows how inconsistencies could reflect attempts to harmonise divergent traditions maintained by different groups (1997: 56–65). This is a salutary reminder of the fact that these traditions are primarily 'origin legends' and 'charter myths', designed to justify the political and social arrangements of later times (cf. Hooker 1976: 169; Osborne 1996: 32–7). They are also affected, almost as soon as they are recorded, by poetic and scholarly attempts at rationalisation and harmonisation (e.g. the well-known account of the Dorians' movements in a series of stages before entering the Peloponnese: Herod. 1.56.3, on which see Hall 1997: 62). The traditions' function as 'charter myths' explains why they make the Dorian leaders bypass all other regions and centres to establish Argos and Sparta, for these were the most significant Dorian centres of the Peloponnese by Archaic times apart from Corinth, whose foundation legend is notoriously separate from the main Dorian tradition (a difficulty that has never been satisfactorily explained by believers in the historicity of the legends, cf. Hall 1997: 57–9). But the archaeological evidence suggests that none of these sites became truly prominent until after the Postpalatial Period, during which Tiryns and to a lesser extent Mycenae remained the leading centres in the Argolid and no major site can be identified in central Laconia or the Corinthia. Similarly, nothing in the archaeology of Boeotia or Elis can be convincingly linked to claims of their settlement by new peoples following the Collapse.

From an archaeological point of view, following Desborough, and more recently Eder (1998), in placing any population movements at the end of the Postpalatial Period, might seem to have more attractions. But Desborough's attempt to identify his 'Sub-Mycenaean culture', characterised especially by cist cemeteries, as that of non-Mycenaean people invading from the neighbourhood of Epirus (1972: 109–11, but see 337) raises major problems. The proposed distinction between Mycenaean and Submycenaean burial customs is far from clear-cut (see Chapter 6), for the vases and metalwork typical of the cist cemeteries can also appear in chamber tombs. Also, many of the best examples of cist cemeteries are found in Attica and Euboea, which according to the traditions were not successfully invaded by newcomers, whereas such cemeteries are notably lacking from classic 'Dorian' areas such as the south

Peloponnese (pit and cist graves are now reported from Sparta and Amyklai; see Raftopoulou 1997, 1998) and Crete. There are also significant variations in burial customs between different cist cemeteries, undermining the suggestion that they represent a homogeneous culture (Dickinson 1983: 66–7; Mountjoy 1988: 29–30). Interestingly, what seem to be Mycenaeanised but not fully Mycenaean groups that buried their dead in cists can be identified on the northern Mycenaean border, as at Spathes (Andreou *et al.* 2001: 295–6) and Agrilia (Feuer 1983: 232–47). But these have few links in metal types with the classic 'Submycenaean' cist cemeteries. Indeed, the published material from Agrilia provides no obvious warrant for the date of *c.* 1200 usually cited, and it could fall well into the EIA (Donder 1999: 94 suggests that the square shafts of three pins indicate a Geometric date).

There remains one distinctive archaeological feature that has been associated with the traditions of the Dorian invasion – the appearance of a class of handmade burnished (hereafter HMB) pottery, very unlike any ware of the preceding phases (see especially Kilian 1988: 127–33; Lemos 2002: 84–5). But as Rutter emphasised in a valuable survey (1990) the whole debate about this material is premature. For pottery that can be classified in this way has now been discovered in a whole range of contexts, not only within the Aegean (including at Troy) but also at Cypriot and Syro-Palestinian sites. The variations observable suggest that the term actually covers a variety of classes that may not all have the same origin, but the closest parallels for the material found in Crete (recently summarised in D'Agata 2001: 346 n. 11), where such pottery appears as early as LM IIIA at Kommos, and for well known groups from the mainland (Tiryns, Aigeira, Lefkandi) are south Italian and Sardinian, not Balkan. This, together with the very varied, often extremely small quantities in which it has been found, makes it even less likely that it reflects a reversion on the mainland to making domestic pottery in the household when wheel-using potters who survived the Collapse could no longer cope with demand, or production by farmers to supplement their uncertain 'income' (Small 1997, with earlier references), although it does seem sometimes to be made from 'local' clays. Rather, its appearances seem most likely to represent trade links and possibly small groups of (specialised?) immigrants.

It first appears on the mainland at Mycenae, Tiryns, Midea and Nichoria in pre-Collapse strata (for Midea, see Demakopoulou *et al.* 2003: 10, 14), it continues to occur in Postpalatial contexts at Mycenae and Tiryns in some quantity (though at most a very few per cent of the total deposits), and also at other sites (notably Korakou, Lefkandi, the Menelaion, and Aigeira). But with very rare and often uncertain exceptions it is totally absent from Boeotia, the western Peloponnese, and most of the Aegean islands. There is no strong reason to link it with Epirus (it is clear from unpublished work that Kilian had abandoned this idea and accepted the Italian parallels: J. Maran, pers. comm.), but even if there were it would be hard to link it with the Greek tradition of migrations, since, as pointed out above, it is a purely modern, if long-standing theory that any of the migrating groups came from Epirus.

Nevertheless, it might seem that the traditions concerning migration cannot be totally ignored, for the evidence of the Linear B tablets strongly suggests that an 'East Greek' dialect was originally spoken in areas of the Peloponnese where 'West Greek' dialects are found in Classical times, and also in Boeotia, where the Classical dialect seems to mix Aeolic and 'West Greek' forms. The specifically Dorian dialects also have a peculiar distribution on the mainland, from Megara in the Isthmus of Corinth down the east and across the south of the Peloponnese, which has commonly been taken to confirm the story of a Dorian invasion and certainly requires explanation. As previously noted, Hooker (1976: 173, 179) and Chadwick (1976b) have presented a quite different interpretation of the distinction between 'East' and 'West Greek', arguing that speakers of the latter were descended from the lower classes of the Mycenaean population, who had revolted to throw off their masters, among whom, in Chadwick's view, 'East Greek' had developed as an elite mode of speaking and writing Greek.

But there are many objections to this theory, archaeological, linguistic and historical. The archaeology simply does not warrant Hooker's separation between a Mycenaean ruling class and 'Helladic' subjects. In particular, what Hooker would see as the re-emergence of buried 'Helladic' traits like cist burial is not a feature of the immediate aftermath of the Collapse, as his theory must surely require, but rather of an advanced stage of the Postpalatial Period. Further, archaeology cannot demonstrate that Greek was the exclusive language in all parts of the regions classified as Helladic and Mycenaean. Our information on the linguistic make-up of the prehistoric Aegean is in fact extremely limited, and derives from material that is associated with the upper strata of society, whether the non-Greek language(s) of the Minoan civilisation or the Greek used in Linear B. It is perfectly possible that Greek only became the virtually exclusive language of the southern Aegean in the course of the Postpalatial Period and EIA, not only in Crete but elsewhere (as must also have happened in the Greek-speaking parts of Cyprus).

Chadwick's identification of 'West Greek' features in the Linear B texts, taken to indicate the existence of a population speaking 'West Greek' in the palace territories, has not found favour with other linguistic specialists (cf. Vanschoonwinkel 1991: 281–8), and the significance of the distinction between 'East Greek' and 'West Greek' remains a matter for considerable debate (Hall 1997: 161–2). More crucially, this theory fails to explain why 'West Greek' dialects should have become dominant only in certain Mycenaean regions – for 'East Greek' dialects were current in Arcadia, Attica and Euboea, regions as Mycenaean as the Peloponnese or Boeotia, and also in the heavily Mycenaeanised Cyclades, in Classical times – or why some regions should have become specifically Doric in dialect, others only generically 'West Greek'. Neither do Hooker or Chadwick satisfactorily explain why

'Dorians' should later appear to constitute the ruling group in several parts of the Peloponnese and in Crete, dominating much more numerous populations that are excluded from the Dorian tribal system.

It seems better to consider that, just as the Greek language is now thought to have taken shape within Greece, many features of Dorian identity (including, perhaps, the specific features of the dialect) were developed within the Peloponnese. The very name of one of the three standard Dorian tribes, Pamphyloi ('people of all tribes'), hints at the artificiality of the grouping, as perhaps does the fact that in Crete other tribal names are attested as well as the standard three. The collapse of traditional Mycenaean culture surely produced appropriate conditions for the creation of new identities like Dorians and Ionians, some of whom also shared a distinctive tribal organisation. But attempts to account for these and other features that have been considered typically Dorian or Ionian, like particular festivals, and are shared between different Classical Greek communities, should be separated from attempts to explain the dialect distribution, with which they may originally have had little connection. All that can safely be said is that many of these features were established by the sixth century, when historical information begins to become more readily available.

To sum up, it would be extremely rash to assume that the traditions of population movement preserve any useful historical information, either in the dating of the movements, based on much later scholarly calculations, or in their nature. That local warfare was involved in the establishment of new political centres and systems of social organisation in various territories during the Postpalatial Period and EIA may seem likely enough. But that these involved the simultaneous immigration of homogeneous population groups, already organised along similar lines to what is attested in historical sources, should be considered extremely doubtful. It remains possible that there is truth in the claims that some groups moved from the rougher parts of central and northern Greece into the Mycenaean heartland, but when this happened and in what circumstances remain matters for speculation. It certainly seems more likely that any such movements happened, at the earliest, late in the Postpalatial Period, when conditions were probably deteriorating again, rather than at its beginning.

Towards an explanation

Thus, none of the traditional explanations advanced seems to be broadly acceptable, but some may contain germs of truth. If it is accepted that the violent destructions of many Mycenaean centres indicate some form of warfare and that these destructions could well have been spread over decades, Hooker's suggestion (1976: 177) that they represent a prolonged period of major internal unrest, which could have involved both warfare between Mycenaean states and internecine strife within them, seems eminently plausible. This unrest might have stemmed not only from growing stresses upon the economic and social systems of the palace societies but also from the personal ambitions of rulers or over-mighty subjects, leading to disputes over territory or resources, even to civil wars, which could provide a plausible explanation for the successful capture and destruction of major citadels, since the armed forces of the affected state would be divided. In a growing climate of instability, there could have been secessions by provinces of the major states, 'peasant revolts', which like later historical examples could in fact have been regional movements led by local personages of some importance, and opportunistic raids and even seizure of territory by poorer groups that lived on the borders of the palace societies. Current ideas of what may have been happening in the final stages of the Hittite Empire, including pressure from the growing power of Assyria, civil war between different branches of the royal family, secession by previously dependent territories, increasing turmoil in the westernmost regions of Anatolia, and finally the sacking of the capital by the Kaska people of the northern mountains, provide tempting and roughly contemporary models (cf. Bryce 1998: ch. 13, especially 372–3 on western Anatolia, and 377–9).

Moreover, even if Halstead's model of the palace economy is accepted and it is assumed that the ordinary settlements' agricultural economy was not organised from the palaces, a localised but severe drought, or some other problem that produced real food shortages over a wide area, could well lead to civil disturbances, as a semi-starving populace demanded supplies that they imagined the palace administration to have in their control. This could produce a breakdown of order and seizure of stores by force. But once these were dissipated, survivors would be no better off, and would have to disperse in a continuing search for food. The evidence for food shortages in the Hittite Empire in the late thirteenth century and later, when Alashiya may also have been affected, shows that these could occur, though the earlier shortages were alleviated with Egyptian help (*CAH* II.2: 146; Bryce 1998: 356–7, 365). Such a sequence of events can hardly be imagined as happening all over Greece, but might account for features like the quite exceptional level of site abandonment perceptible in Messenia, although the Linear B texts of Pylos give no clear hint that there is anything wrong in the agricultural system. It is also possible that peoples living in the poorer parts of Greece, who might suffer the most from naturally caused food shortages, were launching desperate raids simply to get food. The establishment of quite considerable forces to guard the coasts at various points, as set out in the *o-ka* tablets of Pylos (of which Figure 2.2 is the first – see Ventris and Chadwick [1956] 1973: 188–94, 427–30; Chadwick 1976a: 175–7), might represent defence measures taken against an outburst of raiding of this kind. But it must be admitted that all this is speculation; to my knowledge, there is no positive evidence for catastrophic drought in the Aegean itself.

It is not too hard to imagine that a series of what may originally have been local disturbances, but in important regions, could have had a cumulative effect, in which the growing instability of the palace societies was variously exploited until they finally collapsed. Natural disasters like earthquakes, localised droughts leading to famines, or epidemic diseases could have acted as catalysts for trouble or have exacerbated an already deteriorating situation. It should be emphasised at this point that the often repeated view that Athens survived the Collapse unharmed is based entirely on negative evidence, i.e. that there is no positive evidence of a fire destruction on the Acropolis (indeed, it is only a hypothesis, though a plausible one, that Athens was the centre of a fully developed palace society: no Linear B material has been found there, and its placing in the first rank is based largely on its 'Cyclopean' fortifications). But even if it was such a centre, and did survive, Athens alone could hardly have maintained the whole network of overseas connections upon which the Aegean palace societies depended for many of their raw materials and luxury goods (the impressive LH IIIC Early finds from Kanakia on Salamis, *AR* 48 (2001–2002) 14–15, have no necessary bearing on the position of Athens at this time).

If its rulers tried to maintain such contacts for themselves they were bound to fail, for the stable conditions in the Near East which had surely helped the Aegean palace societies to flourish were gone. Whatever view one takes of the activities of the 'Sea Peoples' and the chronology of events in the Near East relative to the Aegean, there can be no doubt that this was a period of major instability there. One of the great regional powers, the Hittite Empire, collapsed completely, the other, Egypt, was seriously weakened, and the whole east Mediterranean littoral seems to have been in turmoil. Some cities were destroyed and never reoccupied, like Ugarit, though Ras ibn Hani nearby was reoccupied on some scale. If the Collapse preceded these developments, they would have dealt a further blow to any surviving, or reviving, organised societies in the Aegean; if they preceded or overlapped with the Collapse, they could well have contributed significantly to its effects. Either way, the system of links which bound the Aegean to the Near East must effectively have been destroyed. Whether it made it inevitable that something like a dark age would ensue will be considered in the next chapter.

Bibliography

For recent general comments on the Aegean palace civilisations see Dickinson (1994a: chs 4 and 9), Wardle (1994), Deger-Jalkotzy (1996) (specifically on Mycenaean palace civilisation), Shelmerdine (2001), which surveys the Third Palace Period on the mainland and summarises the evidence of the Linear B documents relating to palace administration and economy on pp. 358–62, 380 (for Crete at the same period see Rehak and Younger 2001: 441–58, 471–2). On the use of seals for administration see Krzyszkowska (2005: ch. 10). Very important papers relating to the palace economy can be found in Voutsaki and Killen (2001); see also Galaty and Parkinson (1999) and Foxhall (1995: 239–44) on the farming regime.

The Ahhiyawa question is discussed in Niemeier (1998) (especially sections 2 and 5); see also references in Bryce (1998) and useful comment in Hope Simpson (2003). On the 'Mycenaean hegemony' see also Thomas (1970: 190).

On exchange see Cline (1994, 1995), also Mountjoy (1998: 47–9), Sherratt (2000, and 2001: especially 216–24, 230–34). For the Uluburun wreck, with a detailed summary of finds, see most recently Pulak (1998) (some valuable comments are made in Sherratt 2000: 83–4), and for the Cape Gelidonya wreck Bass (1991: 69–73); both provide full bibliographies. For the Point Iria wreck see most recently Pennas *et al.* (2000–01).

On the Collapse, Vanschoonwinkel (1991) contains much useful analysis and comment; see also Shelmerdine (2001: 372–6, 381). The classic discussion of the 'Sea Peoples' by Sandars ([1978] 1985), and more revisionist comments in Bryce (1998: 367–74) lose much of their value in the light of points made in several papers in Ward and Joukowsky (1992), also in Drews (2000). For general discussions of civilisation collapse which are particularly relevant to the Aegean and/or the Near East, see Renfrew (1987: 133–6) and Tainter (1988).

The latest comments on HMB ware are the contributions given by Belardelli, Guzowska and Yasur-Landau at Laffineur *et al.* (2005), on which I have drawn for some statements made in this chapter.

Hall (1997) is a valuable guide to modern analysis of the Greek traditions about the movements of peoples, the arguments that have been used to identify these in the archaeological record, and the philological arguments concerning the Greek dialects. The most recent attempt to justify theories of Dorian invasion is Eder (1998), reviewed by Voutsaki in *CR* 50 (2000) 232–3.

3

THE POSTPALATIAL PERIOD

With the onset of the Postpalatial Period Aegean prehistorians are faced with the characteristic problem of the whole period covered by this book – shortage of information. It becomes necessary to rely on the evidence from relatively few sites (see Figure 3.1), which play a major role in the discussion more because they have been extensively investigated and publicised than because they were in fact the most important sites of the period. For example, while it is clear that Lefkandi and Perati were significant sites in their day, there is no reason to suppose that they were without parallel. On the contrary, it is becoming increasingly likely that other sites already becoming known from preliminary reports may have been equally significant, and may alter perceptions of the period just as radically (e.g. the Elateia-Alonaki cemetery, hereafter referred to as Elateia). They also exemplify a phenomenon that will become typical, for LH IIIC Lefkandi is effectively known only for its settlement, Perati for its cemetery. This contrasts tellingly with the Third Palace Period, in which no really important site is known from its cemetery alone and relatively many significant sites have provided evidence from both sources. But information from settlements is at a premium throughout the Postpalatial and EIA sequence, and this is undoubtedly the most important limitation on trying to give a rounded account. Also, those settlements which have produced most information are generally those which did not continue into later times, allowing the early remains to be preserved; the evidence from such 'failed sites' could be misleading, therefore.

The first stage of recovery

Following the approach taken in Chapter 2, the developments of the Post-palatial Period must principally reflect the activities of the survivors of the Collapse and their descendants. This partly undercuts the basis on which doom-laden descriptions such as Schweitzer's rely, written from the view-point that attributes the Collapse to the damage caused by the invading Dorians:

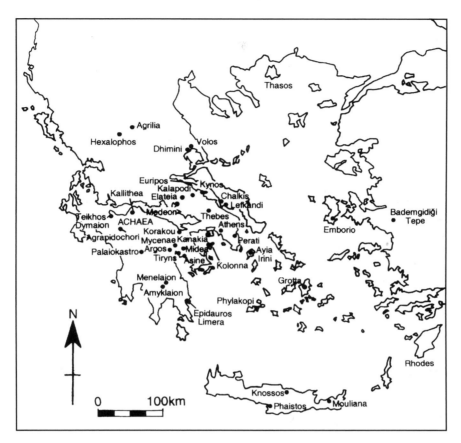

Figure 3.1 Important Postpalatial sites and regions.

The twelfth century was a century of chaos. Citadels and palaces were destroyed, whole populations migrated by land or by sea, population decreased and the survivors retreated to wretched but easily defensible settlements, trading links within the Aegean and beyond it collapsed, the level of culture was rapidly depressed and impoverished, and it was as though prehistory, which had long been left behind, had suddenly returned.

(Schweitzer 1971: 22)

An analysis which attributes the Collapse to the effects of drought and famine uses similar language:

Virtually all the Mycenean palace-centres in Greece were sacked, either by neighboring Myceneans or by their own starving subjects

59

> . . . Refugees streamed into Achaea, Kephallenia and Attica while
> parts of the Peloponnese became almost totally unoccupied. A wave
> of Peloponnesian emigrants sailed to Cyprus . . . After two or three
> generations, the weather patterns probably returned to normal . . .
> But the Mycenean culture could not be restored. The catastrophes
> had produced a breakdown of the entire political, social, and economic
> structure of Mycenean Greece.
>
> (Stiebing 1980: 17–19)

Yet, as Desborough emphasised long ago (1964), archaeology shows that the
Collapse was actually followed by a degree of recovery and, in parts of the
Aegean, a final flourishing, although he viewed this as relatively short-lived,
giving way to decline within the second half of the twelfth century (1972:
24–5). By 1990 Rutter was able to argue that there was still considerable
cultural vitality in the twelfth century, and that final decline did not take
place until the eleventh (1992: 70). This reflects the now commonly accepted
view that the Early and Middle phases of LH IIIC lasted much longer, and
therefore the signs of a last flourishing should be dated much later, than
Desborough had imagined. As argued in Chapter 1, the Postpalatial Period
probably ought to be allotted the best part of two centuries, not much less
than the Third Palace Period before it. The period should be seen, then, not
as a relatively brief and dispiriting epilogue to the history of the Aegean
BA, but as a potentially very significant stage, with distinctive characteristics, which could have exercised considerable influence on the later course
of development.

It is clear that the Collapse did not involve an irreversible breakdown of
society. The palaces had gone, and were not rebuilt, but organised efforts
at reconstruction and new building can be identified at various sites. At
Mycenae itself there was certainly reoccupation of some parts of the citadel,
but the uppermost terraces may simply have been abandoned in their ruined
state (as is also reported from Midea; see Walberg 1998b: 178), and lower
down, in the Cult Centre area, no attempt was made to clear the destruction
debris, which was levelled to form the basis for new but not very substantial
structures (Taylour 1981: 10–11). But at Tiryns the fortification wall was
repaired, and not only the Lower Citadel but the whole settlement below
the citadel seems to have been constructed on a new plan, which involved
expansion into new areas in the north (Kilian 1988: 135; Maran 2002). Some
of the buildings in this settlement were quite substantial, although the
ordinary houses were not of remarkable quality (Papadimitriou in Lemos and
Deger-Jalkotzy 2003). Again, much of the Upper Citadel was left uncleared,
but the important Building T, now firmly established as of LH IIIC date, was
built over the Great Megaron, though how soon after the destruction is not
clear. New structures were built at Korakou, including the large House P
(but Blegen's plan combines two architectural phases; see Rutter 1974: 547),

the many-roomed structures at Kanakia on Salamis continued in use (*AR* 48 (2001–2002) 14–15), and at Lefkandi the first LH IIIC phase, which seems to have involved an effective rebuilding of the settlement, included substantial two-storeyed buildings of several rooms. But at Dhimini the large LH IIIB2 complex of palatial character (Chapter 2, p. 25), which suffered severe damage in one part and intense fire in another, was only partly brought back into use for a short time in LH IIIC Early before being abandoned for ever.

The surviving communities were not, then, totally lacking in energy or resources, but in most regions there were clearly limits to how much could be undertaken, and it is surely significant that there was no real attempt to rebuild the palaces, for this is the clearest sign that the type of society that they represented had disappeared. It is questionable whether even a shadow of it survived, for it is noteworthy how muted the signs of recovery are at most of the great palace centres of the Third Palace Period, where they are identifiable at all. Tiryns, which may have become as large as any of the major thirteenth-century centres and quite probably displaced Mycenae as the leading centre of the region, is the one clear exception. Here the construction of Building T, planned to include the previous throne emplacement in the Great Megaron, strongly suggests that an attempt was made to re-establish a hierarchy centring on a *wanax*-like ruler (Maran 2001). Forms of organised government must have been re-established elsewhere also, but Kilian was surely right when he suggested that there was a substantial levelling down of the previous hierarchy (1988: 135; cf. Maran 2001: 120–1). Indeed, the whole basis for the authority to govern must have been renegotiated, for in the turmoil of the Collapse previously established authorities will surely have forfeited most if not all respect, because of their clear failure to control the situation. Further, they are likely to have lost any monopoly on the use of force, and therefore the ability to enforce obedience.

Thus, the new ruling classes of the surviving major settlements, whether or not they included elements of the old and even represented themselves as their legitimate successors, as apparently at Tiryns, will have had to establish new relationships with the populations that they wished to control and to rebuild a position of authority (see Maran 2001: 117–18 on a possible change in ruler ideology to be observed in the replacement of the central hearth by a row of columns in Building T at Tiryns, a feature also noted by Walberg in the reconstruction of the Midea 'megaron'). The new rulers will also have had to establish the boundaries of their control and negotiate with each other. Their power is unlikely to have been as firmly based as that of the ruling classes of the palace societies, and the new principalities are unlikely to have been as stable or extensive, or to have wielded as much influence, as the old. In fact, the Collapse was followed by a highly significant shift in the distribution of centres of recognisable wealth and, presumably, power.

Population movement

The re-establishment of some degree of stability will have been made more difficult by a notable feature of the Postpalatial Period – mobility of population. It has been traditional to suggest that there was extensive migration from the mainland in various directions, to Achaea and Cephallenia in the west, and the Dodecanese, Crete, Cyprus and Cilicia in the east (cf. Desborough 1972: 20–1, repeated e.g. in Morris, I. 1997: 540, 549, and widely in Karageorghis and Morris 2001). The argument for eastward movement has become associated with a long established theory that the 'Sea Peoples' were, or included, displaced Aegean groups (see a useful summary of the arguments in Niemeier 1998: 47–8, various papers in Oren 2000, and Yasur-Landau 2003), and it is still often suggested that organised groups moved to Cyprus at the beginning of the Postpalatial Period (see recently Karageorghis 2001).

But there are many grounds for questioning this interpretation, not least that until recently it has been based largely on pottery, which does not in fact demonstrate what it has been claimed to do. For the local Mycenaean ware of Cyprus was already developing in Late Cypriot II before the Collapse, and the more elaborate Late Cypriot IIIA pottery which succeeds it, generally termed Mycenaean IIIC:1b in Cypriot studies (a usage obsolete in Aegean terminology), does not represent the typical pottery range of mainland Mycenaean sites. Rather, it is best described as a blending of a selection of Mycenaean, and to some extent Minoan, shapes and motifs with local traditions and Near Eastern influences; the Mycenaean element is strong, but it seems to have connections with different regions and phases in the Aegean (on all this see Kling 1989: 170–6, also 2000). Further, many of the identifiable links cannot be dated at the beginning of the Postpalatial Period, as would be naturally expected if a Collapse-inspired migration is in question. The sudden appearance of sites like Maa-Palaiokastro in Cyprus does not, then, have to be explained in terms of settlement by Aegean 'refugees'. It has been seen as a cooperative venture between Cypriots and Mycenaeans (Karageorghis and Demas 1988: 265–6), and might have been a 'port of trade', as a notable concentration of 'Canaanite' amphorae suggests (C. Bell, pers. comm.).

The local pottery of 'Mycenaean IIIC:1b' type found at Palestinian sites like Tel Miqne and Ashdod could also have pre-Collapse beginnings (Sherratt 1994: 67–8) and does seem to be largely a selection from Cypriot Mycenaean (cf. the 'Mycenaean' pottery from Cilician sites; Sherratt and Crouwel 1987). It forms a notable part of what certainly appears to be a new cultural complex (Killebrew 2000: emphasised on 244; Yasur-Landau 2003: especially 588), for many of whose features Aegean parallels have been cited. But some of the Aegean parallels cited represent types that are also new in the Aegean at this time, like the 'mourner' figures on the lips of bowls, while other features, like the high proportion of pig bones in the settlement strata, have no necessary connection with the Aegean (where pig is the least well represented domesticate in the bone material). Also, well known Aegean types like tripod cooking pots, storage stirrup jars and pithoi are worryingly absent (Yasur-Landau 2003: 592). Quite simply, these do not look like standard Mycenaeans, and if this new cultural complex represents organised movement into Palestine from anywhere, it is surely from Cyprus, not the Aegean, let alone the Greek mainland, and Cyprus is the most likely place for the complex to have taken shape, though in Palestine local Canaanite elements were incorporated.

Undoubtedly the establishment of the Greek language in Cyprus must imply some kind of movement from the Aegean, but this could have taken place over a long period and represent something more like an 'economic' migration which increasingly Aegeanised the population (Sherratt 1992: 325–6; cf. Catling 1994: 133–4). Coldstream (1998c: 6–7) envisages 'migrations' in the eleventh century, seen as a movement of 'optimists and opportunists', who 'arrived in whole communities' to found new settlements. But it remains a problem to understand how such movements were organised at the Aegean end, and how the people who moved at such a late stage, when evidence for contact with Cyprus is much slighter than before, had acquired any knowledge of where they were going (I owe these observations to my Ph.D. student Guy Middleton). I would rather suggest that the situation may have had analogies with the later Greek colonisation movement in the central Mediterranean. Despite the foundation legends, which speak in terms of single organised voyages, in reality this surely involved a continual stream of migrants, who did not own their own ships, to the new settlements (cf. Osborne 1997: 258 on Pithecusae).

Mycenaean pottery was valued and locally imitated in other regions also, Macedonia and south Italy, and its appearance here in post-Collapse contexts is probably to be explained as a local development, where it is not actually imported, as it is rarely. In south Italy local Mycenaean pottery of LH IIIC Early type has been found at several sites (Mountjoy 1993: 174). Locally made material of remarkably late-looking Mycenaean style has recently been reported from Apulia, and might represent a 'refugee' settlement (Benzi 2001). But the evidence does not seem to represent a significant population movement: no local semi-Mycenaean culture developed here, and the 'Hellenisation' of south Italy had to wait until the eighth century.

In contrast, there are grounds for supposing that there was significant movement of population within the Aegean region after the Collapse. This may particularly have taken the form of concentration at major sites, which would explain the indications of expansion at Tiryns, Asine and maybe Argos. All could have absorbed population from the smaller settlements of the Argolid, which were now apparently abandoned. Other plausible examples of new or greatly expanded settlements include Lefkandi: Xeropolis (apparently covering the whole hilltop of 6 ha); the settlement represented by the large cemetery at Perati, which belongs entirely to this period; Emborio on Chios; and apparently Bademgediği Tepe in western Anatolia (Meriç and Mountjoy 2002), which with Emborio and other scattered finds may reflect movement across the Aegean. Identifiable increases in the number of tombs in use during LH IIIC at relatively many sites in the north-west Peloponnese, over an area centred in western Achaea but stretching down to the Alpheios valley, also on Cephallenia, Naxos and Rhodes, have also frequently been taken to reflect immigration, although they could represent the concentration of population at certain sites (for Rhodes see Benzi 1988: 261–2). Certainly, there is increasing evidence from Achaea that the population was already considerable in LH IIIA–B. Equally, the marked changes in settlement pattern in LM IIIC Crete and the establishment of many substantial new sites (Figure 4.3) seems to reflect movement among the native population, although it has been argued that a group of apparently foreign phenomena in early LM IIIC, including the dominance of the deep bowl in the ceramic repertoire, instead of the long-established cup, and the appearance of a new type of cooking jar and of Psi figurines, could reflect an influx from some Mycenaean region(s) (D'Agata 2001: 346). In contrast, it may be noted, Athens has produced no evidence to substantiate the notion, ultimately reflecting Thuc. 1.2, that it was a centre for 'refugees' from other areas.

There remain various questions, including that of motivation. The traditional explanation, especially for apparent movements out of the Argolid and other central parts of the mainland, was that they represented movement away from the threat of subjection to new rulers, or simply from piratical raiding and possible massacre or enslavement. The argument that there was a threat from the sea may be a viable explanation for the very marked movement in Crete away from low-lying coastal areas to defensible sites, often well inland (Nowicki 1996: 284–5, also 2000: 264–5; Wallace 2003b: 257). But here Borgna draws attention to the possible role of social breakdown and stresses that there are marked variations between east and south Crete, where the abandonment of previous settlements is most marked, and north and west Crete, where major nucleated settlements survived (2003: especially 155–60).

A 'flight from the coast' has also been suggested sometimes for the Cyclades and the mainland. Several Cycladic sites were indeed in rather inaccessible and easily defensible positions (Osborne 1996: 200 – but these are mainly late), but the continuing use of Grotta on Naxos for burials provides a counter-example, suggesting that a population was still based in the immediate neighbourhood, close to the shore. Many sites in positions at or close to the shore on the mainland and nearest islands also continued in occupation (e.g. Tiryns, Asine, Kolonna, Lefkandi, Chalkis, Volos), as did Kastri near Palaikastro in eastern Crete. Thus, any theory positing a universal and continuing threat from the sea seems implausible.

It seems very unlikely that such coastal sites were themselves pirate bases, although this has been suggested for both Cycladic and Cretan sites (Nowicki 2000: 264–5, also 2001: 29–31, 37). No community of the size suggested by the spread of material at most of them could support itself largely or entirely from piracy or land raiding (cf. Desborough 1972: 128 on Karphi). However, an explanation of the movement in Crete as driven by purely economic motives has difficulties. It has been suggested that the move into the hills in the well-studied Kavousi region, to sites where there was perennial water and good arable land, was driven by a new need to be self-sufficient in food, responding to a breakdown in trade (cf. Haggis 1996: 410; Coulson 1998: 41). But it is implausible that in LM IIIA-B, when sites clustered in the plain, this region was dependent on imported food, and it has been pointed out that the LM IIIC sites in fact have less access to much arable land and are more difficult to approach than those of other periods, so hardly represent a 'natural' settlement pattern (Wallace 2000: 90–1, also 2003a: 605; Nowicki 2000: 232).

It has also been suggested that lowland sites like Knossos were the bases for new and aggressive rulers, perhaps 'heroes' returned from Cyprus, whose activities might even have caused the movement to hill sites (Catling 1995; *NorthCem*: 647–9; but the movement is earlier than SM), or at least of new settlers from the mainland taking over territory already deserted because of a previous threat from the sea (Nowicki 2000: 265). But as Kanta and Stampolidis emphasise (2001: 105), the material culture of these sites is not different in any distinctive way from that of the upland sites. Nowicki's suggested sequence is also far too dependent on linking successive phases with supposed historical events and displays an unconsciously compressed view of the chronology. In speaking of settlements being founded 'exactly at the same time' (2001: 32) he is falling into the trap of assuming exact contemporaneity between sites that show material of the same pottery phase, when they could have been established at different points over several decades and still show similar pottery. Kanta has also reasonably questioned the claim to date surface finds by fabric to specific phases within LM IIIC (Karageorghis and Morris 2001: 83). There is no reason to suppose, in fact, that the 'movement to the hills' was a planned response to a particular situation, but it could be seen as an increasingly popular response to the breakdown in social order emphasised by Borgna.

Certainly the 'refuge site' interpretation does have its most credible examples in Crete (cf. Wallace 2003b: 257; Nowicki 2000: 230–1 and 2001 on the choice of defensible sites). It seems almost inconceivable that Katalimata in east Crete could be anything but a 'refuge site', probably for the occupants of Halasmenos (on these sites see Haggis and Nowicki 1993; Coulson and Tsipopoulou 1994; Tsipopoulou 2001); Kato Kastellas in the Zakro gorge may be of the same type (Vokotopoulos 1998) (for these and other Cretan sites see Figure 4.3). But the sites that are most difficult of access might be best interpreted as intended for emergency occupation only, by the occupants of closely associated sites which were much better placed in relation to water, arable land, and communications (Haggis and Nowicki 1993: especially 334–6). Given the variability of site placing and site size within Crete, it may ultimately prove necessary to devise explanations for each region individually.

Even if the movements within Crete reflect a response to strongly felt insecurity, this need not have affected the whole Aegean. The new mobility could often reflect attraction towards perceived centres of security and prosperity. For even if the palace societies as a means of social organisation had been deliberately abandoned, if not actually overthrown, their disappearance must have been profoundly disorienting. The overall structures that had shaped most people's lives and experience of the world in the spheres of political and social relationships and public religion had gone. Many settlements that had been occupied for centuries, if not millennia, no longer existed or were shadows of their former selves, and patterns of contact that had existed for equally long had been disrupted. This view of the period admittedly runs counter to the rather rosy picture of a time of new opportunities and widened horizons, once the 'dead hand' of palace bureaucracy was lifted, that is offered in, e.g., Muhly 1992 and 2003 (cf. also Morris, I. 1997: 540, which speaks of a LH IIIC 'renaissance' and describes the period as 'perhaps a golden age for local aristocracies, freed from palatial control'). But, with the exception of Tiryns, there is no sign of a sudden burgeoning of local enterprise, let alone a 'golden age', in the regions likely to have been run by palaces; and if some persons managed to rise to positions of new power and wealth in the Postpalatial Period, a far larger proportion of the surviving population may have seen their prospects as uncertain, if not depressingly meagre.

In such circumstances, anywhere that seemed to offer the security and relative prosperity of the past might be attractive. Traders and craft specialists in particular might have moved to sites where they hoped to maximise the chances of increasing their wealth, and such persons may be considered the most likely to contemplate moving out of the Aegean altogether. Traders, it may be noted, would have the advantage of access to if not control of ships, a factor of considerable relevance as pointed out on p. 63. But it seems probable that ordinary farming families moved also, if originally over smaller distances. But once the first move had been made, renewed moves might be easier to contemplate, and an atmosphere might be created in which a readiness to move might be considered perfectly normal. In fact, mobility might well be considered the most significant feature of the Postpalatial Period, for it not only represents a continuing destabilising factor, it underlines the limits on the coercive power of those trying to re-establish authority. Free movement of population would be undesirable from a ruler's point of view, since it would entail continuing uncertainty over the size of the population available to produce food and provide labour and, if need be, the elements of an army. But it was plainly beyond their power to prevent it.

Such mobility may have had an effect on the total level of population. For, while it is risky to make precise estimations (see further Chapter 4), it is very hard to doubt that the population of the Aegean had declined significantly, perhaps very significantly, by the EIA and that this decline started in the Postpalatial Period. Losses during the period of worst disturbance could have been very serious, especially if localised famines were one cause of the turmoil. Wrigley has pointed out how harvest failures or simply big swings in yield over just a few years could have very serious effects on population level in more recent pre-industrial societies (1969: 62–3). These effects could then have been compounded in the ensuing conditions of insecurity, so that the shifting of parts of the population, either within the Aegean, e.g. to Crete or Anatolia, or beyond it, to Cyprus, was accompanied by a failure to reproduce itself at the same level.

The character of the Postpalatial Period

As noted, the Postpalatial Period was long, and it has become common to divide it into successive phases of recovery, flourishing, and decline. It was also a period in which material culture often shows marked regional and local characteristics, in contrast with the considerable degree of homogeneity typical of the Third Palace Period. Is it nevertheless possible to identify characteristics that typify the whole age and might, as suggested on p. 60, have had a marked influence on future development? In my view, certain common threads can be traced.

One obvious point is that it is no longer possible to identify with certainty a group of leading sites in the Aegean, but certain regions can be suggested to have played a significant role on the basis of their ability to be active in exchange, create a degree of wealth, and influence other regions. The substantial remains from Tiryns and other sites in the Argolid, along with the development there of very elaborate forms of decorated pottery, especially the Close Style, provide a reminder that this region, for so long the effective leader of the Mycenaean culture, still had some importance. Links have been noted with Attica, Boeotia and Euboea, which are still strong in the LH IIIC Late phase, when they extend as far as Paros and Chios (Mountjoy 1999: 53). But in general the leading centres and regions of the Third Palace Period are poorly represented by finds of significance, although exceptional finds such as the probably Italian bronze vessel from Pylos T. K-2 (Harding 1984: 205; see Figure 3.2) show that they could still attract attention, perhaps in this case as a by-product of exchange with the Adriatic.

But other regions seem to have been more important. It has been plausibly argued that at the beginning of the Postpalatial Period there were close links between the Dodecanese, Crete – which becomes important again in this

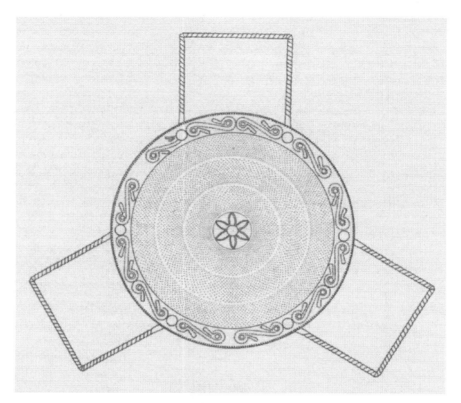

Figure 3.2 Bronze vessel, probably Italian, from Pylos tomb K-2. D. 28.7–29.3 cm,
H. 9.5 cm. Courtesy of the Department of Classics, University of
Cincinatti, and Dr S. Stocker.

period, especially the north and east – and Cyprus, and that contacts with
this network stimulated a recovery in the central Aegean, both in pottery
style and generally (Sherratt 1982: 187–8, also 1985). A resulting 'miniature
Mycenaean *koinē*' spreading from Rhodes to Perati, in which Naxos was a key
link, was identified by Desborough (1964: 228), but this has more recently
been seen as a region of independent centres with abundant but varied interconnections (see Vlachopoulos 1998 on the Cyclades). A more confined area
in the east Aegean, including Chios but excluding Rhodes, does have a
markedly homogeneous pottery style (Mountjoy 1999: 45, 50, 967–9). The
cemetery of Epidauros Limera in eastern Laconia shows links to the central
Aegean, especially in the occurrence of the distinctive and widely found
octopus stirrup jar type (two apparently locally made; Mountjoy 1999: 252),
and may be the conduit for the exotic influences and types, including octopus
stirrup jars, that are found at the important inland cemetery of Palaiokastro
(see most recently *AR* 43 (1996–1997) 33, and Mountjoy 1999: 296–9 on

the pottery). Another region interconnected by the seaways, whose focus seems to be the Euripos strait, takes in Lefkandi, quite probably Kynos (Pyrgos Livanaton), Mitrou near Tragana in Locris, and many substantial but unexcavated coastal sites in eastern Boeotia and western Euboea; it has pottery links extending at least as far as Volos and Ayia Irini on Kea (Popham and Milburn 1971: 348), but curiously few with the central Aegean.

Further west in central Greece there are also sites of significance, represented by their rich cemeteries, such as Medeon and Elateia; the latter, strategically placed at an intersection of land routes, has produced likely Argive, Achaean, and Cretan vases, including a remarkable octopus stirrup jar which has faience beads inlaid into the handles (Deger-Jalkotzy 2003). But this region may not have been as important in this period as that centring on Achaea, which has strong connections with Cephallenia, Elis and much of the Alpheios valley and probably incorporated Messenia, where little material has been found (Mountjoy 1999: 54–5 sees these connections as strongest in the LH IIIC Late phase, when they extend to Aetolia and Phocis; cf. Eder 2003: 41–3, which identifies Achaean-linked pottery in Albania). These western parts of Greece have recently been argued to have maintained significant contacts with Italy and to have acted as an intermediary, passing on goods and influences to other parts of the mainland (Eder 2003: 44–9; Borgna and Cassola Guida 2005; Eder and Jung 2005), so that a mutually enriching system was created, until the final collapse of any polities of significance.

The constant references made to interconnections within and between these regions underline the crucial importance of exchange in the Postpalatial Period. The fact that very many of the important settlements were situated on or close to the sea emphasises the degree to which prosperity depended upon it, which may be further reflected in the representations of ships on several vases. As well as elaborately decorated pottery containers and other fine vessels originating from the various Aegean regions, types of weapon and a wide variety of forms of jewellery, seals, and other items originating from east and west were distributed in small but significant quantities over much the same area of exchange activity as before, extending from Cyprus and the east Mediterranean shores through the Aegean to the Adriatic, Italy and Sardinia. The essentially foreign practice of cremation may also have spread along the exchange networks (see further, p. 73). All this testifies to a degree of vitality, as emphasised in Rutter (1992).

Instability

So far the picture is positive, but there are negative factors which also need stressing. First and foremost, the Postpalatial Period was an age of insecurity and uncertainty. The clearest indications of this are provided by the evidence, not only for mobility of population but also for a decline in its size. The whole class of small sites identified in the previous period and a good many that seem more substantial appear to have been abandoned, and, as the history of various excavated sites shows, this process was not confined to the immediate aftermath of the Collapse, but continued through the Postpalatial Period. Many substantial settlements that survived strongly into the Post-palatial Period were abandoned before its end, not to be settled again in the EIA, if ever (e.g. Midea, Korakou, Teikhos Dymaion, Phylakopi), and Tiryns, which was a substantial town for much of the period, seems to have dwindled by its end to a group of associated villages or hamlets (Kilian 1988: 151). While it is very dangerous to assume that the extremely marked drops in the numbers of identifiable sites in various regions between LH IIIB and LH IIIC (cf. the maps in Popham 1994a: 282–3) represent a proportional drop in the total population, it is hard to doubt that, taken together, the evidence reflects a genuine decline in population, which could have had a strong influence on the development of EIA society (see further, Chapter 4).

The reasons for the decline are debatable, but are likely to have been bound up with a continuing sense of insecurity. The opportunistic banditry and piracy which probably accompanied the widespread breakdown of order in the Collapse could well have continued in the Postpalatial Period as minor but endemic problems, and represent the commonest form of violence that a community might fear. As noted, this may particularly explain the widespread move inland and upland in Crete. It could have inspired the abandonment of small outlying farms and settlements for the security to be found in large settlements, and also the choice of defensible locations for many settlements, although this was by no means universal. The evidence for very extensive fire-destructions at various important sites during the Postpalatial Period, if interpretable as the results of warfare, indicates that attacks on a substantial scale were not unknown. Other evidence for the greater prevalence of inter-communal violence may be found in the relative prominence of weapon burials and of scenes of warriors, sometimes in chariots, and warfare on pictorial pottery (Figure 3.3): even if these more closely reflect ideology than reality, the fact that such an ideology was prevalent is significant. Inciden-tally, the prominence of the chariot in this pictorial material is a strong argument against supposing that it had been rendered obsolete at the time of the Collapse by new military tactics, as proposed in Drews (2000) (a point made by Prof. J. Rutter in his teaching, cited here with his permission). The notable changes in types of military equipment that can be identified in this period (Rutter 1992: 67–8) may also be considered significant.

Whether or not insecurity was the cause of the abandonment of so many settlements, the psychological effects of such an abandonment are likely to have been severe. Rutter's comment, 'Despite some major shifts in how people were distributed in the landscape and what was probably a substantial decline in the overall population, the Aegean world weathered the actual palatial collapse of ca. 1200 B.C. well enough' (1992: 70), surely makes far too little of these. There is no reason to imagine, with Thucydides (1.2), that

Figure 3.3 The Warrior Vase from the House of the Warrior Vase, Mycenae. H. 41 cm. Courtesy of the National Archaeological Museum, Athens.

prehistoric populations were always ready to move on under pressure from stronger groups and settle elsewhere. They are more likely to have made the decision to leave their farms, burial grounds, and shrines with extreme reluctance, even more than the Classical Athenians showed at the beginning of the Peloponnesian War (Thuc. 2.16.2); for these movements, if to other sites or even other regions, were surely intended to be permanent.

This apparent willingness to move from sites that had been occupied for long periods emphasises what a catastrophic effect the Collapse must have had. It might be expected that much of the surviving population was psychologically traumatised, particularly that part of the population which had been dependent on palace administrations for its sustenance, about whose fate one can only speculate, and this effect could well have inhibited recovery and new development. At the least, the survivors would have been plagued with general uncertainty about what the future held, as well as by specific concerns such as the continuing availability of the basic metals and other commonly traded commodities. In regions that were not strongly affected, on current evidence, such as Achaea, the effects need not have been so marked, but there would surely have been considerable uncertainty felt about the new, more unstable world in which they were now living – and if people arrived as refugees or new settlers from other regions, they will have brought their feelings of loss and disorientation with them.

Such reactions are likely to have been most strongly felt in the period immediately after the Collapse and in those mainland regions where the disruption had been greatest and the decline from the past most marked. The strength of such feelings would surely have diminished over time, with the birth of new generations which had known nothing else, but the tradition that in the past things had been considerably better would survive, enhanced by the remains visible on every side. The confidence-sapping effect of living 'in the ruins of the former great towns, in the shadow of the departed greatness' (Desborough 1972: 25) should not be underestimated. To see or simply to know that settlements, fields, terraces and plantations lay totally abandoned all around them would surely have been equally depressing to a population that consisted largely of farmers.

Continuity and change in material culture

The effective destruction of the previous social order should have had other results. An openness to innovation, in the adoption of new burial customs, styles of dress, and types of artefact, might well be considered a positive feature. But it also suggests a loss of confidence in inherited cultural types and traditions and the attribution of greater prestige to exotic novelties (some of which, like Type II swords and fibulae, had begun to appear before the Collapse). The tendency to invest the exotic with prestige is, of course, a commonly recurring feature in all societies, but it seems particularly evident in the Aegean in this period. The prominence of exotic items in what may be considered elite burials gives evidence of a hunger for status symbols, which could have drawn special impetus from the now much more marked cultural imbalance between the Aegean and the Near East and the growing rarity of locally made elaborate craftwork. Items likely to come both from the Near East and from Italy or central Europe seem to play this role, and perhaps also Aegean-made valuables of much older date such as the Perati seal-rings. Again, the need for such status symbols can be argued to reflect an insecure society, in which the use of 'heirlooms' suggests that some were still trying to appeal to traditional systems of displaying rank and status that others were discarding.

Nevertheless, the overwhelming impression given by the material culture is of the continuance of past traditions in a whole range of features, house plans and fittings, ordinary pottery and artefacts for domestic use, burial customs and religion, as identified in the ritual use of figurines. The apparently immediate disappearance of arts which had been particularly closely associated with the palaces is readily explicable: writing would be of no use to the new rulers, who are unlikely to have had complex administrative practices, and the most elaborate forms of architecture, furniture, precious vessels and jewellery required resources that they could no longer command. But there is strong evidence for the continuing production of some luxury items, such as the typical gold and glass relief beads and, it seems likely, simply decorated sealstones in steatite and fluorite, most clearly at Elateia (this is a controversial area: see Pini in Dakoronia *et al.* 1996: xxi–xxv; Krzyszkowska 2005: 235 is not very explicit, but notes that some examples in late contexts are in mint condition, 270–1). But such items are no longer found everywhere (relief beads are rare at Perati, for instance), so that the prosperous no longer had access to a similar range of finely crafted goods in every part of the Aegean. Very probably this was because production was now centred in small workshops, which had limited and not necessarily regular access to raw materials.

The evidence of burial customs will be considered in detail in Chapter 6. Here it seems important to stress that while the types of tomb identifiable are overwhelmingly those current earlier, particularly chamber tombs, the changes in the manner in which they were used may suggest 'a society in dissolution' (Cavanagh and Mee 1998: 135). The appearance of cremation as a minority rite at a wide range of sites is a notable feature. The practice may have spread from Anatolia: a few certain and likely Third Palace Period cremations have been found in the Mycenaean-style cemetery of Müsgebi in Caria and in the Dodecanese, as also in Crete and at a very few mainland sites (Cavanagh and Mee 1998: 75–6, 94; for Crete see Desborough 1964: 187–8, and Kanta 1980: 325). But since cremation also appears in Italy in the local Middle Bronze Age, the possibility that some Postpalatial examples, especially in the west Peloponnese, reflect influence from there cannot be discounted, since there were lively links between Italy and the Aegean in the Postpalatial Period (Eder and Jung 2005). Certainly, while Postpalatial cremations are commonest at sites in the central Aegean koinē and in Crete, they also occur in the west Peloponnese (Kallithea, Klauss, Koukoura, and Lousika: Spaliareika in Achaea, Agrapidokhori in Elis, and Palaiokastro in Arcadia), and at Khania near Mycenae, Argos and Thebes (Cavanagh and Mee 1998: 93–4), as also in cemeteries of apparently Postpalatial date on Thasos (Koukouli-Chrysanthaki 1992: 822) and maybe in inland Macedonia. The rite itself represents only a partial departure from traditional practice, in that except at Khania and Argos these cremations are found within traditional forms of tomb, alongside inhumations. The rite's widespread distribution implies a readiness on the part of some members of many different communities to adopt what was an essentially foreign custom, but whether this involved adopting new ideas about death and the afterlife remains questionable, although it is hard to believe that no ideological element was involved (see further, Chapter 6).

Another interesting and probably significant development is the increased prominence of weapon burial (Cavanagh and Mee 1998: 95 cite most

Mycenaean examples known to date; cf. also Papazoglou-Manioudaki 1994, and Deger-Jalkotzy forthcoming). Like cremations, these are generally found in traditional types of multiple-burial tomb, chamber tombs and, in Crete, stone-built tombs; the majority are inhumations, but some are cremations. Typically, they are accompanied by a sword, sometimes decorated and most often a Type II form, one or more spearheads and a knife. There may also be items of bronze armour or other war-related fittings such as shield-bosses, scabbard ornaments, or boar's tusk plates that were probably attached to helmets in the traditional way, but only rarely are elaborate vases or more valuable goods found.

It was a characteristic feature of Mycenaean culture from its beginning to bury weapons with some adult males, but the Postpalatial burials differ from classic early Mycenaean examples like those in the Shaft Graves and Dendra tholos, for they are normally found in tombs that rarely have any special features, alongside other burials which were provided with unremarkable goods, though there are cases where more than one warrior burial has been found in a grave (e.g. two from the Lousika: Spaliareika tomb; Papazoglou-Manioudaki 1994: 180). Mouliana T. A is exceptional in containing not only four swords and other weapons, but several bronze vessels and other metal items, including two pins and a 'stud' of iron. The distribution pattern of weapon burials is also very peculiar: there is a very marked concentration in Achaea, especially the Patras region (Papadopoulos 1999), and more than one has been found in the cemeteries associated with Grotta on Naxos and in eastern Crete, where 'Siteia' is the reputed provenance of several swords. But other examples, and sword finds that indicate their presence, are widely scattered, and surprisingly there are none at all in the eastern Peloponnese, although Type II swords have been found there in non-funerary contexts. Finally, they are a feature of the developed phases of the Postpalatial Period. These features make it difficult to see these burials as members of a well-established ruling elite, but they may well reflect the emergence at this stage of leaders whose power derived from their military role (Deger Jalkotzy forthcoming).

This points up one of the notable features of the Postpalatial Period, that a ruling elite marked by really distinctive forms of tomb or building is impossible to identify. The tholos tomb effectively went out of use as an elite tomb type, although small and unremarkable tholos-shaped or vaulted rectangular tombs continued to be built in stone, whose contents do not differ significantly from those of other contemporary tombs (the rectangular Mouliana tombs are a partial exception, being small but notably rich). The most elaborate buildings might have several rooms and be two-storeyed, and there are examples of the use of columns and painted wall plaster (especially in House W at Tiryns), but only the large complex at Dhimini previously noted (p. 25) seems comparable with the more substantial buildings of the Third Palace Period, let alone the palaces, and this originated in LH IIIB2. Equally, no major achievements in public architecture can be attributed to the period (the Tiryns dam is most probably to be dated earlier; Maran 2002 *contra* Zangger 1994: especially 207). Clearly, no class capable of mobilising the resources needed to support such endeavours existed, and membership of any elite may have been more dependent on personal achievement than on inherited position.

Similar features can be observed in the field of religion. While Mycenaean religious sites of the previous period were modest in their dimensions and fittings, the Unterburg shrines at Tiryns (Figure 8.2: 1) and Room XXXII in House G at Asine are completely unremarkable apart from the use of pillars, while at Phylakopi and Ayia Irini the old buildings were simply kept in use, though becoming increasingly dilapidated. The most substantial structure likely to have had cult use is the 'megaron' at Midea, which was remodelled and used for a considerable part of the Postpalatial Period (Walberg 1998a). Again, relatively many structures can be identified in Crete, but they are generally unimpressive as architecture (D'Agata 2001: 348–50). Moreover, votives were only exceptionally of any material other than clay. The occurrence of large and elaborately decorated clay figures, especially bovids, which are very popular at certain sites, particularly in Crete (Zeimbekis 1998: especially ch. 4), could well be taken to indicate that this was the most prestigious type of votive available even to leading members of communities. This may reflect shortage of skilled craft specialists as well as of materials, but it indicates that only limited advantage was taken of another common arena for social display.

Thus, in general, the evidence suggests that the Postpalatial Period was characterised by limited achievement, which may be linked to a substantial shake-up in, if not complete breakdown of, the previous social hierarchy through which resources were mobilised. If this is accepted, it is not surprising that the one area where considerable evidence for artistic development can be identified is pottery, which was relatively cheap to produce in terms of both time and resources. Already in the LH IIIC Early phase Cretan and Dodecanesian centres were producing finely decorated stirrup jars, container vessels which were designed to have their contents shaken from them in small quantities, and so would have held liquids like perfumed oil, or valued local products like fish sauce (Rutter 1992: 64), and this practice spread more widely in LH IIIC Middle, when various centres seem to have advertised their identity through individual styles. There was a concurrent production of large ceremonial vessels, especially kraters, with elaborate, often pictorial decoration, which less often found their way into the exchange networks, but which were apparently produced at many sites from Volos to the Menelaion. The elaborate styles used on such vessels influenced each other and the decoration used on smaller shapes in a manner reminiscent of the much later Orientalising styles, and give an impression of artistic vigour and inventiveness. But it should not be forgotten that the great majority of pottery was much more simply decorated, and that, unlike in the

Orientalising period, no comparable movement can be detected in other crafts. Thus, although this was a real and positive development, it was limited, and had no long-lasting effects, for sooner or later all these elaborate styles disappeared.

The final decline

The disappearance of elaborate painted pottery is most easily explained as reflecting a decline in local patronage and in the level of exchange, for which finely decorated containers were produced. Both could be linked to the evidence for the continuing abandonment of sites and apparently continuing decline in the population. For the level at which crafts were practised would depend upon the size and wealth of the population that supported them, while the kind of entrepreneurial trader imagined to dominate exchange in this period, whose main motivation would be personal profit, would not long continue to plan voyages into or around the Aegean, if his potential markets were disappearing. This dwindling of exchange would in turn adversely affect the prosperity of the communities at which it was directed and those through which it passed, which could inspire further abandonments. It seems likely that such self-perpetuating processes lay behind the final decline of many mainland and central Aegean communities in the Postpalatial Period. They could well have prompted population movements that were the basis for the traditions of Greek settlement in Cyprus, where a dominant Greek-speaking presence had been established by historical times (but see Catling 1994: 136–8 for other explanations), and in the eastern Aegean, as related in the stories of the 'Ionian migration' and other traditions, though these may belong to a later period still. The traditions never suggest a motivation for such movements, but if this analysis of the final stages of the Postpalatial Period is correct, the basic one could have been simply hope of better prospects, closer to the still civilised Near East.

This final decline did not affect all regions equally. Crete, where many late LM IIIC and SM settlements and cemeteries can be identified, retained much of its BA heritage and seems in general to have prospered more than other parts of the Aegean, perhaps because of its position along the route to the central Mediterranean, which was still being travelled by Cypriot traders (see Chapter 5). This route might also have contributed to the apparent survival of communities that continued to use chamber tombs in Achaea and Cephallenia after these had been abandoned in more central regions. But the continuation of Mycenaean types of tomb seems to be a general feature of the more northern and western parts of the mainland, identifiable as far east as sites in Phocis bordering on Boeotia. Mycenaean shapes frequently continued in the pottery of these outlying regions when they had been abandoned elsewhere, and one can find other apparent survivals like the three female figurines from Elateia T. 58 (Alram-Stern 1999).

In general the final LH IIIC phases, including Submyc, seem to represent the culmination of processes that had been continuing throughout the Postpalatial Period, the abandonment of sites and a decline both in population and in the range and quality of craft products, but they also show significant changes and innovations in material culture. Now, and not before, the use of metal dress-fasteners and the burial of inhumations or ash-containers individually in pits and cists became the dominant practices of whole communities. Some Postpalatial cult sites were abandoned, as in the Tiryns Unterburg and at the Amyklaion (the abandonment of the Phylakopi shrine complex must fall earlier, no later than LH IIIC Middle). Kalapodi and the Ayia Irini 'temple' survived, but the dedication of figurines ceased. The practice of burying figurines with the dead had already disappeared much earlier from several regions, such as Achaea and Cephallenia; now the whole class seems to have ceased manufacture, as do other absolutely characteristic Mycenaean types such as the steatite 'whorls'/buttons/clothing-weights. Even the 'standard cooking-pot jug' changed (Popham 1994a: 303).

To interpret these developments in terms of 'a considerable, even fundamental change in population, involving the arrival of people of non-Mycenaean origin' (Popham 1994a: 303) represents an approach that has already been questioned. But there can be no doubt that the population of many significant central mainland regions was effectively ceasing to be recognisably 'Mycenaean' in material terms, preserving only some traditions in decorated pottery. In other areas of the mainland more of the Mycenaean tradition survived for some while, as some Minoan traditions were to do for even longer in Crete. No clear-cut line can be drawn culturally, any more than chronologically, and comments such as 'central Greek material culture changed abruptly in the early and mid-eleventh century' (Morris, I. 1997: 541) give a false impression, for there was no abrupt or radical break. But the material remains suggest that significant cultural changes were occurring, whose cumulative impact would produce a markedly different picture from what had seemed typical even in the Postpalatial Period.

Bibliography

The classic though now heavily outdated discussion of the period is Desborough (1964); cf. also Desborough (1972: 19–25). The most extensive recent survey is Popham (1994a), still traditional in its approach but useful for detail. Rutter (1992) is valuable, but concentrates on particular aspects. There are useful comments on Crete in this period in Rehak and Younger (2001: 458–64, 472). The most detailed comments on the complex interconnections visible in the pottery are to be found in the various chapters of Mountjoy (1999).

Several papers in Kyparissi-Apostolika and Papakonstantinou (2003) provide up to date discussions of LH IIIC and contemporary material from various sites and regions; see particularly Eder (2003).

Further comment on various facets of material culture will be found in Chapters 4–8.

4

THE STRUCTURE AND ECONOMY
OF COMMUNITIES

The environment and natural resources

The Aegean environment has been discussed by many authors. For the purposes of this book, there is little point in going into great detail, since all authorities are agreed that by the beginning of the EIA the landscape is likely to have been very similar to today's. This would have involved considerable changes from its original state, as a result of natural processes like rise in sea-level, tectonic activity, erosion and alluviation, as well as millennia of cultivation and other exploitation of resources. By the end of the BA, the sea had risen sufficiently to create more or less the pattern of islands and coastlines known in Classical times, although because of local silting and alluviation the shoreline was actually receding in some places. For example, bays near Iolkos and Troy were becoming dry land, and Tiryns was increasingly distant from the shore.

Episodes of erosion may have been triggered during the BA by a combination of unusually severe weather conditions and over-exploitation of hillslopes, but although it has been argued that this had marked local effects in the EBA, there is no trace of anything comparable later, except, perhaps, on some Cycladic islands (see Davidson and Tasker 1982: 89 on Melos). In fact, the effects of all natural processes were basically local and gradual, and the most spectacular change is likely to have been that caused by the eruption of the Thera volcano in the early LBA, which took out the centre of the original island. But it had become habitable again before the end of the Third Palace Period, and the wider effects of the eruption in the south Aegean were short lived.

Recent work on climate change suggests that the Aegean was distinctly less arid in the Early Holocene and that the typical Mediterranean regime of very dry summers established itself gradually during the BA, becoming particularly marked from the thirteenth century (Rackham and Moody 1996: xvi–xvii, 39; Moody 2003 suggests that aridity was worst in the tenth century and persisted to *c.* 800). There could have been noticeable fluctuations during this process (cf. Rackham and Moody 1996: 41: 'It is a fallacy

79

to assume (as most scholars do) that the climate remained constant at other periods when little was being written down'). In any case, as Osborne has pointed out (1996: 54–5), climate is extremely variable in Greece, not only from year to year but between neighbouring localities, which produces a considerable variety of ecological niches. Thus, even a slight general change in climate could have marked local effects, particularly on vegetation. But the view that a change to wetter conditions would have a marked general effect on erosion processes seems to have little to recommend it: sudden deluges are likely to have greater impact (Rackham and Moody 1996: 23–4). Variations in climate could be one of the factors governing the choice of places to settle and of agricultural regime to pursue, even one of the forces impelling population movement, but hypotheses supposing such effects remain speculative at present.

It is increasingly being argued that the effects of human exploitation have not been as uniformly and progressively deleterious to the Aegean environment as used to be suggested. One might expect that demand for timber, for building and even more for fuel, could cause shrinkage of woodland, especially on the smaller islands where this resource would always have been limited, but the most marked changes in vegetation more often reflect climatic change (Rackham and Moody 1996: 126, 127, 137). One change will reflect human activity: the widespread establishment of domesticated olives and other fruit trees; although no longer intensively exploited after the collapse of the palace economies, they surely remained common in some regions. The capacity of woodland to regenerate in periods of diminished human activity has been underestimated (Rackham and Moody 1996: 137–8), and this is very likely to have been a feature of the EIA (see Zangger *et al.* 1997: 593 for a notable increase in deciduous oak in the Pylos region). But the resulting landscape will still have been much more similar to that of Classical and later Greece, down to modern times, than to what might be reconstructed for the beginning of the BA (Wallace 2000: 96 fn. 17 notes Cretan evidence that the range of maquis and garigue species was similar to the modern one).

The larger types of wild fauna identifiable on the Greek mainland in earlier BA contexts (Dickinson 1994a: 28) may have become rare by the end of the BA, but the commoner species could have increased in numbers again during the EIA. Red deer are certainly well represented in the Nichoria EIA deposits, while roe deer, wild pig and fox are attested. The absence of hare and wolf (never clearly attested at Nichoria) is surely attributable to the potential for variation in relatively small samples, a factor pointed up by the study of a large sample of LM IIIC–LG bones from Kavousi in Crete. These include quite a number of hare, badger and agrimi bones, a very few of fallow deer, weasel, wild cat and beech marten, and even some fish bones and crab remains, but no red deer, although these are reported elsewhere – even wild pig and wild cattle are claimed at Khamalevri (Table 4.1; on Kavousi, see further Snyder and Klippel 2000: 68). At Assiros in Macedonia, in strata ranging from the later LBA to the earlier EIA, hare and all three species of deer are attested (Halstead and Jones in Wardle 1980: 266). Classical and later sources in fact indicate that wolf and perhaps bear survived in southern Greece, most probably only in the more mountainous regions, and even a form of lion in Macedonia-Thrace.

The BA population must have built up a great store of knowledge about the environment, its resources and the methods of exploiting them, covering the qualities of different types of land and the techniques needed to farm

Table 4.1 Faunal remains from Cretan Postpalatial–EIA sites, with proportions of main species

Site/date	Sheep/goat (%)	Pig (%)	Cattle (%)	Other (percentages included where known)
Kavousi: Kastro (mostly LM IIIC–PG)	82.2	7.7	8.6	Horse (< 1 per cent), fallow deer (< 1 per cent), agrimi (< 0.1 per cent), dog, small quantities of hare, badger and other small wild animals; shellfish
Kavousi: Vronda (LM IIIC)	70.0	15.9	5.0	Horse (1 per cent), agrimi, dog, hare
Monastiraki: Halasmenos (LM IIIC)	72.9	16.7	5.2	Horse (2.1 per cent), dog
Khamalevri (LM IIIC)	41.3	15.0	7.4	Indeterminate medium mammals (15.7 per cent) and large mammals (3.6 per cent), horse (1.3 per cent), fallow deer (1.4 per cent), red deer (1.3 per cent), indeterminate deer (9.1 per cent), wild pig, wild cattle, dog, hare, badger
Khania (LM IIIC)	56.0	26.0	9.0	Horse, fallow deer, red deer
Kommos Temple A (SM–PG)	55.0	10.0	35.0	Hare, red, deer, dog, marine shellfish (individually quantified)
Other SM–PG in Kommos sanctuary area	55.6	—	44.0	Hare, marine shellfish (individually quantified)

(*Source*: After Wallace 2000: 97, table 3).

81

them successfully, the properties of plants, and the distribution and uses of materials, including potter's clay, types of stone and wood, colouring materials, metal ores and other minerals. But it is questionable how much knowledge about the distribution of the rarer materials, which may have been largely the preserve of specialists, was transmitted to later times, if it is accepted that there was widespread abandonment of localities during the twelfth and eleventh centuries. This, along with the disappearance of the finer crafts and their practitioners, could well have resulted in a loss of local knowledge, while the dwindling of contacts within the Aegean reduced the opportunities for the dissemination of information. Thus, the various fine stones used in the BA for the manufacture of vessels, sealstones, jewellery, inlays, and architectural features had all gone out of use by the end of the BA, to remain unused in some cases, like *lapis lacedaemonius*, for many centuries. Changes in technology will also have had an effect: although stone implements continued to be made, it seems that obsidian was no longer in demand.

This point has particular significance for the use of metals. The Aegean is not copiously supplied with sources, but large polymetallic zones, principally containing silver, lead and copper ores, and sometimes iron also, have been identified in northern Greece and the Laurion region of Attica, and smaller sources are found throughout the Aegean islands (Stos-Gale and Macdonald 1991: 254–5, see also Stos-Gale 1998: 718). Smaller copper sources are also to be found in Thessaly, Euboea and the east Peloponnese (but Stos-Gale *et al.* 1999: 105 emphasise that the Peloponnesian sources are negligible, apart from Hermione, and that there is no correspondence between their lead isotope compositions and those of items from Nichoria), and iron sources varying from small to extensive are also quite widespread (as shown in Snodgrass 1980b, fig. 10.2). But it cannot be assumed that, because sources existed, they were exploited, although just such an assumption has often been made for copper and iron sources in Euboea and Boeotia (recently, Tandy 1997: 64; see Bakhuizen 1976: 45–52 for the claimed sources, but in *AR* 40 (1993–1994) 35 Bakhuizen reports that no traces of ancient exploitation of the richest iron source could be found). The patterns of ancient exploitation are erratic. For example, the Siphnian silver sources apparently exploited in the earlier BA seem to have effectively gone out of production by the LBA, but there was clearly renewed working on a large scale in Archaic times (Herod. 3.57); however, the associated copper or iron ores seem to have been ignored, at least in the Classical period (Gale 1979: 43–4). Similarly, on Thasos the local copper and iron ores seem not to have been heavily exploited in the EIA. Indeed, the copper used on Thasos may have come from a wide variety of sources (Koukouli-Chrysanthaki 1992: 784–801).

Small gold sources that could have been exploited in the EIA have been claimed in the Aegean (Lemos 2002: 134), while Laurion may have been the source of almost all the silver and lead and much of the copper used in the LBA. But this depends on accepting the results of the lead isotope analysis technique of 'fingerprinting' metal ores, which no longer seem as definite and clear-cut as when first presented (see references in the chapter bibliography), and the possibility that north Aegean sources were exploited should not be discounted (Stos-Gale and Macdonald 1991: 255–62). There is likely evidence for continued exploitation of Laurion in the Postpalatial Period, since several artefacts from Perati nearby are of silver (claimed to be from Laurion in Stos-Gale and Macdonald 1991: 271), while a lump of copper slag comes from T. 137 (Iakovidis 1969: 237, 239). But there may have been an interruption in working thereafter, for from the time that mining can be certified again, the mid-ninth century (Coldstream 1977: 70), it seems to have concentrated exclusively on silver. No Laurion copper has so far been identified in post-BA contexts, and given that copper ore is reported to be still present in large quantities at Laurion today, the simplest explanation is that when mining recommenced at Laurion it was no longer thought worth exploiting. This could have been because Cypriot copper had become so relatively cheap and efficiently distributed as to drive the Laurion product off the market, or because there was far greater profit in producing silver. There is also evidence for iron-working at Laurion (e.g. Photos-Jones and Ellis Jones 1994: 338, 355–6), but it is not very early and may relate only to production for local purposes.

In fact, there is virtually no evidence bearing on when Aegean sources of iron were first exploited; *contra* Morris 1992: 117–18 and following, it is highly unlikely that sources were being searched for, let alone exploited, much before the beginning of the EIA (cf. Sherratt 1993: 917). Nor is there much evidence for the origin of the iron used in local metalworking (see further Chapter 5, pp. 147, 149). Markoe (1998: 234–5) cites Varoufakis for indications that west Cretan sources of iron ores were being exploited by the eighth century, if not before, and iron slags from Asine suggest an origin from the Hermione source (Backe-Forsberg *et al.* 2000–1: 31–4). The finding of two iron smelting slags at Nichoria suggests that ore was brought to the site, perhaps from western Crete or from across the Messenian Gulf (*Nichoria I*: 184, table 12–1, see 216–17 on sources), but there is nothing to demonstrate either origin. This is an area in which more data are badly needed.

It might seem unlikely that metal sources, particularly one as rich as Laurion, would have been ignored in the EIA, when the level of trade was far lower and resources may have been too scanty to allow the purchase of supplies brought from far away. But there are various possible explanations for a temporary cessation of production in Postpalatial and EIA times, apart from the general insecurity of the period and perhaps a shortage of skilled labour. These include reaching the water level, the petering out of sources, particularly in the Cyclades where, in contrast to Laurion, ores are typically found in scattered veins and pockets (Z.A. Stos, pers. comm.), and the need for timber, especially for fuel, which was required on a vast scale for smelting (cf. comments in Muhly *et al.* 1982: 28, 116, 357; Wertime 1983; but Pickles and Peltenburg 1998: 84 express scepticism over arguments for a timber shortage in the Near East). If local timber supplies were temporarily exhausted, mining could hardly continue on a large scale without potentially costly importing from elsewhere, which would only be worth while if the results were really profitable. The indication from Nichoria that ores might be moved for smelting to sites far from any likely source may well have this explanation.

Patterns of settlement

All this helps to establish the background against which the EIA population lived their lives, but it is much harder to discuss the detail of those lives, because settlement evidence for the EIA proper is extremely rare. Even at those sites which have been investigated on some scale, few substantial structural remains have been found, and published data deriving from scientific analysis of any kind, whether of animal bones, plant remains, metal items, or pottery, are notably scanty. But the greatest problems are undoubtedly posed by the shortage of evidence for the very existence of sites. New discoveries are making it possible to place more dots on the map that represent sites occupied during some or all of the time between *c.* 1050 and *c.* 800 (Figures 4.1, 4.1a), but as in the Postpalatial Period many dots represent certain or likely burials rather than the settlements which produced them. Even including these, the distribution remains remarkably thin by comparison with the Third Palace Period, and it is still very difficult to identify any at all in some major provinces, such as Laconia, for a considerable part of the EIA.

In this respect, however, an important difference between Crete and the rest of Greece must be signalled. For in Crete the evidence for the progressive abandonment of many major BA sites is balanced by that for the establishment of very many new settlements, especially during the twelfth century (Figure 4.3), many of which continued in use into the EIA. The rarity elsewhere of indications of the existence of settlements has led to the belief that population had dwindled very considerably (see further, p. 93), although other explanations have been advanced. It has been suggested, for example, that the population concentrated at those sites that were best placed in relation to good arable land, as part of a long-term cyclical pattern of expansion and contraction of land exploitation. On this model, in the contracted phase, settlement is concentrated in the best land and the economy centres on grain agriculture, while in the expanded phase the population spreads out into farms over a wide territory, establishing an intensive pattern of exploitation for cash crops in demand in an external market, such as olive oil (van Andel

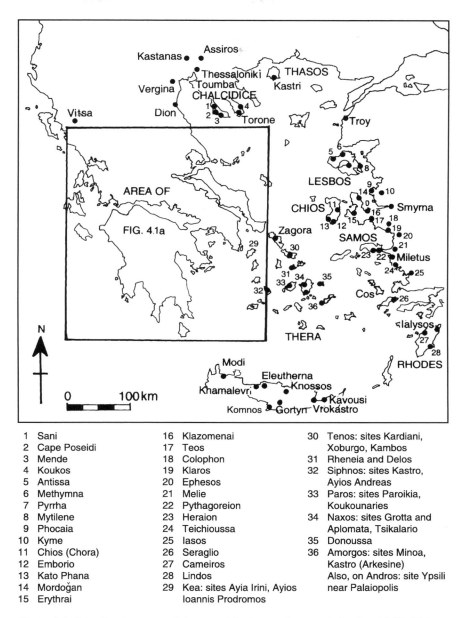

1	Sani	
2	Cape Poseidi	
3	Mende	
4	Koukos	
5	Antissa	
6	Methymna	
7	Pyrrha	
8	Mytilene	
9	Phocaia	
10	Kyme	
11	Chios (Chora)	
12	Emborio	
13	Kato Phana	
14	Mordoğan	
15	Erythrai	
16	Klazomenai	
17	Teos	
18	Colophon	
19	Klaros	
20	Ephesos	
21	Melie	
22	Pythagoreion	
23	Heraion	
24	Teichioussa	
25	Iasos	
26	Seraglio	
27	Cameiros	
28	Lindos	
29	Kea: sites Ayia Irini, Ayios Ioannis Prodromos	
30	Tenos: sites Kardiani, Xoburgo, Kambos	
31	Rheneia and Delos	
32	Siphnos: sites Kastro, Ayios Andreas	
33	Paros: sites Paroikia, Koukounaries	
34	Naxos: sites Grotta and Aplomata, Tsikalario	
35	Donoussa	
36	Amorgos: sites Minoa, Kastro (Arkesine) Also, on Andros: site Ypsili near Palaiopolis	

Figure 4.1 Distribution map of sites outside the southern mainland, *c.* 1050–800.

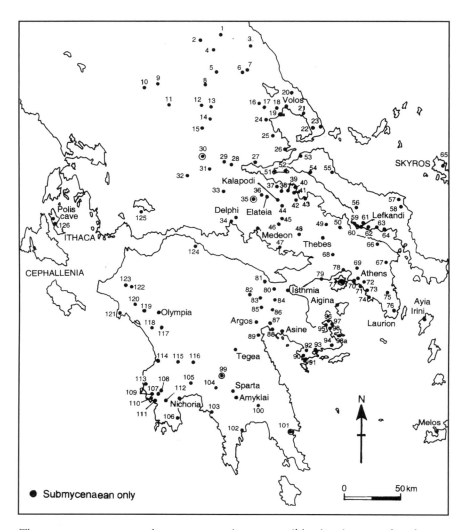

These maps attempt to show as many sites as possible that have produced some evidence of use between c. 1050 and c. 800, including those whose latest or sole material is Submyc, except in Macedonia, Thasos and Crete, where only some of the more significant sites have been shown. The sites have been derived from a variety of sources, and their positioning is approximate in some cases. I have little doubt that the maps are still incomplete. My main sources have been Desborough (1972), Coldstream (1977), Catling (1998), Mountjoy (1999) and Lemos (2002), supplemented principally by Sackett et al. (1966) (Euboea), Coulson (1986) (Messenia), Eder (1999) (Elis), various publications by Mrs Ph. Dakoronia for modern Phthiotis and Locris, and useful information from Dr I. Georganas on Thessaly.

1 Retziouni	40 Livanates: Kynos (to west	82 Phlius
2 Elasson: Chyretiai	is Palaiokastro)	83 Cleonai
3 Homolion	41 Atalanti	84 Athikia
4 Argyroupoli	42 Kastraki	85 Mycenae
5 Larisa (nearby are	43 Mitrou and Tragana	86 Berbati
Mesorachi, Platykambos,	Lokridos	87 Tiryns
Lykoudi)	44 Hyampolis	88 Nauplia
6 Marmariani (to south,	45 Orchomenos	89 Lerna
Kastri Ayias)	46 Vranezi	90 Vista (C12)
7 Chasambali	47 Mali	91 Halieis
8 Krannon	48 Askra	92 Kranidhi roadside (B17)
9 Trikkala	49 Paralimni	93 Hermione
10 Phiki	50 Rhitsona	94 Sambariza
11 Karditsa (nearby are	51 Likhas	95 Megalochori: Methana
Kedros and Paliouri)	52 Yialtra	96 Kounoupitsa
12 Ktouri	53 Oreoi	97 Oga
13 Palaiokastro	54 Rovies	98 Loutra
14 Pharsala	55 Kerinthos	98a Kalauria
15 Domokos: Neo Monastiri	56 Psakhna	99 Pellana
16 Velestino: Pherai	57 Kyme	100 Geraki
17 Aerinos (approximate)	58 Oxylithos	101 Epidauros Limera
18 Sesklo	59 Chalkis	102 Mavrovouni
19 Megali Velanidia	60 Nea Lampsakos	103 Kardamyli
20 Lestiani	61 Phylla	104 Volimnos
21 Maleai	62 Eretria	105 Antheia and Aithaia
22 Argalasti	63 Magoula	106 Kaphirio
23 Theotokou	64 Amarynthos	107 Pylos
24 Phthiotic Thebes	65 Skyros cemeteries	108 Volimidia
25 Nea Halos (to northwest,	66 Skala Oropou	109 Beylerbey
Platanos)	67 Marathon	110 Tragana
26 Pteleon	68 Panakton	111 Koryphasion and
27 Stylis	69 Menidi	Osmanaga
28 Lamia	70 Palaia Kokkinia	112 Koukounara
29 Bikiorema (nearby is	71 Mounychia	113 Ordines
Tymbanos)	72 Mount Hymettos	114 Rizes
30 Arkhani	73 Aliki	115 Malthi
31 Ypati	74 Anavyssos	116 Tsoukaleika
32 Perivoli	75 Merenda	117 Gryllos
33 Pavliani	76 Thorikos	118 Samikon
34 Itea	77 Salamis: Arsenal	119 Salmoni
35 Amphikleia	Cemetery	120 Lasteika
36 Ayios Athanasios: Modi	(unplaced on Salamis:	121 Ayios Andreas
37 Agnanti	Tsami/Tani)	122 Keramidia
38 Aï-Georgis	78 Eleusis	123 Elis
39 Megaplatanos (nearby is	79 Megara	124 Derveni
Palaiokastro and to north	80 Corinth	125 Gavalou
is Roustiani)	81 Vello	126 Aëtos

Figure 4.1a Distribution map of sites on the southern mainland, *c.* 1050–800.

and Runnels 1987: 167–8). It is unlikely, however, that any settlement's economy effectively depended on such markets, like some examples discussed in Purcell (1990: 51–2). There may be some truth in this cyclical pattern, but the case is best for historical periods when much more sophisticated marketing systems, incorporating the use of coinage, were operating, and the evidence, such as it is, does not lend itself readily to the production of hypotheses that apply throughout the Aegean. Moreover, it is noticeable how many of the most prosperous EIA sites are either close to the sea or evidently have overseas contacts, which suggests that these were important in the EIA, against a common assumption (see further, Chapter 7).

Against any view that the population did not dwindle significantly, but simply concentrated in the best land, it has to be pointed out that the surviving settlements did not even maintain the size that many evidently had in the Postpalatial Period, as might be expected if there was no major drop in the total population. Rather, they often seem to consist of separate small patches of settled area, which can hardly represent more than a few households each. These are frequently distributed around a central acropolis, as at Tiryns and Argos (cf. Kilian 1988: 146–7 figs. 19a–b, 151; and more recently Papadimitriou 1998: 118–19 figs. 1a–b for Tiryns, and Lemos 2003: 139 fig. 10 for Argos), although at Nichoria such an obvious centre is lacking.

Such a pattern of settlement has often been deduced wherever a scatter of cemeteries has been found, on the assumption that each cemetery was attached to a settled area, and this pattern has been compared to that suggested to be typical of 'old Greece' in comments by Thucydides (1.10.2) and Aristotle (*Politics* 1252b.28). Many sites have such a scatter of cemeteries: apart from those already mentioned, Asine and Skyros are good examples (Lemos 2003: 137 fig. 8, 169 fig. 17; see also Coldstream 1977: 174 on Corinth). But at some which have several distinct cemetery areas the existence of a substantial nucleated settlement has been posited, among them Knossos (Coldstream 2000; see *NorthCem*: 713 ill. 27 for the cemeteries) and Lefkandi. At Athens, Papadopoulos has argued that occupation was concentrated on the Acropolis itself, while a potters' quarter was established in the Agora (2003: ch. 5). It remains hard to explain why several cemeteries, including that of the Kerameikos, should be situated well over 1 km from the Acropolis (Figure 4.2), but at Lefkandi too the known cemeteries are all several hundred metres from Xeropolis (Lemos 2003: 141 fig. 12).

It certainly should not be taken for granted that separate cemeteries necessarily represent separate areas of occupation, but the evidence of Tiryns cannot be easily dismissed, for unlike Athens and Argos it was not a major city of the historical period, where it might reasonably be argued that earlier remains have been largely effaced by later building activity. Papadimitriou's analysis of the finds at Tiryns (1998) draws a picture of separate habitation areas, distinct even on the acropolis, which steadily increased in number over the Submyc-G phases. But there were certainly some substantial nucleated settlements: notoriously, Smyrna was provided with a fortification wall datable as early as the late ninth century, which argues that it had a considerable population to defend.

Although the quantities of material found at a mainland site are not

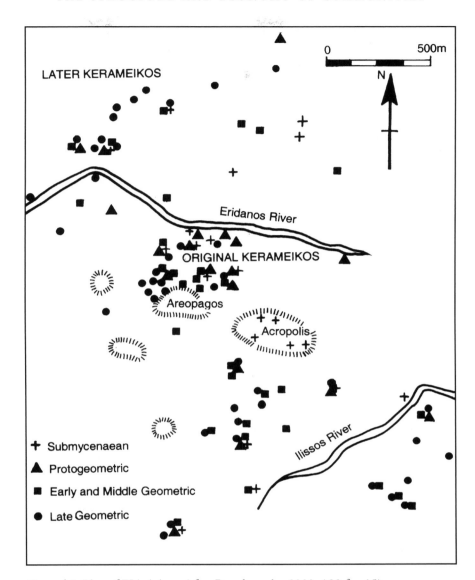

Figure 4.2 Plan of EIA Athens (after Papadopoulos 2003, 199 fig. 15).

always such as to certify that the settlement was substantial, in the great majority of cases this seems the most likely interpretation, since the identifiable sites very often developed into a later *polis*, township, or major village. New surveys constantly reinforce this impression. Thus, the intensive survey on the Methana peninsula produced PG evidence from four sites (Mee and Forbes 1997: 57, 59; cf. Foxhall 1995: 246). All were considered reasonably extensive and three of them are evidently the 'natural' centres of settlement, having been the largest sites of the Mycenaean period and continuing in occupation to become the main centres of population after the EIA. Similarly, among the sites studied in the Pylos Regional Archaeological Project (PRAP), Pylos itself and the two other largest identified Mycenaean sites (Beylerbey, close to Pylos, and Ordines, both considered likely to be among the administrative centres attested in the Linear B texts) are the most prominent among those which produced traces of Postpalatial and EIA occupation (Davis *et al.* 1997: 451–3).

But in no mainland region does the evidence allow the clear definition of a settlement pattern, let alone a site hierarchy. In a very few areas enough sites have been identified to suggest at least the major components of a pattern. In the central Argolid, for example, continuous occupation at Argos, Tiryns, Mycenae and Asine is virtually assured. Several islands have produced evidence of two or three separate PG settlements, if not more, as on Lesbos (Lemos 2002: 238–40). Relatively many sites that were significant in both LH IIIC and PG have been identified in western central Greece, and also in south-central Euboea, where there is a series of substantial sites along or near the coast from Psakhna north of Chalkis to Amarynthos (cf. Sackett *et al.* 1966: 106–7). An apparent gap in their settlement histories – since the PG pottery reported seems in almost all cases to be LPG if not SPG – may prove to be no more real than at Lefkandi: Xeropolis. Here new excavations (*AR* 50 (2003–04) 39, also 51 (2004–05) 50–1) have produced evidence that makes it almost certain that there was continuity of occupation from LH IIIC, as already seemed likely on the basis of the cemeteries and the fill of the 'Heroön' (*Lefkandi II,1*: 91; cf. Lemos 2002: 140, 146). But the closer context of Lefkandi remains a little obscure. There is no other significant settlement in its immediate neighbourhood, but there is evidence for smaller sites like Phylla nearby (*AR* 44 (1997–98) 65), and by a late stage of PG Chalkis, Eretria and Skala Oropou were certainly in occupation. But important sites like Nichoria and Athens still stand in virtual isolation at present, without close satellites.

The picture is wholly different in Crete. As stated above, many new settlements can be identified in the twelfth century, particularly in eastern Crete (D'Agata 1999b: 182 n. 7 provides a useful summary, concentrating on the main sites). Over 130 LM IIIC settlement sites are shown in Figure 4.3. Typically they are in upland settings, often quite remote and sometimes in regions not apparently exploited much in the BA, and they are reasonably substantial, ranging *c.* 1–4 ha in estimated extent (Wallace 2000: 90, 92 fig. 15; see Table 4.2). Their greater visibility may reflect the fact that the great majority were eventually abandoned, unlike many, perhaps most of the significant EIA sites of the mainland and islands. The areas of occupation at these sites can be either nucleated and quite substantial, as at Karphi, or grouped in small and separate but close clusters which seem to form a single

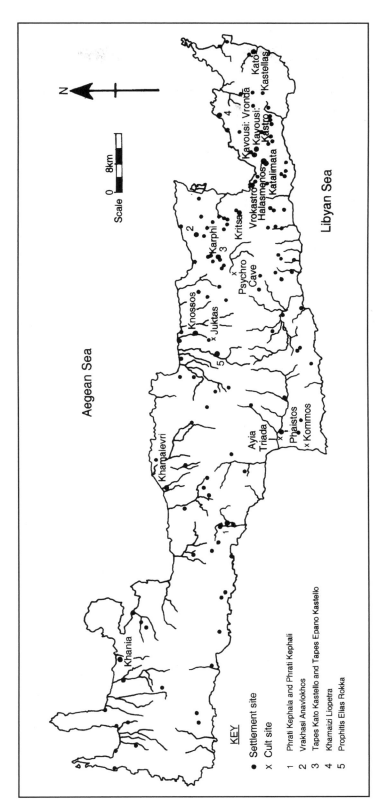

Aegean Sea

Khania

Khamalevri

Ayia
Triada
Phaistos
× Kommos

Knossos
× Juktas

5

Psychro
× Cave

Karphi
3

2

Kritsa

Vrokastro
Halasmenos
Katalimata

Kavousi: Vronda
Kavousi:
Kastro

Kato
Kastellas

Libyan Sea

N

Scale
0   8km

KEY

● Settlement site
× Cult site

1 Phrati Kephala and Phrati Kephali
2 Vrakhasi Anavlokhos
3 Tapes Kato Kastello and Tapes Epano Kastello
4 Khamaizi Liopetra
5 Prophitis Elias Rokka

Figure 4.3 LM IIIC sites in Crete (after Wallace 2000, 61 fig. 1).

settlement unit, as often in the Kavousi region (Haggis 2001: 45–51; Figure 4.4). These clusters are much more widely spaced, up to 0.5–1 km apart, than the pattern of distinct settlement areas placed in close relation to each other already noted at some mainland sites, but Haggis (1999, 2000) seems to believe that the two classes reflect comparable phenomena, representing the typical settlement pattern of the EIA.

The site clusters, which Haggis interprets as the bases of extended families, with possible interrelations between clusters, may be a distinctly east Cretan phenomenon. Wallace notes that sites in central Crete are much

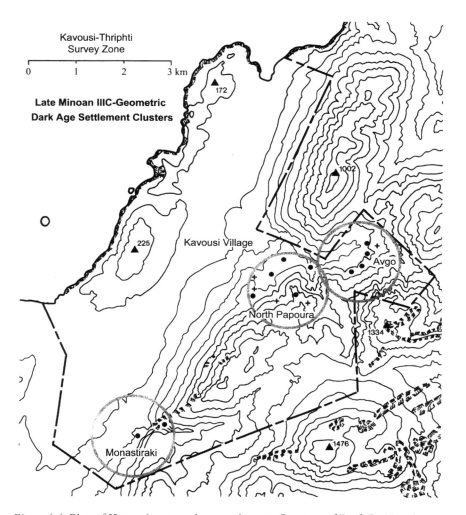

Figure 4.4 Plan of Kavousi area settlement clusters. Courtesy of Prof. D. Haggis.

more widely spaced and more nucleated than in the east, where notional one-hour catchment areas around them often overlap. She also draws attention to cases where small sites seem to depend upon a large one, as at Karphi (2000: 83–5), although she cannot detect an overall hierarchical structure in the distribution of sites of different sizes (2000: 90). Of the sites founded in LM IIIC, more than half, particularly those of the more remote, 'defensible' type, were abandoned in the tenth century in a process of localised population nucleation; a very few new settlements were also founded at this time (Wallace 2003b: 257–9). The later settlement pattern of the eighth to sixth centuries derived directly from this nucleation; some settlements became very large, the centres of the later *poleis*.

The size of the population

As has been seen, the evidence gives a general impression that outside Crete settlements were smaller as well as fewer than even in the Postpalatial Period, let alone earlier in the LBA, and thus that the total population of the Aegean in the EIA could have been very low. Belief in such a low level of population, following massive decline during the Postpalatial Period, has effectively become standard. To a great extent this picture has been established through the influence of Snodgrass and Desborough. Snodgrass originally interpreted the archaeological evidence to indicate that the Aegean population had fallen by over three-quarters by the end of the BA (1971: 367), and was ready to propose that whole regions and islands remained largely or completely deserted for much of the eleventh and tenth centuries (1971: 89, 131). More recently, he has not been so specific, but believes that all the indications point to a low population ([1971] 2000: xxx–xxxi). Desborough believed that the population had dropped even more catastrophically, being by c. 1100 'about one-tenth of what it had been little over a century before' (1972: 18). But he was reluctant to accept total desertion of any region (cf. 1972: 172 on the Dodecanese, 241 on Laconia), apparently preferring to believe that all communities were tiny and thus hard to locate. Both based their arguments essentially on comparing crude totals of sites identified for the different periods, though Snodgrass has recently emphasised the consistent failure of survey to turn up more than a handful of EIA sites in many parts of Greece ([1971] 2000: xxx). Both accepted that there was substantial emigration during the Postpalatial Period, especially from the Mycenaean heartland, and drew attention to evidence for further destruction and abandonment of sites in the final stage of the BA to explain the continuing low level in the EIA.

This has been a very influential interpretation: estimates of a drop by as much as 75 per cent have recently been suggested by I. Morris (1997: 540, over c. 1250–1100) and Tandy (1997: 20, over c. 1200–1000). But not all are convinced. Papadopoulos implicitly denies the 'intimations of poverty and the depopulation of the countryside inherent in the traditional view of the period' (1996a: 254). He would undoubtedly prefer the view that, rather than concentrating at the known surviving sites, from which in the course of time it recolonised the countryside, much of the population dispersed to the countryside. Dietz seems to argue similarly, though to judge from his reference to Asine he does not seem to contemplate a very wide dispersal:

> the depopulation during the Submycenaean period and the following earlier phases of the Protogeometric period, so well proved on almost all major sites, was just as much a result of a change in the pattern caused by the return to a predominantly rural economy as of immigrations. Peasants of the Dark Age lived close to their fields, not to the citadels . . . But it must be admitted that only at Asine does this view seem to be clearly supported.
>
> (Dietz 1982: 102)

More often, it is suggested that the settlements in the countryside were too small to be archaeologically recognisable, or that there are other reasons why EIA settlement evidence is not being recognised.

Since the size of the population must form a crucial element in any picture of the period, the possibility that the data are being systematically misinterpreted in some way, or that there is some other embedded error in our approach, deserves serious consideration. But we can surely dismiss any suggestion that sites are hard to identify because the population became nomadic or semi-nomadic for a period around the time of the transition from the Postpalatial Period to the EIA, returning to their villages only to bury the dead (Thomas and Conant 1999: 32, see also 43–4, 92). It is impossible to imagine any circumstances in which this would seem a better way of supporting themselves than continuing to farm as their ancestors had done for uncounted generations (see pp. 98–102 on pastoralism).

Although not infrequently the sites identified as abandoned are actually cemeteries, and it could therefore be argued that this need represent no more than a change of burial place, the majority are considered to be potential settlements, found in survey. But survey evidence needs to be handled carefully, as pointed out in Chapter 2 (p. 40). In fact, it has always been a fundamental problem that the Postpalatial and EIA phases are far harder to identify by survey than those of the Third Palace Period or Classical times, because they lack forms of pottery that are both common and readily diagnostic (cf. Foxhall 1995: 249 n. 46 on the relative ease with which sherds can be identified as LG, compared with PG). But it is a noteworthy fact that, unlike the sites in Methana mentioned on p. 89, many of the Mycenaean sites identified in various regions by survey, especially the small ones, have produced no evidence of use in the EIA or even in Archaic or Classical times. In fact, some appear to have been abandoned for ever, as has been demonstrated for quite substantial sites by excavation. It seems unlikely, then, that the rarity of sites can be explained simply in terms of the difficulty of identifying diagnostic pottery. If the evidence is taken at face value, there was a considerable shift in settlement pattern in the final stages of the BA, and no pattern comparable to that of the Third Palace Period reappeared for a very long time.

But should the evidence be taken at face value? The idea that post-depositional factors have made small sites effectively invisible has considerable attractions. It could be argued that many EIA structures were too flimsy, and much of the pottery of too poor quality, to survive. This could explain the difficulty of finding structural remains at excavated sites whose cemeteries seem to certify a settlement of some size, although at sites that became significant local centres of the historical period this might be due more to the constant process of rebuilding over many centuries, which has meant that even Archaic house remains are rarely preserved. This would be more readily explicable if the early wall foundations were not particularly substantial or well built, so relatively easy to dismantle. It would then be no accident that some of the best preserved EIA structural remains are from sites that had been abandoned by the end of the period or soon afterwards, as at Nichoria, where natural wash-deposits seem to have protected them, or were protected by deliberate filling and covering, like the Lefkandi 'Heroön'. In contrast, on Lefkandi: Xeropolis, which to judge from the spread of surface material was a large site, the PG-G building levels are largely missing from the top surface of the site except in one area. Probably this is due a combination of natural erosion, which might be exacerbated by the removal or rotting of a thatched roof, later stone-robbing, which would remove even the foundations, and agricultural activity, which would disturb the strata generally.

This is to assume, of course, that EIA structures were built in the traditional Aegean manner, basically of mudbrick on stone foundations with wooden features and some form of thatched roof, all of which are perishable or degradable, so that only the stone foundations usually survive, and if structures did not even have stone foundations all trace of them could have been lost. Mazarakis Ainian has suggested (1997: 100) that the simple oval buildings found at some EIA sites derived from even simpler huts built completely of perishable materials, developed in the immediate aftermath of the collapse of Mycenaean civilisation. But such a departure from traditional building methods would require explanation, especially since the traditional methods are still widely found in the Postpalatial Period. The only real possibilities are the arrival of a new population unused to building in this manner, an idea associated with the highly questionable notion of invasion by nomadic pastoralists, or the reduction of the population to a condition of such complete poverty and hopelessness that any makeshift structure would do, which reflects an equally questionable picture of the period.

The types of house do change markedly with the end of the BA, outside

Crete. One-roomed houses become common, and the most elaborate are constructed on the old 'megaron' plan, very often apsidal (axially arranged porch, main room and storage room). Wood may have played a more significant role in the structure of some, as suggested for Nichoria Unit IV–1 (*Nichoria III*: 31), but they still seem to have had stone wall foundations of the standard kind, if often narrow and poorly built. This is shown by excavations at Asine, Nichoria, Lefkandi, Mitrou, Volos: Palia, Assiros, Thessaloniki: Toumba, Smyrna (Lemos 2002: 148) and many sites in Crete. Remains of other types of structure can sometimes be found, as at Smyrna, where a one-roomed semi-rectangular structure dated *c.* 925–900 has been uncovered, whose narrow (30 cm) wall consisted mainly of one thickness of exceptionally broad mudbricks, though a layer of small stones and pithos sherds was used to strengthen the wall on one side (Akurgal 1983: 17, see pls 4–5). This building is quite small (*c.* 4 × 2.5 m) and has been thought to represent the poorest type of house at Smyrna, although the substantial quality of the construction does not immediately suggest poverty. More plausible examples of truly flimsy structures are the circular huts, founded on sand and clay, reported from Eretria, which may date to *c.* 800, but it remains unclear whether these were permanent dwellings (Snodgrass 1987: 202), and this report seems unique so far.

Since until now BA excavations have nearly always taken place at what have proved to be substantial sites, it would be possible to maintain that at small sites the structures could have lacked stone foundations altogether, and that this tradition continued into the EIA. But it has seemed hard to accept that the material culture of such hypothesised small sites consisted so much of perishable items in the EIA that they are undetectable even by intensive survey methods, when these have detected small sites of the BA and other periods. In particular, it has seemed most unlikely that pottery, an essential commodity both earlier and later, went out of use. Here, however, important arguments advanced by Czech archaeologists could be helpful (Bintliff *et al.* 1999: 155–8). These suggest that if well-preserved pieces of pottery are found on the surface it is because they have been brought up relatively recently and, indeed, have probably already been incorporated in a soil matrix of later but still ancient date, through continued activity on the site. This would certainly explain why clearly prehistoric pieces can sometimes be found on an otherwise apparently Classical-Roman site (as has been noted several times by the Boeotia Survey Expedition). But when on or near the surface, coarse pottery will be relatively quickly destroyed by a combination of natural and agricultural processes, unless it is very hard-fired; it is preserved much better below the plough-soil level, especially in graves, pits, etc. Thus, a period in which a large proportion of the pottery is coarse and/or low-fired could well be severely under-represented in surface finds.

This is an attractive argument, but the difficulties in applying it to the Aegean EIA should not be overlooked. While there is evidence that an increasing proportion of the pottery from the end of the Postpalatial Period and the earlier EIA at some sites was indeed handmade coarse, this fabric was not wholly dominant. Wheelmade pottery was still produced in apparently considerable quantities. Kalapodi provides the best evidence, for full statistics are given: in the relevant strata, the handmade wares, including pithos fragments, constituted from around 20 to over 45 per cent of all pottery (Jacob-Felsch 1996: 73), but no more. The evidence from Asine and Nichoria suggests a comparable picture, while at Lefkandi coarse ware was considerably less common proportionally (see Chapter 5, p. 000). Thus, there is no reason to suppose that Kalapodi is exceptional because it was a sanctuary site. Moreover, at Kalapodi the handmade coarse ware was normally quite hard-fired, to judge from the samples (Jacob-Felsch 1996: 111–12), and the quality of the equivalent ware at Asine also seems generally good, although the Nichoria material is poorer, and the cooking pots from the Lefkandi 'Heroön' deposit are remarked upon as often unevenly fired (*Lefkandi II,1*: 58; other coarse shapes are generally described as evenly fired). (see Lemos 2002: 84–97 for a general account of PG handmade pottery.)

It could be argued that at small sites coarse ware would be proportionately much more common, but it is doubtful whether their occupants would have used nothing but coarse ware when wheelmade pottery was still available, if possibly harder to acquire because produced in smaller quantity. Such sites certainly used wheelmade pottery in the Third Palace Period, as indicated by surface finds, although this may reflect the greater level of prosperity (Foxhall 1995: 249 n. 46). Ultimately, it is not possible to conclude more than that in some regions much of the coarse and even of the fine ware (whose quality is also not remarkably high at Nichoria, for example) might be vulnerable to the processes mentioned. A combination of the vulnerability of the more poorly fired pottery to soil processes and the difficulty of recognising the relatively rare pottery of better quality, for lack of really distinctive diagnostic types, might still make small farm sites effectively invisible.

Such arguments are inevitably speculative. Even if they are accepted, it seems unnecessary to suppose that a large proportion of the total population was based at small sites in what would normally be poorer land, when the much diminished size of the major centres would mean that the better land in which these were based was not being fully exploited. It is more plausible that there was a considerable contraction in the total land area exploited, and that any separate farmsteads were established reasonably close to the known settlements, which would seem advisable for reasons of security, as well as for access to craft specialists like potters. The population of such farms, then, is unlikely to have represented the majority of the total population in any particular region; indeed, its size is impossible to estimate.

Overall, it seems safest simply to accept the general impression that population was low, without any commitment to precise figures, because these entail highly questionable deductions from the numbers of sites and/or burials identified. Neither does any increase in the numbers of settlements give a reliable indication of a possible rate of increase in the population. For the potential population of a settlement can only be estimated from a good indication of its size, whereas, even at an excavated site, the evidence has rarely provided more than a simple indication of occupation in some part of the EIA. Cemetery evidence is an equally dubious basis on which to construct estimates, for, as will be argued in Chapter 6, it should not be assumed that the number of graves bears any direct relation to the size of the living population (if that were so, we should have to account for an enormous drop in the population in the seventh century, when graves are notoriously hard to identify in many parts of Greece). Thus, it is extremely unwise to argue that the known datable graves provide any basis for arguing that population remained static at a very low level for most of the EIA, only to begin growing extremely swiftly in the eighth century (as most recently proposed in Tandy 1997).

The most that can be said is that the data do give some indication of the orders of magnitude involved, and as such do point in the direction of a low population for much of the EIA. That population, having dropped substantially, can remain at a low level for over a century has been noted for much later times by Wrigley (1969: 77, with specific reference to the fluctuations in the population of England between the mid-fourteenth and mid-eighteenth centuries), so the population of the Aegean could have remained fairly static for a considerable time. But the data cannot be considered very trustworthy, particularly when the picture for the ensuing Archaic period is taken into account, for here there is a notable mismatch between the archaeological evidence for sites and the historical evidence for the existence of substantial populations.

The nature of the farming economy

Snodgrass has offered another explanation for the rarity of identifiable settlement sites and the short life of some excavated sites and cemeteries, that the Aegean population had adopted a much more pastorally oriented economy, which would tend to exhaust the land and thus encourage periodic changes of residence (1987: 187–209). This is the most recent version of a theory that has for long been prominent in accounts of the period, and which Snodgrass himself has suggested in earlier work, on partly different grounds (1971: 378–80, also 1980: 35–6). But he does not link this with any idea that specialist pastoralism, involving transhumance, was a long-established adaptation to the natural environment in the Aegean, let alone with theories that the Dorians and similar 'invading' population groups were nomadic pastoralists or had a strong interest in pastoralism (Jameson et al. 1994: 291, 373), thus avoiding the telling criticisms of such ideas set out by Cherry (1988). Rather, he argues that 'To practice large-scale stock-rearing from a few fixed bases could have seemed a perfectly reasonable response' to the circumstances that he envisages for the period. Similarly, Jameson *et al.* (1994: 291) suggest a recent commitment to pastoralism on the part of the supposed resettlers of the southern Argolid, although they note that specialist pastoralism is a high risk activity, which is surely the opposite of what one would expect at this period.

However, such hypotheses fail to provide a good theoretical basis for identifying material features that should indicate a pastoralist culture (Cherry 1988: 28; Wallace 2003a: 602–3). Many of the arguments commonly used are, as Cherry shows, either unjustified backward projections from medieval times or wholly arguable assumptions. For instance, there is no basis for associating the apsidal house-plan specifically with pastoralists, given its constant occurrence all around the Aegean from the EBA onwards. The apse may rather be a functional feature, designed to facilitate thatching a pitched roof (Coldstream 1977: 304). Again, the offering of animal figurines to the gods is no new phenomenon of the EIA but has a long history in the BA, and surely reflects in part a belief that animals are the most valued type of offering. It is notable that in the BA and later such figurines most often represent cattle, even when the bone evidence suggests that sheep and goats were the dominant domestic species and the most commonly sacrificed; this must surely relate to the symbolism involved (Zeimbekis 1998: ch. VI). More significantly, Wallace has calculated that only extremely small populations could have been supported at the Cretan sites she has studied, if their economies had been wholly based on animal-rearing (2000: 94 and table 7; see Table 4.2), whereas the sheer extent of surface remains at the sites suggests that their populations were quite substantial, and they are sited in areas of good agricultural land, though not necessarily with easy access to it.

The only evidence cited until recently from actual EIA animal bone collections as indicative of a pastoral economy, that from Nichoria, has been expected to bear too much weight. It comes from a site in an exceptionally well-watered region, so that the evidence may well indicate a specifically local adaptation to the rich pasture available (cf. McDonald and Rapp 1972: 175) rather than provide a pattern for the Aegean as a whole. Mancz (1989), who dealt with a much larger sample than is considered in Sloan and Duncan (1978), confirms the relatively high proportion of cattle bones previously identified in the EIA deposits, and notes that the rearing of cattle in quantity would be appropriate to the unusually favourable environment. She confirms that this is balanced by a notable drop in the quantity of pig bones, and argues that the relative unpopularity of the pig may reflect the fact that it is the least useful of the major domesticates, because it produces fewest secondary products. She also comments that meat consumption may not have been high overall, for animals were generally slaughtered at quite an advanced age, which could suggest that they were not especially numerous. In general, she interprets the evidence as suggesting a mixed farming community that

Table 4.2 Estimated populations of some Cretan Postpalatial – EIA sites

Site(s)	Phrati: Kephala and Kephali	Vrakhasi: Anavlokhos	Kritsa: Kastello	Tapes: Epano and Kato Kastello	Khamaizi: Liopetra	Prophitis Elias: Rokka/Korphi
Total 1-hour range	1,100	1,300	1,263	1,518	848	1,579
Total available arable	620–789.5	663.5–874	580–942.8	473–962.4	445.4–588.1	1,508.4–1,521.8
Population supportable on 100 per cent cereals, annual fallow	517–658	553–728	484–786	394–802	371–490	1,252–1,268
Population supportable on 100 per cent animals (minimum) – assuming only cleared land grazed (or all land grazed, in parentheses)	12–16 (22)	13–17 (26)	12–19 (25)	9–19 (30)	9–12 (17)	25–30 (32)
Total population supportable, assuming only cleared land grazed (or all land grazed, in parentheses)	531 (539)–674 (680)	566 (579)–745 (754)	496 (509)–805 (811)	403 (424)–821 (832)	380 (388)–502 (507)	1,282 (1284)–1,298 (1300)
Estimated site size	c. 1.5 (Kephala) and c. 1.0–1.5 (Kephali)	c. 1.5?	c. 3.0	c. 2.2 (Kato Kastello) and c. 1.0 (Epano Kastello)	1.5–2.0	Not possible to estimate, minimum 1.5
Estimated population for site(s) (minimum)	c. 521–570	c. 313–375	c. 625–750	c. 479–575	c. 313–500	c. 625–750

Source: After Wallace 2000: 83, table 1.
Note: All land measurements are in hectares.

was no longer part of a much larger society, whose requirements might have affected modes of animal exploitation. This community was therefore able to make the most efficient use of domestic animals consistent with a relatively small population.

There seems no obvious reason to dispute these plausible if undramatic conclusions, which fit what Cherry has suggested (1988: 27). They completely undercut reconstructions of 'Dark Age' Greece's farming economy and diet such as that of Tandy (1997: 35–8), which is heavily dependent on Sloan and Duncan's assessment of the Nichoria evidence and on Wright's outdated interpretation of the olive pollen peak from the Osmanaga lagoon core (see criticisms and a more recent view in Zangger et al. 1997: 582–4, 592–3; also Foxhall 1995: 244). Tandy was led by these to suppose that diet was based largely on red meat and olives, which, he argues, would not be particularly beneficial to health and so might explain the low level of population. This is a good example of Snodgrass's 'positivist fallacy' (1987: 37–8): because animal, especially cattle, bones predominate in the archaeological record, Tandy assumes that the animals they represent dominated in the actual economy, and equally that because little trace of cereals has been found, they must have been insignificant. This takes no account of the fact that animal bones survive in the archaeological record far better than plant remains, which are rarely found in significant quantities in contexts when agriculture was unquestionably the basis of the farming economy. An older analysis by Fågerström also interprets developments at Nichoria to reflect EIA social development in microcosm (1988a: 42), seeing the occupants of Nichoria contemporary with Unit IV–1 as a 'band of pasturalists [sic]/ hunters (and probably also warriors) led by a basileus, robbing cattle from their neighbours and feasting at the great house at Nichoria', who disappear to be replaced by an agrarian society centred on Unit IV–5. To be blunt, this is romantic fantasy.

Preliminary reports of the much larger Kavousi bone assemblage from the Vronda and Kastro sites show a very high percentage of sheep/goats, fitting the normal Aegean pattern, and smaller samples from other sites show a very similar picture (Table 4.1); the lower-lying sites may have higher percentages of pigs and cattle. Interestingly, the Kavousi evidence is also interpreted to suggest that sheep were managed for their meat rather than secondary products, being preferentially slaughtered before the age of three. There was evidence at the later of the two Kavousi sites, Kastro, for consistent extraction of marrow, which together with the extensive evidence for butchery of all species, wild and domestic, might indicate a determination to get as much food out of animals as possible (Snyder and Klippel 2000: 70–80). In turn, this would suggest that meat was highly valued but not abundant, and thus that domestic animals were not particularly numerous. Hunting, for which the evidence is relatively prominent from both Nichoria and the Kavousi sites, particularly for red deer, would of course also have supplied meat.

Thus, neither at Nichoria nor in Crete can the bone evidence be considered to give much support to theories that domestic animals were very common, let alone that they were intensively exploited for secondary products, though both of these features would be typical of a specialised pastoralist economy. But in any case such an economy would only make sense if it formed a symbiotic relationship with settled agricultural communities that provided a large demand for secondary products like wool, cheese or hides (Jameson *et al.* 1994: 291). Yet there is no evidence that EIA communities within the Aegean could provide demand on any scale, and to market such products on a large scale to the more developed Near Eastern economies would surely require precisely the kind of centralised organisation that was lost with the Collapse.

To discuss other questions that could be raised, such as whether the short-lived sites that Snodgrass considers significant are in fact well-placed to be centres of pastoralism, seems superfluous (Wallace 2003a provides strong arguments against this view for Crete). The hypothesis that a heavy concentration on pastoralism could be a viable economic adaptation in the Aegean region needs much better support before various pieces of evidence that might reflect pastoralist behaviour can be brought into the argument. Unfortunately, the whole topic is tainted by the long-standing belief that the tales of conquering invaders in Greek tradition can be taken to represent historical fact, and can only be squared with the shortage of archaeological evidence for the EIA if these were pastoralists (supposedly hard to detect archaeologically), who came from Epirus or other territories on the northern border of the Mycenaean world. In turn, this belief has an undesirable subtext which opposes undisciplined, rather barbarous but vigorous pastoralist groups to organised but weak, even decadent, agricultural civilisations, which echoes to some extent the antitheses made between Dorians and Ionians in the ancient world and the attribution of 'racial' characteristics to these groups in early modern scholarship (cf. Hall 1997: ch. 1).

If theories about pastoralism are discounted, very little that is not speculative can be said about the rural economy of the EIA. The few studies of bones and plant remains from archaeological sites (notably Nichoria and Kavousi; Wallace 2000: 96–7 summarises the evidence for domesticated plant species known from EIA Crete), the distribution of known settlements, which strongly suggests that cereal agriculture was still the basis of farming, and the Homeric poems together tend to suggest that a style of mixed farming was prevalent, very similar to what has been postulated for pre-palace societies in the Aegean, for ordinary Third Palace Period communities (see Chapter 2, p. 37), and to a great extent even for Classical Greek communities (cf. Foxhall 1995, Donlan 1997: 649–50, 654–5). This would encompass the growing of one or both of wheat and barley, surely also pulses and other vegetables, and probably in many parts at least some orchard cultivation, especially of vines and olives (but in the PRAP survey area olive pollen decreases markedly after *c.*1200, not to rise strongly until after *c.* 800; Zangger *et al.* 1997: 594).

All the major forms of domesticated livestock would have been kept on a relatively small scale, but since cattle and horses require considerably more and better quality pasture than sheep and goats they were probably rare at ordinary village level. Horses were a real luxury, probably maintained for chariot teams and riding. Donkeys and mules were probably much commoner, and would have served as carriage and draught animals as well as for riding. Oxen would have been maintained for ploughing and heavy load-pulling, and they may well have been confined largely to the estates of the relatively rich, though available for hire by the more prosperous villagers (Halstead 1999c), while much agriculture at village level could have been of the labour-intensive hoe-based 'garden' type. No doubt the intention was for communities, even, perhaps, the individual holders of large estates, to be self-sufficient in basic foodstuffs and to have enough livestock to provide reasonable quantities of wool and hides, as well as meat.

Donlan (1997: 654–7) argues from the Homeric evidence, which he believes to apply to a time no later than *c.* 800, that the economy practised by the 'chiefs', Homer's *basileis*, was different. On his interpretation, although they had large estates that included orchards, they concentrated particularly on pasturing livestock on a large scale, so that their wealth was reckoned largely in terms of their herds, and they were able to do this because of the low population and low demand on the land. Although this is making assumptions whose basis is questionable, as is evident from the previous discussion, there may be some truth in this picture. But although the main uses of these livestock in Homer are in socially prestigious feasting or as sacrifices to the gods, in reality they may have been equally valuable as items to be exchanged for services or commodities, or hired out to tenants and share-croppers. In particular, 'wealth', as measured in the possession of metal objects and other luxurious or exotic items, can only have been acquired by marketing the surplus products of fields and herds; but the evidence does not suggest that agricultural products could have been produced, processed and marketed on the scale of the palace societies, for, as noted above, this would require a level of organisation that seems to be entirely lacking.

However, it may be considered plausible that there was always an intention to produce a surplus in some products of farming, for without it the communities would have nothing to exchange for commodities that they needed but did not have available locally. At this point it needs stressing that there is absolutely no evidence that the economy was or became reciprocal and redistributive, in the sense that the 'chiefs' took in everything and redistributed it, as argued by Tandy (1997: especially 106–11). This view seems to depend partly upon the notion that such an arrangement suits the kind of society prevalent by the ninth century, when Tandy argues that a return to cereal production created scope for much more redistribution than before (1997: 112–13), and partly upon what can be argued to be mis-interpretations of archaeological finds, of the Homeric references (e.g. the position of Eumaeus in the *Odyssey* is completely misunderstood: he is a slave, sending pigs from his master's herd to the palace, not a 'citizen' under social obligation to contribute from his own herd), and of anthropological studies (see the strong criticisms of Tandy's arguments by Schaps in *Bryn Mawr Classical Review* 98.11.01). As Schaps points out, 'reciprocal, redistributive, or market activities may occur in any economy' (further comment relevant to the nature of the EIA economy will be made in Chapter 7, and on that of EIA society generally in this chapter and Chapter 9).

Settlement arrangement and architecture

As already noted, settlement evidence is at a premium for almost the entire period covered by this book. Even remains of Postpalatial (twelfth to eleventh century) phases are relatively few, though enough to indicate that essentially the older types of building continued. Substantial multi-room structures were still built, as at Lefkandi (where they can be two-storeyed), Korakou (House P) and House W and other structures at Tiryns (Figure 4.5). The last may even be the centre of a more complex group of structures, continuing the tradition of Mycenaean palaces in a simpler form. Excavations in the north of the Lower City at Tiryns have also indicated a distinctive Postpalatial feature, the arrangement of several structures around a courtyard (Maran 2002), but there is as yet no clear evidence that these occur else-where. Other new features observed at several of the major sites involve details like a preference for pisé walls, the use of unbaked clay vats, and the building of hearths from potsherds (French 1999); not all of these continued into the EIA.

Old traditions also continued in Crete, where a large portion, even all, of the settlement plan has been uncovered at several sites, mostly in east Crete (especially Karphi, Kavousi: Vronda and Kavousi: Kastro, Vrokastro, Katalimata and Halasmenos). These suggest that from the Postpalatial Period onwards a Cretan settlement was typically made up of aggregated blocks of structures, although these might have developed progressively from an original core and originally multi-roomed houses could be subdivided by blocking off linking doorways. At upland sites made up of several natural terraces, separate structures were established on each terrace. The blocks may be divided by identifiable streets and have areas resembling courtyards at intervals (Figure 4.6). The parallels with the LB town plans of Crete (Dickinson 1994a: 60–3) are evident, although there is less regularity, the buildings have fewer rooms and very rarely show any trace of a second storey, and the general standard of architecture is lower than in the LBA. Nevertheless, the houses are commonly rectilinear in outline, with frequently square or

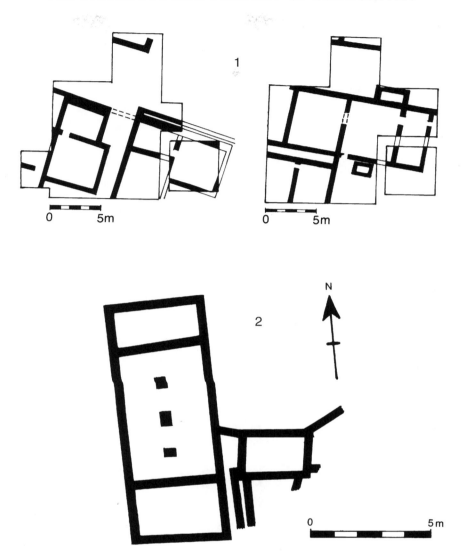

Figure 4.5 LH IIIC structures: stylised representations of (1) Lefkandi phases 1 and 2 (after Popham and Sackett 1968: fig. 12), and (2) Tiryns House W (after K. Müller *et al.*, *Tiryns VIII*, Mainz 1975, Beilage 4).

rectangular rooms, of which there may be one, two or several, and the rooms are often axially arranged in a manner that seems to become common in Crete from LM III onwards, and has been thought to reflect Mycenaean influence, though this is not forced. The rooms can be quite regular in dimensions, and frequently have internal fittings, including roof-posts set on

105

stone bases, benches, hearths, and ovens. Some buildings stand out as exceptionally elaborate, like House A/B at Kavousi: Vronda, Building G at Kavousi: Kastro, and that centring on Room AA at Phaistos (Cucuzza 1998: 65–7), and might be the dwellings of elite families if not 'chiefs'. Some sites have also produced evidence that substantial terrace walls and even, perhaps, circuit walls were built during the period, but there are no signs of other communal architectural undertakings. (See Hayden 1987 for a discussion of LM III architecture; also Rehak and Younger 2001: 460–1.)

The contrast with the rest of the Aegean is marked. Only Zagora, apparently founded before the end of the tenth century (Lemos 2002: 207) but essentially of eighth century date, provides a parallel to the 'block' type of settlement. It has produced notable evidence for built-in features like benches and windows, and the house walls and, probably, roofs are built of stone slabs (Coldstream 1977: 306–11 provides a useful summary). The stone blocks incised with trident marks found in a wall of PG date at Volos, on which Desborough lays some stress as evidence of fine stone architecture (1972: 261, 353) remain mysterious, and the possibility that they represent reused Mycenaean blocks cannot be ruled out; there is certainly no other evidence of the use of shaped stone in building. Otherwise, what evidence there is suggests that settlements were made up of free-standing houses built in the standard way with basically mudbrick walls and thatched roofs, rarely remarkable in structure or fittings, and that these houses were not arranged

Figure 4.6 Plan of Karphi (after J.W. Myers, E.E. Myers and G. Cadogan, *The Aerial Atlas of Ancient Crete*, Berkeley, University of California Press 1992, fig. 15.1).

on any kind of regular settlement plan, though this is hard to demonstrate conclusively because only Nichoria has produced remains of more than one or two structures in any phase. The evidence gathered by Mazarakis Ainian (1997: ch. 1) suggests that on the mainland simple one-roomed structures that are often oval (really rectangular with rounded corners) and apsidal-ended structures arranged on the hall-and-porch principle, in which the apse could function as a storeroom, were particularly common. The curved walls may, as suggested (see p. 99), have been intended to facilitate thatching the roof. Such buildings are hard to parallel in the Cyclades, and do not appear at all in Crete, though they are found at Smyrna.

The apsidal-ended plan was used for most of the largest structures known from the earlier EIA apart from Megaron B at Thermon, now demonstrated to be rectangular (*AR* 45 (1998–99) 43), including the Lefkandi 'Heroön' (Figure 4.7; fully discussed in Lemos 2002: 140–6), the probable shrine at Cape Poseidi, and buildings at Asine and Nichoria (Units IV–1 and IV–5), which have been identified as the houses of elite families if not 'rulers' (on Nichoria see Mazarakis Ainian 1992). This plan continued to be widely popular in G times, especially for what are arguably early temples. The 'Heroön' is most interesting in its demonstration of the limits of EIA archi-tecture, as far as they are known today. There are difficulties in the view that it is a purely mortuary construction (see especially Mazarakis Ainian 1997: 48–57), but the seemingly unfinished state of the building, its barely trod-den floors, and most of all its position in an otherwise purely funerary area weigh heavily against the view that it was originally a ruler's house. Perhaps it is best seen as something like a replica of such a house, built only to be covered up in a remarkable act of conspicuous consumption (as argued in Lemos 2002: 145–6, following *Lefkandi II, 2*: ch. 7). Originally *c.* 50 m long by 13.8 m wide, it is by far the largest EIA building known, four times the size of Nichoria Unit IV–1. But the lines of its walls are not completely straight, the cross-walls are not precisely at right angles, and the building narrows from east to west. The stone foundations have no monumental qual-ity; the interior walls were coated with a simple mud plaster, and the only suggestion of decoration is the discovery of mudbricks of different colours, which could have been laid in patterns in the walls (*Lefkandi II, 2*: 30, 38). The interior also has a relatively simple plan, though it includes more separ-ate parts than any other building, including a porch, anteroom, long hall, two small rooms that might be bedrooms or stores, a back store-room, and what may be stairs leading to a loft. The big apsidal buildings at Nichoria, although substantial, were considerably simpler in their internal arrange-ment and features.

Nichoria Unit IV–1 (Figure 4.8) shares with the 'Heroön' the feature of timber posts set vertically against the walls, whose purpose is argued to be to help support the roof rafters. In Unit IV–1 such posts were set against both sides of the wall and there was a single central roof-pole, whereas in the

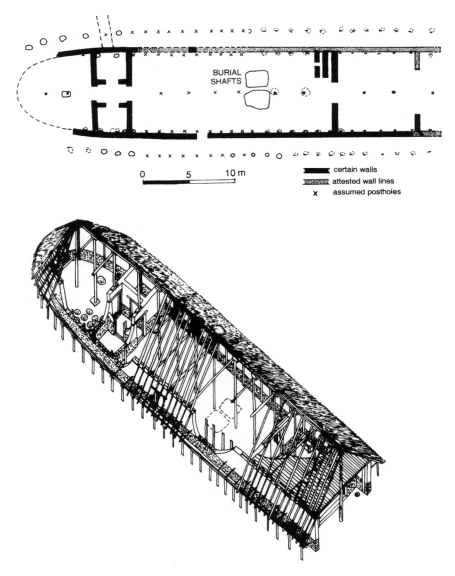

Figure 4.7 Plan and reconstruction of the Lefkandi 'Heroön' (after *Lefkandi II,2*, pls 5 and 28).

'Heroön' the posts were on the interior only, and the row of posts outside was at a distance of 1.8 m from the wall, forming a veranda, and are argued to have supported a horizontal tie-beam which carried the outer ends of the rafters, running around all sides except the entrance. A row of posts running

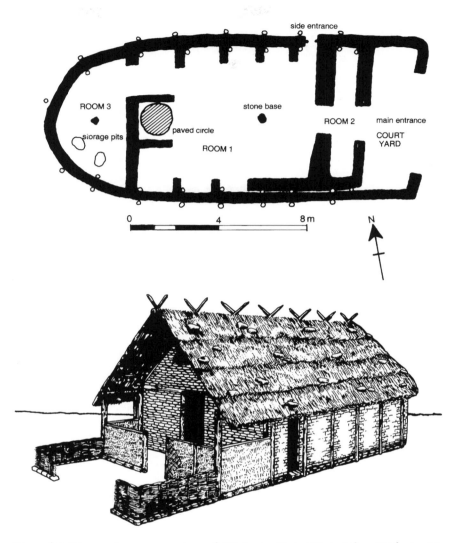

Figure 4.8 Plan and reconstruction of Nichoria Unit IV–1 (after *Nichoria III*, figs 2–22, 23). Courtesy of the University of Minnesota Press.

down the centre of the building gave further support to the superstructure. These supporting posts seemed to have varied in shape, those in the 'Heroön' being roughly rectangular, except the central row, and they were not unusually large, averaging about 20 cm in width/diameter; but considerable quantities of timber would have been required, especially in the 'Heroön'. This use of timber on a large scale seems a typically mainland feature, which

109

is not paralleled in Crete so far. It may reflect the relative availability of materials, although there should still have been substantial stands of timber in parts of Crete.

Social structure

Relatively large buildings like the Lefkandi 'Heroön', Nichoria Unit IV–1, and the most elaborate structures in Crete could well have been the homes of real-life counterparts to the Homeric *basileis*. They thus demonstrate the resources that these could command, at least for some purposes, but also the limits, both practical and conceptual, to what could be achieved at the time. But how much control any such 'chiefs' or elite had over the rest, how embedded social distinctions were, and whether it was easy or hard to rise in the social scale, remain questions beyond the capacity of the known settlement evidence to answer on its own. The most that can be said is that the largest and most elaborate buildings do not represent a completely different level of architecture compared with the rest. Also, in Crete, at least, most houses seem reasonably substantial, suggesting that the gulf between the putative 'chiefs' and many of their followers was not immense. Haggis (2000) thinks in terms of a dominant family in each settlement cluster, which would form a segment of the whole community, accompanied by a wide if uneven spread of wealth; but this might be a feature of the Cretan settlements only. The apparently marked difference between the layout of settlements in Crete and the mainland may indeed be significant, reflecting an important distinction in the prevailing types of society, but again the evidence is too limited for this to be more than a speculation at present.

The existence of this difference warns against the assumption that EIA society was uniform, a point which Whitley has stressed, surely rightly, in an interesting paper (1991b, see also 1991a: 184–6) that includes an attempt to explain the phenomenon of short-lived settlements. Snodgrass has drawn attention to the fact that several major EIA settlements were abandoned so early that their ancient names remain unknown (1987: 172–3, 189–90; others could be added, especially in Crete). His use of this evidence in support of the argument for a predominantly pastoral economy has been rejected (see p. 102), and some of the sites that he lists, like Zagora and Emborio, were quite late foundations (Coldstream 1977: 305–6), but the phenomenon deserves attention. Whitley suggests that some (but not all) of these 'unstable settlements' reflect a particular type of society, potentially recurrent in the EIA Aegean, in which 'big men' compete to attract supporters, who move to be physically near them and may disperse again if the 'big man' loses his source of power or dies. The Lefkandi 'Heroön', Nichoria Unit IV–1, and Building A at Kavousi: Vronda (for which see Day *et al.* 1986: 360–6; Mazarakis Ainian 1997: 208–9) are suggested to be examples of the central buildings occupied by such 'big men', and the situation in Ithaca depicted in the *Odyssey* is interpreted to represent such a system in reality.

But, apart from the major problems involved in any attempt to interpret the Homeric picture as a realistic depiction of a working society, there is an inherent difficulty, that Whitley's examples do not in fact show the kind of local instability that the model seems to demand, for the evidence at various sites suggests that they were long-term centres of significance. The Toumba cemetery at Lefkandi suggests that an elite group continued to associate themselves with the 'Heroön', and so were presumably based close by, over several generations, while Unit IV–1 at Nichoria was used for long enough to have the floor relaid and undergo various changes in the internal arrangement, if not an expansion in size (Coulson's interpretation of the apse as a later addition has been plausibly questioned; see Mazarakis Ainian 1997: 77), and it was succeeded by the equally impressive Unit IV–5 (*Nichoria III*, figs. 2–26, 27). At Mitrou, continuity was such that the large apsidal building A utilised walls and perhaps even column bases of the larger LH IIIC building B (*AR* 51 (2004–05) 51). At Kavousi the Vronda settlement was certainly more long-lived than Whitley implies, and its decline may be explained in terms related to its membership of a site cluster (Haggis 1993: 148 (in use LM IIIC-SM/PG), 150). In all, the 'unstable settlement' hypothesis is intriguing, but it needs better support in the archaeological evidence before this can be taken to reflect a potentially significant form of Aegean social arrangement.

It has already been noted in Chapter 3 that a comparable pattern of foundation, or more often considerable expansion, of a settlement, followed by abandonment after a relatively short period, can be traced in the Postpalatial Period. It was argued there that the Postpalatial motivation for movement of population might be attraction towards perceived centres of prosperity. The abandonment of settlements would represent the corollary, movement away from settlements perceived to be failing. It was also suggested that towards the end of the Postpalatial Period there was movement to the east Aegean and Cyprus in hopes of better prospects. These may indeed have been 'boom' regions of the tenth century, although the finds from Torone and Mende suggest that the north Aegean also attracted considerable interest and, plausibly, settlement. It is hard to believe at one and the same time in a very low population and a considerable level of emigration, but it may be easier to postulate a degree of mobility among what population there was, that was quite exceptional by comparison with the greater part of the BA. It might then be possible to see the whole period from the Collapse into Archaic times as characterised by a general readiness to move, and sometimes to found new settlements, on the part of individuals, families, and larger groups (cf. Osborne 1996: 119, 1997: 256–9; also Purcell 1990, although this gives more credence to theories of population movement, especially on 41, than is allowed here).

111

Short-lived sites could be the equivalents of the 'boom towns' of the nineteenth-century North American frontier, although they clearly had longer lives than many of these. It would follow that failed settlements may have been much commoner than the later traditions concerning migration and colonisation suggest, and also that Thucydides' picture of the unsettled state of Greece, in which he linked the Ionian migration with the colonisation of Italy and Sicily, placed centuries apart on the standard chronology, as examples of the same phenomenon (1.12.4), might not be too far from the truth. But while the traditions presented these movements as events completed in a brief space of time, we should rather see them as long-term processes. The major change represented by the 'colonisation movement' would then be a readiness to go well beyond the boundaries of the Aegean to found new settlements.

Bibliography

On the natural environment, short accounts are given in Dickinson (1994a: ch. 2), Osborne (1996: 53–8) and Sauerwein (1998). Rackham and Moody (1996) is concerned specifically with Crete, but contains many valuable and salutary remarks on themes of relevance to the whole Aegean, particularly on climate, erosion, and the supposed degradation of the natural vegetation.

The distribution of ore sources in the Aegean has recently tended to be discussed in connection with publication of the results of lead isotope analysis by N.H. Gale, Z.A. Stos (formerly Stos-Gale) and colleagues (see especially Stos-Gale and Macdonald 1991). The presentation and interpretation of these results has attracted considerable criticism; a useful debate can be found in *JMA* 8:1 (1995), with valuable general comments by Muhly (54–8) and Pernicka (59–64).

The data relating to plant remains are summarised in Hansen (2000: especially tables 3.2–4, 'Geometric'), with bibliography; for sparse IA material from Assiros note Halstead and Jones in Wardle (1980: 266) which also refers to the bone material. For major studies of IA bone material see especially Sloan and Duncan (1978) and Mancz (1989) (Nichoria), and Klippel and Snyder (1991), updated in Snyder and Klippel (2000) (Kavousi). On the likely farming regime, see useful comments in Foxhall (1995), more generally on 'traditional' farming in Greece (Foxhall 1998; Osborne 1996: 60–3), and specifically on pastoralism (Cherry 1988; Forbes 1995; and (for Crete) Wallace 2003a). Journal articles by Wallace (2000, 2003a) contain a wealth of data and discussion relevant to the themes of settlement and economy in Crete, with case studies of settlements occupied in LM IIIC particularly (cf. also 2003b), a cogent analysis of developments in settlement pattern and use over the whole period from LM IIIC to Archaic. For remarks on likely settlement pattern at several important sites see Whitley (2001: 88–9).

Mazarakis Ainian (1997) gives a comprehensive and very fully illustrated account of EIA architectural remains, which updates and often corrects earlier studies like Drerup (1969) and Fågerström (1988b). Significant references for individual sites are: Tiryns (98), Asine (68–72, 98, 107), Nichoria (74–80, 98–9), Lefkandi (48–57, 105), Eretria (58–63, 102–3, 252–5), Assiros (43, 98), Thessaloniki: Toumba (234–5, 249), Koukounaries (82–3, 99, 107, 255), Zagora (121–5), Smyrna (99–100, 256–7), Kavousi (208–12), Karphi (218–20), Vrokastro (213–15); references for Cape Poseidi, Thermon, and Kommos can be found in the Chapter 8 bibliography.

For recent discussions of the Lefkandi 'Heroön', see Pakkanen and Pakkanen (2000) and Lemos (2002: 140–6).

5

CRAFTS

(For locations of place-names cited in this chapter, see Figures 3.1, 4.1 or 4.3)

Introduction

In comparison with what is available for the BA, the picture presented by the evidence for EIA crafts is generally uninspiring, and has contributed greatly to the traditional picture of a 'dark age'. Many of the advanced crafts attested earlier in the BA disappeared during the Postpalatial Period, as noted in Chapter 3, and the only significant innovation, iron-working, is represented by a limited range of rather simple forms. The great majority of artefacts belong to one of a few broad categories, pottery, weapons, implements, dress-fasteners and other jewellery, and, much rarer and mainly late, figurines of clay and bronze. Items of other categories and/or made in other materials are not commonly found. This must partly reflect the rarity of extensive settlement excavations, but while it is natural to assume that many household items continued to be made of readily available materials like stone, wood, bone and clay, as they had been in the BA, items of bone, even pins, are surprisingly rare, and most items of clay can be related to the production of textiles, a basic craft which obviously survived, although cloth itself very rarely does (Barber 1991: 197 cites evidence). Likely spindle-whorls are quite commonly attested, including makeshift ones made from Mycenaean kylix-feet or other sherds. A study of those from Nichoria suggests that they were mostly used for spinning wool rather than linen (*Nichoria III*: 287), but linen has been identified at Lefkandi, both in the 'Heroön' burial (Popham *et al.* 1982a: 173) and other graves, and in a PG grave at Tiryns (Hundt in Kilian-Dirlmeier 1984: 300). Potential loom-weights are rarer: unperforated spool-like objects found at Nichoria and elsewhere have been identified as loom-weights (*Nichoria III*: 290–1; see Wells 1983b: 237 for an Asine example), while perforated examples in a range of shapes, some apparently 'home-made', were found at Lefkandi (*Lefkandi I*: 82–3).

A basic array of ground stone pounders, rubbers, mortars, quernstones, whetstones, etc. have been identified at various sites, though rarely in great quantity. Whetstones have also been found in some graves with high-status warrior associations (*NorthCem*: 536–7). It must seem implausible that such absolutely essential domestic implements would cease to be made, although some found in EIA levels may be much older survivals, like three Neolithic stone tools found in an LG context at Lefkandi (*Lefkandi I*: 81–2) and another at Nichoria (*Nichoria III*: 292). But it may have been otherwise with the craft of chipping or flaking stone and obsidian blades. Blitzer suggests that dependence on chipped stone tools lessened through the BA (*Nichoria II*: 727), and strongly implies, on the basis of the Nichoria evidence, that the craft of producing chipped stone tools was moribund, if not completely obsolete, by the EIA (*Nichoria III*: 291). Certainly, chipped stone implements are extremely rare, if not totally absent, in the EIA settlement deposits of Lefkandi: Xeropolis, Kalapodi, Karphi and Kavousi. Even at Nichoria, where the EIA deposits have been excavated most extensively, they are rare in comparison with the quantities from BA strata, and none are from unmixed contexts, whereas ground stone items appear in some number in pure or predominantly EIA contexts (see catalogue in *Nichoria II*: 730–43 and 743–54 respectively).

However, Runnels has mounted a strong argument (1982) that the craft of chipping stone blades survived, partly because examples have been found at sites where there is little or no previous prehistoric occupation, like Zagora and Halieis (obsidian implements have also been reported from contexts at Skala Oropou dating as late as the eighth to seventh centuries; see *PAE* 1996: 111). It seems likely that the simple straight-edged blade, the commonest BA form, continued to be produced, especially in obsidian, also rough chert flakes that were probably used in threshing sledges. Nevertheless, the absence of examples of the common BA denticulate blade type, surely produced to edge sickles, in later contexts may be considered significant, and together with the general rarity of finds indicates the very limited nature of this survival.

Overall, the evidence suggests a marked dwindling in the range of crafts practised. It has sometimes been suggested that the evidence from durable materials like clay and metal is deceptive, and that lively artistic traditions could have been maintained in perishable materials like wood and cloth. The patterns on the great krater from the Lefkandi 'Heroön' (Figure 5.11), particularly the sets of circles linked by strips of pattern, bear a resemblance to embroidery, but the surviving pieces of cloth from the male burial are decorated with much simpler rectilinear patterns (*Lefkandi II,2*: 20; Barber 1991: 197), and the colour contrasts that seem to have been favoured by the use of different materials together in necklaces and pins would be most effective against a background of relatively plain cloth. Perhaps the most plausible pointers to the existence of such classes of craftwork belong to the ninth and eighth centuries, particularly the complex patterns of the developed Geometric pottery style, some of which could well derive from weaving or wickerwork (cf. Barber 1991: ch. 16; Boardman 1998: 24). The possibility that elaborate textiles were produced earlier cannot be ruled out, but without further tangible evidence this has to be considered speculative.

In the circumstances, it is not surprising that so much has been written about the Attic PG style, for little else of the eleventh and tenth centuries can honestly be considered deserving of much attention from the artistic point of view, and while there is detectable improvement in the ninth century and even more in the eighth, the picture is still dominated by the evidence of pottery. Of course, it should not be forgotten how much the general picture has until very recently depended on the evidence from a very few published cemeteries, particularly those of the Kerameikos at Athens, which can now be recognised to be unusually frugal in their provision of grave-goods. In any case, grave-goods represent a highly selective range of items, and their evidence cannot be unhesitatingly assumed to offer a full picture of the range of crafts, or the range of items in any one craft.

Because of the limitations, conclusions can still be altered very significantly by a single major find. For example, at Lefkandi the clay mould fragments from Xeropolis (Figure 5.1) provided the first clear indication that bronze tripods of some kind were being locally produced by *c.* 900 (*Lefkandi I*: 93–7), while the remains of the 'Heroön' have demonstrated the ability to work wood on a previously unsuspected scale. But although the 'Heroön' offers a warning that we may be lacking evidence for a significant level of cultural behaviour and craft activity, it also offers reassurance that this was not of a completely different nature from what had been deduced previously. Similarly, when the range and number of contexts begin to increase markedly in the ninth and eighth centuries, the picture is notably enriched, but not changed out of all recognition.

Of course, information on the level of artistic and technical skill in a society is not the only or the most important information that can be gained from the study of its artefacts. Properly analysed, they can yield valuable data concerning the nature and level of demand and patronage, openness to innovation, effective wealth, access to raw materials, internal and external connections, even social stratification and the status of craft specialists. Certain salient points relating to the last can be made. First, it seems extremely unlikely that there were full-time craft specialists of the kind imagined to have produced the finest BA work. On all the evidence, institutions like palaces that could support full-time specialists and provide them with raw materials did not exist, while elite individuals or families are unlikely to have had the need to have their services permanently available or the resources to do so. Specialists are much more likely to have been of the part-time kind, who farmed also, as has been argued to be typical at ordinary settlement level in the BA (Dickinson 1994a: 96).

As in the BA, few traces of the processes of craft production have been found apart from stray finds of slags and pottery wasters, so there can only be

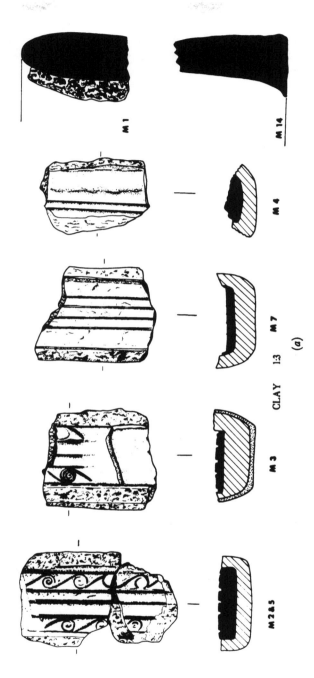

Figure 5.1 Moulds for bronze tripod legs from Lefkandi: Xeropolis. L. *c.* 7–11 cm. Courtesy of the British School at Athens.

speculation about the circumstances in which craftworkers practised their trade. Papadopoulos has now published good evidence for a craftworkers', especially potters', quarter in the area of the later Agora at Athens (2003: ch. 2; see Figure 4.2, 'Original Kerameikos') from the beginning of the EIA onwards, but this is exceptional. Specialists of this ordinary kind are likely to have been quite widespread, and may be detected in the evidence for local traditions, such as the distinctive type of Cretan spear (Snodgrass in *NorthCem*: 577, 580), the individual types of iron sword at Halos in south Thessaly and Vergina (Kilian-Dirlmeier 1993: 113–15), and the observable differences in the development of dress-fastener types between Athens and Lefkandi (H. Catling in *Lefkandi I*: 263–4). But it may be noted that overall there is a high degree of uniformity in the metalwork types produced in the Aegean, in notable contrast with the situation in continental Europe (Harding 2000).

There may have been itinerants hoping to make a living from their craft alone, like those referred to in *Odyssey* 17.382–5, although of the classes named there only carpenters are concerned with the working of materials. New metalworking techniques, particularly the working of iron, are most likely to have been spread by such itinerants, since they could hardly be learned except through personal contact, and they may well be responsible for the appearance of similar metal types through much of southern Europe and the Mediterranean. Itinerants could in fact be responsible for such exceptional finds as the iron sword from Lefkandi: Toumba T. 14, which differs from others here and at Athens in being very close to the earliest bronze Type II form (*Lefkandi I*: 254), the tripod leg moulds from Lefkandi, and the well-known gold earrings from a mid-ninth century Athenian grave (Coldstream 1977: 56; see Figure 5.2). Despite the Near Eastern techniques that they display, the Athens earrings do not have close Near Eastern parallels (though this could simply reflect the rarity of finds), and are unique in the Aegean. If they are not imports, the smith who made them must either have been of Near Eastern origin, or trained by someone who was. Before the end of the ninth century, skilled metalworkers from the Near East may even have been settling in Crete, but the evidence commonly cited has been critically appraised by Hoffman (1997: especially chs 3–4). She accepts that knowledge of techniques may well have been introduced by such immigrants, but has made a good case for questioning common identifications, particularly the supposed North Syrian jeweller buried in Tekke T. 2 at Knossos.

Specialists with the high level of skill indicated by the Athens earrings and Tekke jewellery cannot have been common. Indeed, conditions might well seem inimical to the fostering of artistic talent, so that the most promising craft specialists may have travelled to Cyprus or further east to find more suitable outlets for their abilities. Also, the general impression given by the finds is that materials of the more valuable and exotic kinds were in short supply. Items of semi-precious stones, amber, ivory and glass are all extremely

Figure 5.2 Gold earrings from Areopagus T. H 16: 6, Athens (end of EG II). H. 6.5 cm. Courtesy of the American School of Classical Studies at Athens: Agora Excavations.

rare in most contexts, especially in the more central Aegean regions (faience is rather more common, though not abundant except at Lefkandi), and the few occurrences datable in the eleventh and tenth centuries are often, if not always, either Near Eastern imports or recycled BA items. Even gold and

119

silver are rarely reported between about 1050 and 950. Silver items are particularly rare, outside Crete, but here we are entitled to argue for a gap in the evidence, since a silver-extracting furnace of PG date has been identified at Argos and, as noted in Chapter 4, the Laurion source was evidently being worked again by the mid-ninth century, so quite probably earlier (the silver produced may have travelled mainly to the Near East; see Chapter 7, p. 203). Snodgrass has put forward a case for a shortage of the ingredients of bronze, but this is open to serious criticism (see further, pp. 144–5). In fact, the evidence from the few extensive settlement strata suggests that bronze, lead and iron were commonly available, if not in the quantities that seem to have been circulating in the BA. But the limiting factors may have been more the regularity of exchange, and the need to find goods to exchange for raw materials like metals, than any shortage of the metals themselves.

Limitations on what materials were available would inevitably restrict what craft specialists could achieve, but there is little indication of ambition to achieve for a considerable part of the EIA. Indeed, it may be suggested that, rather than a metals shortage, there was a skills shortage. This could account for the slow spread of the new skill of iron-working, the continuing use of items of obsolete types, and the fact that many of the more elaborate finds from the richest graves, at least outside Crete, are plausible imports, whether contemporary products or 'antiques' that had come back into circulation. Signs of deficient metalworking skill have been noticed on common items like spearheads (Snodgrass 1971: 224, and see 245–6 on the Amyklaion examples), fibulae (Catling in *Lefkandi* I: 236), and an iron dagger in Elateia T. 44, which consists of the blade and hilt of two different weapons crudely riveted together (Deger-Jalkotzy 1999: 198). The reported use of hammer-forging to produce bronze weapons at Agrilia (Feuer 1983: 238, 240, 246–7; see Figure 2.1 for this site) may be a purely local phenomenon at a remote site, but rings of bronze wire and plate often seem crudely made. It is also significant that indications of comparable decline have often been detected in the standards of pottery production and decoration.

Morgan has drawn attention to the special associations of much of the metalwork found on settlement sites, either with elite residences or hoards (1990: 196–7). It is important to remember that metal items were originally prestige objects – metal itself was a convenient means of storing capital, as many Homeric references suggest – and bronze at least could largely retain such associations even when it had become a utilitarian metal, used to make mundane items such as farming implements, craftsmen's tools, fish hooks, and house fittings like door hinges. For it remained the material of prestigious weapons, armour, and vessels intended for ceremonial and display purposes, and the one most commonly used for all kinds of jewellery and dress ornaments. In fact, with the effective disappearance of other precious materials such as ivory and faience from the Aegean by the end of the Postpalatial Period, and also of other means of display such as monumental buildings and tombs, metal items would have become the single most significant indicators of wealth and social status, especially because their manufacture entailed the use of materials that had intrinsic value attributed to them, unlike the materials of decorated pottery. This is surely the context in which not only the provision of metal items as grave-goods but also the introduction of iron, much the most significant technical innovation of the period, should be viewed.

Naturally, those items which show some intention to achieve monumentality, or are unusually elaborate or of precious metal, are most likely to have been made for the wealthiest and highest-ranking members of the community. But it should be remembered that, if fluctuations in supply prompted general frugality in the use of metal, wealth might be demonstrated by what, to our eyes, looks a meagre show, as with the single or paired pins or fibulae, especially those made of iron, that are quite often the only grave-goods found in PG burials. Equally, simple as they generally are, decorated vases may have been considered much more prestigious than those that were only coated or banded with paint, let alone domestic handmade vessels, so that the provision of even a single such vessel could have signified considerable status. Admittedly, items placed in the grave will not have been selected purely for reasons of display (see Chapter 6). But the possibility that what seem poor burials may, in their context, have been considered rich, and the items in them may have been correspondingly valued, should never be forgotten.

What follows will be an attempt to provide an up-to-date survey within a roughly chronological framework of three broad categories, pottery, metalwork, and dress and jewellery, which is intended to cover all items worn as dress-fasteners and ornaments. Clay figurines are so rarely found after the Postpalatial Period, until the eighth century, that discussion of them seems best reserved for the chapter on religion, to which they are most relevant, but bronze figurines will receive some attention under metalwork. The emphasis will be on range and trends, with some comment on relevance to social conditions and development, more on which will be found in Chapter 4. The rare examples of technical innovation or elaboration will be discussed in their chronological context, since they are too few to merit separate consideration.

Pottery

By the time of the period covered in this book, pottery had been an indispensable element of material culture in the Aegean for several thousand years, and many of the typical characteristics of Aegean pottery had been established for a very long time. One of the most fundamental is the division between light buff, yellow or near-white fine wares, often decorated with paints varying from red through brown to black, and domestic wares of coarser fabric, which are generally fired darker shades, especially brown and grey, may well be polished or burnished, and can be decorated with incised patterns or applied clay but are very rarely painted. There were also large, open-mouthed storage jars known as pithoi, made of much thicker fabrics that contain many large inclusions; these were generally light-surfaced and quite frequently had applied clay bands on the shoulder bearing incised or stamped patterns. In the Third Palace Period the potter's wheel was generally used to produce the fine wares, and frequently a large proportion of the coarse wares as well. Fabrics were normally hard-fired, pot surfaces were often polished or burnished with an implement, and paint was very often glossy. A wide range of abstract patterns and stylised naturalistic motifs was used in decoration, along with banding; generally the decoration was very neatly drawn, although examples of clumsy work can occur in any phase. Several categories of plain or monochrome coated fine ware were also produced.

The potters of the Postpalatial Period continued these traditions to a great extent, but the quality of the early Postpalatial pottery is often noticeably poorer than before, since the fabric was not fired so hard, the paint quality was often uneven, and the decoration was generally rather unimaginative. But most pottery continued to be wheel-thrown, a considerable range of shapes was still produced in both fine and coarse wares, and the proportion of paint-decorated fine ware was greater than before, as coating much or all of the vase surface, including the interior of open vases, increased in popularity at the expense of plain fine ware. A high level of quality was attained again with the best LH IIIC Middle wares, which probably fall in the second half of the twelfth century and show an impressive degree of innovation in decoration. These consisted mainly of container vessels, especially stirrup jars (Figure 5.3), and shapes which have obvious functions connected with drinking, such as the jug, sometimes found in the form of a hydria with strainer attachment, the krater, which had already been produced in large and elaborately decorated forms in the Third Palace Period, and the amphora. The fine styles might also be applied to deep bowls and to specialities like pyxides and kalathoi, but surprisingly rarely to drinking vessels, whose decoration was much simpler (the smaller deep bowls could well have functioned as drinking vessels, however). Comparable elaboration can be found at a roughly similar time in Crete, as represented particularly by octopus-decorated stirrup jars and by the 'Fringed Style', popular on kraters but also found on other shapes, especially pyxides (Figure 5.4).

Often, considerable care was taken with the production of these fine classes, which were clearly designed to be luxury wares: the creamy surface and neat brushwork of the Argive Close Style (Figure 5.3: 1) have been particularly remarked on. Vases in these styles were frequently used as grave-goods, especially stirrup jars, which often were 'imports' at the sites where they are found. Kraters do not seem to travel so often, perhaps because they were often of considerable size. They were usually made of heavier fabrics than the smaller vases, but they could be decorated with two or three different colours of paint, as on the famous Warrior Vase from Mycenae (Figure 3.3),

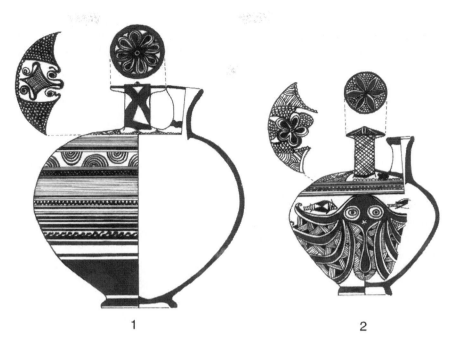

Figure 5.3 Elaborate LH IIIC stirrup jars: 1 Close Style (Asine), 2 Octopus Style (Perati) (after Mountjoy 1999, figs 44: 340, 219: 439). Scale 1:4.

Figure 5.4 LM IIIC Fringed Style pyxis from Kritsa. H. *c.* 34.5 cm (after *BSA* 62 (1967) pl. 90b).

and their decoration included not only scenes of human activity but also of mythical animals that sometimes formed part of more complex scenes. Such scenes could appear on other shapes as well, but more often these were decorated with animals, particularly birds and octopuses (Figure 5.3: 2), arranged in zones or displayed across broad areas of the vase. These might be combined with elaborate abstract patterns based on antithetic spirals or streamers, which could also form the main decoration of even the finest vases. One interesting technical feature may be noted: the compass, long used to decorate other materials like metal and bone in the Aegean, was sometimes used to draw the circles representing octopus eyes on Naxian LH IIIC stirrup jars (Vlachopoulos 1998). The ordinary pottery was often decorated with no more than simple banding or coating; spiral patterns, wavy lines and other geometric motifs were popular, while the stylised floral and marine motifs common previously were rare (Figure 5.5).

The cultural decline generally identified in the late Postpalatial Period, probably extending over the late twelfth and much of the eleventh centuries, affected the pottery in many ways. Tendencies that had already been visible earlier became much more marked. Pottery was frequently fired unevenly, the decoration was carelessly applied in paint that is often streaky or matt, and even the vase shaping could be poor. But, as has been pointed out more than once, there is considerable variation, even within regions: Submyc vases from Athens are well-shaped, but those from Lefkandi often clumsy, and standards vary between different Argolid sites (Mountjoy 1999: 57; compare Figure 5.6: 1–5). The quality of Cretan fabrics is somewhat better than elsewhere in the Aegean, and more care was taken with the decoration (Figure 5.6: 7), but the paint is generally matt and sometimes faded. The lower quality of the pottery may reflect the potters' response to a decline in demand for more elaborate and so, presumably, more expensive vases. It might also reflect the migration of more talented potters to regions where such a demand still existed.

Nevertheless, although by the beginning of the EIA a much greater proportion of the pottery was of coarse fabric, fine ware, now generally painted in some way, continued to be normally wheel-thrown. Iolkos is remarkable in having a distinctive paint-decorated but rather coarse handmade ware, which includes kantharoi, kraters and jugs. But this ware, well known from the Marmariani tholoi further north and almost certainly derived from Macedonia (Desborough 1972: 213), seems to have been developed quite late in PG. There is also a unique local class of handmade decorated pyxides at Asine. But most handmade wares are decorated, if at all, with incised patterns or plastic features, and are of relatively coarse fabric. In general the coarse wares were handmade, but small quantities of wheelmade coarse ware have been noted at Kalapodi, Iolkos, and in the Lefkandi 'Heroön' deposit. The coarse wares were much more varied than the rare occurrences in tombs might lead one to expect, and often of quite good quality. While what is

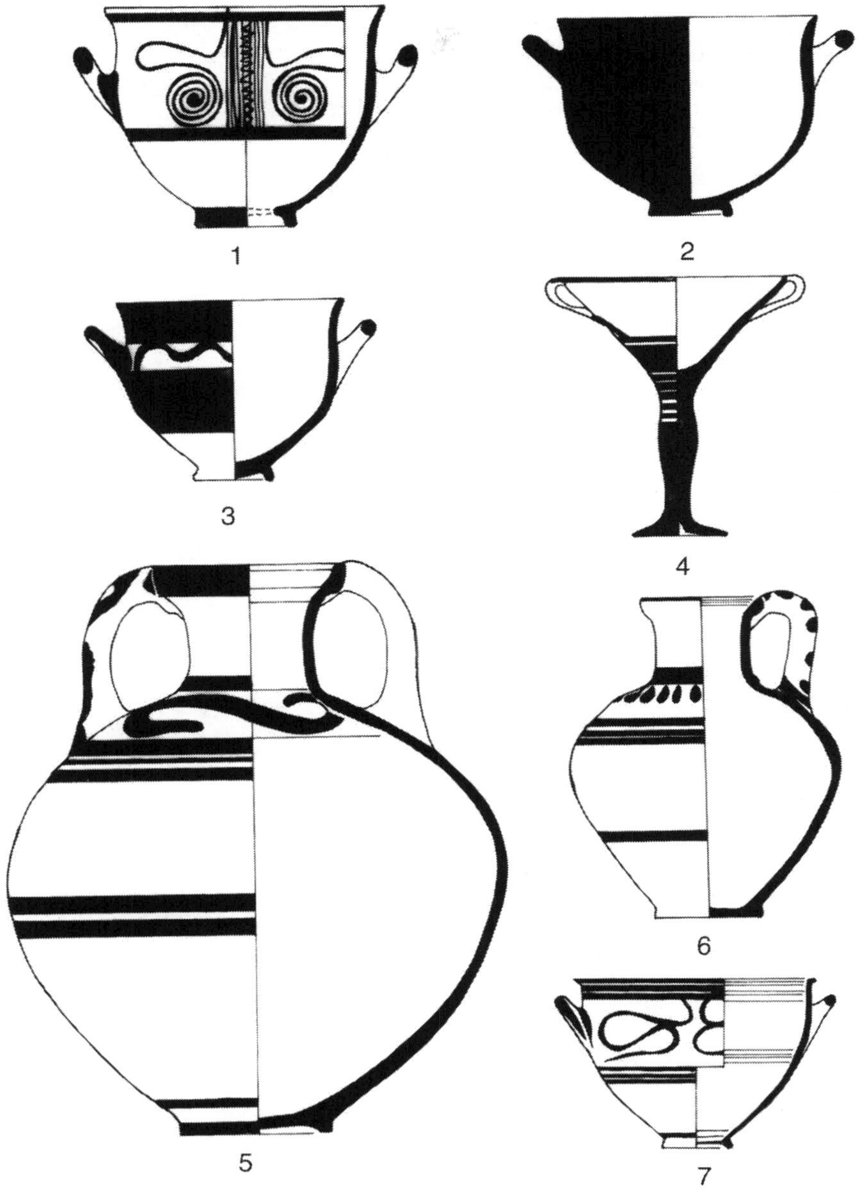

Figure 5.5 Typical LH IIIC vases: 1–3 LH IIIC Early, Middle (Developed) and Late deep bowls; 4 LH IIIC Middle (Advanced) kylix; 5 LH IIIC Early neck-handled amphora; 6 LH IIIC Middle jug; 7 LH IIIC Middle krater (1–4, 6 after Mountjoy 1999, figs 274: 64, 274: 75, 58: 442, 225: 80, 217: 416; 5, 7 after Mountjoy 1986, figs 171, 226:1). Scale 1:6.

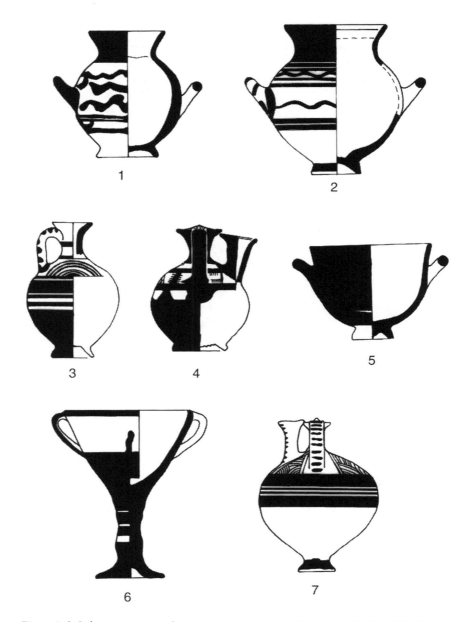

Figure 5.6 Submycenaean and contemporary vases: 1–2 amphoriskoi, 3 lekythos, 4 stirrup jar, 5 deep bowl, 6 Ithacan kylix (after Mountjoy 1999, figs 278: 98, 239: 612, 241: 628, 60: 462, 244: 656, 174: 23); 7 SM stirrup jar (after *BSA* 53–54 (1958–59) 262, fig. 28: VIA1). Scale 1:4.

often called the cooking pot, a broad-mouthed jug- shaped vessel, is found in variants everywhere (Figure 5.8: 8), other cooking-related shapes like braziers, basins, trays and stands have sometimes been identified, and a considerable variety of shapes from amphorae to small bowls, often derived from the wheelmade pottery, is known (Lemos 2002: 84–97). All domestic deposits also contain fragments of large pithoi.

In some cases what is classified as coarse might be better called 'rough plain', as with the Kalapodi 'kitchen ware' (Jacob-Felsch 1996: 78–80) and the hand-made pottery of Iolkos, since in appearance it is closer to the light-coloured plain wares than to the generally darker coarse wares, and it can include versions of fine shapes, like small bowls and kylikes at Kalapodi and skyphoi at Kaphirio in Messenia (Coulson 1986: 47). The fine burnished handmade of PG Asine also seems hardly classifiable as coarse (Wells 1983b: 158–9), while at Tiryns what appears to be the HMB fabric can be traced through from pre-1200 deposits to G times, improving in quality into a fine though often unburnished ware that seems to be the same as the fine plain handmade G ware well represented in the Argolid (Papadimitriou 1998: 123–5).

Sorting out the handmade fabrics and their possible relationship to the HMB ware(s) that appeared near the end of the Third Palace Period (see pp. 52–3) will require more work. Reber (1991) distinguishes central Greek Dark Ware, Argive-Corinthian Ware, and Attic Incised Ware, all starting in Submyc, while Jacob-Felsch argues that the Kalapodi burnished handmade derives from a local tradition not directly related to HMB (1996: 77–8). It may be noted that a considerable variety of coarse wares is found in the MPG 'Heroön' deposit at Lefkandi, including some hard-fired semi-fine that may be imported, but if pithos fragments are excluded they only constitute some 8 per cent of the total, an exceptionally low figure that nevertheless fits the indications from the much smaller LPG and SPG deposits at Lefkandi, and might suggest that coarse ware formed a smaller proportion of total production at leading centres in the EIA than in the BA.

The discovery of the massive MPG deposit filling the Lefkandi 'Heroön' (the total cited in *Lefkandi II,1*: 159 table 17, is 18,530 sherds, once residual and modern pieces are discounted, an enormous quantity compared with all other published deposits) has completely skewed the picture of our sources of information, though it may yet be paralleled by the well deposits in the Athenian Agora, when they are fully published (Papadopoulos 2003 contains useful information). The other domestic deposits from various sites, ranging from Kalapodi to Nichoria, may provide a picture that is closer to the norm, but for a clear idea of many of the decorated shapes in fine ware it is necessary to turn to the graves, which complement the evidence of the domestic deposits by containing complete examples of the whole range of smaller open and closed decorated vases, also of the larger shapes that were used as crema-tion urns where the practice of cremation was prevalent. Less frequently they include examples of coarse cooking pots and similar.

Apart from local peculiarities like the handmade pyxides of Asine and the kantharoi popular in the north-west from Ithaca to Elis, and BA survivals like the kylix (particularly noticeable at Nichoria, on Ithaca (Figure 5.6: 6) and in eastern Crete) and stirrup jar (in Crete; see Figure 5.6: 7), all the local pottery industries produced a similar range of shapes in the EIA, such that the same terms can be used in describing them (cf. Figure 5.8). Only in Crete do the shapes vary significantly in form, although classifiable in similar categories. The main open fine-ware shapes were the deep bowl (now commonly called skyphos), cup, kantharos, and krater. The main closed shapes were types of jug, very often in the trefoil-lipped form called the oinochoai, and amphora, including the small amphoriskoi, also the hydria, pyxis, normally lidded, and lekythos, a small narrow-necked closed vessel that seems to have taken over the function of the stirrup jar except in Crete, where it hardly appeared before the ninth century and is a largely funerary type.

Most of the main shapes occur in large and small forms; most consistently large are the kraters, which are always relatively elaborately decorated and often seem intentionally monumental. The belly-handled amphora is also a shape that is frequently elaborately decorated, more so than the equally common neck-handled variety, although both were used as cremation urns, especially at Athens. It has been traditionally believed that the neck-handled form was reserved for men and the belly-handled for women, at least in the mature phases of PG, but the evidence might warrant reappraisal. Certainly, when vessels were used as grave markers at Athens in G times the belly-handled amphora was used for women, but the krater for men. Massive kraters are also associated with male burials at Lefkandi, in the 'Heroön' and Toumba T. 79, and seem to have more social significance than amphorae, in that they were surely used for ceremonial feasting in life. But they rarely appear inside the grave except in Crete, where they could be used as cremation urns. The pyxis, which obviously functioned as a box, can also have very elaborate decoration, though this is more of a feature of the G styles.

As noted previously, the pottery used in funerary contexts gives a good view of the range of decorated shapes and motifs. By the end of the BA, it seems that all the more elaborate forms of decoration had virtually disappeared from Aegean pottery. Even the spiral was increasingly rare, and apart from wavy lines and zigzags, only groups of arcs, variously filled triangles, chequerboard, vertical wiggly lines, dashes pendent from a band (languettes), and grouped bars and bands were generally used (see Figure 5.6). Overwhelmingly these motifs were arranged in horizontal registers, rarely more than one on a vase; the rest was covered with spaced single or grouped horizontal bands or more general areas of coating, giving respectively a 'light ground' or 'dark ground' appearance. This concentration on abstract pattern was to continue for several centuries. The patterns might be arranged in increasingly elaborate compositions, but naturalistic forms and figures of any kind were extremely rarely introduced; most examples come from Crete, which otherwise produced very simply decorated vases. In such circumstances, the main differences between and within decorated wares depend on how well the motifs were painted and arranged, and this has tended to be the focus of discussion, particularly with regard to the development of the Protogeometric style.

This deserves attention, partly because it has been given special historical significance. The discussion must concentrate on the central regions of the Aegean area, where innovations can be most clearly identified. In a wide arc south and west of these regions, stretching from Crete through the south and west Peloponnese to north-west Greece, local traditions continued that show little knowledge of or influence from developments in the centre. It does not seem likely that Submyc pottery as defined by Desborough and Mountjoy lasted for very long without change. As noted in Chapter 1, various distinctive shapes well known in Late Cypriot IIIB pottery have been identified in the 'late' Submyc graves at Athens and Lefkandi, also in EIA contexts in the Argolid. Another widespread feature is an increasing tendency to raise vases, particularly bowls and cups, on conical or flaring feet, which can be identified not only in Attica, Euboea and the Argolid but also at Kalapodi, Iolkos, and even in Nichoria DA I. This has been seen as possibly Cypriot-inspired by Desborough (1972: 54, more firmly on 145), and certainly was an increasingly popular feature of Late Cypriot IIIB (Pieridou 1973). A type-fossil of Athenian late Submyc and EPG graves, the lekythos decorated with hand-drawn semi-circles, the innermost of which is filled (Figure 5.6: 3), has a comparably wide distribution, appearing in graves at Lefkandi, Corinth, Theotokou in Thessaly, Tragana in Messenia, and Grotta on Naxos (Figure 7.1).

These complex distribution patterns suggest that there was still scope for interconnections and exchanges, which provide a background to the development of the PG style. Desborough presented this as an essentially Athenian phenomenon. He explained one of the main features of the style, concentric groups of circles and semicircles, as drawn by a 'multiple brush' linked to a compass, which he considered an Athenian invention, and he argued that the Athenian potters also developed a 'faster wheel', which allowed the production of more attractive ovoid shapes, and began to take more care with the preparation of the clay and paint than they had in Submyc times. Although he laid emphasis on the importance of links with Cyprus as stimulating this 'awakening', he evidently saw the development of PG as an expression of Athenian self-confidence and 'native genius' (1972: 45), and interpreted the appearance of PG traits elsewhere as reflecting an expansion of Athenian influence in the LPG phase.

Popular though this interpretation has been, it is vulnerable at several points. Papadopoulos and his collaborators have produced a perfectly plausible 'pivoted multiple brush' and demonstrated by experiment that it works (Papadopoulos et al. 1998), but there can be no such thing as a 'faster wheel' (Eiteljorg 1980; Papadopoulos 2003: 220). Greater skill, or care, in using the

129

wheel is all that can be deduced, and in this case the Athenian potters were simply regaining the level of the best BA potters. Further, as noted above, the compass was already being used for pottery decoration in Naxian LH IIIC, and although it is not easy to trace after that until the beginnings of PG, it is perfectly possible that the idea of using a pivoted multiple brush based on the compass as an implement for decorating pottery spread independently of the Attic style.

A distinctive type of neck-handled amphora decorated with groups of compass-drawn concentric circles, or more rarely semicircles (Figure 5.7), that has been identified at north Aegean sites (Catling 1998b), may well be relevant here. It has not been reported from Athens and may have originally been a product of central Greece, but quickly spread to be manufactured in Thessaly and later Chalcidice, before becoming confined to Macedonia, where it lasted into the eighth century if not beyond (cf. Jones in Jacob-Felsch 1996: 118 on Kalapodi examples; Catling 1998b: 176–7). In the north Aegean there is no compass-using style, as Catling emphasises (1998b: 163), but only this one shape displaying such decoration, so it seems difficult to

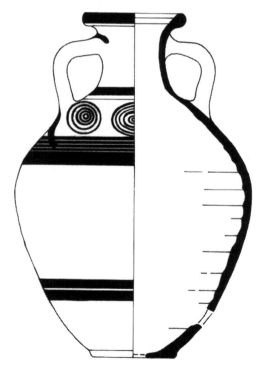

Figure 5.7 North Aegean amphora decorated with compass-drawn circles (after R. Catling 1996, fig. 1a). Scale 1:4.

130

suggest that the origins of the PG style are to be sought in the north Aegean. But the remarkably early date for the context of a Group I amphora with this decoration at Assiros (Chapter 1, p. 20) suggests the possibility that these amphorae were produced quite independently of Attic influence.

Evidence for the independent adoption of the features considered typically PG by Desborough can be assembled from several sites. At Asine, the material from the earliest PG deposits includes what are surely local experiments with the pivoted multiple brush, quite un-Attic in character, on skyphoi, amphorae and other shapes, and there are comparably primitive pieces from Iolkos (Wells 1983b: 184 fig. 133, 146–51; Sipsie-Eschbach 1991: pls 29: 1, 57: 4, 64: 2). At these sites, semicircles seem to have been considerably less popular than circles at first, in contrast with Athens, perhaps because they were harder to draw with precision (cf. Snodgrass 1971: 48). Similarly, when evidence for the multiple brush appears on Ithaca and Crete, and at Nichoria, it was not used to produce anything very Attic-looking in style (Desborough 1972: 228–9 on Crete, 346 on Ithaca). At Nichoria semicircles are apparently more popular than circles when evidence of the instrument's use first appears in DA II, but these may well derive from the hand-drawn semicircles that are popular in DA I (*Nichoria III*: 68). Equally, what may be considered typical PG features in vase manufacture generally, the preference for ovoid closed shapes and for high, often conical feet, especially on open shapes, can appear in areas which have no clearly marked connection with Athens; as already noted, these seem to be widespread tendencies before the development of PG.

It must nevertheless be admitted that in most regions the adoption of these features did not result in the emergence of a definable style, if by style is meant a clear attempt to aim at particular effects and to produce recognisable standard types that combine shape and decoration in a particular way. Apart from the ubiquitous monochrome and wavy line-decorated skyphoi, such standard types are very hard to identify in the domestic material of most regions. Decorative motifs seem almost to have been applied at random, though chosen from a narrow range, and the material often includes examples of poorly conceived and executed decoration and clumsy shaping. Even at Asine, where decorated pieces are quite common, the decorated material has a strong experimental flavour and only weakly defined character. Only in the Lefkandi 'Heroön' deposit are the monochrome and wavy line-decorated skyphoi, so common elsewhere, markedly outnumbered by pattern-decorated skyphoi and other shapes. This can be taken to symbolise a feature which Lefkandi shares with Athens, as against the rest of the Aegean as it appears at present – the capacity to develop a recognisable decorative style.

There can be no doubt that the Attic potters evolved the finest PG style, which influenced local potters to varying degrees in the north-east Peloponnese, Euboea, the Aegean islands, Ionia, and at Knossos, all regions where likely or certain Athenian vases have been found (Catling 1998a). Its most distinctive feature is in fact the fine glossy black paint, produced by a complex three-stage firing process (Papadopoulos 2003: 220–2), but it also offers the clearest examples of a concern for balance, both in the articulation of the shape and the arrangement of the decoration, and for the overall effect, in which contrasts between the black paint and the light buff to brown surface of the clay were important. But, although it certainly made use of very few motifs, principally circles and semicircles, and the majority of pieces are decorated with a studied simplicity (Figure 5.8), this was not always so. To the early belly-handled amphora from Kerameikos T. PG 12 (Figure 5.9) may be added the even more elaborate later example (83 cm high) from the Lefkandi 'Heroön' (*Lefkandi II,1*, pl. 80). It seems that this shape, as well as the poorly known krater (Lemos 2002: 49–50), attracted relatively elaborate schemes of decoration, a pattern repeated in the G style.

The Lefkandi potters clearly used many ideas first found in the Attic style, but these do not appear until the phase classified as MPG (Lemos 2002: 11 on EPG, 15–16 on MPG). There seems to be no local phase of experiment with the compass equivalent to Attic EPG, and it is therefore supposed that the ideas represent influence from Athens. But in Euboea an individual version of the PG style developed (Figure 5.10). The wide range in the mass of material from the Lefkandi 'Heroön' argues strongly that Euboea, if not Lefkandi itself, was the centre of the 'Thessalo-Euboean' style: the more limited material of comparable date from sites like Iolkos and Torone does not offer a strong argument for placing this centre in eastern Thessaly or Chalcidice. This style's influence can be detected over a very wide area, taking in not only the rest of Euboea, Skyros, and eastern Thessaly, but sites in Macedonia and Chalcidice, eastern central Greece (notably Kalapodi), and eventually the more northern Cyclades (Lemos 1998: 49). Some closely similar types have even been identified in the MPG material of Cos (*Lefkandi II,1*: 16, 20, 46). The potters' interest in innovation is especially apparent in the considerable variety of shapes and wares, and in the decorative schemes seen in the numerous krater fragments from the 'Heroön' deposit. The krater found by the grave is particularly remarkable for its quite un-Attic approach to the arrangement of motifs, which gives as much prominence to rectilinear forms rarely used in Attic PG as to circles, and includes the unique stylised trees placed under the handles (Figure 5.11).

Another innovation traceable at Lefkandi as early as the 'Heroön' deposit is the application of pendent semicircles to skyphoi and krater-bowls (*Lefkandi II,1*: 22, 24). There are several examples of each, showing considerable variations in profile and other details, which suggests that these are still experimental. This constitutes a strong argument for placing the development of the famous pendent semicircles skyphos here and not in Macedonia (as suggested by Papadopoulos 1998: 365–6), while one example suggests that the carinated profile characteristic later may have been adopted from the

Figure 5.8 Typical Attic LPG vases: 1 neck-handled amphora, 2 oinochoe, 3 lekythos, 4 skyphos, 5 cup, 6 pyxis, 7 kantharos, 8 PG coarse ware domestic jug (after Lemos 2002, figs 33.1, 35.3, 34.6, 32.4, 33.4, 33.7, 31.4, 33.9). Scale 1:6.

Figure 5.9 Attic EPG belly-handled amphora from Kerameikos T. PG 12, Athens. H. 52 cm. Courtesy of the Deutsches Archäologisches Institut, Athens.

similarly high-rimmed cup (compare *Lefkandi II,1*, pl. 48: 57 and 155). Later, but not before LPG, the same motif was applied to plates (Figure 5.12), which may have been developed specifically for export to the Near East (see further Chapter 7, p. 210–11). The Lefkandi potters also developed individual shapes like the strap-handled bowl and minor fine wares like the incised Black Slip ware, that seems to be linked with north-east Aegean Grey Ware, and Red Slip ware (*Lefkandi I*: 347), although these were not widely distributed elsewhere. If, as has been argued (e.g. Desborough 1972: 293; Boardman 1998: 13), the quality of Attic PG reflects in some way important developments in the Attic community, then these features peculiar to Lefkandi could surely be interpreted to say something equally important about society there. But it is questionable whether the evidence of pottery should be pushed this far.

Despite the wide spread of types characteristic of the Euboean style, especially the open shapes, Euboean influence did not continue strong outside

Figure 5.10 Typical Euboean PG and SPG vases: 1 EPG amphoriskos, 2 MPG skyphos, 3 LPG pendent semicircle skyphos, 4 LPG cup, 5 LPG oinochoe, 6 SPG I lekythos, 7 SPG IIIA pendent semicircle skyphos (1, 4–6 after *Lefkandi I*, 309 fig. 12B, 294 fig. 7G, 317 fig. 15D, 314 fig. 14F; 2 after Lemos 2002, fig. 66.3; 5, 7 after *Lefkandi III*, pl. 100: Toumba Pyres 34,1 and 14,1). Scale 1:4.

Figure 5.11 MPG krater from the Lefkandi 'Heroön'. D. *c.* 88 cm, H. *c.* 80 cm. Courtesy of the British School at Athens.

Skyros and Thessaly, and the future was to belong to Attic. For unquestionably it was the Attic potters who developed the Geometric style, which was to have a much more profound influence on pottery production throughout the Aegean than the preceding Protogeometric style, widely distributed though that was. It is unnecessary to consider the changes of the Geometric style in detail, since these have been set out elsewhere (especially Coldstream 1968), but some salient features may be pointed out. Some new forms and variants were introduced, but the basic classes remained the same. The most elaborate vases were still the kraters and amphorae, which became decorated with complex systems of bands and panels that eventually covered most of the vase. The motifs were now mainly rectilinear; many had already been current in LPG as subsidiary motifs, but it was two new ones, the meander and multiple zigzag, that were to become dominant. The style began with a preference for dark ground schemes, already well established in Attic LPG, in which the decoration was confined to narrow bands or small panels between large areas coated with a rich black paint.

As the style developed, the decorated zones expanded and became more numerous (Figures 5.13, 5.14). The effect, on the most elaborate vases of the MG I phase (*c.* 850–800), the amphorae used as cremation urns and grave

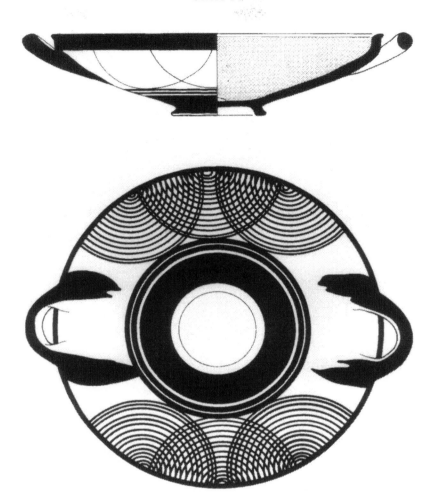

Figure 5.12 Plate (LPG or SPG I) decorated with pendent semicircles from Lefkandi: Toumba T. 42. D. 17.4 cm, H. 4.5 cm. Courtesy of the British School at Athens.

markers for what has been argued to be an increasingly selfconscious elite (Figure 5.15), is extremely impressive in its careful balancing of light and dark areas and arrangement of the patterned zones used on the different parts of the body. In the eighth century the essentially abstract style of decoration began to be enlivened with stylised plant motifs, posed animals (Figure 5.14: 1), which came to be repeated as a zone-filler, and scenes of human action. These show clear allusions to elite preoccupations – horses, hunting, warfare, funerals – and the best examples are found on the truly monumental grave-marker vases first developed by the Dipylon Painter, whose workshop

137

Figure 5.13 Typical Attic EG–MG I vases: 1–2 EG I oinochoe and shoulder-handled amphora, 3–4 EG II oinochoe and skyphos, 5–7 MG I pyxis, lekythos–oinochoe, and shoulder-handled amphora (after Coldstream 1968, pls 1d, 1a, 2d, 2b, 3g, 3l, 3m). Scales: 5 (over 1:5), 1–4, 6 (1:6), 7 (1:8).

Figure 5.14 Typical MG II–LG vases: 1–2 Attic MG II pyxis and skyphos, 3 Attic
LG Ib skyphos, 4 Atticising Corinthian MG II krater (after Coldstream
1968, pls 4e, 5e, 10b, 17f). Scales: 1, 4 (1:6), 2–3 (1:4).

founded the Attic LG style (Coldstream 1968: 29–41, pls 6–7, also 1977: 110–14). On these the panels and zones showing ritual mourning for the dead and the procession to the grave were placed at the centre of carefully worked out schemes of intricate geometric decoration (Figure 5.16); on the kraters used to commemorate male scenes of warfare were also prominent. These developments may have been inspired by customer demand for more elaborate work, and clearly drew on the increasingly familiar Near Eastern artworks, the source of the commonest animal types as well as of some very individual scenes on later vases (Carter 1972). But most scenes of human activity were a native development with only a few precursors, mostly found in north Crete.

Figure 5.15 MG I belly-handled amphora from Kerameikos T. G 41, Athens. H. 69.5 cm. Courtesy of the Deutsches Archäologisches Institut, Athens.

Figure 5.16 LG Ia grave-marker amphora NM 804 from the Dipylon cemetery, Athens. H. 1.55 m. Courtesy of the Deutsches Archäologisches Institut, Athens.

The increasing skill and elaboration detectable in Attic LG pottery can also be identified elsewhere in the Aegean, not only in the painted ware but in the improving quality of the plain and domestic wares, though these are harder to document. It is easy to get lost in the details of style and influence that can be seen in the increasingly rich material, but certain features stand out. In the ninth century the Attic style was closely followed in most of the neighbouring regions and had detectable influence in others, but it was largely ignored in Euboea, where an essentially PG style was continued, and was hardly known in the south Peloponnese and western Greece. In the second half of the ninth century developments in north-central Crete, as represented principally at Knossos, produced the notably

141

idiosyncratic PG B style, which combined ultimately Minoan, PG, G and Near Eastern influences in extraordinary medleys that included some of the earliest post-BA figured scenes, notably representations of goddesses (Coldstream 1984), on vessels with strong elite associations such as cremation urns, kraters and giant oinochoae. But these seem to have had no influence outside Crete.

In the eastern Peloponnese Attic influence continued strong in the earlier eighth century (Figure 5.14: 4), but later the local styles began to diverge more from the Attic standard and established their own areas of influence. Other regions of the Peloponnese had also established definable styles by this time, but these owed little to standard PG, let alone G. 'Laconian PG', of which a local form can now be identified at Tegea (see p. 19), may not have become fully established until the ninth century, and the same may well be true of what has been defined as Achaean PG. Both make much use of triangular and diamond motifs, usually cross-hatched, but their open shapes are quite distinct. Messenia, however, if Nichoria is typical, continued its impoverished 'DA' style with few innovations (but something very like 'Laconian PG' was produced at Kaphirio south of Nichoria; Coulson 1986: 41–8). Ithaca also shows little further development (see Figure 5.17 for examples of all these styles).

From the middle of the eighth century, styles that clearly relate to the final, LG, development of the Geometric tradition began to be produced almost everywhere, even in Euboea, which had continued its SPG tradition until this point although beginning to incorporate reproductions of some Attic MG types (*Lefkandi I*: 40–3), and in the regions which had never produced a true PG style. Figured scenes appeared widely on what was evidently the best pottery, with some interesting choices of theme – shipwrecks and men holding horses are represented more often outside Athens than in the Attic style – but scenes intended to tell a story are rarely if ever clearly identifiable. This growing popularity of figured decoration allowed more scope for differentiation than the standard geometric patterns, but these were also treated differently in different centres, and there seems to have been a deliberate intention to produce distinctive wares. Many local preferences in shapes, combinations of motifs, styles of composition, and the general appearance of the fabric can be identified. By the later eighth century, for the first time in centuries, all parts of the Aegean were decorating their pottery with variants of the same style. But the growth of interest in the possibilities of figured decoration, though still largely confined to a few themes, was paralleled by a loss of interest in intricate geometric patterns, although it survived in subsidiary zones well into Archaic times.

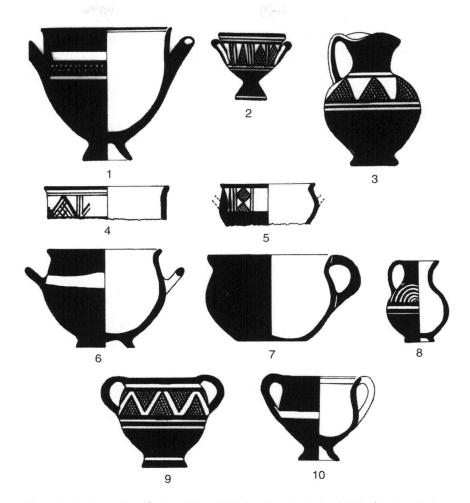

Figure 5.17 Examples of other PG and SPG styles: 1 Argive MPG skyphos (Asine),
2–3 Argive LPG skyphos and oinochoe (Tiryns), 4–5 Laconian 'PG'
skyphoi (Amyklai, Sparta Heroön), 6–7 Messenian DA II skyphos and
cup (Nichoria), 8 Messenian DA II oinochoe (Antheia), 9 Achaean 'PG'
kantharos (Derveni), 10 Ithacan PG kantharos (Polis) (1–3 after Lemos
2002, figs 28.4, 56.6, 57.7; 4–5 after Coulson 1985, figs 1: 12 and 2: 30;
6–7 after *Nichoria III*, figs 3–23: P1565 and 3–34: P907; 8 after Coulson
1986, fig. 6.33; 9 after Coldstream 1968, pl. 48h; 10 after Mountjoy
1999, fig. 175: 32). Scale 1:4.

Metalwork

Metal objects form the second great class of EIA finds after pottery, in settlement deposits and graves, but they are neither very common nor technically elaborate between the end of the Postpalatial Period and *c.* 900 at most sites. The cemeteries in the Athenian Kerameikos have been used to suggest that before *c.* 900 even items of common metals were rare, but finds from other cemeteries in Athens and elsewhere give a different impression, which is strengthened by the material from the PG settlement levels at Asine, where nine metal objects, mostly bronze, were found in a small area (Wells 1983a: 227, 255, 278), and more generally (since it covers a much wider chronological range) by the evidence from Nichoria. Here 119 complete or fragmentary objects, pieces of scrap and residues from working or casting (one gold, seventy-nine bronze, thirty-one iron, and eight lead) have been catalogued as of EIA date, though some from mixed strata might equally well be Mycenaean (*Nichoria III*: 273–87). The bronze items have a particularly wide range and include several that contain notably high percentages of tin, a feature also noted in some of the analysed items from the Lefkandi cemeteries (*Lefkandi I*: 456–8).

These data have an obvious bearing on Snodgrass's 'bronze shortage' theory (1971: 237–49, cf. 1980a: 50–1). This posited that an interruption in the supply of tin, because of a breakdown in communications between the Aegean and the Near East, forced the development of iron technology in the more progressive parts of the Aegean (including Lefkandi), where iron was used for items that would normally be made in bronze. In contrast, in the remoter parts (which should include Nichoria) old bronze items continued in use and types obsolete elsewhere may have continued to be produced, using the metal of recycled BA artefacts; thus, metal technology was 'frozen' in the state reached before the breakdown. Snodgrass originally considered the period of 'bronze shortage' to have had maximum limits of *c.* 1025–950, but more recently ([1971] 2000: xxvii) he has confined it to no more than a 'brief transitional phase', presumably a generation or so. The idea that there was shortage of the constituents of bronze has also been used to explain the development of iron technology in the Near East, and has been heavily criticised in that context in Pickles and Peltenburg (1998: 80–1), but it could still be imagined to apply to the Aegean.

However, it is questionable whether there was any significant interruption in supply at all. The marked variations in tin content revealed by analysis of Aegean EIA bronzes show that the metal for these is unlikely to have been produced simply by melting down BA artefacts (although LB bronzes could also vary considerably in their tin content). It is more probably the result of new alloys (Waldbaum 1987; Kayafa 2000). The low percentages of tin found in some analysed Elateia bronzes (Dakoronia 2003) could reflect the addition of extra copper to old bronzes melted down, suggesting that some of what was in use was 'recycled', presumably through tomb robbery. The use of new supplies of metal to make alloys is also suggested by the exceptional quantities of lead found in many of the Lefkandi bronzes and of iron in both Lefkandi and Nichoria bronzes, which could reflect the exploitation of new copper ores. Significant quantities of lead and iron have been noticed even in G bronzes, especially in the copper bodies of tripod vessels (Kayafa 2000; cf. *Lefkandi I*: 447–59).

Further, Snodgrass's approach did not take sufficient account of the symbolic value of iron (a point he now acknowledges: [1971] 2000: xxvii). Iron was not at first a utilitarian metal, but rather exotic and prestigious, and it evidently had high value originally in the Near East. Even in the thirteenth century, when iron ores were evidently being exploited in Anatolia, and ostensibly functional (but probably mainly ceremonial) items, including weapons and tools, were being made of it, especially in Hittite territory (Yalçin 1999: 181–4), the metal was thought appropriate for god-images, dedications and royal gifts (Gurney 1990: 67–8). The fact that working iron into anything like a blade involved a technology quite different from that used for bronze would also surely contribute to its mystique.

Near Eastern attitudes are likely to have had great influence on the Aegean, and the iron objects found in Postpalatial contexts are more likely to have been valued as prestige items than as technical improvements on their equivalents in bronze (see further, p. 146). The choice of iron for locally made items may then reflect a continuation of this attitude. Thus, pins and other ornaments of iron in the mainly early (late Submyc-MPG) Lefkandi: Skoubris cemetery are normally from 'rich' graves which contain many other items. That iron in fact had comparable prestige throughout the EIA is suggested by the occurrence of iron fibulae and pins, sometimes gilded or otherwise elaborated, alongside more numerous bronze examples in rich graves (e.g. in the Lefkandi 'Heroön' and the Toumba cemetery; see *Lefkandi III*, table 1), by the manufacture of iron versions of the most elaborate G pin shapes in the Peloponnese, and by the practice of providing important male burials not simply with weapons but also with whole collections of iron items (see Coldstream 1977: 146). Various Homeric references support this picture (cf. Sherratt 1994: 78), especially the standard line describing a hero's treasure, used five times, 'bronze and gold and much-hammered iron'.

Taking these points into consideration, together with the evidence for the occurrence of bronze items in quantity at relatively remote sites, especially the Elateia cemetery, it seems most likely that, as suggested on p. 120, all the common metals continued to be available in the Aegean, presumably circulated through exchange and perhaps the movement of itinerant smiths and prospectors. This does not mean that enough metal was always available everywhere to fill demand, and another major limiting factor could well have been an inability to assemble sufficient resources to pay for it. This, together with likely variations in burial customs, should explain the phenomena noted by Snodgrass.

The introduction of iron

It has been evident for some time that many once widely held beliefs concerning the spread of iron technology must be discarded. It cannot be seen to derive from a dispersal of knowledge following the collapse of the Hittite Empire, although there are strong indications that within that empire its production and distribution were palace-controlled (Muhly *et al.* 1985). But the skill was known in other centres, even Egypt, in all probability (Waldbaum 1980: 77, 79), and the most significant developments may well have taken place in Cyprus, where iron-working was evidently being expanded in the thirteenth century. Here there is no evidence for central control of production and distribution. Rather, the producing workshops seem to have been autonomous, which would inevitably increase the scope for the spread of iron objects beyond the exalted circles in which they apparently circulated before *c.* 1200. Indeed, it is most likely that iron's prestigious associations were a driving force behind the spread of iron-working, because early iron products could not have been superior to good bronzes (Muhly *et al.* 1985: 68).

However, iron did have some practical advantages that may have been realised fairly quickly. To make a usable item required only one metal, not two as with bronze, and iron ores were more widely available. Iron items were also lighter than their equivalents in bronze, more rigid, and could take an edge better and be re-sharpened more easily. Once the value of carburisation was realised and the basic techniques of forging to produce a form of steel had been worked out, as had apparently happened in Cyprus by the twelfth century (Pickles and Peltenburg 1998: 84; a form of steel may even have been produced in Anatolia in the thirteenth century, see Yalçın 1999: 183), iron was more likely to become favoured for practical weapons and implements as well as ornamental items. But the spread of iron-working is likely to have been a lengthy process, if only because it would require movement by experts who could recognise ore sources and work the metal. One might also suspect that the elite attempted to limit its availability because of its prestige value (cf. Crielaard 1998: 191).

The earliest iron items to become widespread in the twelfth century were knives with bronze-riveted hilts of ivory or bone; one example even has rivets capped with gold or silver (Karageorghis 1982: 299). It has been plausibly argued that these could have been made from the iron blooms that appeared as a by-product of smelting copper from iron-rich ores (Pickles and Peltenburg 1998: 79–80, 90–1). They would thus have been quite cheap to produce, but would be highly prestigious items, which would have great value for display, like the iron knives and daggers used earlier as royal gifts in the Near East,

146

and like them could have been used in ceremonial gift exchange that might have ultimately commercial motivation. It is surely no accident that the earliest examples in the Aegean appear at important sites like Perati, Lefkandi and Knossos. The suggestion that these knives were all Cypriot (Sherratt 1994: 68–9) does have some difficulties. As Waldbaum has pointed out (1982: 330–2), the one-edged knife had only become established in Cyprus relatively recently, and the examples vary considerably in form (Snodgrass 1980b: 346), which might suggest production in different regions, but perhaps only haphazard rather than organised production (cf. Hoffman 1997: 140–1 for doubts as to whether all examples in Crete are imports). It is also relevant that other iron items of likely Cypriot origin are not particularly common in the Aegean, although a find from Cyprus suggests that the first Aegean iron daggers and short swords could have been based on a Cypriot type (Karageorghis 1982: 299).

However, despite Waldbaum's arguments (1982: especially 336–8), there seems little reason to suppose that iron-working developed independently in the Aegean. Not only does the Aegean lack evidence of a metallurgical background comparable to that in which iron-working seems to have developed in Cyprus and the Near East, but iron items are hardly found in the abundant settlement strata of the Third Palace Period in the Aegean, as might have been expected if there was a developing local industry (Muhly *et al.* 1985: 77–9 refer to evidence from a workshop in a LH IIIB2 context at Tiryns that could indicate local iron smelting, but more detail is needed), and iron is not mentioned in the Linear B texts (I owe this point to Dr E.S. Sherratt). EIA settlement strata are now better known than when Waldbaum wrote, but iron items remain very rare in these also. Even at Nichoria, where they are commonest, the only identifiable implements are knives. It still seems most likely, then, that iron-working developed in the Aegean under the stimulus of external influences, which need not have been exclusively Cypriot (Matthäus 1998: 141). It is also perfectly possible that the Cypriot parallels of the early iron items in the Aegean reflect the movement of Cypriot-trained smiths rather than trade, and some pieces may have been locally made by such persons even in the twelfth century.

The few items of iron apart from knives that are found in contexts of the Postpalatial Period in the Aegean (Figure 5.18) are mostly ornamental, pins, rings and one large bracelet (Snodgrass 1971: 221, lists almost all examples). A fragmentary sickle blade of a well-known Near Eastern type was the only iron item in the Tiryns Treasure, which probably dates around the end of the Postpalatial Period; this was surely hoarded for its metal rather than any special value as an implement. A sword is reported from a presumably LH IIIC context, a cremation in a hydria at Arcadian Palaiokastro (*AR* 43 (1996–97) 33), but no details are available. But around the transition to the EIA proper other weapons are found, two swords from Athens graves and several daggers from Athens, Lefkandi, Tiryns and Knossos (*NorthCem*:

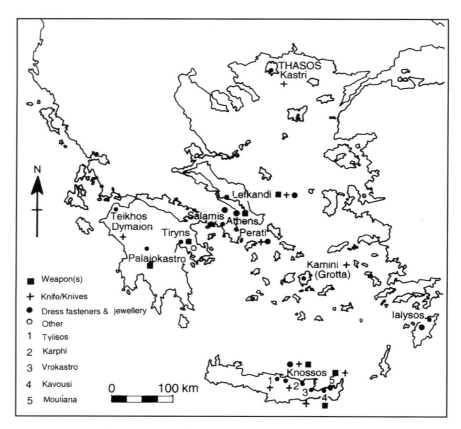

Figure 5.18 Distribution map of iron items from certain and probable pre-1000 contexts in the Aegean.

528–9). All have shapes derived from the bronze Type II sword form and most are iron-riveted. Such blades may well have been produced first in Cyprus (see p. 147; also Snodgrass 1980b: 347), and the earliest Aegean examples resemble a Cypriot version of Type II. The daggers, like the older knives, were surely primarily intended for show (several have ivory hilt-plates), since they are too short (reported lengths vary from 21–31 cm) to have been much use as weapons except at very close quarters. But the swords, while no doubt being display items, could well have been effective weapons (one, from PG T. 2 in the Kerameikos, is 48 cm long).

Together, these finds suggest that iron was becoming more common in the leading regions of the Aegean, and was being worked at some centres by the middle of the eleventh century. The earliest items that are plausibly local products essentially duplicate some of the commoner and more easily produced bronze forms, and they represent a further narrowing down of the range of weaponry from what had been current in Postpalatial times. No attempts were made to reproduce in iron the last types of the indigenous Aegean sword and dagger tradition in bronze, although these were clearly still current in the Postpalatial Period, or many of the previously known forms of spearhead, not even the 'flame-shaped' form only recently introduced. Perhaps this was because it was mainly current in western Greece (Catling 1968: 106–7), where iron-working was probably slow to become established. Nor was iron used for the earliest forms of fibula, or indeed for any fibulae of Postpalatial date, although it became popular for the simpler forms of pin and ring and was occasionally used for other ornaments. But in the course of the tenth century the range of iron items expanded: known types include spear, javelin and arrow heads, spear butts, axe blades, chisels, horse bits, and some fibulae. But the more complex forms of fibula and finger ring, 'phalara' (see p. 157), tweezers, and the rare vessels and armour facings continued to be made of bronze or copper.

It is very difficult to establish how quickly iron-working spread through the Aegean region. The reported evidence from many areas is so scanty or so hard to date closely that no conclusions can be safely based on it. In Thessaly iron items certainly appear in PG contexts. Here there could even have been some stimulation from Macedonia, where the local iron sources may have begun to be worked as early as *c*. 1000 (Snodgrass 1980b: 350), but the types found at Iolkos are standard forms with no specifically Macedonian links. In Messenia, however, it cannot be assumed that local iron-working was established very early. An iron pin with attached bronze globe from a tomb near Pylos, a well-known PG type elsewhere, suggests that Aegean iron types were reaching Messenia before *c*. 900, but the best evidence for local working comes from DA II contexts at Nichoria, the phase to which iron finds from other Messenian sites certainly or probably belong (Snodgrass 1980b: 353–4; see Coulson 1986: 30 for DA II material from Malthi, which offers a more likely context than LH IIIC for the iron objects and slag reported). As noted in Chapter 1, this phase may well belong largely in the ninth century. There are also plausible indications of a late arrival at Elateia, where relatively many tombs were in use in PG times but iron is represented by a very few daggers and pins, while bronze items of many kinds are extremely common. Overall, the evidence suggests that the area where iron-working became established only expanded relatively slowly from original bases in Crete and the central mainland, and iron items may only have become really commonplace in the ninth century, when local sources were beginning to be exploited.

By the end of the EIA, a much clearer distinction had become established between iron as the practical metal and bronze as the ornamental. Although iron continued to be used quite frequently for pins, it was not used for armour and other ornamental fittings, vessels, or figurines. To a great extent this may be explicable in terms of the technical difficulties involved in

forging such items in iron, but it may owe a lot to bronze's more immediately attractive appearance, which made it a natural choice for forms of
display item that were too large or common to be made of precious metal.
That iron persisted as a material for jewellery and dress-fasteners for as long
as it did may be due to a liking for colour contrasts, which can be detected in
its simplest form in the common practice of providing iron pins with heads
or attachments of bronze, bone, or ivory (and also threading faience beads
onto them at Lefkandi).

Vessels

Limited resources could explain the near-disappearance of metal vessels in
the EIA, but the position is not clear-cut. There are certainly no indications
that any tradition of making vessels of precious metal continued in the
Aegean after the Collapse, or was revived at any time in the EIA. But there is
a good deal of evidence for the survival and likely continued manufacture of
bronze vessels (as they are conventionally called, although the bodies are
probably copper and only the cast attachments of bronze). The possession and
display of metal vessels would surely have been one of the most potent status
symbols in the EIA, as is corroborated by their prominence in the epic tradition, and it is no accident that the types most commonly found can be
readily associated with ceremonial feasting and drinking.

There are substantial groups of Postpalatial bronze vessels from the Tiryns
Treasure and Mouliana T. A, but sporadic and generally fragmentary finds
thereafter, relatively many being from the cemeteries of Knossos. The most
elaborate of these are of types that seem to have originated in Cyprus
c. 1250–1150, especially rod tripods (Figure 5.19: 1) and four-sided stands,
and Catling originally argued that all Aegean examples were products of that
period and so, when found in later contexts, 'heirlooms', as he has argued for
the Lefkandi 'Heroön' amphora (*Lefkandi II, 2*: 87). 'Antiques' might be a less
tendentious term, which can cover examples relatively recently brought back
into circulation by tomb robbery. But Matthäus has argued for local Cretan
production of both rod tripods and four-sided stands into G times (1988,
also 1998: 129–33). Catling has conceded that the clay mould fragments
from Lefkandi (Figure 5.1) have reopened the question on rod tripods,
although he still prefers the 'heirloom' explanation (*NorthCem*: 569). These
moulds were used for casting decorated strips that could serve as legs for rod
tripods (as Matthäus believes, 1998: 130) or tripod cauldrons, and come
from a context no later than *c.* 900. They show clear stylistic links not only
with the rod tripod from Fortetsa T. XI, a context of similar date, but with
tripod cauldron legs of the earliest Olympia type (*Lefkandi I*: 96–7). The
argument for Cretan production of rod tripods is given added strength by a
clay imitation of the shape, dated SM/PG, from Arkadhes, which has also
produced an imitation of a different type of stand (Kanta and Karetsou 1998:

150

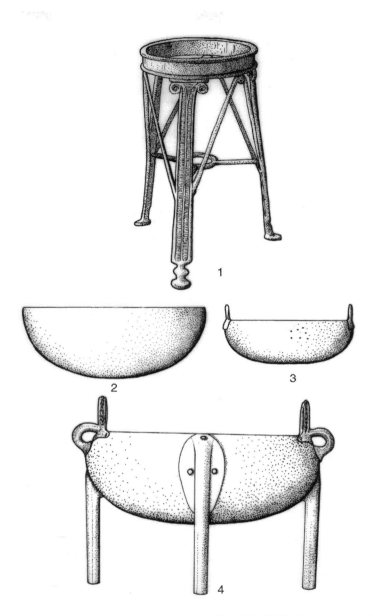

Figure 5.19 Bronze vessel types: 1 rod tripod (after E.H. Hall, *Excavations in Eastern Crete, Vrokastro*, Philadelphia 1914, fig. 80), 2 bowl, 3 two-handled bowl, 4 tripod cauldron (all after Matthäus 1980, pls 49: 418, 4: 28 (both Tiryns Treasure), 72: 6 (Mycenae, PG?)). Scale 1:8.

161–2), and Hoffman has accepted the case for the production of rod tripods, while wanting better evidence for the stands (1997: 116–20).

LPG–G tombs at Lefkandi and Knossos and other mainly Cretan contexts, especially the Idaean cave, have produced decorated bowls that seem to be Syrian or Phoenician, other bowl types that may be Cypriot, and lotus-handled jugs that are Egyptian or Egyptianising Phoenician. On present evidence, the last are likely to be 'antiques', since the type was not made in Egypt after the New Kingdom (Carter 1998), but hardly 'heirlooms', for, as Whitley points out (2002: 226), this would require their being passed down in a family for exceptionally many generations between the times of their manufacture and burial. There are also rarer, generally late types which have Near Eastern parallels (Matthäus 1998, especially 128–9, 134–8; see also Hoffman 1997: 123–35). With these should be mentioned the remarkable collection of faience vessels from Lefkandi tombs dating near *c.* 900, probably Phoenician or Syrian work in an Egyptian tradition (Popham *et al.* 1982b: 242–5; see Figure 7.2).

The commonest type of bronze vessel that could have been locally produced is the simple hemispherical bowl (Figure 5.19: 2), which is very common in Cyprus but could easily have been adopted and produced in the Aegean as a ceremonial drinking vessel. After examples in the Tiryns Treasure and Salamis Submyc cemetery, they are not found again until contexts near the PG–G transition, especially at Athens and Knossos, but such a simple form could well have been produced continuously. Rare examples of other shapes are known, e.g. a skyphos from Knossos that seems to imitate the Attic PG shape (*NorthCem*: 566) and a small plain jug from Drepanon in Achaea (*AR* 20 (1973–74) 18 fig. 29) which may not be earlier than the eighth century. Both are simple forms that could well have been more common than these isolated finds suggest. Fragments of vessels, including a small handle, and of a possible stand have been identified at Nichoria (*Nichoria III*: 279–8, 308), but some identifications are tentative and their dating is rather insecure.

There is a case for arguing that cauldrons, with or without tripod legs, not only survived in the Aegean but continued to be manufactured in some places. Matthäus has suggested that a tripod cauldron found at Mycenae (Figure 5.19: 4) is of PG date (1980: 118–21). Its closest parallels are two clay imitations of cauldrons from Kerameikos PG T. 4 at Athens and a Cypro-Geometric I bronze example from T. 58 at Palaepaphos-Skales (Karageorghis 1982: 298). Catling has also noted the long life of the plain cauldron type, which surely derives from the LB cauldron tradition. This is well represented in the Tiryns Treasure (Figure 5.19: 3), but can be traced through an example from Tylissos that should date near 1000 to examples from Knossos and Eretria dating to later eighth- and early seventh-century contexts (*NorthCem*: 560). Clay imitations that could date well before the end of the ninth century, both of tripod cauldrons of this type and of legless cauldrons that faithfully preserve features noted on some Tiryns Treasure examples, have also been found in the Knossos North Cemetery (*NorthCem*: 372–3). While these forms may have been represented only by such clay imitations (which are very rare) and by BA survivals between the Tylissos cauldron and the ninth century, the possibility that they continued to be produced, especially in Crete, should not be ruled out, especially if this is accepted for rod tripods. Certainly, it seems likely that the development of the increasingly large bronze tripod cauldrons that are the most elaborate product of eighth-century metalworkers began no later than the second half of the ninth century. It has also been suggested, on the basis of evidence from Eleutherna, that the famous 'shields' of the type best known from the Idaean Cave were actually cauldron lids (Stampolidis 1998: 181–3).

Figurines

Bronze figurines were not a feature of Mycenaean culture. The few found in Mycenaean contexts are undoubtedly of Near Eastern origin and may, as suggested by the contexts of examples associated with the Phylakopi shrines, be entirely of Postpalatial date. But in Crete there is some evidence that small solid-cast figurines of cattle and perhaps humans were dedicated at various ritual sites in the Third Palace Period, and it is often believed that this tradition continued unbroken through the EIA, although this cannot be demonstrated from stratified contexts. In the most recent study, three bronze cattle from Ayia Triada are thought possibly LM IIIC-SM, but the majority, including humans (all male?), animals (mostly cattle), a winged human-headed quadruped, and two wheels that may come from a model chariot, are probably to be dated between PG B and Early Orientalising (D'Agata 1999a: 48, 166–70). At present there is little evidence to suggest that this Cretan tradition had any influence elsewhere in the Aegean, where the development of bronze figurines could have begun in the ninth century but is likely to have been mainly a feature of the eighth. It could well be related to the growing interest in representations of human and animal figures that seems to have been inspired by Near Eastern imports.

Figurines were used almost exclusively as sanctuary dedications, and as a result they are not often found in stratified contexts, and their dating owes much to hypothesis. New excavations at Olympia have produced pottery evidence that the ashy stratum that represents the earliest cult activity here is likely to go back to the tenth and even eleventh century (Eder 2001), but the material from this stratum has a considerable range, and it is unlikely that any of the clay figurines are as early as the pottery. The earliest-looking bronzes (Schweitzer 1971: figs. 117–23) may derive inspiration from the clay tradition, although bronzes from Ayia Triada dated to PG B are not wholly dissimilar (see D'Agata 1999a: 167; Figure 5.20: 2). They are so primitive-looking as to seem the first local attempts in a new craft (Figure 5.20: 3). The leaving of casting sprues on the feet is a feature that can be paralleled in

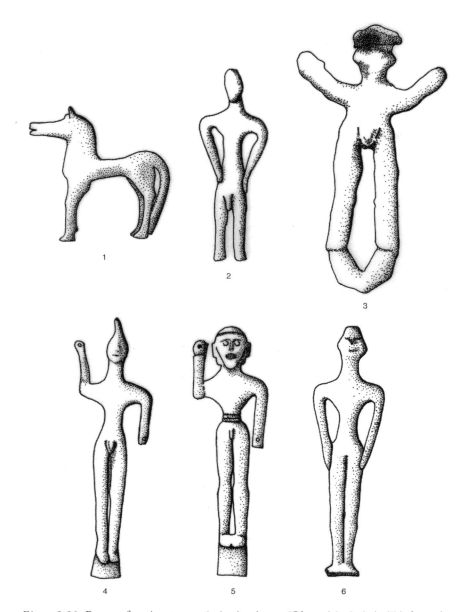

Figure 5.20 Bronze figurine types: 1 Argive horse (Olympia); 2 Ayia Triada male, dated end of PG B; 3 Olympia male (god?), pre-800?; 4 Corinthian warrior/horse-leader, LG (Olympia); 5 Argive warrior/horse-leader, LG (Olympia); 6 Corinthian female (goddess?), LG (Delphi) (1 after Coldstream 1977, fig. 48 right; 2 after D'Agata 1999, pl. 103: E1.5; 3–6 after Schweitzer 1971, figs 118, 126, 136, 130). Scale 1:2.

Near Eastern practice, apparently to allow fixing to a base, but is very rare in Crete (cf. Hoffman 1997: 115), which may indicate the source of the crafts-men or at least the technology. The tentative dating of these pieces before 800 may receive some confirmation from two bronze fragments of what may be a figurine base and animal tail from Nichoria, which could well be of ninth-century date (*Nichoria III*: 282, 308; these are from mixed lots, cf. 193 (Section J), but a DA II dating is the latest likely). A primitive human figure modelled in clay, set on a base or lid, from Toumba T. 38 at Lefkandi, dated SPG II-IIIA and so in the middle to late ninth century (Popham *et al.* 1982b: 232–3, pl. 29e), also has stylistic resemblances to the earliest-looking Olympia pieces.

Although the earliest looking bronze figurines from Olympia have features in common with the terracotta examples that may represent deities (Figure 8.4: 4, 7), the warrior/horse-leader and standing, originally naked female types soon became the commonest humanoid forms (Figure 5.20: 4–6). The horse predominated among animal figurines on the mainland (Figure 5.20: 1), although bulls and birds were quite common also, but cattle were most popular in Crete, to judge from Ayia Triada. Various kinds of group are known, but these may all date very late, even past 700. Although many were evidently made to be self-standing, others were intended to be attached to the rims and handles of the great tripod cauldrons mentioned in the previous section, and so must be contemporary with these. At present it seems as if in the eighth century there were several local schools of figurine-making in the Peloponnese and another in Athens, but elsewhere they are rare.

Weapons, armour and implements

Another class of items, whose associations are also linked to status and are prominent in tradition (that is, those which have to do with warfare), shows notable changes. Even in the later LBA, weapons had become generally plain, lacking the elaborate ornament and fittings found on many early LB swords, daggers, and sometimes spearheads, but in the Postpalatial Period there seems to have been a revival of the tendency to decorate swords, both with cast ribs or channels on the blade and with ornamental hilts. These features can be found on several Type F and G weapons in Postpalatial graves (a sword from Hexalophos T. A even has a small gold band round the hilt, as does an accompanying knife), and the earliest iron knives and daggers are normally provided with ivory or bone hilt-plates fastened with bronze rivets, surely responding to a wish for display. Surprisingly, the fine Type II bronze swords rarely show such features, although their sheaths might be decorated (see Papazoglou-Manioudaki 1994: 181–2 for a clear example from Achaea; Figure 5.21: 1; also possible parallels there and in Cephallenia).

This may well indicate that the iron items are imports, while the bronze swords are locally made, for with the full transition to iron weapons,

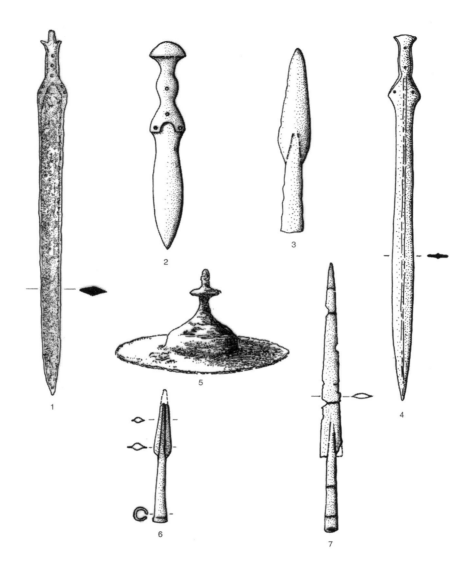

Figure 5.21 Weapon types: 1 bronze Type II sword, LH IIIC (Krini, Achaea); 2 iron dagger, SMyc (Athens); 3 iron spearhead, PG (Athens); 4 iron sword, SPG I–II (Lefkandi); 5 bronze shield boss, Submyc (Tiryns); 6 iron spearhead, EG I (Athens); 7 iron pike, probably eighth century (Fortetsa) (1 after *BSA* 89 (1994) 178 fig. 4; 2–4 after Lemos 2002, figs 5: 10, 2 and 4: 1; 5–7 after Snodgrass [1971] 2000, figs 77, 84 top centre, and 94 right). Scale 1:4.

presumably local products in most cases, this tendency seems largely to disappear. Ivory hilt-plates are found on only one full sword, of LPG date, from Lefkandi, Toumba T. 26, and only in Crete does it remain common to find bronze rivets, quite often with bone hilt-plates (Kilian-Dirlmeier 1993: 107–9). Several of the smaller blades also have midribs, which seem intended to strengthen the blade. Spear and javelin heads are even more consistently plain.

The only other potential area of display for the warrior is defensive armour, but after the bronze helmet-facings from the Tiryns Submyc 'warrior grave' nothing can be identified except for the bronze 'phalara', which appear rarely in Postpalatial and very early EIA contexts, then again from LPG onwards, being particularly abundant at early sanctuaries (Figure 5.21: 5). While there seems no doubt that these could be used as belt attachments, the argument that some were shield-bosses remains plausible (see most recently *NorthCem*: 522–4). The ancient BA helmet-type plated with boar's tusk did not outlast the Postpalatial Period, possibly reflecting a scarcity of the material as well as a loss of skill. Helmets could of course have been decorated impressively with non-metallic horns, plumes, etc., such as are depicted on Postpalatial figured vases. But, if this tradition continued, it seems to have been the one area, apart from the possession of fine metal weapons and perhaps the use of the chariot, in which the status associations of warfare might be commonly demonstrated.

As well as being plain, EIA weapons and implements were notably homogeneous. Snodgrass's account of the Knossos North Cemetery ironwork (*NorthCem*: 596) is typical. Generally, in each class one form is dominant over the whole period, even more so if purely eighth-century forms such as the one-edged sword are ignored. Iron swords, dirks and daggers are all variants of the Type II form (Figure 5.21: 2–3). The noticeable variations often seem to reflect local traditions, so that Kilian-Dirlmeier's Type 3 weapons are exclusively Cretan, while Type 2 is a long-lived and mainly Athenian form. Really long swords, ranging up to 90 cm in length and occasionally decorated with ribbing, bone or ivory hilt-plates, or bronze rivets, can date as early as LPG and seem to be a specifically mainland feature, especially prominent at Athens, while shorter forms were definitely preferred in Crete.

Similarly, iron spearheads generally conform to a fairly long-socketed, round-shouldered shape with curving edges, but Cretan examples have distinctive squared shoulders and straighter edges (Figure 5.21: 4, 6–7, *NorthCem*: 580–1; Snodgrass 1964: 126–7). Where the blade is slender, or tapers evenly to the point instead of widening a little way down the blade, or is small in proportion to the socket, Snodgrass argues that it should be identified as a javelin head (1964: 137–8, *NorthCem*: 581, 582), although many javelin heads identified at Knossos are over 30 cm long, which would seem large for a throwing weapon and exceeds that of many items identified as spearheads from the mainland (*NorthCem*: 581–3; cf. *Lefkandi I*: 254–6).

What Snodgrass identifies as spearheads have a range of around 30–45 cm at Knossos, and some mainland spearheads are as large or larger, especially in G phases, although shorter ones are still found.

These variations between Crete and the mainland could indicate different styles of warfare, depending on whether the spear or sword was used as the primary thrusting weapon, but it seems very likely that many 'spearheads' were attached to weapons that could be used equally for throwing or thrusting, as suggested by the Homeric evidence and the G and early Archaic representations of warriors carrying two spears (cf. Snodgrass 1964: 138). Representations of spears being thrown in fact go back as far as the unique Kynos LH IIIC kraters showing sea battles (Wedde 1999: 473, pl. LXXXVIII, A4–6).

Other metal types are not represented frequently enough for any conclusions on development or local preferences to be sound. The commonest are iron axes, which can appear in single-bladed, double-bladed, or trunnion axe form, often in association with 'warrior' burials which can also include groups of iron spits (*obeloi*). It is implausible that they were weapons, given the concentration of the epic tradition and G depictions upon swords and spears, but it is likely that they carry some status-related symbolism, like the iron spits and plausibly also the bronze graters found in some Lefkandi graves (on graters see Popham *et al.* 1982b: 240–1; Ridgway 1997). Iron arrowheads are better represented than when Snodgrass surveyed them (1964: 144–56), for examples of his Types 2 and 5 have been found in Lefkandi graves (see *Lefkandi III*, pl. 148g–h), as well as a new form at Knossos (*NorthCem*: 584), but the total number of occurrences is still small. Other iron forms, listed on p. 149, are known from even fewer finds, and mainly have significance as evidence for the varying range of items produced in iron by the ninth century. Occasional bronze items found at sites where iron had become established for weapons and tools may sometimes be contemporary products, like a bronze spear from the Knossos North Cemetery which imitates an iron shape (*NorthCem*: 571), that may have been made purely for burial or dedication, but in most cases are more likely to be BA survivals, or recycled from tomb robbery.

Dress and jewellery

Dress, particularly women's dress, and jewellery form an area in which the archaeological material has long been thought to show marked change between the LBA and the EIA. There are indeed some notable changes, especially the virtual disappearance of beads and, in most regions, of what have commonly been described as steatite whorls or buttons but are more likely to be clothing-weights or attachments (Iakovidis 1977; Hughes Brock 1999: 280–1). But traditionally most emphasis has been laid on the supposed change from sewn and buttoned Mycenaean and Minoan dress to pinned 'Dark Age' dress, which has often been given cultural significance. For the pinned dress, imagined to consist of a blanketlike length of material sewn along one or both sides, perhaps folded over at the top like the later Greek peplos, and pinned at both shoulders, has been related to evidence for pinned dress in central Europe (e.g. Hood and Coldstream 1968: 214–18) and argued to be introduced by a new ethnic group, usually identified as the Dorians.

But this interpretation has been disputed for some time (cf. Snodgrass 1971: 226–8, following Deshayes), and in her survey of Peloponnesian pins Kilian-Dirlmeier has argued a case for a continuous tradition of pin use on the mainland from MH times (1984: 31–65, 296–7). She accepts that these may sometimes have been worn in the hair, like elaborate Aegean pins (Higgins 1980: 62), but argues that they could also have pinned shrouds or funeral dress and that this should reflect some real use in life. The reported Hittite liking for wearing one or two bronze pins at the shoulders of a dress (Macqueen 1986: 100) could be cited as a possible parallel and potential influence. In Kilian-Dirlmeier's view, the apparent increase in the numbers of pins in late Postpalatial and EIA times simply reflects the change from multiple to single burial in tombs, which would allow pins to survive in good condition more frequently (1984: 81–2).

Her case for continuity is strengthened by the similarity of the ribbed decoration, knobbed heads and swellings on the earliest EIA metal pins, especially her Type A (Desborough's Type B, 1972: 297; see Figure 5.22: 1–2), to the decoration of many LH and even MH bone pins, which provide more plausible parallels than the Near Eastern examples cited by Deshayes (see Kilian-Dirlmeier 1984: 68). However, her postulated derivation of her Type B pins (Desborough's Type A) from Mycenaean pins with separate, sometimes globular heads (1984: 76) is less convincing, since none of these clearly shows the characteristic swelling or attachment some way down the shaft. In general, she argues forcefully against the idea that the use of pinned dress represents an intrusive foreign custom, pointing out that in most cases the earliest pins, even when found in pairs, were not created as a pair but differ very markedly in type and length, which suggests that the manner of wearing such pins only became standardised in the Aegean after a period of experimentation. This is not what one would expect if it was introduced by a population group among whom it was an established custom.

These are powerful arguments, but they fall short of proving that most Mycenaean pins were used as dress-fasteners, as opposed to being worn in the hair or in a head covering, as reports of finds near skulls suggest, and as might seem particularly appropriate for examples shorter than 10 cm. Only a few were reported as having been found on or near the shoulder, and none as having remains of cloth attached, in contrast with several EIA pins. Many of the best Mycenaean examples come from early contexts, whereas it is very hard to identify examples in contexts of the Third Palace Period until its

159

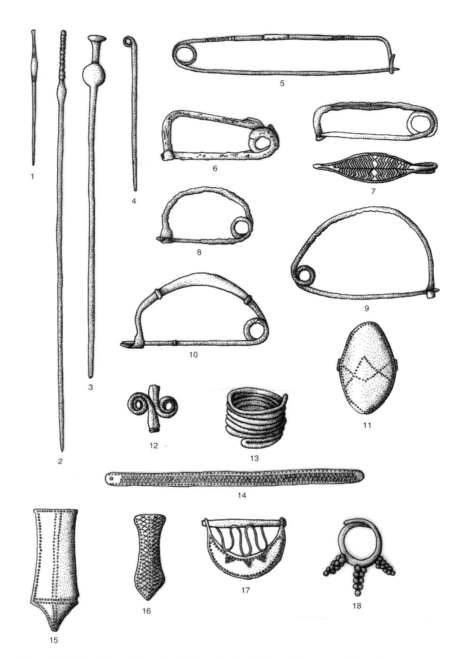

Figure 5.22 Early jewellery: 1–2 Type A pins (Elis and Argos), 3 Type B pin (Argos),
4 roll-top pin (Lefkandi), 5 violin-bow fibula (Mycenae), 6–7 stilted and
leaf-bow fibulae (Perati), 8–10 arched fibulae (Perati, Nea Ionia: Volos,
Elateia), 11 shield ring, 12 ring with spiral terminals (Nea Ionia: Volos),
13 double wire ring, 14 headband, 15–16 attachments, 17 pendant, 18
earring (14–18 all Lefkandi) (1 after Eder 2001, pl. 13a; 2–3 after
Deshayes 1966, pls 24: 3, 87: 6 top; 4, 16, 18 after *Lefkandi I*, pls 136:
11, 232g: right, 231d; 5 after K. Demakopoulou (ed.), *The Mycenaean
World* (1988) pl. 258; 6–8 after Iakovidis 1969, figs 121: M 229, M 108,
122: M 71; 9, 12 after Batziou-Efstathiou 1999, figs 27 and 25; 11, 13
after Desborough 1972, pl. 60c, e; 15, 17 after *Lefkandi III*, pls 138a,
136b). Scales: 1–10 (1:4), 11, 14–16 (1:2), 13, 17–18 (lifesize), 12 (over
lifesize).

final phase, LH IIIB2. Several of those cited by Kilian-Dirlmeier are certainly or plausibly Postpalatial, or not demonstrably earlier (including an undoubted pair from Mycenae T. 61 – see Figure 5.22: 5 – on which Kilian-Dirlmeier 1984: 65 places some emphasis), and most of the datable bone pins have a similar range. Also, Mycenaean frescoes give no hint of the existence of metal dress-fasteners, although here it might be objected that the frescoes only show members of the elite in ceremonial dress, and can give no reliable indication of what they or ordinary Mycenaeans might have worn every day. But given the very numerous excavations of Mycenaean settlement strata and tombs that were in use in the Third Palace Period, this lack of evidence should be taken seriously, particularly since Mycenaean single burials which might be expected to preserve pins in situ are not uncommon, in pits dug within chamber tombs or separately.

In sum, the argument that a form of pinned dress was common in Mycenaean times is not supported by sufficient evidence. But pins of some kind were certainly known, though more in the Peloponnese than further north (Donder 1999), and could have been adapted to new purposes late in the Mycenaean period. It needs emphasising how limited our sources of information are: once the EIA proper is reached, Athens, Lefkandi, Argos, Tiryns, Asine, Knossos and Iolkos have produced virtually all the useful material. It should also be noted that the rich range of ornaments found on female burials in the Vergina graves (well described in Snodgrass 1971: 253–4) and at Vitsa (Coldstream 1977: 186), which includes headgear, belt ornaments and even anklets, has relatively few links with Aegean material, though including types of pin and fibula. Other graves known to have material of this period have not been fully published or, as often in Crete, were used so frequently that burial groups have usually been thoroughly disturbed. Thus, it is only a hypothesis that similar customs to those attested at the productive sites were followed throughout the Aegean area. In fact, many EIA burials that are likely to be female are not provided with any kind of dress-fastener at all; even the rich female burial in the Lefkandi 'Heroön' had none on her body, although a collection of nine pins lay above her left thigh and a single iron pin above her right.

Dress-pins may in fact have begun to become fashionable in response to the appearance of the first fibulae, whose only function would be to fasten cloth. For, although few of the earliest form typologically, the violin-bow (Figure 5.22: 6), are closely datable, they clearly began appearing in the Aegean in the late Third Palace Period: at least two from Tiryns date before the destruction at the end of the period, one of a notably developed form (Kilian 1985: 152 – III B 3, V A 1, cf. 190), while the leaf-bow variant (Figure 5.22: 7) appears in Crete before the end of LM IIIB (Kilian 1985: 183–4, 191). The distribution of the violin-bow type, while having marked concentrations at Mycenae and Tiryns – which compares interestingly with the distribution of metal and bone pins – includes a wide scatter from the western side of Greece, which suggests that they were introduced through maritime links with Italy. Here early production is demonstrable, and although chronological priority to the Aegean is not assured, the relatively swift appearance of fibulae in Alpine areas and the northern Balkans is more easily explicable if this reflects influence from an Italian rather than Aegean source (the fringes of the Alps may indeed have been the region where fibulae and other supposedly 'northern' metal types, Type II swords, 'flame' spears, and long pins developed; Harding 2000). Many of the earliest, Postpalatial, examples in the Aegean and Cyprus may have been Italian products, as an unusual multiple-loop type found in a Cephallenian tomb and the Psychro cave in Crete surely must be (Kilian 1985: 171–3). But they are very varied, and may reflect production in several centres and the exchange of ideas and features by smiths over most of their region of popularity. This would explain the relatively swift development of variants and of the new arched shape, current well before the end of LH IIIC on the evidence of Tiryns and Perati (Mountjoy 1988: 23–4); this may even be an Aegean or Cypriot development (*NorthCem*: 525). It seems plausible that fibulae swiftly became fashionable as a new and exotic status symbol, but one that was relatively widely available. Surprisingly many of the earliest type come from settlement contexts, which suggests that they were already quite numerous.

Both pins and fibulae often occur singly in Postpalatial burial contexts, which suggests that they were used to pin cloaks, shawls, or funeral shrouds, but in PG graves they are often found in pairs, sometimes in larger groups. Here, though, we encounter a basic problem of interpretation. It has been commonly assumed that arrangements of pins in the grave represent the manner in which they were commonly worn in life to fasten a basic peplos (for an exception see Jacobsthal 1956: 109), but the difficulties of this view are seldom explored. Not only would fibulae be a far less cumbersome way of fastening dress than straight pins (and graves often do contain fibulae only), but some pins are so long (30–40 cm and more, e.g. Figure 5.22: 2) that wearing a pair for any length of time would surely have been uncomfortably constricting. Moreover, when found *in situ* in graves, pins are characteristically positioned with the point downwards and the head resting on or near the shoulder. This arrangement, while probably the most natural way to insert pins into wrappings on a prone body, would in life surely risk allowing the cloth to slide off the pin. The broad heads, attached globes, and swellings on the shaft that are found on most pins may well have been intended to prevent this, but they could only do so if the pin was inserted with point upwards, the position often found in European burials (cf. Kilian-Dirlmeier 1980: 253 fig. 52 and Piggott 1965: 105 fig. 58: 1, 3 – but on fig. 58: 2 the pins point downwards) and shown in Archaic vase paintings (Jacobsthal 1956: 106–9). The dress material is supposed to be sufficiently heavy to counteract any tendency for the pin to slip out; alternatively, the pins were actually placed more or less horizontally on the shoulder to counteract this tendency.

What then was the function of pins? It is unlikely that they were purely funerary, since examples have been found in settlement contexts at Karphi, Asine and Nichoria. Cases where pins and fibulae are found in graves together could be interpreted to suggest a style of dress in which pins were worn in the position generally found in graves, with head uppermost, because the fibulae provided the actual dress fastening. Thus, they could represent a form of ceremonial dress, suitable for a burial but only occasionally worn in life, in which pins would have been worn on an outer garment. It could then be suggested that, at its most basic, EIA women's dress consisted of a simple, presumably sewn, garment that did not need metal fasteners, but that an outer robe that did require to be fastened could be worn over this, and perhaps a cloak, shawl or veil as well.

The wearing of more than one layer of clothing, and of metal fasteners on the outer layer, would then be a sign of wealth and status, as might be expected (and as can be seen in the later Archaic kore statues, some of which preserve traces of metal fasteners at the shoulders; Jacobsthal 1956: 105). The presence of multiple dress-fasteners, both pins and fibulae, in rich graves might reflect the remains of such elaborate dress (Hundt identified the remains of two different garments, one of light scarflike material, on one Tiryns pin; see Kilian-Dirlmeier 1984: 303). But equally, in many cases such arrangements could simply represent a show made for the burial, in which most or all that the dead person possessed, or, if a child, might have expected to possess in adulthood, was fastened to the dress or shroud. Indeed, often enough, as in the 'Heroön', a collection of dress jewellery was simply placed among the grave-goods, not even in a potentially functional position. The possibility that the longest pins were used to secure shrouds is strengthened by the case of T. 57 in the Iolkos: Nea Ionia cemetery, where two were placed diagonally across the upper body (Batziou-Efstathiou 1999: 119 fig. 7, 120), but the fact that these fastenings are mainly found in likely female burials, and not all of those, shows that this was not a universal practice.

The general impression given by the finds is of early variety, that may reflect a desire to display exotic forms, followed by the establishment of a more standardised range, typical of PG graves, in which indications of local traditions can be detected. Thus, massively long pins seem to be a particular feature of Athens and the Argolid, and are occasionally found elsewhere, but not at Lefkandi or Knossos. Often these are of Kilian-Dirlmeier's Type B (Desborough's Type A), with a disc-head and usually globular swelling some way down the shaft (Figure 5.22: 3); many combine an iron shaft with bronze globe (Type B3). This variant was equally popular at Athens, Argos and Tiryns, so can no longer be thought specifically Athenian, but at Lefkandi it is notably rare. Some examples, especially in the Argolid, had an attachment of bone or ivory instead of bronze.

Pins with ivory or bone heads at the end of the shaft and no swelling or attachment are also found, notably in a SM grave near Knossos, and versions of Kilian-Dirlmeier's Type A, with an oval swelling down the shaft, usually flanked by ribbing or grooving (Figure 5.22: 1–2), are particularly common in northern and central Greece, though also found at Athens, in the Peloponnese and at Knossos. At Lefkandi there seems to be a local undecorated variant of this type, which demonstrates that it had a longer life than used to be thought. Others that fit neither of these types occur sporadically, especially the roll-top pin (Figure 5.22: 4), which has a long history in the Aegean and Near East (a new example is reported from a LH IIIB context at Elateia; Dakoronia *et al.* 1996: xix). Lefkandi has also produced several examples of pins, usually iron, with disc-like heads but no attached globe, which are often gilded and combined with fibulae and other dress jewellery.

Fibulae vary comparably, with no obvious patterns in the distribution, except their remarkable rarity in the PG graves of the Kerameikos (but not the Agora) at Athens, also of Argos, Tiryns and Asine. The violin-bow, leaf-bow and arched types (Figure 5.22: 5–10) can all be identified widely in the Aegean area. Within the broad groupings, fibulae were variously ornamented almost from the start, through making the bow of twisted wire, introducing angles or knobs into its shape, and decorating it with incised patterns. As with the pins, it seems to have taken time for more standard forms to appear and pairs to be made (Kilian 1985: 189). A sequence has been detected at Elateia, where relatively many have been found, in which the violin-bow form which has a bow of twisted wire appeared in LH IIIC Middle, to be succeeded as the commonest form by the leaf-bow type, and then in Submyc by the arched type, which seems to develop naturally from the progressive raising of the bow (Dakoronia 2003). By this time fibulae were commonly found in pairs or larger groups, sometimes mixing different types; but single examples, which may have pinned cloaks or shawls, continue to be found on the left shoulder or chest, including with male burials (cf. *AR* 34 (1987–88) 13, a PG warrior burial from Marathon).

Pairs of fibulae are usually found at or near the shoulders, and at Lefkandi are quite often combined with pins. The disposition of goods at Lefkandi also suggests more complex arrangements, including a third fibula on the chest, several arranged across or down the body as if to fasten a dress or shroud, even one or more around the head to hold a veil or other head-covering (Catling 1985). Even the simplest of these arrangements is hard to match in early graves at other sites, and although the Lefkandi arrangements are outstanding in their generosity with metal items it cannot be assumed that the more complex faithfully reflect any style of dress in life. Equally, there is no reason why extra fibulae should not have been worn ornamentally.

Pins and fibulae were not, however, the only forms of early metal jewellery. In fact, finger-rings of metal wire or sheet were much commoner than either: for instance, one or more rings were found in seventy of the Athenian tombs classified as Submyc (including Desborough's EPG) in Styrenius (1967), whereas pins and/or fibulae appeared in barely half this number.

The wearing of rings seems to have begun increasing in popularity in the Postpalatial Period, when it is represented especially by the mainly silver rings of Perati, but examples in gold, silver and bronze are found elsewhere (Papazoglou-Manioudaki 1994: 185). The first iron examples appear in Submyc graves, but the majority of earlier EIA rings are of bronze. They are often found *in situ*, usually only one or two on each hand, but sometimes in larger numbers, even more than one to a finger. This might represent simply the emptying of the dead person's jewellery box. They are not confined to women's and children's burials, but can be found on men, at least in early phases, as with the warrior burials at Tiryns and Marathon (see p. 164).

There are many variants, but few really distinctive forms. Many are simple broad or narrow bands of sheet or twists of wire, sometimes decorated by ribbing, that hardly seem to require any foreign inspiration, although Cypriot influence has been claimed (*Lefkandi I*: 221; Lemos 2002: 133 notes similarities in types and working techniques). More notable but less common are two types that occur early, the 'shield rings', which have an oval bezel, usually decorated with a simple dot repoussé pattern, and are widely thought to derive from the BA seal-rings (Figure 5.22: 11), and the rings with spiral terminals (Figure 5.22: 12), which belong to the group of items often supposed to have a 'northern' origin. Kilian-Dirlmeier (1980) has opposed this view, pointing to the chronological gap between the European Tumulus Culture examples and those from Greece, and suggests a local origin. But after the Shaft Grave era ornaments involving wire spirals are not part of the Mycenaean tradition, whereas this is a marked feature of European bronze-work (Harding 1984: 203, see 141–2 on the rings), and the distribution has a distinct bias to the central and northern mainland, enhanced by new finds (one from Megaplatanos: Sventza in Locris apparently has a LH IIIB context; Ph. Dakoronia, pers. comm.). Many come from the Elateia cemetery, where more have been found, from LH IIIC Late onwards, than in the rest of Greece put together (Dakoronia 2003). It seems more likely that this type was originally European, although, given the considerable variety between examples, some may have been made in Greece. But its occurrences are too sporadic to be given great cultural significance, and after its appearances in late Mycenaean and early EIA contexts it is not found in southern Greece until Geometric times, though occurring at Vergina.

The only other common metal finds are the widespread circlets and spiral twists of wire, normally of bronze or even gold (Figure 5.22: 13), thought to have been worn in the hair or as earrings. There are also some wire bracelets, and the rare wheel-shaped ornaments found in certain Postpalatial contexts at Argos and Knossos (where the object may have been the head of a wooden pin) are worth mentioning for their Italian links (*NorthCem*: 526–8). The typical LB steatite items identified as clothing weights can still be found, presumably reused items passed on in the family or recovered from older tombs. Found in ones and twos, they may have been used as decorative belt tags and the like (cf. especially Volos: Nea Ionia Ts. 177 and 197, where they are found by the knees; Batziou-Efstathiou 1999: 122–3), though use as spindle whorls is not ruled out (E.S. Sherratt, pers. comm.). At Elateia alone they are reported in quantity, but like the steatite necklaces and pendants found here (Dimaki 1999) these may be of Postpalatial manufacture and reused later (as argued for a steatite seal and necklace found with PG burials in Elateia T. 58 by S. Deger-Jalkotzy in an unpublished paper; cf. Dimaki 1999: 206). As has been suggested in relation to the sealstones (Chapter 3, p. 73), this probably represents a localised Postpalatial industry, which, together with the evidence for reuse, is quite exceptional, although old sealstones were sometimes recovered and reburied elsewhere, especially at Knossos.

One of the great surprises of EIA jewellery is the general scarcity of beads (Higgins 1980: 75), even of humble materials like clay and bone, which implies that necklaces were rarely worn, though the beads and other pendants or 'amulets' which are occasionally found in ones and twos were probably worn strung around the neck. The contrast with sites beyond the 'Helladic' area is remarkable: at Vergina the rich ornamental tradition includes beads of bronze and what was reported as amber, actually sard (carnelian) (Snodgrass 1971: 253–4; Coldstream 1977: 45), and at Elaphotopos (probably post-LB) chalcedony, amber and tiny bronze beads are reported. Beads of amber, faience, and semi-precious stones like carnelian and rock crystal are indeed reported from LH IIIC contexts, some perhaps 'recycled' from burials of earlier date, but in general the number of occurrences dwindles over the Postpalatial Period, though there is plausible evidence for the continued manufacture of gold beads in simple shapes to its end. These occur in four sets of different sizes from the Tiryns Treasure, surely too many to be interpreted purely as hoarded survivals, also in a necklace of globular beads combined with incised steatite ones from Elateia (*BCH* 120 (1996) 1202), and in two types, which Higgins suggests are Cypriot-inspired, from the SM T. 200 from Knossos (*NorthCem*: 539). The Knossos tomb also contains glass and faience beads (*NorthCem*: 193–4). But beads of gold or any other metal are lacking thereafter until the female burial in the Lefkandi 'Heroön', where thirty-nine globular gold beads are combined with two of faience and one of crystal in a necklace with a damaged antique Mesopotamian gold pendant as centrepiece. This necklace seems an early example of a liking for contrasts of colours and materials which seems particularly typical of Lefkandi, but may be a general feature of the period, seen at its simplest in the fitting of globes of different materials on iron pins (see p. 163). In the rich Lefkandi graves that follow, gold beads remain rare, though examples found are often elaborate (see Figure 5.23).

In contrast, segmented faience beads are common at Lefkandi (the earliest come from Skoubris T. 16, put at the transition between Submyc and PG), and can be found in hundreds, even thousands. These are surely Near Eastern imports, like the much rarer glass beads often found with them, and are found in a whole range of colours. Amber and crystal beads, whose origin is less clear, can appear with them. Faience beads also appear in small numbers in PG graves in the Argolid, but not before EG in Athens, on current evidence. In general, where small groups of beads are found they are plausibly interpretable as elements of necklaces, though strings could have been worn around the wrist or arm. But it remains uncertain whether the much larger groupings could represent garments to which they were sewn, or multi-strand bands that formed massive chest-covering necklaces or were worn like belts. Just as probably, they were simply deposited as a sign of wealth and status, as the marked variations in numbers between different graves might suggest.

The 'Heroön' burial also provides the earliest examples of a distinctive Lefkandi tradition, dress ornaments of gold sheet or foil: two discs were found over the breasts with a lunate shape between them, all decorated with patterns in repoussé dots or lines. Smaller disc ornaments have been found in LPG graves at Lefkandi and also on Skyros. The latter have long been thought to be Mycenaean survivals, but implausibly, since their closest parallels are of the Shaft Graves phase and considerably more complex in style. It is easier to attribute them to a Lefkandi school of goldwork whose existence is amply attested by other finds in graves there from LPG onwards and from Skyros, which has close cultural relations with Euboea at this time (cf. generally *Lefkandi III, 1*: pls 136–8, 157; Lemos 2002: 133–4). Most notable are the peculiarly shaped 'attachments' and long rectangular bands, generally identified as headbands (but found on the head or face and on the chest in Skyros graves; Sapouna-Sakellaraki 1997: 40), both often decorated with patterns of repoussé dots (Figure 5.22: 14–16). The headbands may derive ultimately from Cyprus (Higgins in *Lefkandi I*: 219), but the attachments remain without parallel. They seem from evidence in Toumba Ts. 39 and 42 to have been attached to the headbands by gold foil ribbons to form complex head-dresses (Popham *et al.* 1982b: 236). Early types of pendants and earrings that are better represented in the SPG graves (Figure 5.22: 17–18) also appear, some decorated with simple granulation. This technique is generally thought to have been reintroduced to the Aegean from the Near East, but is not found elsewhere before the mid-ninth century. Toumba T. 63 also contained a set of remarkable tubular beads with attached wire spirals (Figure 5.23 – part of a complex arrangement of ornaments worn on the upper body, to judge from *Lefkandi III, 1*: pl. 19).

Although many of the sheet or foil ornaments and rings are relatively flimsy, it is hard to believe that such an array of items, often decorated, was manufactured purely for ornamenting dead bodies (as Higgins argues for headbands, 1980: 96), unless they were deliberately flimsy copies of much sturdier items worn in life. This is possible, but they could also represent items reserved for special ceremonial occasions, and so unlikely to be subject to much wear and tear. The rings are certainly carefully made (*Lefkandi I*: 221), but the attachments can seem unfinished (Popham *et al.* 1982b: 236).

Figure 5.23 LPG gold necklace with pendant from Lefkandi: Toumba T. 63. L. *c.* 9.9 cm. Courtesy of the British School at Athens.

Whatever the explanation, this array is currently without parallel in the Aegean before the end of the tenth century. Only Knossos has produced any significant pre-900 goldwork (Desborough 1972: 229–30), and this makes a meagre show by comparison. Gold is also uncommon in Cyprus, which shares a 'sense of economy' with Lefkandi in the use of very thin sheet plate (Lemos 2002: 133). Thus, the important dead of Lefkandi were buried with unparalleled ostentation in the later decades of the tenth century, which may well reflect the wearing of more elaborate dress in life, perhaps under the influence of closer contacts with the Near East than other parts of Greece, even Knossos, enjoyed.

In the ninth century, there was no essential change in the style of dress, to judge from the finds, although fibulae are more commonly found in the Kerameikos graves and the more complex arrangements of ornaments hypothesised for Lefkandi earlier now have some parallels elsewhere (e.g. Kilian-Dirlmeier 1984: 160–2). Pins and fibulae were made to be more substantial and elaborate. The former now had shanks that were square or rectangular for much of their length, unlike the earlier round-shanked types, and the bows and plates of fibulae were made larger and more decorative. Some leading regions developed individual styles: the finest pins were made in the north Peloponnese, with increasingly elaborate heads (Figure 5.24: 1–2), while new types of fibulae seem to have been developed particularly in the Attica-Euboea region, provided with even more elaborate knobs and

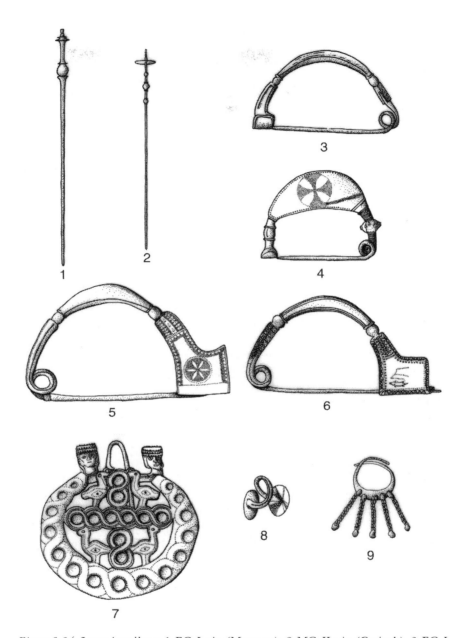

Figure 5.24 Later jewellery: 1 EG I pin (Mycenae), 2 MG II pin (Corinth), 3 EG I fibula (Mycenae), 4–5 SPG II and III fibulae (Lefkandi), 6 EG II/MG I fibula (Athens), 7 PG B pendant (Knossos), 8–9 LPG/SPG and SPG IIIA earrings (Lefkandi) (1, 3, 6 after Snodgrass [1971] 2000, figs 92(a), 91(a); 2 after Coldstream 1977, fig. 27c; 4–5 after *Lefkandi I*, pls 249: 5, 4; 7 after *BSA* 92 (1967) pl. 11: 2; 8–9 after *Lefkandi III*, pl. 136f, d). Scales: 1–6 (1:4), 7 (1:2), 8–9 (3:2).

ribbing and enlarged flat bows or square catchplates which could be decorated with patterns, animals, even figured scenes (Figure 5.24: 3–6). The square-catchplate form was to spread widely and produce local variants, while other local traditions that can be seen to be well established in the eighth century, such as the fibula with globes on the bow found in Crete and later in the east Aegean, were probably being developed in the ninth.

Surprisingly, in Crete the pins and fibulae mostly remained simple and undeveloped, but a new type of short pin with elaborately moulded head was made at Knossos in gold, silver and bronze, and before 800 a workshop was established here producing very sophisticated gold items, especially pendants (Figure 5.24: 7), decorated with Near Eastern techniques of filigree, granulation, and inlays of amber and rock crystal (Higgins 1969: 150–1; *NorthCem*: 540). However, although the products of different regions were beginning to circulate, only one piece outside Crete, from Ithaca, can be linked to this workshop. In Thessaly, northern types, particularly the spectacle fibula, can be found at some sites, a development which has been linked, along with the appearance of Macedonian types of pottery, to local population movements (cf. Coldstream 1977: 43–5); but the spectacle fibula was to become widespread in central Greece also.

The material of most pins and fibulae continued to be bronze, but gold also began to be used for fibulae, mainly the square-catchplate type, at Lefkandi and in Attica, also for other items, especially elaborate earrings, which are predominantly of types that can be linked with the Near East (Higgins 1969: 148–9). The most ornate of these ornaments are found in Attica, where a tradition of headbands like those of Lefkandi, but decorated with geometric patterns and (in the eighth century) animal and human themes, was also established from the mid-ninth century, but without any trace of Lefkandi-style attachments. In fact, the jewellers working in the territory of Athens seem to have taken the lead from those of Euboea by *c.* 800, although Euboean evidence is largely lacking after the Lefkandi cemeteries go out of use, until the rich late eighth-century graves from Eretria. But the Athenian jewellers had no discernible influence elsewhere in the Aegean, any more than the Knossian jewellers of the 'Tekke School' did. There was still nothing so elaborate in the Argolid, where gold items remained extremely rare and simple, although there was very fine bronze-work, and there is little trace even of advanced bronzes in other parts of Greece where any material has been found. But the discovery of an elaborate necklace of bronze and glass beads in a grave at Gavalou in Locris (*AR* 33 (1986–87) 27), which may be ninth or even tenth century in date, suggests that more elaborate types may have been current than is evident at present.

To some extent, it seems that by this time new types of ornament were being used to demonstrate wealth and status, especially headbands and earrings. Some necklaces, bracelets, more substantial spiral ornaments worn in the hair, and fine finger-rings with bezels are also known, and seals of ivory and stone begin to appear in the eighth century. But these represent essentially localised traditions which rarely had wide influence, although variants of the square-catchplate fibula spread over much of the Greek world and a type of earring with conical or cymbal-like terminals, first found around the end of LPG at Lefkandi (Figure 5.24: 8), also spread more widely in the ninth and eighth centuries. The crescent-shaped 'Eleusis Group' earrings found in Attica (Higgins 1969: 145–6) also have a Lefkandi predecessor (Figure 5.24: 9).

The forms traditionally associated with dress also continued. Fibulae, mainly bronze, are popular grave-goods in a variety of forms for the rest of the EIA, but pins only occur commonly in the Peloponnese, and the most elaborate forms were now beginning to be dedicated in sanctuaries, which also become a major source of fibulae and sometimes of other jewellery items. But during the eighth century there seems to have been a movement away from the practice of providing elaborate metal jewellery as grave-goods in places where it had been customary, only partly compensated for by its occurrence in new regions such as Epirus, on the edge of the Greek world, and the east Aegean, especially Rhodes (Coldstream 1977: 96–7, 186, 250). From then it becomes harder to trace the history of forms, old or new.

Bibliography

Dickinson (1994a: ch. 5) surveys BA crafts, particularly the more elaborate, and includes comments on Postpalatial developments.

Pottery

(1) LH IIIC and Submyc. Rutter (1978) provided the first real updating of the studies by Desborough (especially 1964: ch. 1, and 1972: 30–45). See also Rutter (1992: 62–7) and Mountjoy (1986: chs 8–11) (which concentrate on the central mainland; for briefer accounts with more information on other regions see Mountjoy 1993: 90–117). There are brief but useful comments in Sherratt (1982: 187–9, 1985) and Morgan (1999: 254–6) on Submyc.

(2) LM IIIC and SM. A useful outline of LM IIIC is given in Popham (1967: 349–51), and there is much information in Kanta (1980: ch. 4), and in papers in Hallager and Hallager (1997 – see especially Mook and Coulson, Rethemiotakis, Borgna, Prokopiou, and general comments on 405–6). A stratigraphical sequence continuing into SM at Knossos is discussed in Warren (1983: 69–83). On SM see particularly Desborough (1972: 57–63) and *NorthCem* (ch. 5).

(3) PG. Lemos (2002: ch. 2) supersedes the classic accounts in Desborough (1952, and 1972, Section III); the most succinct up-to-date account of the decorated pottery is Boardman (1998: ch. 2). *Lefkandi II, 1* provides the most

complete account of a large deposit published so far and much information on the PG styles in many parts of Greece.

(4) G. Coldstream (1968) is the classic survey of the decorated styles, most recently summarised and updated in Boardman (1998: ch. 3).

(5) The material published in Papadopoulos (2003) includes good evidence for the working practices of EIA Athenian potters.

Metalworking

On the early working of iron, see papers in Wertime and Muhly (1980), especially those by the editors, also Snodgrass (1980b), Waldbaum (1980, 1982), Sherratt (1994), Pickles and Peltenburg (1998), and for a recent view of the Anatolian material Yalçın (1999). Snodgrass ([1971] 2000: 213–17) offers one of the clearest discussions of technical factors. Lemos (2002: 101–3) provides an up-to-date summary, though without some references cited above. Kayafa (2000) provides a valuable survey of evidence relating to bronze-working.

Metal vessels

On the early material see Matthäus (1980: especially 35–8 (Mouliana T. A), 56–8 (Tiryns Treasure), 118–21 ('PG' tripod cauldrons)), and on the Knossos material *NorthCem* (559–69), which cites comparable material from elsewhere in the Crete and the Aegean.

Bronze figurines

Schweitzer (1971: ch. VI) gives a very detailed discussion, but the dating is surely too high; see Coldstream (1977: Part II, under the relevant regions), and on Olympia (Heilmeyer 1979), on the Cretan material (Naumann 1976; Verlinden 1984; D'Agata 1999a). The last fully publishes the Ayia Triada material and queries some previous datings.

Weapons, armour and implements

Lemos (2002: 119–26) is an up-to-date survey of PG weapons and armour.

Jewellery

Higgins (1969, and 1980: chs 11–12) is basic; for pins specifically see Kilian-Dirlmeier (1984). Lemos (2002: ch. 3) gives a valuable discussion of the various classes of jewellery, centring on the PG material.

Cloth

For the latest discussion see *NorthCem* (ch. 15), which centres on the Knossos North Cemetery material; also *Lefkandi I* (227–9) for finds from the Lefkandi cemeteries.

6

BURIAL CUSTOMS

Introduction

Graves and the material from them provide the greater part of our information about the whole period covered by this book, from the Collapse onwards. Traditionally their evidence has been used mainly in discussing whether types of burial and artefact, as reflected in the grave-goods, are evidence for the supposed movement of population groups into or within the Aegean in this period, and in estimating the relative wealth, external connections, and sometimes population size of the communities to which the graves belong. More recent attempts to utilise analyses of cemeteries and grave-goods to throw light on processes of social development, particularly at Athens, during the EIA (Morris 1987; Whitley 1991a) represent a welcome change from old preoccupations, but have produced some highly critical reactions, which indicate that these studies are vulnerable to criticism on methodological grounds, quite apart from critics' doubts about the appropriateness of their theoretical approaches and the historical conclusions drawn (see Papadopoulos 1993 generally, especially 187–8 for citations of reviewers' criticisms of Morris, and reviews of Whitley by Shennan in *Antiquity* 66 (1992) 276–7, Morgan in *JHS* 113 (1993) 206–7, and Morris in *AJA* 91 (1995) 157–9). Nevertheless, they raise important questions about the significance of changing patterns of funerary ritual in different periods and regions, and Morris has focused attention on what is one of the most fundamental questions in any discussion that makes use of the evidence of burial customs: what proportion of the population do archaeologically retrieved burials represent?

This question had barely been considered in the context of the EIA before Morris's work. The tendency was simply to assume that the small numbers of burials recovered reflected a small population. The possibility that a section of the population was socially excluded from using archaeologically detectable types of burial was considered by Snodgrass, but dismissed on the grounds that

174

the cemeteries which we do have represent a fairly complete range of ages and sexes, while their general poverty is such as to make it an almost laughable claim that they should represent any kind of elite or privileged group.

(Snodgrass 1980a: 21)

However, more recently he has basically accepted the implications of Morris's analysis, that for the bulk of the EIA the poorer adult males and many women and children did not receive the kind of formal burial that has been preserved, and even 'poor' burials represent something beyond the reach of the majority ([1971] 2000: xxviii). Morris's analysis of the Athenian cemeteries does indeed suggest that in many phases the range represented is by no means 'fairly complete', although it has to be admitted that there are few reliable data relating to the age and sex of EIA burials, whether at Athens or elsewhere in the Aegean. Non-adult burials, especially those of small children and infants, seem to be generally rare, if more in some phases than others. This is also widely evident in the LBA, in notable contrast with the high proportion of such burials found in MH contexts (Dickinson 1994a: 222). It constitutes a strong argument for the existence of types of burial that are hard to identify archaeologically (Morris, 1987: 62 rightly dismisses any suggestion that these variations reflect rises and falls in the standard of living). Nevertheless, EIA children's and adolescents' burials have been recovered, both on settlement sites, if not consistently (e.g. none are reported from Nichoria), and in cemeteries, where even infant cremations are sometimes identifiable, as at Torone (Musgrave 1990: 284). At Seraglio on Cos the burials of young children predominate among the EIA graves discovered (Desborough 1972: 172–3). Clearly, then, there was no question of the exclusion of *all* non-adults from the accepted types of formal burial, and, given that what are apparently children's burials are often well provided with goods, one might well imagine that those who did receive such burials belonged to a select group.

The possibility that similar considerations affected the burial of adults is plausible. Indeed, it has been suggested in Chapter 2 (p. 39) that there might have been a Mycenaean class of dependants who were not entitled to burial in chamber tombs or even the less commonly found cists and pits. Of course, any suggestion that the section of the EIA population excluded from standard formal burial derived from a comparable Mycenaean class would run counter to Morris's and Whitley's interpretation of the Submycenaean burials of Athens as representing persons of all ages and statuses. Morris (1997: 542–3) lays particular emphasis on his view that it was at the beginning of the EIA proper that a new ritual system was introduced, in Athens and elsewhere in central Greece, that involved the exclusion of children and the poorer class of adults from formal burial and the reflection of an 'egalitarian' ethos in the burial customs followed for the formal burials of the elite.

But he never explains why this new system came to be introduced at this particular time, and he and Whitley seem to have fallen into the same trap as others in assuming that because preserved burials of the Submycenaean phase are relatively numerous they can be taken as a representative sample of the total population. Moreover, their arguments are heavily dependent on the assumption that the burials preserved from EIA Athens form a statistically usable sample, although both were unable to include the largest group of PG burials yet found there, the Vasilissis Sophias cemetery, still very poorly known (*AR* 30 (1983–84) 7. As well as Submyc burials sixty-two amphora-cremations and eleven inhumations of PG date are reported; cf. Figure 4.2). Along with other evidence, this find, though admittedly over 2 km from central Athens, must call into question the common tendency to assume that the Kerameikos can be regarded as Athens' premier cemetery and its practices as embodying the dominant ethos.

A further common assumption is that some Athenian cemeteries have survived complete. It is true that the city region has been extensively sampled through excavation. But it is surely significant that this has produced virtually no graves at all from the enormously long period of prehistory before LH III during which Athens was occupied as a sizeable centre. This serves to emphasise that the survival of graves is affected by many factors apart from the chances of discovery, and if not completely random is at least variable enough to provide a dubious basis for any statistical analysis. The most significant factor affecting survival is probably the continual disturbance of the soil by agriculture and building. When graves are positioned away from settlements and agricultural land, like the LB rock-cut chamber tombs which needed to be cut in particular types of rock, or are quite elaborate stone structures, like other LB graves, they have a high capacity for survival, although their discovery will often be a matter of chance (as with the Elateia cemetery, situated in a relatively remote area). But the majority of graves throughout prehistory and history are likely to have been forms of pit, which there is no need to place at any great distance from settlements; there may even be ritual reasons why graves should be placed near if not within them. The chance that such graves will be disturbed by later activity of some kind, even by the use of the same area for later burials, as frequently at Athens, is high, and in such cases older graves were certainly not always respected. Often they were built into or over, and one may suspect that they were frequently plundered of anything valuable. Therefore, to describe known cemeteries as 'fully excavated' (e.g. Morris 1987: 76, 77) is misleading. At most, what has survived has been fully excavated, and even to demonstrate this may not be easy. This is shown, for example, by the continuing discovery of significant graves in the Kerameikos and in the Toumba cemetery at Lefkandi (cf. *AR* 41 (1994–1995) 4, 31), and the evidence that the Submyc–PG Erechtheiou Street graves at Athens (Brouskari 1980) were part of a larger cemetery area that has only been partially investigated (Whitley 1991a: 201–2).

176

Despite this, it must seem rather unlikely that, if the class excluded from standard formal burial actually constituted the greater part of the population, its burials should be quite so difficult to identify. The archaeological record does not provide any clear trace of the charnel pits that Morris thinks the most likely form of disposal. The recent discovery of disarticulated human bones at Thessaloniki: Toumba, clearly from informal intramural depositions (reported by Prof. S. Andreou in Wardle 2000), represents the kind of evidence that one would hope for, but this is not a phenomenon reported so far from sites further south. Other possible examples of 'informal' burial that Morris cites (1987: 106–8) seem mostly explicable as evidence of secondary burial practices or as simpler forms of primary formal burial. For example, the intramural burials of Postpalatial Tiryns and Lefkandi might be thought to represent a lower class than chamber tomb users, but at Lefkandi they are associated with notably substantial buildings and two in fact had grave offerings, while a third wore a stone amulet which may be compared with examples in the Elateia chamber tombs (Musgrave and Popham 1991: 273; cf. Dimaki 1999).

It seems preferable to assume that the EIA burials found do represent the practices of the larger part of the population, with the proviso that non-adult burials are certainly under-represented, and to accept that their general rarity fits the common patterns of recovery more closely than the large numbers of Third Palace Period burials identifiable. In Crete, where the majority of graves are of relatively complex forms and involve quite elaborate burial rites, these certainly could represent a select group, as is suggested by the relatively low numbers calculated to have been buried in the large Knossos North Cemetery over a period of more than four centuries (*NorthCem*: 659–60, between 422 and 671?) and the generally similar burial customs that were followed (*NorthCem*: 720). Nevertheless, detectable variations in wealth of grave goods and the presence of imports suggest a system of ranking, which could fit quite well with Morris's distinction between aristocratic and non-aristocratic '*agathoi*' (1987: 94).

Another question of great significance and considerable complexity raised by Morris and Whitley relates to the significance and functions of grave-goods, which not all finds in or at the grave need be, since pottery might have been used in rituals during the funeral ceremony or in later observances. This is an enormous subject, on which widely differing views have been expressed, but I have most sympathy with a post-processualist approach which is gaining ground, particularly in early mediaeval studies (I am indebted to my wife, Dr T.M. Dickinson, for advice on this point; cf. Houby-Nielsen 1995 on later Athens, especially 130, 145, and Morris 1987: 38–42 generally). This does not see grave-goods as primarily the treasured possessions of the dead and/or as intended for their use in the afterlife, nor yet as faithful reflections of the status of the dead person according to a regular system of rules that dictated what grave-goods should reflect a particular social status. Rather, they should be interpreted as incorporating statements by the *living*, who use the burial of a household or group member consciously or unconsciously to proclaim their social position and aspirations. On this view, the goods themselves are drawn from an accepted set of items that carry social significance and are used in life, not manufactured purely for the grave, so could well include possessions of the dead. In the Aegean context, grave-goods may have become a more significant focus for making statements of this kind as the chamber tomb and other multiple-use types were abandoned, since this meant that the place of burial itself had considerably less potential to impress.

But it would be too reductionist to imagine that grave-goods are simply expressions of the status of the burying group. The provision of goods may embody a whole complex of ideas, often not coherently formulated and even potentially contradictory. In particular, when grave-goods of unusual elaboration or quantity are provided for children, adolescents, and even young adults, this could have been partly intended to propitiate the spirit of the dead for being deprived of the opportunity to live a full life, and would not only express grief in an expensive material form, as funerary statues and tombstones were used to do later in Greek history, but provide symbols of the status that should have been achieved. Also, it should be remembered that the grave itself preserves only 'the material residue of burials rather than the totality of rituals associated with the funeral' (Hall 1997: 130, citing Leach). This point has particular relevance when it is remembered that a considerable percentage of excavated graves held no recognisable grave-goods. Rituals of mourning, bearing the dead to the grave, and completing the burial, secondary rituals conducted with the remains of the dead, and observances at the grave on later occasions could well have offered an even better field for making social distinctions than the grave's layout and contents. Also, the placing of the burying place in relation to the inhabited landscape and to other graves may have had considerable significance, and the attention of anyone in the grave's neighbourhood may have been drawn to it in various ways, not all of which have left tangible remains.

The Postpalatial Period

Burial customs in the Postpalatial Period superficially appear to continue those of the Third Palace Period (see pp. 38–9), but the analysis by Cavanagh and Mee (1998: ch. 7) reveals various significant differences. Most often, Postpalatial use of chamber tombs represents the continuing use, or reopening, of older tombs. The establishment of a new cemetery at Perati, which eventually consisted of nearly two hundred and thirty tombs, is quite exceptional, although small groups of new tombs are found elsewhere, e.g. the Aplomata and Kamini tombs at Grotta on Naxos, and new tombs were quite often built within established cemeteries in some regions, especially

Achaea and other parts of the north-west Peloponnese, Phocis and Locris, Cephallenia, and Rhodes.

The Perati cemetery provides by far the largest and best reported body of data on Postpalatial patterns of use (Figure 6.1; Iakovidis 1969, 1980), and its evidence is instructive, although it is worth remembering that over a quarter of the graves had been robbed. Tombs were smaller and less well constructed than previously, and twenty-six were actually pits, interspersed among the chamber tombs and containing one or at most two burials, including four of infants. Although relatively many tombs were used in more than one phase of the cemetery, they often held only two or three burials, and sixty-one tombs held only one. Thus, the reuse of tombs was apparently becoming a rarer and much diluted practice, although it should be noted that, unlike the cremations, the inhumations have not received osteological analysis, which has demonstrated in chamber tombs elsewhere that many more burials may be represented than are identifiable simply by skull-count (Mee and Cavanagh 1984: 55). As repeated use became a rare practice, one might expect that ritual practices associated with such use would cease to be prominent, including the secondary burial practice identified by Voutsaki and others (Voutsaki 1995: 60, with references cited there, cf. 1993: 75–7 for more extensive discussion of the Argolid material, and Cavanagh and Mee 1998: 76, 116). Cremated remains, often representing more than one body, were placed in ten of the chamber tombs in a variety of ways, generally in a pot but sometimes loose on the floor or in a pit (T. 1 pit 2 held three, including that of a small child). The richest grave-goods tend to be found in

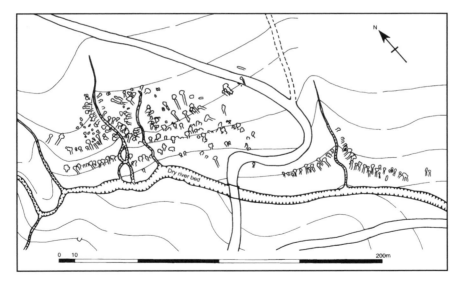

Figure 6.1 Plan of Perati cemetery (after Cavanagh and Mee 1998, fig. 7.7).

179

the largest tombs, but the association was by no means universal, and some relatively large tombs were not well provided. The total absence of a tholos tomb, such as might have been expected at such an evidently important site earlier in the LBA, is worth noting, serving as a reminder that, as already noted in Chapter 3, tholoi had effectively gone out of use as an elite tomb type.

Comparable patterns can be traced in many other cemeteries, especially the tendency to make chamber tombs smaller, but in some regions there is a detectable tendency to use them for more burials over a shorter period than had previously been customary. Often these burials were placed within pits and niches. In the case of the Cephallenian 'cave-dormitories', which are large and contain regularly arranged rows of pits, the tombs were clearly constructed to be used in this way and must have been intended for considerably more than a single family or descent-group. This might reflect the development of new types of social group that were defining their identity by being buried together, but if so it seems a localised feature, which is traceable in older Cephallenian tombs, that often contain many pits, less regularly arranged, and at Derveni in Achaea, but is without close parallel elsewhere. Tombs containing numerous pits occur in other cemeteries, like Elateia, but the numbers buried in these tombs seem to fit the usual Mycenaean patterns, although up to thirty or forty burials have been reported from some reused monumental tombs (Cavanagh and Mee 1998: 96 n. 53), and two tombs at Elateia held about one hundred and sixty apiece, though these may have been buried over a very long period (Dakoronia 2003). Such cases may represent a new pattern of use, rather than simply economy of effort, but they are never universal in a cemetery, as they seem to be on Cephallenia.

The appearance of cremation is one of the more remarkable features of Postpalatial burial customs. As noted in Chapter 3, it is widely spread, but in general thinly represented. However, a recently reported tumulus at Argos (Piteros 2001) held no less than thirty-six urn cremations of LH IIIC Middle-Late date, as well as eighteen inhumations. Cavanagh and Mee suggest that the sporadic Postpalatial occurrences may reflect the movements of individuals (1998: 97), but it is not easy to reconcile this with the fact that, except in the Khania burial tumulus, 2.5 kilometres south-west of Mycenae, which contains eight LH IIIC Middle urn cremations only, cremations nearly always accompany more numerous inhumations in the same tomb, rather than being confined to separate tombs, as might be expected if they represented immigrants. Moreover, though cremation seems to have been widely popular in Anatolia, it was not the major or sole rite of any community in the Postpalatial Aegean, so it would not necessarily be the natural rite for migrants within the Aegean to take to other sites.

Further, the general occurrence of cremations in the same tombs as inhumations hardly suggests that adopting the rite entailed any basic change in beliefs, since it was the living users of these tombs who would have organised the cremations, so that any ideological element involved must have been acceptable to them. One may rather suspect that, like weapon burials, cremations should be associated with attempts to assert status, and the rite may have been chosen because it offered greater potential for flamboyance at the funeral. It may be significant that the majority of Perati cremations were found in the richer tombs and were adult males, and that some weapon burials at other sites, especially the later ones, were cremations. On the other hand, the Argolid cremations in tumuli have nothing spectacular in the way of grave-goods. The piecemeal adoption of this and other novelties does support Cavanagh and Mee's suggestion that a degree of continuity in practice from the Third Palace Period was accompanied by the increasing breakdown of previous traditions and the development of new ones, often localised. Further changes in burial customs in the early EIA reveal that this was a continuing process.

Because the funerary practices of the Postpalatial Period are thinly documented at Athens, and totally lacking at other sites where supposedly typical Submyc cemeteries have been identified, such as Lefkandi, it is easy to get the impression that the burial customs of Submyc cemeteries represent a sudden and radical innovation. But, when all the evidence for variation in burial practices in the Postpalatial Period is taken into consideration, the widespread move to single burial near the end of the period might more plausibly be seen simply as the culmination of the already established trend to use chamber tombs for very few burials. The gradualness of the change is suggested by the fact that at some sites, like Argos, the last use of chamber tombs, generally for only one or two burials, seems to overlap with the appearance of cist and pit cemeteries (Dickinson 1983: 66). Moreover, as will be clear from the distribution, large parts of the Aegean have produced little or no burial evidence dating between Mycenaean and G times, including such important provinces as Laconia and Ionia, while other regions are represented by no more than one or two sites that cover only part of the EIA. Even in the central mainland and Aegean islands it is more the absence of evidence for other forms of grave than a large body of positive evidence that allows the presumption that single burial, normally in pits or cists, was the dominant form over the whole area. Such single burials have in fact been found at sites from Thessaly and Skyros to the Dodecanese, but they are hard to identify before G times on the western side of the mainland.

Although found at a wide spread of sites, single-burial cemeteries certainly did not immediately become the norm everywhere in the Aegean at the end of the Postpalatial Period. The chamber tomb tradition in its local forms probably continued for a while at Epidauros Limera in Laconia and Palaiokastro in Arcadia, where Submyc-looking pottery occurs, and at several sites in Achaea and Cephallenia, where the cemeteries may go out of use even later, although it is hard to say precisely when. More remarkably, this tradition certainly lasted right through the EIA not only in central Crete but in the Phocis–Locris region, although here, at the typical site of Elateia and elsewhere, newly cut chamber tombs were small and generally poor in quality, and tended to hold very few burials. In appearance these can resemble large pits (Figure 6.2), but they could still have dromos-like entrances (not at Delphi: Desborough 1972: 203).

Other forms of multiple burial did continue. Small stone-built tombs of tholos type that might be used for several burials were popular in the peripheral regions of Messenia and Thessaly (for Thessaly see Georganas 2000), and although none can be dated particularly early, they presumably derive from the LB tholoi. Similarly, the LB vaulted rectangular tomb type persisted in parts of Crete, especially the east, and is also found at Asarlik and Dirmil in Caria (Lemos 2002: 182–3). A tradition of multiple burial in large cists on Thasos continued through the EIA, but it has many individual features and it is not clear if it owed anything to influences from the south Aegean. The tumuli of Vergina may also be considered a form of multiple burial in a local tradition, traceable at other Macedonian sites (Snodgrass 1971: 160–3; Lemos 2002: 183), but the graves within them

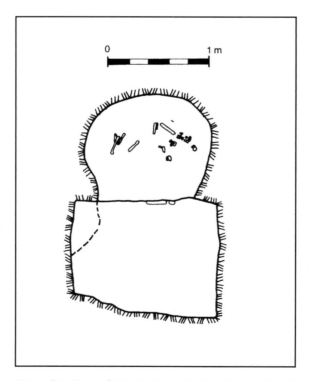

Figure 6.2 Plan of Elateia Type B chamber tomb (after Deger-Jalkotzy, with Dakoronia, 1990, pl. VII fig. 12).

normally contain only one burial, and there are cist cemeteries elsewhere in Macedonia.

This survival of older forms in some parts of the Aegean and the indications that the move away from multiple burial was gradual must call into question Snodgrass's singling out of the practice of single burial in pits and cists as a basic feature of an underlying 'Greek' continuity from MH to the EIA (see p. 196). There are in fact some notable differences. In particular, MH burials, whether of adults or children, were normally intramural until a late stage, but in the EIA extramural cemeteries, large or small, seem the rule. Grave-goods of some kind are also much commoner in EIA graves than in MH. The preference for single burial may in fact be part of a more widespread movement away from traditional forms in the east Mediterranean. In Cyprus, which had considerable contacts with the Aegean in the Postpalatial Period, there is a comparable movement to single burials in shafts, although some chamber tombs of the traditional local form remained in use, and when chamber tombs on the Aegean model were adopted in the eleventh century these were rarely used more than once (Niklasson-Sönnerby 1987; Vandenabeele 1987).

The significance of this move to single burial remains debatable. The natural expectation is that it reflects important social change, as the switch to multiple-burial tombs in the early Mycenaean mainland is believed to have done. Yet single burial had remained an acceptable form of disposal of the dead on the mainland during the LBA, and repeated use of tombs continued to be typical of some regions in the EIA, as previously noted. Moreover, types of grave normally used for single burials can occasionally be reused once or twice, and can coexist in the same region with tombs used for several burials, some of which may be very old tombs brought back into use. The fact that many of the cemeteries are at new sites has been thought a sign that the cemeteries are those of newcomers, as Desborough argued (see the discussion in Lemos 2002: 184–6). But it is just as likely that the new sites were chosen because pit and cist burial did not require sites very far from the inhabited areas, and, if they were placed in land that was part of Mycenaean settlements, that this was the best way of using land that might have been laborious to clear for agriculture. Such developments may also reflect social change and perhaps the establishment of new hierarchies in the settlements concerned, which would be a plausible setting for the establishment of new cemeteries that are not single-burial, like the Knossos North Cemetery.

The Early Iron Age

Just as the single-burial cemeteries of the end of the Postpalatial Period can be argued to represent the culmination of trends developing during it, so those of the beginning of the EIA proper do not seem to represent a major change of direction, but rather continuity. In fact, they frequently continue previously established cemeteries, and it is not always easy to place individual graves on one side or the other of the indistinct dividing line between Submyc and PG (Chapter 1, p. 15). One major development is the adoption of cremation as the predominant rite in certain communities, to be discussed further on pp. 185–9. But this is only one facet of the notable variability in types of burial that can be associated with particular sites, which seems considerably more marked than in Mycenaean times. Variations can be seen in the form of grave, the choice of inhumation or cremation, the manner in which cremated remains are buried, and the arrangement of the body if inhumed.

The Submyc Pompeion cemetery in the Kerameikos area provides a typical example, including many of the main types. Cists built of stone slabs, though much the commonest form, are mingled with pits, which can either be covered with slabs or filled with stones or simply earth. There are a few cremations, usually but not always inurned, and there is one burial in a wooden coffin from the end of the phase. Although some graves seem to form rough rows they are remarkably varied in their orientation (for a recent plan see Mountjoy 1988: fig. 21). This variability continues into PG at Athens, although inurned cremation becomes much more popular. There may be more apparent uniformity at other sites: e.g. in the earliest Lefkandi cemeteries, Khaliotis and Skoubris (Figure 6.3), the cist grave is dominant, as also at Argos and Asine, and at Knossos rock-cut chamber tombs are almost universal, although other types of rock-cut tomb, the shaft and pit-cave, are

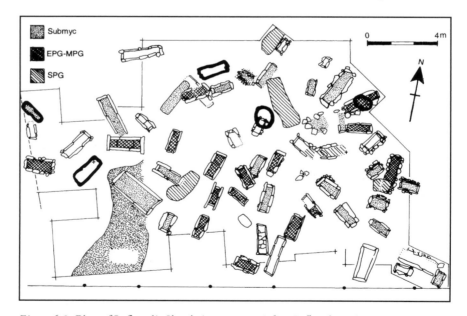

Figure 6.3 Plan of Lefkandi: Skoubris cemetery (after *Lefkandi I*, pl. 75).

found among the earliest SM graves. But in general, the more burial evidence that is preserved from a site, the more variations can be identified.

Very similar patterns of grave-good deposition to those of the Postpalatial Period continue into the EIA, visible in both single-burial and multiple-burial cemeteries, inhumations and cremations. If accompanied by goods at all (as many were not), burials were generally provided with one or more vases, rarely over four. A burial that has more is usually definable as 'rich' in other ways, such as the presence of generally several metal dress-fasteners and rings, which can also sometimes appear without pottery as the sole grave-goods. While such metal jewellery is quite often found in women's and children's graves, it is rarely found with those identified as men. Sometimes men whose main goods are weapons, and occasionally items of armour, may wear rings, even a fibula that presumably pinned a cloak, but only a few men were distinguished in this way; many were provided simply with pottery. Items of precious materials like gold, silver, and glass, and exotic imports like the Near Eastern beads and seals found at Perati, were generally extremely rare.

The considerable variability in provision led Morris to speak of 'virtual symbolic anarchy' in the Submyc phase, going on to say, 'The overall impression is that Mycenaean styles of life being abandoned . . . but no alternative vision of social order had yet taken hold' (1997: 541). Similarly, Whitley states, of Submyc burials:

> Persons were not defined as types . . . There was no mechanism of selectivity in operation, either in defining symbolic forms or in determining who was and who was not to be given visible burial.
>
> (Whitley 1991a: 181)

But this is to set up the distinctions that they have identified in PG–G Athenian practice as expected norms. In fact, the impression given by the finds does not differ markedly from that presented by LB or even earlier cemeteries. In these, also, graves of different sizes and quality of construction, even sometimes of different types, can be grouped together in cemeteries, and there are equally wide variations in the range, quantity and quality of the goods placed with the dead. The clearest visible distinction between Mycenaean and Submyc is that burials which might once have been grouped within a single tomb now seem to be buried in separate if closely placed graves, forming miniature cemeteries that could gradually merge to form extensive grave-fields. The major difference from standard Mycenaean patterns of grave-good deposition is that figurines, necklaces and sealstones have disappeared as grave-goods practically everywhere, while the steatite items identified as clothing weights have become very rare, and when they occur may well be recycled from older graves.

The shift to single burial at the end of the Postpalatial Period partly coincided with another shift that affected far fewer communities, the adoption

of cremation as a favoured form of burial. On current evidence, this movement was particularly strong at Athens, Lefkandi, Medeon, Torone, and
Knossos and other sites in central Crete. Other cremations dating before
c. 900 have been found in small numbers elsewhere in Attica, in the Vranesi
tumulus in Boeotia, at Argos, Elateia, Halos in Thessaly, Grotta on Naxos,
Asarlik and Dirmil in Caria, and quite commonly in east and west Crete (see
Desborough 1972: 234–5); there are a very few at Vergina and on Thasos.
But at most of these sites inhumation was clearly equally or more common,
so that these cases seem to reflect a pattern, continuing from the Postpalatial
Period, of the appearance of cremation as an occasional choice, although
cremations of EIA date are not always found in regions where Postpalatial
examples had occurred (e.g. Achaea and Elis).

But even at the sites where cremation was clearly very popular the picture
is not clear cut. At Athens cremation only became standard in the course of
the PG period: even in the Kerameikos several EPG burials are inhumations,
and there is an adult inhumation in the Agora as late as MPG, while outside
Athens the PG weapon burial at Marathon is an inhumation (*AR* 34 (1987–88)
13). At Knossos inhumations continued through the SM phase and probably
into the local PG, so quite late in the tenth century (*NorthCem*: 651–2), and
at Lefkandi it is becoming increasingly clear that many graves thought
to have held token remains of a cremation actually held inhumations
whose bones have completely decayed (Lemos 1998: 53), particularly those
cases where dress ornaments were laid out as if upon a body. At Torone
inhumations make up over 10 per cent of the burials found, and seem to
range in date over the whole period of the cemetery. Only at Koukos near
Torone, which may be later than Torone, and 'native' in showing no evidence
of a local Greek pottery tradition, does cremation seem to be the sole rite,
though it occurs in various forms: the ashes may be put in a pit, in a vessel
placed in a stone cist, or in a pithos or smaller pot (Lemos 2002: 184).

It is generally common for different forms of cremation to be found at the
same sites. At Athens inurned cremations, of the form already found in the
Postpalatial Argos and Khania tumuli particularly, are commonest. This
involved placing the ash-holder vessel, normally an amphora, in a hole at the
bottom of a pit, and covering it, usually with an open vessel (Figure 6.4);
some part of the funeral pyre might be raked into the pit, and goods might
be placed within or outside the amphora. But sometimes urns were placed in
a hole which was not within a pit, and some cremations were placed loose
within the pit, whether brought in from the pyre or burnt *in situ* (Whitley
1991a: 102). Cremations where the remains were left on the pyre or placed
loose in pits or cists have been identified at other sites, including Vranezi,
Grotta and Vrokastro, and a variant of this rite was practised at Medeon,
which involved the construction of the pyre over a pit, into which it was
allowed to fall, the remains then being covered with earth. At Halos a unique
cemetery of tumuli that contained varying numbers of cremation pyres

Figure 6.4 PG pit-and-hole cremation in the Kerameikos cemetery, Athens.
Courtesy of the Deutsches Archäologisches Institut, Athens.

covered by stone cairns began to be used towards the end of PG, continuing
to Archaic times (Georganas 2002). But inurned cremations seem to be the
norm at Torone and are commonest in Crete, and they occur increasingly
frequently in the Aegean as the PG phase progresses. The discovery of many
pyres in all the Lefkandi cemeteries guarantees that cremation was popular
here, but while some seem to conform to what had been supposed to be a
standard practice of placing a token amount of the cremation along with
unburnt grave-goods in a cist or shaft, some may have been left on the pyre,
and a few were inurned. Lefkandi has also produced the most elaborate EIA
cremation, the burial of a male's ashes in an antique bronze amphora in the
'Heroön' with associated horse sacrifices, but, as if to emphasise the potential

187

variability of practice, this was accompanied by a richly arrayed female inhumation (Figure 6.5).

Explaining the shift to cremation is no easier than explaining the shift to single burial. The fact that it was not completely adopted even at the sites where it was popular does not suggest that any general change in beliefs about the dead and life after death was involved, and there is a lack of pattern in its occurrences, already foreshadowed in its appearance as a minority rite among inhuming communities in the Postpalatial Period. It does occur particularly at sites that have continuing overseas connections, and it is

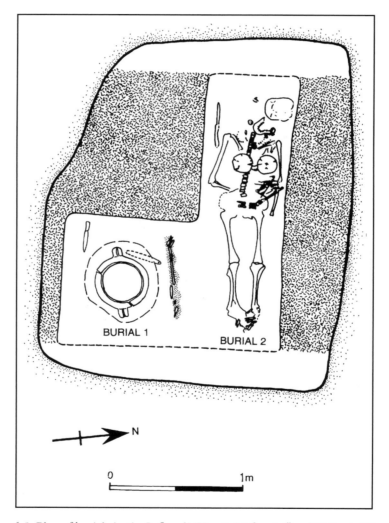

Figure 6.5 Plan of burials in the Lefkandi 'Heroön' (after *Lefkandi II,2*, pl. 13).

noteworthy that reportedly it was becoming popular in Syria–Palestine at much the same time as in some Aegean communities (Aubet 2001: 65). Although it might seem natural to assume that its adoption reflects a desire for a more prestigious burial rite, this was clearly not universal. At Lefkandi, as noted, the rich female burial in the 'Heroön' was inhumed, and several later rich burials are certain or possible inhumations. At Athens, while the Kerameikos burials surely include leading members of the community, they are not distinctly richer or more elaborate than the inhumations of the Agora region, which include some quite well-provided children. Many of the later Kerameikos cremations are distinguished by the presence of animal bones in the fill, that presumably reflect a sacrifice and ritual meal at the funeral, but this feature is also found with several burials in the Erechtheiou Street cemetery and one or two in the Agora. To sum up, cremation may have high-status associations at the sites where it was adopted, but it does not seem to have been absolutely required for high status burials.

If a close link between particular types of grave or burial rite and high or low social status seems unlikely, it is even less plausible that the various types reflect different 'ethnic' groupings (cf. Hall 1997: ch. 4). It is quite possible that particular variations were used locally as a way of stressing the individuality of a group or community and its links, or lack of them, with its neighbours, but the mingling of different types in the same cemetery, without any obvious patterning in distribution, seems to argue against this idea in many cases, since the natural expectation is surely that groups wishing to emphasise their individuality or their higher status would do so in the placing of their graves as well as in the grave-type and features of the actual burial. The most plausible indications of such behaviour seem to belong to a much later stage (see Hall 1997: 137 on the eighth-century Argolid; but Georganas 2002 reasonably proposes this to explain the unique features of the Halos cemetery).

The feature that emerges from a consideration of all the earlier EIA burials, apart from their variability of type, is their relative simplicity and lack of overt display. There are few traces of elaboration in the grave itself, except where the traditions of chamber tombs and stone-built tombs survived, and few burials were provided with more than a small number of pots, with a basic set of dress-fasteners quite often if female, a weapon sometimes if male. Even the cremation urns were decorated carefully, though not with exceptional elaboration. Notably, few males were provided with more than pottery, and the richest burials in terms of range and number of goods are female. When children are provided with more than pottery, these too most often seem to be female, to judge from the presence of dress-fastener sets. In the Kerameikos, female cremations also consistently outnumber males through the PG phases, although in each phase there is a sizeable group of adults whose sex cannot be distinguished. A higher proportion of the female burials have produced evidence of animal sacrifice, and the first burials to be given vases as grave-markers, at the end of PG, are female. Given that these societies were surely male-dominated, it could be argued that the leading males were proclaiming their status and that of their households primarily through the burials of their wives and children, only sometimes claiming for themselves the distinction of a weapon burial. Indeed, identified weapon burials can seem too young to be heads of households – e.g. the young men buried in the double cremation of Kerameikos T. A – and, like many of the Archaic Athenian burials marked by statues or reliefs, may represent burials carried out by their parent(s).

This concentration of visible wealth in the burials of adult females and children shows interesting similarities to the pattern detectable much earlier in MH graves, which were also normally single burials, although the incidence of grave-goods is higher than in MH times. Again, this is probably best not interpreted as the re-emergence of buried 'Helladic' traits, as Snodgrass would have it ([1971] 2000: xxvi, 186, 385), but as evidence for the existence of similar social patterns to those prevalent in the MH period, which probably involved only a loosely defined social hierarchy. In considering the Athenian material, both Morris and Whitley see evidence of an egalitarian ideology within the burying group, but Whitley nevertheless draws attention to indications of 'tensions and contradictions' within the community, in the form of 'stylistic preferences or differences in quantity of artefacts deposited' (1991a: 115–16). This sounds a plausible enough setting for the considerable range of minor variations in grave-goods that can be observed at many sites, which may reflect subtleties of distinction that we can no longer grasp. But, though the basis for ranking may have been considerably more fluid than in the Postpalatial Period and before, there seems little reason to doubt that it was still a fundamental feature of the EIA societies in some form. It certainly needs to be emphasised that the closely defined 'burial personae' identified in the PG Kerameikos burials particularly by Morris and Whitley do not seem to have analogies in other cemeteries: if this is a genuine Athenian feature (Papadopoulos 1993 has criticised their over-reliance on the Kerameikos evidence), it serves to demonstrate that Athens was unusual rather than typical.

The one clear exception to the general rule of limited display in the grave is provided by the Lefkandi 'Heroön' (Lemos 2002: 166–8 focuses on the burials). As noted in Chapter 4 (p. 107), Mazarakis Ainian's theory (1997: 48–57) that this was originally a ruler's house, later used as the site of a simultaneous burial of the ruler and his wife, has difficulties, not least that it is situated near an otherwise funerary area. It may be better to treat it as a house replica. Even this distinguishes it from the heroes' burial places described in the *Iliad*, as does the accompanying female burial, but the Homeric parallels are otherwise close, as has often been noted, and Morris interprets it as an effort to claim for the man the status of ancient heroes already celebrated in tradition (1997: 544). Perhaps this does not give full weight to the female burial, which fits the general EIA pattern in being more richly provided in terms of grave-goods than her putative husband: despite its splendid container, an antique Cypriot bronze amphora, the male burial was provided only with iron weapons and razor, a whetstone, and the cloth robe and bands found in the amphora, while the female had a rich gold necklace, gilt earrings, and large gold ornaments attached to the upper part of her dress, as well as the metal pins and ivory-handled knife laid around her body. Other exceptional features of the burial, the sacrifice of four horses, the massive krater placed by the grave (which can only have been used in the funeral ceremony, rather than as a grave-marker and libation receptacle, if the building was filled in afterwards) and the heaping of a mound over the structure, can be paralleled – the first two occur in later burials in the Toumba cemetery – but the combination is unique, and perhaps always was. From later analogies one can imagine that the associated ceremonies were also elaborate, involving mass mourning and even funeral games.

Nevertheless, it is difficult to believe that this was the only example of giving such exceptional honours to a burial in the EIA. Indeed, it has been compared with richly provided burials, several of them cremations, at Knossos and in Cyprus (Catling 1995; cf. Matthäus 1998: 140–1 and Crielaard 1998: 188–91). It is implausible that the Homeric descriptions should derive from a single actual example, and perhaps more likely that, if they reflect real practice, they relate to Ionia rather than the mainland (although it has recently been suggested that 'Homer' was a Euboean; Morris and Powell 1997: 31). But although PG tholoi seem to have been built for apparently elite burials in Thessaly (Georganas 2000), these are family tombs used for many burials, and examples of impressive burial tumuli are generally later. There are, however, various examples of possible veneration of the dead in some form of ancestor cult, the earliest of which are the enclosures surrounding LPG graves at Grotta on Naxos (Lambrinoudakis 1988; Mazarakis Ainian 1997: 188–9, who assembles other examples of apparent cult of the dead, see 352). The Grotta graves themselves are not remarkable in form or contents, but ceremonies were evidently performed at them for a considerable time. Perhaps the Lefkandi 'Heroön' should be seen partly as the most magnificent surviving example of such cult, although if the building itself was not used as a shrine, as Mazarakis Ainian argues, there is only inferential evidence for cult at the edge of the mound. Certainly, the Grotta enclosures are a reminder of the undesirability of suggesting a single common culture of funerary customs in the EIA Aegean.

The Toumba cemetery, which developed at the east edge of the mound over the 'Heroön', provides further striking examples of exceptional practices at Lefkandi. Although the positioning of the cemetery suggests claimed relationship with the 'Heroön' couple, there is considerable variation in the orientation of the graves and other features (Figure 6.6), and they were often superimposed. Some hold inhumations, though the bones have often

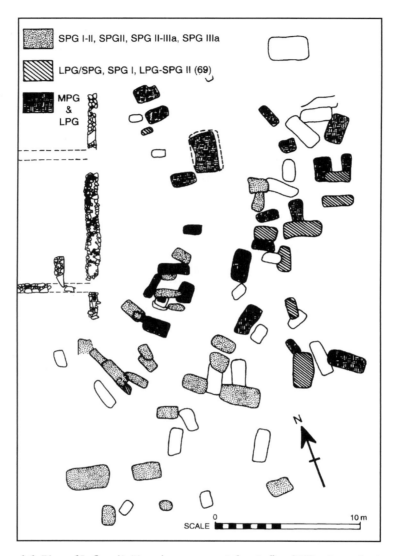

Figure 6.6 Plan of Lefkandi: Toumba cemetery (after *Lefkandi III* colour plate).

decayed, others cremations, and a few, even the richest, were clearly or probably reused (see Popham *et al.* 1982b: 230 on T. 39). There is an unusually high proportion of weapon burials, both urn cremations with the sword wrapped around the amphora neck, as in Athens, and inhumations in shafts. These generally date in or close to LPG, while some of mainly ninth-century date seem to be cremations left on the pyre (*Lefkandi III,1*, table 1: pyres 8,

192

13, 31). Only T. 79B is particularly unusual, consisting of a cremation contained in a bronze cauldron, that was placed in a niche opening off the bottom of a shaft (in Popham and Lemos 1995 this is not distinguished from T. 79A, with which the pottery and some other finds are associated, but this is clear from *Lefkandi III,1*, table 1 and the captions to pls 76–9). A number of graves are readily comparable, in terms of grave-goods, with those found elsewhere, including at Palaia Perivolia, the other main Lefkandi cemetery of tenth- and ninth-century date, but some, dating from as early as the later tenth century, are richer than any other burials of this date preserved in Greece, both in the profusion and elaboration of gold and other ornaments and in the presence of precious vessels and other imports, mainly of Near Eastern origin.

Even the latest and most elaborate of the Athenian PG burials cannot match these, but, as with the 'Heroön', it would be dangerous to assume that they are truly unique. In fact, there is a group of notable tombs at Knossos which all contain Attic LPG pottery, especially drinking vessels, together with bronze vessels that were sometimes used as ash containers, and many weapons and other items of iron. Plain urns are more commonly used for the cremations, but these are distinguished by being set into stone slabs arranged on the tomb floor. Elaborate dress-fasteners, jewellery and other small items of precious materials are rarer, though they do occur. This emphasis on weapon burial is seen by Whitley as particularly characteristic of Knossian society throughout the EIA and one of the few regular features, given the general eclecticism in burial assemblages (1991a: 187–9). Snodgrass offers an analysis dividing the graves into a series of groupings according to what iron types are present (*NorthCem*: 575–7), but points out the problems caused by the widespread damage to and probable plundering of earlier assemblages in reused tombs. This has not only affected the survival of bronze vessels (*NorthCem*: 559), but perhaps particularly the goods of female burials. Higgins points to scanty survivals of fine quality jewellery datable to the ninth and eighth centuries (*NorthCem*: 540–1), but the quantities of ordinary fibulae are also notably small, and the most elaborate pins are Orientalising in date. There may, then, be a difference in social patterning here: it is noteworthy that a similar emphasis on weapon burial and a relative lack of rich female burials can be found at Argos, most markedly in the eighth century, although the female burials were provided with some very fine pins.

In the ninth and eighth centuries, especially the eighth, the quantity of material grows considerably, and evidence is available from a much larger area of Greece. On the view taken in this book, this growth should not be taken to reflect an exactly commensurate growth in the population, although this was probably increasing (see Chapter 4, p. 98), but rather a growth of prosperity that encouraged a larger section of the population to follow the most visible form of burial rites. The types of grave and burial rite change generally in minor details, if at all, but there is an almost bewildering amount of local variation, with neighbouring centres following different customs. As before, the more evidence there is available, the less uniformity is visible (cf. the varied evidence at Nichoria, *Nichoria III*: 266–70). The area over which cremation is found widens only slightly, to include several of the Cycladic islands, Rhodes, and outliers like Colophon and Halos. Increasingly, these are pyre cremations, as are some of the earliest graves found at Eretria east of Lefkandi (Coldstream 1977: 88). But inhumation remains generally dominant, and even begins to reappear in Attica and at Medeon. There is the same range of grave-types, dominated by forms of cist and pit. But pithoi, for whose use for children's inhumations there was some evidence previously, became increasingly favoured for adult burials at Argive sites and elsewhere in the Peloponnese, also at Seraglio on Cos. Burial tumuli covering inhumations or cremations are increasingly common, but their distribution does not suggest any obvious patterns of diffusion. The significance of these variations is still unclear, since they are often mingled together in the same groups of tombs and so cannot be convincingly related to social or 'ethnic' divisions. It is noteworthy that in contrast to the apparent situation at Argos, pithoi were being used for richly provided burials, some of them with weapons, in several parts of the Peloponnese by the eighth century, including Sparta (Raftopoulou 1998). Even at Argos, no clear distinctions can be drawn between the users of cists, pits and pithoi (Hall 1997: 122–8).

Like the graves, grave-goods do not change markedly. There is a more widespread readiness to be relatively lavish with bronze and iron, but items of precious metal and exotic imports remain very rare outside the cemeteries of Euboea, Attica and Knossos (some small gold items are now reported from Amyklai; *AD* 51 (1996) B 129–31). The Koukos cemetery is also notably rich in goods, including iron weapons, bronze fibulae, a few gold ornaments and glass beads. In several regions, burial with weapons and other warriors' accoutrements, including armour, horse gear and iron spits, seems to become increasingly important. This is clearest at Argos and Knossos, but such burials can be found elsewhere, to the end of the eighth century and beyond, most notably in the West Gate cemetery at Eretria (Coldstream 1977: 196–7). It may represent an important element of the prevailing ethos, and its growing rarity at Athens during the eighth century may well be counterbalanced by the prominence of scenes of battle and warrior processions on the vases used there as grave markers and grave-goods.

These and other indications, such as the popularity of providing gold headbands for the dead, both male and female, at Athens, contribute to a picture of the intensification of display by local high-status groups, which seem to be increasingly drawing attention to themselves through their burial customs and using these to compete with each other. This can take various forms apart from the provision of numerous and/or valuable grave-goods, including the use of tomb-types which require much labour to construct, like tumuli and stone-built tombs, of elaborate rites of mourning and

194

procession, as depicted on the Athenian grave-marker vases (see Figure 5.16), the provision of grave markers, and the use of exceptionally elaborate types of pottery, especially as cremation urns and, at Athens, as grave markers. The use of increasingly massive vases as grave markers is a particularly Athenian development, that lasted from the beginning of the ninth century into the seventh and has no real parallels outside Athens's territory, except perhaps the massive krater found in the shaft of Toumba T. 79A at Lefkandi (but this could have been used in the funeral ceremony, as argued for that from the 'Heroön').

The reuse of tombs for second and sometimes third burials in the Argolid is surely another way of drawing attention to the burying group, and the increasingly large numbers of identifiable burials of children could well also be interpreted in this fashion, as a form of display which was accessible to more than the richest social stratum. But other arenas for competition were being developed by the eighth century, particularly religious dedications, and the marked decline in seventh-century evidence for burials may reflect the diversion of resources to this area. The strongest argument against Morris's interpretation of this phenomenon at Athens in local politico-social terms is surely that it is widespread, although by no means universal: for instance, the cemeteries of Knossos have produced very rich evidence of seventh-century use. Equally, the switch from grave-goods as a focus for display to other aspects of burial customs, such as grave markers, including eventually sculpted monuments, and elaborate sacrificial rites, is not confined to Athens, but not universal. The picture of local diversity that one is bound to derive from a consideration of the EIA evidence certainly continued to Archaic times.

Bibliography

Morris (1987: ch. 2) is a useful discussion of general theory about the interpretation of burial customs.

Cavanagh and Mee (1998) is the most comprehensive modern account of Mycenaean burial customs; Lewartowski (2000) is a useful supplement.

For general discussions of EIA burial customs see Snodgrass (1971: ch. 4), Kurtz and Boardman (1971: chs 3 (Athens) and 9). The material is discussed in detail throughout Desborough (1972) (Submyc–PG) and Coldstream (1977) (G), which provide site gazetteers with references. Coldstream often refers to PG material, and Lemos (2002: ch. 5) provides valuable up-to-date summaries of all PG burial sites within her area of coverage, often referring to Submyc and SPG material; particularly useful are the sections summarising material from Athens, the Argolid, Lefkandi, Skyros, Elateia, Atalanti (Locris), Thessaly, Cos, northern Greece (especially Vergina) and Chalcidice (Torone and Koukos).

7

TRADE, EXCHANGE AND FOREIGN CONTACTS

Introduction

By the beginning of the LBA commodities, artefacts, and knowledge of technological developments had already been circulating in the Aegean for a very long time, and were increasingly being accompanied by more abstract features such as writing and weight systems, religious symbols, even perhaps elements of ideology. Much of this derived from local sources, but a significant element can be certainly or plausibly derived from outside the Aegean. During the LBA the Aegean's contacts with the outside world intensified, as its most important centres became more closely tied into the long-range, mainly maritime, exchange systems that were being developed from bases in the east Mediterranean. Aegean external contacts were especially strong with this region, but certainly extended to the central Mediterranean, as far as Sardinia, as well as to neighbouring parts of the Balkans and further but less directly into continental Europe (see Figure 2.4). The potential significance of these European links should not be underestimated, since the Aegean was well placed to play an intermediary role between the Near East and other parts of the Mediterranean and Europe. In fact, the link with the central Mediterranean may never have completely lapsed in the EIA, and many have wished to lay stress on links with 'the north' in explaining new developments at the end of the BA and in the EIA. But the Aegean's links with the east Mediterranean and the Near East more generally remain the best documented and were probably the most significant, although as noted in Chapter 2 it would be straining the evidence to explain them in terms of a core-periphery model, and this region remains the most likely source of new ideas and of influences that went beyond the spheres of exchange and technology in the EIA.

Long-distance exchange seems, from the evidence of shipwrecks, written sources, and depictions in Egyptian tombs, to have been concerned particularly with metals and other raw materials, but there is evidence for the movement of other commodities in bulk. A useful reminder of the kind of perishables that these could include is provided by the tale of Wenamun, supposedly sent from Egypt to Byblos in the early eleventh century to get cedarwood. His cargo of goods to be used in the exchange is described as consisting of large quantities of clothing, ropes, ox hides, sacks of lentils, and baskets of presumably dried fish, and a quantity of gold and five silver vessels, that may have been intended for use as ceremonial gifts (Åström 1989: 203). Real-life counterparts to this list can be found, such as the Nilotic perch bones from Hala Sultan Tekke (Åström 1989: 204) and remains of foodstuffs, including olives, from the Uluburun wreck (Pulak 1998: 201, 210), but mostly foodstuffs and liquids are represented by the pottery containers that would often have held them, and it is rare for even scraps of textiles to survive.

It has already been argued in Chapter 2 that long-distance exchange played a very significant role in the Third Palace Period, supporting the position of the elite and to a substantial degree the general level of prosperity in the Aegean, and in Chapter 3 it has been suggested that it also played a crucial role in the Postpalatial Period. But for the EIA it has been commoner to lay stress on internal processes as the mainspring of Aegean development, and to interpret evidence for extra-Aegean contacts and exchange as indicative of the expansion outwards of Greek enterprise. But, as in the BA, there is every reason to suspect this Aegeocentric bias. While internal processes, including growth in population and social change, could account for an increase in the basis for prosperity and in contacts within the Aegean, the form in which this prosperity was displayed still depended to a great extent not only on foreign items and materials but arguably on foreign ideas. Indeed, it is increasingly often suggested that the Near East exercised considerable cultural influence in the LBA and later, being the source not only of new technology and artistic motifs but of narrative themes, features of social organisation and ritual practice. The argument has been taken to unacceptable extremes by Bernal (1987, 1991; cf. Cline 1994: ch. 6, and Whitley 2001: 105), but in more restrained forms, which stress western Asiatic rather than Egyptian parallels (e.g. Burkert 1992; Morris 1992; West 1997), it cannot be ignored. In particular, S.P. Morris has argued (1997) that influences from the Near East, exercised through the medium of Phoenician activity in the Aegean, played a particularly important role in the EIA, and this hypothesis has been repeated and expanded in relation to specific material by Papadopoulos (especially 1997).

There are basic difficulties involved in the verification of such claims, which are based on very heterogeneous material, by no means all of which can be associated with specifically Phoenician culture. The tendency to link anything Near Eastern or 'Levantine' with this name and the deductions drawn often involve questionable arguments, as Hoffman has demonstrated (1997: especially 15–17, ch. 3 *passim*, 250–1, 254). Moreover, the question whether the literary sources constantly cited offer genuine evidence must be faced. While the Homeric references to Phoenician activity in the Aegean region can surely be accepted as authentically ancient, even if their precise significance remains debatable, reports of such activity in much later sources do not necessarily have the same credibility. Thus, the claim that the Phoenicians were the first to colonise Thasos (Herod. 6.47) and founded a cult of Herakles there (Herod. 2.44) finds no obvious archaeological support in the now quite well documented and clearly native EIA culture (Koukouli-Chrysanthaki 1992). This provides no convincing evidence of close links with the Near East, although the early appearance of iron knives with bronze handles could indicate some kind of connection.

Clearly, all traditions relating to the remoter past that are reported in Greek sources cannot be taken at face value as precious scraps of historical fact but require rigorous analysis (cf. Osborne 1997, also 1996: 40 – traditions that the Phoenicians founded sites are often not the only version reported), and there is no reason why those which refer to Phoenician activity should be considered to have intrinsically greater credibility, still less that they should be referred specifically to the EIA. Most often, they are timeless and semi-mythical, reflecting the general failure of Greek tradition to relate supposed events of the past to a clearly defined chronological framework.

West (1997) presents the argument for influences in poetic themes and technique most extensively, but he excludes most of the EIA from the period when Near Eastern influences are most likely to have been transmitted (1997: 625), apparently placing the development of many characteristic features of the epic style and technique no earlier than the eighth century, which seems implausibly late. The parallels identified are most persuasive when they involve very distinctive features, as in the myth of the succession of supreme gods told in Hesiod's *Theogony*, which is notably close to a Hittite–Hurrian myth. But, while hearing some version of Near Eastern poems like the Epic of Gilgamesh could have provided inspiration for Aegean poets, there is no obvious need to suppose that they could not come up with comparable similes, metaphors, themes, and actions without having done so. Frequently what are presented as close and significant parallels may to a less sympathetic eye appear general resemblances only, which could reflect the development of similar patterns of thought and behaviour in societies whose origin, environment and general nature had many similarities, and which had been in contact with each other for a very long period before the EIA (West places surprisingly little emphasis on the potential role as intermediary of the Minoan civilisation, despite its long history of Near Eastern contacts and its profound formative influence on Mycenaean development). Such arguments, then, often involve material that is hard to evaluate, let alone to date (cf. Whitley 2001: 105). But these postulated connections remain a part of the total picture of potential links between the Aegean and Near East, and could support the view that these were more intensive than might be imagined on the basis of the strictly archaeological data, just as can be argued for the BA (cf. Dickinson 1994a: 243–4, 248–9).

Claims for Near Eastern influences in the sphere of cultural behaviour, especially ritual, can be equally difficult to evaluate. Sometimes, they clearly date later than our period, like the custom of reclining to eat, a typical feature of Greek symposia which is unknown to Homer and first represented at the end of the seventh century, as on the 'Eurytios' krater (Murray 1993: 208; cf. Whitley 2001: 208–9). Arguments for the Greek adoption of alphabetic writing, which must reflect contacts with the Phoenician world, very early in the EIA remain purely hypothetical and must be considered implausible, on the grounds that not a single example of Greek writing can be dated earlier than the eighth century. The Phoenician-inscribed bronze bowl from a context of *c.* 900 or not much later in Knossos Tekke T. J, which may date as much as a century earlier than its context to judge from the style of writing, is probably a gift or 'heirloom' rather than the possession of a Phoenician buried in this tomb (Hoffman 1997: 120–3), and remains a nearly unique curiosity (but see Coldstream [1977] 2003: 379 for a bronze bowl from Tragana in Locris that has a neo-Hittite inscription, found with a rich MG II burial).

The significance of a foreign link in ritual is equally unclear. For example, although there are occurrences of cremation in the Aegean before *c.* 1200 (Cavanagh and Mee 1998: 94), it was essentially a foreign custom (as was equally true in Syria-Palestine, where it was introduced in the eleventh century; Aubet 2001: 65). Nevertheless, as argued in Chapter 6, its spread in the twelfth century and thereafter cannot be assumed to represent the adoption of significant new beliefs about death and the afterlife, let alone of a population group (for general comments see Hoffman 1997: 169–71), although one motive for its adoption might be to signal prestigious contacts with the outside world. Other significant influences have been claimed in the field of religion, but these are best reserved for discussion in Chapter 8, although it is worth noting here that the conclusions drawn by Negbi (1988) from supposed parallels between Mycenaean and Palestinian cult complexes, which have been accepted by several scholars (Cline 1994: 54; West 1997: 37; cf. Morris 1992: 109–11), have been effectively refuted by Gilmour (1993).

We are brought back, then, to the most tangible (and most closely datable) evidence of all – that from artefacts and craft traditions. Various general points, that have as much application to intra-Aegean exchange as to the tracing of Phoenician or other Near Eastern activity, need to be made before the evidence is discussed in detail. The first is that discussions of exchange activity in this period and the following Archaic period have typically depended greatly on the evidence of pottery, largely because pottery can so often be given a particular origin. But such discussions are too often infected by the insidious tendency to identify pots with people. For instance, it is very common to estimate the degree of active participation of a particular community in exchange from the frequency or rarity in outside contexts of the typical pottery produced by that community. As extensions of this idea, the level of contact between two communities is sometimes estimated on the basis of such frequency or rarity (see Osborne 1996: 41–4 on the relations of Athens and Lefkandi, largely following Coldstream 1977), or the presence of a wide variety of foreign pottery types may be taken as indicating, for example, that Knossos was 'an exceptionally outward-looking place with a frequently visited port of call' (*NorthCem*: 716). Here it must be pointed out that the examples of Greek wares apart from Attic found at Knossos are thinly spread over a very long period (*c.* 950–700), working out at only one or two per generation, and have a strong tendency to appear in the same few tombs, generally the richest, so that they might rather represent the overseas activities or connections of just a few families. But at Knossos other foreign goods appear also, in greater frequency than at most sites, and overall it seems a reasonable conclusion that some members of the Knossos community had strong links with the outside world.

It certainly should be emphasised that there is no necessary link between the external trading activity of a community and occurrences of its characteristic pottery or of any other artefacts that it might have produced. Notoriously, some Greek cities that were very active in trade in the Archaic period according to literary sources, such as Aigina, did not even produce a distinctive fine ware for very long, if at all. Still less can it be assumed that pottery or other artefacts of a particular origin signal a visit by people of the same origin to the site where they are found. The heterogeneous cargoes from ancient shipwrecks, not merely the BA ones discussed in Chapter 2 but those of Archaic date (e.g. Papadopoulos 1997: 200 (Massalia wreck); Bound 1991 (Giglio wreck)), show how common it was for goods of different origins to be carried on the same ship.

Neither can the quantity, or rarity, of a particular class of pottery overseas be considered a reliable index of the level of trading activity of the community that produced it. At Knossos, Attic pottery is far more common than any other Greek or Near Eastern ware, yet it would surely be ridiculous to assume from this that the EIA Athenians dominated trade with Crete. It may be noted that Papadopoulos, who is justifiably critical of the tendency to deduce a high level of Euboean activity from the rather thin if wide spread of Euboean pots (1996b: 157–8), comes dangerously close to implying that Euboean activity in the north Aegean or central Mediterranean could not have been significant, simply because Euboean pottery is so rarely found. Shaw similarly begs a question in concluding that Phoenician traders were stopping less often at Kommos in the second phase of Temple B, simply because Phoenician sherds are fewer (1998: 20).

On the aspect of quantity, it is worth remembering how very exceptional, and thus potentially misleading, are the quantities of Aegean pottery found abroad in the Third Palace Period. At no other time before the Archaic period was Aegean pottery exported on such a scale, and examples of imported pottery in the Aegean, whether Cypriot or Near Eastern, are also very rare, whether in the BA or EIA. Thus, basing any detailed conclusions on the quantities actually found involves highly questionable assumptions. Even the ninety-seven Attic imports identified from the Knossos North Cemetery for the period *c.* 950–700, to which more must be added from the Fortetsa tombs and the settlement, seem unimpressive when matched against some 300 pieces of Phoenician vessels associated with Temple B at Kommos, dating over a much shorter period (Shaw 1998: 19). In sum, it is a safe assumption that pottery that is clearly foreign to a site indicates that the site had some kind of contact with the outside world, but nothing more can be safely deduced without analysis of the whole context of exchange in the period and the part which pottery might play in it. Only when pottery appears in the form of container vessels can it be taken to represent a significant exchange item directly – and even then the indications that such vessels could be recycled mean that their presence does not necessarily demonstrate a direct link with their home territory.

Finally, the possibility that the presence of foreign pottery does not involve exchange of goods or commercial trade of any kind needs to be borne in mind. Luke's argument that the finds of Greek Geometric pottery in the Near East, from the tenth to the eighth centuries, largely represent sets of prestige vessels given in the context of establishing and maintaining formal 'friendship' relationships deserves serious attention, given the restricted distribution of finds at harbour sites and central places, the range of shapes found, which are largely associable with drinking, and the importance of feasting to the elites of all regions involved (2003: especially chs 4–5). The distribution of similar pottery types within the Aegean itself could often be interpreted in a similar light.

In any case, it is not necessary to rely solely on the presence of foreign pottery to deduce links with the outside world. Throughout the period covered by this book, the basic metals copper, tin, and increasingly iron, would have been in demand. Yet tin sources are unknown in the Aegean, copper sources that can be worked with early technology are relatively rare, and iron sources are hardly ubiquitous. Thus, it is inherently likely that most communities acquired these metals by some form of exchange, and no site that felt the need for them could have been truly self-sufficient. The very presence of metals at a site should suggest that it was linked somehow to an exchange network, and their acquisition could have considerable resemblances to a 'commercial' venture (cf. Athena's presentation of herself to Telemachus in *Odyssey* 1.180–4 as Mentes, a Taphian chieftain, aiming to exchange a boatload of iron for copper at Temese).

The desire for metals, not merely the basic metals but gold and silver, may in fact have underlain much of the exchange activity in the period, especially that involving relatively long distances, and it has often been specifically identified as the mainspring of Phoenician activity in the Aegean and the rest of the Mediterranean. But it is going too far to suppose that evidence for exchange activity always relates to a search for metals, for, as pointed out in Chapter 4 (p. 82), it cannot be assumed that all known metal sources were being exploited at this particular time, and any suggestion that metals were moved purely by foreign traders (as implied by Tandy 1997: 59, although Tandy has surprisingly little to say about metals) may be considered inherently unlikely. Donlan (1997: 652–4) gives a more plausible picture of pre-800 conditions, but still perhaps a rather minimalist one. There is much in Purcell's argument (1990) that contact between the different regions of the Aegean and more generally of the Mediterranean was part of the natural order of things, but for reasons stated above it is harder to make any certain deductions from variations in the visible evidence.

Exchange in the Postpalatial Period

The disappearance of highly organised political units from the Aegean as a result of the Collapse, and the roughly contemporary upheavals in the Near East, must have had a radical effect on the conditions of exchange. Although Egypt, Assyria and Babylonia remained considerable powers for a time, and sophisticated urbanised societies survived in many parts, including Cyprus, the whole system of long-distance international diplomatic relations disappeared, and the disintegration of the Hittite Empire turned Anatolia and Syria into an unstable mosaic of principalities, which would inevitably affect both overland and coastal trade routes. In such conditions, long-distance exchange may have seemed an increasingly hazardous business, which might well deter those who were not focused on obtaining particular goods and commodities. These would be particularly rulers and members of local elites, who could best afford to maintain ships, and would be most able to call on the manpower to crew them, in the absence of any larger state organisation. Like the great rulers before them, these might use traders, who could be other elite members or even relatives, to act as their agents, or take an active role themselves (like 'Mentes'). Nor should it be forgotten that commodities and trade goods could have been moved by small-scale operators who moved over local circuits only, of the kind referred to derisively in *Odyssey* 8.161–4.

In the new conditions, it would be more necessary than ever for those who wanted to carry on trade over some distance to establish personal relationships in places where they wished to trade, to ensure some regard for their interests and security for themselves or their agents and their ships' crews. The natural medium for this would be gift exchange, probably associated with guest friendship in the case of elite persons, which involves the mutual acceptance of a code of honour and system of obligations (cf. Murray 1993: 48–9). Often the gifts involved would be prestige items whose main if not only use would be in ceremonial or ritual contexts. Many of the objects commonly cited as evidence for 'trade', both in the Postpalatial Period and later, could be such prestige items, rather than primary articles of trade, but they may still be taken to indicate a relationship that surely had as its ultimate motive the acquisition of commodities and sometimes manufactured items.

The quantities of foreign items found in Postpalatial contexts, which are rather more conspicuous than in the Third Palace Period, might reasonably be taken to suggest that traders were still visiting the Aegean, especially from the Near East. But this raises the question: what interest could traders based in the Near East have in the Aegean, where no state organisations capable of assembling large quantities of commodities like staple agricultural products or textiles now existed? Some sites, like Tiryns, may have continued to attract traders simply because of their size, but one of the principal attractions may have been metals, especially silver from the Laurion mines and perhaps also from Chalcidice. A position on, or as the destination of, long-distance trade routes particularly concerned with the movement of metals may provide the simplest explanation for the concentration of the bulk of the evidence for exchange at certain sites, particularly those which could have served as way-stations on routes from the Near East to Perati, which probably controlled the Laurion mines, or to the north Aegean via the Euripos, or to the central Mediterranean via Crete and the west coasts of Greece. Many of these sites could have acted as 'gateway communities' or entrepôts, where foreign traders could find tradable surpluses of local goods, and from which foreign goods and commodities could be distributed through local networks. Also ships from the Near East might not have ventured as far as the north Aegean or the Adriatic, but have found it easier to rely on Aegean ships to bring goods and commodities from these distant regions (cf. Popham 1994b: 30). Yet the Cypriots clearly maintained an active interest in the central Mediterranean, especially Sardinia, which seems to have continued without any significant break into the EIA (Crielaard 1998: 191–9).

In this period there is a marked change in the type of evidence available for long-distance exchange. Standardised types of metal ingot and large container vessel apparently disappear from Aegean contexts, although they survived in the Near East (see Crielaard 1998: 195 on ingots). The few fragments of Syro-Palestinian ('Canaanite') amphorae reported from earlier Postpalatial contexts at Mycenae and Tiryns (Cline 1994: 171, no. 310, 172, nos. 320–1) could well be cast-ups, for none have been reported from the settlement strata at Lefkandi or major cemeteries like Perati. Similarly, Aegean storage stirrup jars apparently ceased to be manufactured. Although for much of the Postpalatial Period fine ware stirrup jars may have served the purpose of holding oil, they would mostly have contained far smaller quantities than the storage vessels, though some are of substantial size, and they have a very restricted distribution outside the Aegean. Mountjoy (1993: 174–6) provides an overview of the scanty data available on the distribution of Mycenaean pottery, which makes clear how much of it that is found outside the Mycenaean core area in this period was locally made, whether in

Macedonia, Cyprus, Cilicia, south Italy and Sardinia, or at Troy. The recent discovery of a LH IIIC Early amphoriskos at Ano Komi near Kozani in Macedonia (*AR* 40 (1993–1994) 56, 58 fig. 49) is a reminder how much the present distribution pattern may reflect the chances of discovery, but it remains striking how rarely even the most elaborate types of LH IIIC Early and Middle pottery are found outside the Aegean.

This contrasts very noticeably with their wide if sporadic distribution within the Aegean, which, together with the many detectable cross-influences between the local styles, gives an impression of lively exchanges. Close Style stirrups jars reached as far east as Rhodes, while an 'octopus stirrup jar', perhaps Rhodian, reached Scoglio del Tonno in south Italy. In fact, stirrup jars and other container shapes make up the bulk of the locally produced items demonstrably being moved within and beyond the Aegean, and indicate that commodities like perfumed oil were still being produced and traded. Their generally elaborate decoration was presumably intended to emphasise the luxury nature of the contents and may well have made the vases desirable in their own right. In contrast, the equally elaborate kraters were rarely used as exchange items. One might well place the distribution of such fine vases in the sphere of ceremonial exchange.

Other evidence for continuing contacts with both the Near East and Italy consists mainly of exotic, generally small items such as figurines, beads, seals, amulets, stone weights, pins, occasional bronze vessels, knives (including the first iron examples), even bronze armour scales at Mycenae and Tiryns (Cline 1994: 223; Maran 2004). Many of the items from Perati are of this nature, including a very heterogeneous array of Egyptian, Syrian, Mesopotamian, and Cypriot seals, scarabs, amulets and beads. It is noticeable that the Egyptian items in particular seem to be products of the previous period, but this is not unusual and there seems no need to interpret them as hoarded 'heirlooms', only buried now. There is other evidence that small items like seals and scarabs continued to circulate in the Near East and Aegean long after the time of their original manufacture and that some were reworked, which suggests that they were valued partly for their exotic materials. The bronze 'smiting god' figurines of Near Eastern type found in the Phylakopi sanctuary complex in Postpalatial contexts could have arrived earlier, though no Aegean examples are demonstrably from earlier contexts (Renfrew 1985: 303–10). In all, these items represent a curious mixture of simple trinkets and much more valuable prestige items like metal vessels, but perhaps all carried prestige because of their foreign origin.

Further evidence for a picture of widespread exchanges and contacts may be drawn from the spread of the different types of new metal artefacts, all of which may have originated in northern Italy (see Chapter 5, p. 162). They include long pins, fibulae, Type II swords, and 'flame' spearheads, of which some of the earliest Type II swords may well be imports and Italian types of dagger and knife surely are. These last are found more rarely than the swords and were not adopted as local types in the Aegean, but have an interesting distribution: they are common in Crete (most come from the cave at Psychro), but occur also at other significant Postpalatial centres such as Lefkandi, Phylakopi, Ialysos, and on Naxos (Cline 1994: 225–7, cf. also 230, two Italian razors from Cephallenia and Crete; see Sherratt 2000, fig. 5.1 for the distribution of European types of weapon and knife).

Recent papers have suggested both an economic and social context for these exchanges: Borgna and Cassola Guida (2005) believe that the Italian elite was exporting foodstuffs on a large scale – an interesting idea, but one that requires believing that the Aegean could not produce its own food – while Eder and Jung (2005) draw attention to evidence for shared values between the Italian and Aegean elites, reflected in the exchange of high-quality metal types and perhaps even the movement of small numbers of Italians with specialised skills (smiths, mercenaries) to the Aegean, even before the Collapse. Such ideas have considerable plausibility, but difficulties should not be ignored. For instance, as noted in Chapter 2, an Italian origin has been suggested for HMB ware, but its distribution pattern does not fit that of Italian types of bronzework very well, failing to match the large concentrations of such bronzework found in Achaea and the eastern half of Crete. The European links of the decoration of bronze items from Kallithea and the Submyc bronze helmet from Tiryns may in fact lie a bit further to the north (Harding 1984: 176, 178).

The general impression given by this material is of lively exchanges criss-crossing the Mediterranean, continuing the activity of the Third Palace Period and reaching almost as far. The prosperity detectable in the middle phases of the Postpalatial Period may well, as suggested in Chapter 3, derive largely from this activity. But the evidence also suggests that these exchanges were conducted on a much smaller scale than before, and may have been rather sporadic, opportunistic, and not ultimately sustainable. Far fewer exchanges of elaborate pottery between the Aegean regions can be identified in the final Postpalatial phases, and hardly any pottery of these phases is found outside the Aegean (Coldstream 1988: 38 cites a piece from Tyre closely resembling 'Final Mycenaean' skyphoi from Asine, but E.S. Sherratt, pers. comm., suspects from the description that it is PG). Similarly, fewer exotic items are found in Aegean contexts. But some Near Eastern material may still have been reaching not only Crete but the mainland, e.g. a Syro-Palestinian vessel fragment reported from a LH IIIC Late context at Tiryns (Cline 1994: 217, no. 747, possibly a cast-up). It is not clear how late the Cypriot bronze rod tripod and other exotic items in the Tiryns Treasure, especially the extraordinary 'sunwheels' which include the amber beads that give their name to the very widespread 'Tiryns' type, should be placed, but they could well be as late as this. Also, the distribution patterns of distinctive types of amber bead like the 'Tiryns' and 'Allumiere' types are remarkably widespread, providing another reminder that long-distance exchange is not necessarily documented by pottery (both types have been thought Italian, but have been found as remotely as in kurgan burials at Hordeevka in the Ukraine, as reported by K. Slusarska-Michalik at Laffineur *et al.* 2005).

Exchange in the Early Iron Age

Some discussions barely seem to allow any role for exchange that is not gift exchange in the EIA Aegean. The word 'trade' does not figure, for instance, in Jones (1999), which suggests that a 'leader' would acquire almost everything he and his household (*oikos*) needed by raiding, if it was not produced by the household. This seems an implausibly literal interpretation of the Homeric evidence. More often it is suggested that the Aegean effectively lost contact with the outside world in the early stages of the EIA, and that there was even breakdown in contact between different parts of the Aegean region. It is true that the heterogeneous range of small items that can be linked with the Near East and Italy largely disappears from Aegean EIA contexts, especially the most clearly recognisable, like scarabs, seals, and beads. Near Eastern items also seem to become rarer in Cypriot contexts at a time equivalent to the beginning of the Aegean EIA, and in Italian contexts of eleventh–tenth century date (I am grateful to Dr J. Toms of the Institute of Archaeology, Oxford, for advice on Italy). It is tempting to deduce a considerable decline in the level of exchange, or at least a significant change in its nature, throughout the east and central Mediterranean, although there are other possible explanations, e.g. that such items had simply lost their prestige value. It is also true that for a while in the EIA little or no Aegean pottery can be found outside the Aegean and movement of pottery is often hard to identify within it, but as previously noted too much emphasis should not be placed on this.

The eleventh and tenth centuries

It has been argued (Chapter 5, p. 147) that the craft of iron-working was very probably being introduced from the Near East, perhaps specifically Cyprus, at the time of the transition from the Postpalatial Period to the EIA. Cyprus is also the generally agreed source for certain specific pottery shapes that were particularly popular at this time. Some iron items in the Aegean may be direct Cypriot imports of this date, although others had arrived earlier (see Sherratt 1994: 88, 91–2 for lists; Chapter 5, p. 147); one iron dagger from the EPG Skoubris T. 46 at Lefkandi was even accompanied by a Syro-Palestinian juglet (*Lefkandi I*: 126, 347–8). More general testimonies to continued exchange activity and the spread of types and ideas can be seen at Karphi, to which, despite its relative remoteness, types of jewellery otherwise typical of Submyc and SM contexts, Italian bronzes, a few items of iron, and even knowledge of the Cypriot bronze openwork stand penetrated

(Desborough 1972: 126–7; for the stand see Hoffman 1997: 118, for Italian bronzes Crielaard 1998: 197). Italian bronzes were also offered in the Psychro cave, in the same region as Karphi (Popham 1994a: 285). Though such finds are scanty and often hard to date closely, they strengthen the likelihood that exchange contacts, both within the Aegean, and between the Aegean and neighbouring regions, never completely ceased (cf. Catling and Jones 1989: 184). It has even been suggested that there was actual movement of people from Cyprus back to the Aegean (Desborough 1972: 340–1), who have been suggested by Catling to have established themselves as new rulers at Knossos and perhaps elsewhere (1995). Although no motive is offered for such a movement, the Cypriot links of some of the earliest and richest North Cemetery burials at Knossos are notably strong.

The appearance of cremations and iron knives with bronze handles on Thasos, and of pottery of Submyc and PG styles in the cemetery at Torone, indicates that the north Aegean also had contacts with regions further south. The appearance on Thasos of glass beads, that may have Italian links, and amber beads of the 'Allumiere' type (Koukouli-Chrysanthaki 1992: 822) gives further indications of the island's external connections, more probably made by sea routes than by land routes through the Balkans. Comparable finds come from the Vergina cemetery, which has clear links to the north in its jewellery traditions (Snodgrass 1971: 254), and the pottery of Thasos is strongly linked to that of Macedonia. As suggested above, local metal sources could be the main reason for this perceptible level of exchange activity involving the north Aegean. Thasos seems to have been acquiring copper from Chalcidic sources and further afield (Koukouli-Chrysanthaki 1992: 784–801), so more central Aegean regions could have done the same. The possibility that the wealth of the Koukos cemetery in Chalcidice also relates to exploitation of local metal sources (*AR* 39 (1992–93) 54) cannot be ignored.

The wide distribution in the north Aegean of the distinctive neck-handled amphorae decorated with circles (Figure 5.6) provides an indication that exchange activity here did not only involve metals, since they were surely containers for some substance (Catling 1998b: 176–7 on the sources; recent neutron activation analysis suggests that at least some Trojan examples are of local origin: Mommsen *et al.* 2001: 194). They may have begun as a central Greek type, but were almost certainly produced in Thessaly and spread to Macedonia (Figure 7.1), which seems to be the home of the Group II form, although it has a wide distribution pattern. It is unlikely to be an accident that this pattern overlaps markedly with the area within which the influence of the Euboean PG style seems to be strongest, and that handmade vessels of likely Macedonian origin found their way to Lefkandi, to form part of the 'Heroön' fill (*Lefkandi II, 1*: 65), while a Macedonian style of painted ware became established in eastern Thessaly. Surely this all represents a significant exchange network, but there is no need to interpret the evidence purely in

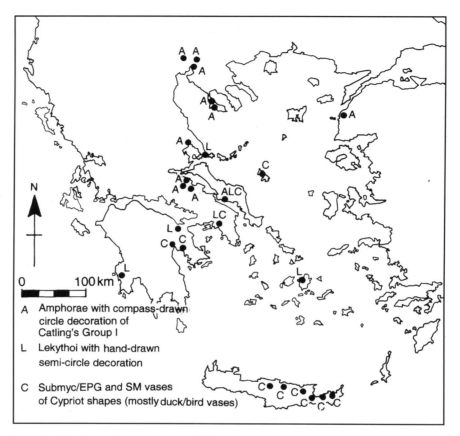

Figure 7.1 Distribution map of special pottery types.

terms of the activity of Euboean traders. Macedonian container vessels could have been carried to other regions in Macedonian or other non-Euboean ships, some of the earliest-looking pottery from the Torone cemetery appears to be Attic or close to it, and Cycladic and Thessalian pottery has also been reported (Papadopoulos 1996b: 157).

Other potentially important evidence of exchange can be traced through the distribution of distinctive pottery types like the Cypriot-linked shapes noted in Chapter 1 (pp. 14–15) and the lekythos decorated with hand-drawn semicircles (Figure 7.1), perhaps even the group of stylistic features considered typically PG (Chapter 5, p. 129), all of which were current around the time of the transition from Submyc to PG. By MPG, what has been called a Euboean 'koinē' of shared pottery shapes takes in a considerable part of Greece (Chapter 5, p. 132; Lemos 2002: 213–17, with map 7). Several shapes found in material from Cos are close to Lefkandi types, and

Euboean vases have been identified in Naxos and Amorgos, and reached the Syro-Phoenician coast, especially Tyre (Coldstream 1998b: 355; Lemos 2002: 228). Attic MPG is also quite widely distributed, forming the bulk of the identifiable imports in the Lefkandi 'Heroön' deposit and appearing on Aigina, Kea, perhaps Naxos, also at Asine, Argos and even Knossos (Catling 1998a: especially 376–8). Lefkandi's external connections are further enhanced by the presence in the 'Heroön' deposit of the newly developed Black Slip ware (Catling 1998a; 55), which also appears in Thessaly and on Skyros and seems to have north-east Aegean links, two pieces that may be Argive (*Lefkandi II, 1*: 89), and a substantial group that look foreign but cannot be derived from a particular source (*Lefkandi II, 1*: 65–7, 90). An apparently Rhodian oinochoe that reached Amorgos (Catling and Jones 1989: 182–3) strengthens this picture of cross-Aegean connections. The occurrence of a skyphos fragment thought to be potentially Argive E/MPG at Tell Afis in northern Syria (not shown on Figure 7.3; Luke 2003: 32, 35 fig. 13) is remarkable, given the possibly Argive skyphos fragments from Lefkandi and Tyre (Coldstream 1988: 38), and a reminder that we may still only be seeing part of the picture.

These patterns are much strengthened in LPG, in terms of the quantities of material, when Attic pottery is found in most of the rich Lefkandi graves, is well represented in the north Peloponnese, the Cycladic islands and Ionia, as far east as Samos, and at Knossos, while Euboean PG types reach Amathus in Cyprus and are quite common at Tyre, including amphorae (which are also found at Ras el Bassit and Tel Dor; Lemos 2002: 228). Both styles also seem to exert considerable stylistic influence in their Aegean areas of distribution. In contrast, very few links of this kind can be identified between the east and west sides of the Greek mainland. A single PG lekythos-fragment from Ithaca may be Attic or north-east Peloponnesian (Catling 1998a: 372 n. 31), while at Antheia in Messenia a complete skyphos that appears to be locally made is claimed to have similar connections (it looks more Argive than Attic), which are strengthened by the presence of several typically PG conical feet (Coulson 1986: 31–2). But no PG Attic or Euboean pottery has yet been identified in Italy; pieces found here that have been classified as PG, and might derive from western Greek regions, are unlikely to date so early in absolute terms.

Two things stand out about this material. One is that it includes not only drinking and pouring vessels, which might have been exchanged as prestige items through their association with ceremonial drinking and libation, but amphorae. These should reflect the exchange of commodities like oil, wine or foodstuffs, which would be prominent among the commodities that most Aegean communities would have available for trade. The other is that, as pointed out by Catling (1998a: 371–2), the distribution patterns of both Attic and Euboean pottery are selective. Attic is absent from the Thessalo-Euboean area, apart from Lefkandi, as is Euboean PG from the Peloponnese.

It cannot, then, be simply a matter of Euboean ships distributing Attic pottery or vice versa. Indeed, Attic pottery could largely have been spread to the Peloponnese and central Greece by intermediaries like Aigina and Corinth (Catling 1998a: 372), and Euboean pottery could have reached not only the Near East but the north Aegean in non-Euboean ships. In general, the evidence might suit a picture of fairly frequent but small-scale exchanges, that did not follow any regular patterns.

Euboeans or Phoenicians?

Although Near Eastern items and probably materials are represented in the grave-goods of the Lefkandi 'Heroön' burials, Near Eastern pottery is strikingly absent from the building fill, which is particularly remarkable because of the very considerable quantities of pottery involved. In fact, only two examples of Cypriot pottery have been identified in Aegean LPG contexts – the well-known flask from Lefkandi: Palaia Perivolia T. 22 and a likely cup fragment from Volos (Sipsie-Eschbach 1991: 52). Evidently luxury oil containers were not yet a trade item, as they were to be later. But there are other luxury items in remarkable quantities from a whole series of graves at Lefkandi datable *c.* 950–825, especially in the Toumba cemetery, including bronze and faience vessels of Egyptian or Egyptianising style and Syro-Phoenician bronze bowls (Figures 7.2, 7.3), masses of faience beads, and quantities of goldwork, some of which shows the technique of granulation that was probably reintroduced from the Near East (Coldstream 1998b: 355–6, also 1998c: 14–15). Other exotic items or materials like amber and rock crystal that must be imported also occur sporadically.

The potential closeness of relations between Lefkandi and the Near East at this time is underlined by the production at Lefkandi from LPG onwards of the pendent semicircles plate (Figure 5.12). The distribution pattern, which

Figure 7.2 Egyptian-style faience vessels from Lefkandi: Toumba T. 39. H. 8.5 cm (ring flask), 8.9 cm (lugged flask), 9.2 cm (other two). Courtesy of the British School at Athens.

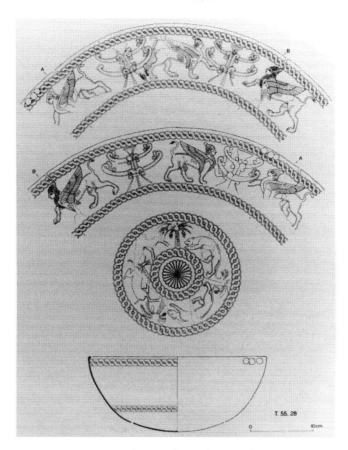

Figure 7.3 Syro-Phoenician gilt bronze bowl from Lefkandi: Toumba T. 55. D. 28.3 cm, H. 12.7 cm. Courtesy of the British School at Athens.

focuses on Lefkandi and Tyre (the type has also been rarely identified at Athens, Asine and Ras el Bassit), has led Coldstream to suggest that it represents a deliberate attempt to produce a high-quality version of a shape that was central to Near Eastern dining practices (1988: 38–9, also 1998b: 354–5). Production of these plates and their distribution in the Near East evidently continued for a considerable period, probably well into the eighth century, and spread to the Cyclades, for one of two sets from rich tombs on Cyprus datable to the early eighth century is apparently Cycladic. This fits with the evidence for Cycladic production of another Euboean shape, the pendent semicircles skyphos, which had considerable distribution in the Near East (Figure 7.4). Similarly, some of the skyphoi in Attic MG I–II style found in the Near East could be Cycladic (Coldstream 1977: 93; but Popham 1994b: 27–8 suggests that many are Euboean). But outside Tyre the PG

211

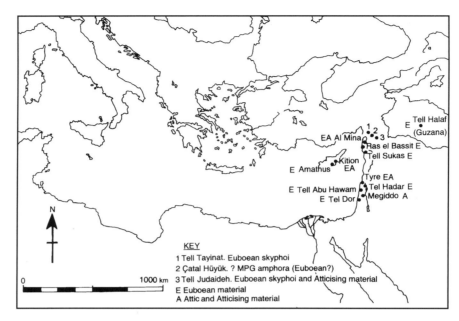

Figure 7.4 Distribution map of pre-800 Greek pottery outside the Aegean (after Popham 1994b, fig. 2.12, and Lemos 2002, 228 and map 8).

vessels found at Syro-Phoenician sites are predominantly amphorae, which suggests that these were imported for their contents, perhaps olive oil (Courbin 1993: 103, 107), and that Tyre may have been the centre of import and distribution of this Euboean pottery (including to Amathus).

The crucial question is the significance of Lefkandi's close Near Eastern links, which are effectively unique in the Aegean for the later tenth century and still quite remarkable for the ninth century, although by then there is some comparable material from Knossos and Athens. It goes without saying that such limited material can hardly support any suggestion of a core-periphery relationship between the Near East and the Aegean at this time. The standard interpretation has been that it reflects Euboean initiative in re-establishing links with the Near East (as in sources cited in Papadopoulos 1997). Coldstream has even suggested that these included personal relations, perhaps intermarriage, between the elites of Lefkandi and Tyre (1997: 356–7). In contrast, Papadopoulos has suggested that it represents the settlement of 'enterprising Easterners' at Lefkandi, that the Toumba T. 79 burial suggested by Popham and Lemos to be a 'Euboean warrior trader' (1995) could be such a settler, by implication that the pendent semicircle plates were commissioned by Near Eastern traders and/or settlers, and that discoveries of Near Eastern items in tenth- and ninth-century Aegean contexts 'accord well with the references, in later Greek literature, of early Phoenician activity in the

Aegean' (1997: especially 192–3, 200 (on plates), 206; cf. Sherratt 2002: 229–30). Courbin has also argued that Euboean pottery was brought to the Near East by Phoenicians (1993: 107–11).

It is always salutary to be forced to acknowledge one's preconceptions, and Papadopoulos's criticisms of the arguments used to support a picture of Mediterranean-wide Euboean activity can often seem reasonable. But I do not believe that anything is gained by substituting ubiquitous Phoenicians for ubiquitous Euboeans as the principal driving force behind the expansion in exchange activity at this time. The peculiarities of Toumba T. 79, especially the presence of Cypriot and Levantine oil flasks and weights, otherwise unexampled at Lefkandi, might well suggest that one of the two burials now distinguished (Chapter 6, p. 193) could have been that of someone deriving from the Near East, whether a visitor or resident. But other features such as the presence of weapons fit local practice, and though the tomb-type is odd, it and the general features of the Toumba cemetery have no obvious parallels with what may be observed in plausibly 'expatriate' Phoenician cemeteries, e.g. at Amathus (Christou 1998).

Furthermore, Phoenicians came from an urban environment, with a sophisticated culture, and it is hard to picture them settling permanently anywhere in any numbers without leaving considerable traces of their presence apart from burials. But as at Thasos, so at Lefkandi: no features have been identified of the kind used to certify or plausibly suggest a Phoenician presence at sites like Kition, Amathus and Kommos, or later in the central and west Mediterranean (cf. Ridgway 1994) – no pottery, whether transport vessels, plates, or other domestic types, no graffiti, no substantial architecture, no distinctive element in ritual behaviour (contrast the Kommos shrine; Shaw 1998: 18–20). The actual rarity of the pendent semicircles plates at Lefkandi and in the Aegean generally is particularly striking if these were designed specifically to suit Near Eastern dining practices, such as one might expect Near Eastern settlers in the Aegean to follow. It seems more plausible that Greek visitors to the Near East discovered that the plate was an 'indispensable domestic chattel' there, than that the information came from Near Eastern visitors to the Aegean (Coldstream 1998b: 354). Even the argument that individual Near Eastern craftsmen, whether from Phoenicia or north Syria, settled in Crete has been subjected to searching criticism by Hoffman (1997), who convincingly questions Boardman's claim (1999: ch. 3 and 272–5) that the links of the relevant material are mainly north Syrian. But such settlement remains a possibility where advanced craft techniques and very Near Eastern artistic styles are seen to be transferred, as in north Crete.

Coldstream's postulated elite intermarriages certainly offer a tempting alternative explanation for the extraordinary quantity of Near Eastern luxury goods in the Lefkandi graves, which are hard to interpret simply as the products of 'trade', and for the evidently close connection with Tyre. But

213

such intermarriages, when made over such a distance, would surely require some important motivation, which in the circumstances could certainly be some form of mutually beneficial exchange, although the prestige element involved in establishing gift-exchange relationships over great distances may well have been a factor. Such explanations might suit the occurrence of such material at Knossos also (*NorthCem*: 716), though this is generally thought less plausible. Such personal links and possibly a similar motivation could also lie behind the presence of distinctively Attic types of burial and of much very fine pottery and other characteristically Attic products at Lefkandi; Coldstream has postulated Attic immigrants ([1977] 2003: 373).

The appearance of Euboean pottery at a restricted group of Near Eastern sites enhances this picture of potentially personal relations, as does the evidence that until the eighth century Euboean pottery is virtually the only kind found in the Near East. For, as Boardman has pointed out (1999: 271), Near Eastern traders could have no reason to pick up Euboean pottery exclusively, when they could encounter a wide variety of other wares in the Aegean that were just as exotic and equally if not more attractive, especially Attic. Coldstream has argued that establishing trade links with the Near East derived from the Greeks' 'urgent need to travel eastwards in pursuit of metal ores and other raw materials lacking in Greece' (1998b: 356). But, as seen already, this did not necessarily require going outside the Aegean for some of the most commonly desired metals, and the value of the goods and materials found at Lefkandi, together with the unique quality of many individual items, might well be taken to suggest that it was Near Easterners, rather than Euboeans, who were 'desperate'. Ultimately, no argument is conclusive, and it seems quite likely that Coldstream is right to postulate that Euboeans and Phoenicians worked closely together ([1977] 2003: 374). Luke (2003: 56–9) provides a judicious survey of the whole topic.

Whichever end of the link was the most active one, the Lefkandi elite clearly profited from it, but it remains something of a problem as to what they had to offer, apart from the prestige of such a distant connection. It has been argued by the Sherratts (as cited in Popham 1994b: 30) that Lefkandi is a natural anchorage for ships intending to go through the Euripos, allowing its inhabitants to exact tolls and payment for services. But if these were Phoenician ships, there is no evidence for their going further. Since as Popham points out, clearly or even plausibly Near Eastern material is conspicuously rare in this region, and there remains the question: what drew them in this direction? As before, metals may be the answer. As noted in Chapter 4, no evidence demonstrates that Euboean sources, which do not include the most valued metals anyway, were exploited, but the establishment of the Thessalo-Euboean stylistic area suggests close relations within much of the north Aegean. To judge from the splendour of the Lefkandi finds, the Euboeans would have been the leading group in this activity, so they could have provided the conduit through which north Aegean materials flowed to other regions (cf. Popham 1994b: 30, 33). They could even have taken silver from Laurion eastwards in ingot form (if it all went into the Near Eastern trade, this would explain the virtual lack of silver items in Attica and Euboea, noted as a problem in Coldstream 1998c: 259–60). This must all remain rather hypothetical, in the absence of analytical data, but it does not seem impossible.

The ninth and eighth centuries

The striking discoveries in the Toumba cemetery at Lefkandi, the North Cemetery at Knossos, and at Tyre undermined Coldstream's original picture of the earlier ninth century as a time of marked deterioration in exchange relations both within and beyond the Aegean, as he has acknowledged, but the fact remains that this evidence is confined to a few sites. The quantity of material available as evidence for exchange in the ninth century also remains small in absolute terms, if anything less striking than in the later tenth. Of the forty or so ninth-century Attic vases from the Knossos North Cemetery, nearly half were found in one tomb (G), and there is only a handful of pieces from other Greek sources. In general, the majority of ninth-century Greek pottery vessels found outside their home context are drinking vessels, although there are some amphorae and kraters (both large and potentially prestigious shapes associable with drinking) and pyxides, and the total quantity is unimpressive, suggesting that such pottery is more a sign of activity than a significant exchange item in its own right. It is noteworthy that Corinthian pottery began to appear at other sites in the ninth century, and was carried across the Gulf of Corinth to Phocis in some quantity (Coldstream 1977: 85, 177–9), but none from the western end of the Gulf or in Epirus has been dated before the early eighth century, and hardly any pieces found in the Aegean date before that (Coldstream 1977: 182; a hand-made aryballos at Knossos is dated MG I, see *NorthCem*: 402). This draws attention to a newly developing centre, but the gradualness of its expansion may be taken as a reflection of general trends.

There are notable peculiarities in the ninth-century distribution of material. Thus, Attic pottery is much the most prominent exported ware in the Aegean, and was clearly valued for its quality. Not only is a much wider range of shapes represented in non-Attic contexts than of any other Greek ware, but some pieces found at Lefkandi and Knossos are as fine as anything found in Attica, if not finer; unsurprisingly, these Attic imports tend to appear in the wealthiest tombs. Yet the Attic pieces found in the Near East are few and unremarkable, and far fewer items of Near Eastern origin are to be found in the Athens graves, despite conspicuous exceptions like the Areopagus woman's grave H 16:6 (Smithson 1968; Coldstream 1977: 55–6), than at Lefkandi. The range of luxury Near Eastern items at Lefkandi is also more impressive than that at Knossos, although this may partly reflect the disappearance or destruction of material during the repeated use of the Knossos tombs. But the oil flasks of ultimately Phoenician type, apparently produced in Cyprus, that began to be imported and produced locally in the Dodecanese and at Knossos during the ninth and eighth centuries (most recently, Coldstream 1998a: 255–8), are only found in one Lefkandi grave (Toumba T. 79A) and never reached Athens. Finally, Euboean pottery is not well represented at Athens or Knossos, where the somewhat more prominent Cycladic imports are of Atticising rather than Euboean style (*NorthCem*: 403–4), nor in Cyprus, but it remains quite common at Tyre.

Altogether, the peculiarities of distribution suggest that exchange may still have been a matter of separate links, sometimes regular, sometimes opportunistic, between particular regions, sites, families or individuals, and that much of the material may relate to the exchange of gifts rather than commodities. The growth of evidence for wealth in the tenth and ninth centuries seems intimately linked to the evidence for external exchange at Lefkandi, Knossos, and at least to some extent Athens. But this is harder to demonstrate for other centres with relatively richly provided burials, such as Elateia or indeed Vergina. The real expansion both in exchange activity and in adoption or adaptation of Near Eastern techniques, types and themes in various areas of art does not seem to begin until late in the ninth century, and gathers pace fast in the eighth century. In this respect, Coldstream's description of the period after *c.* 770 as a 'renaissance' still seems reasonable, but it might best be seen as an intensification of already existing contacts, possibly responding to political changes in the Near East, rather than an effectively new departure.

In the eighth century, particularly its second half, it becomes possible to argue that certain processes were affecting at least the greater part, if not all, of the Aegean area. Thus, in the second half of the eighth century all regions began producing versions of the LG style, although some derived their immediate inspiration not from Athens, where the style originated, but from other major centres such as Argos and Corinth. Corinth's influence became more general late in the century as certain of its pottery types, especially drinking vessels, became so popular as to form an 'export ware' whose distribution can hardly reflect Corinthian activity alone. Materials became much more readily available, particularly bronze, which was used by workshops in relatively many centres that produced figurines and sometimes tripod vessels for dedication, but also gold, amber and ivory, although most ivory items are thought to have been produced by craftsmen who were Near Eastern immigrants or locals under strong Near Eastern artistic influence. Classes of object that clearly reflect Near Eastern influence, whether or not they were made by immigrant craftsmen, started appearing at different centres, such as the gold headbands and jewellery, especially earrings, and a unique group of ivory figurines in Attica, stone seals in the Argolid, ivory seals at Corinth, and a whole range of different products in gold, bronze and ivory from Crete.

Mostly these have relatively confined distributions, but the increasingly international flavour of the exchange of goods and of the influences that could be received by Aegean craftsmen is well reflected in the wide range of sources for imported items apparently dedicated on Ithaca, although the foreign pottery is overwhelmingly Corinthian (Coldstream 1977: 184), the distances over which some items, including pots, could travel (e.g. a Sardinian pot at Knossos; Ridgway 1994: 39), and the fact that the famous Argos panoply combines a Near Eastern type of helmet with a European type of corslet (Harding 1984: 176; Snodgrass [1971] 2000: 271–2). Overall, then, it does seem that the level of exchange within the Aegean and between the Aegean and the Near East was intensifying, and the horizons of many Aegean communities were widening quite rapidly.

Before the middle of the eighth century, if not even in the late ninth, some Greek vases were reaching the central Mediterranean, including Sardinia, often appearing in the same contexts as Near Eastern items and so perhaps supporting Coldstream's theory of Phoenician-Euboean collaboration. These include a few examples of the pendent semicircles skyphos (from Veii, probably Rome, and one site each in Sicily and Sardinia), but are mainly of the chevron skyphos type, originally an Attic form, to which most of the earliest Greek pots from Etruria and Campania belong. As drinking vessels, they might well be interpreted as 'initiatory gifts' in Luke's terminology (2003: 52). Many of them are Euboean, and Pithecusae, the first substantial settlement of Greeks outside the Aegean, which seems to have been established by *c.* 750, has strong Euboean connections (Ridgway 1992). It was surely established primarily with exchange in mind, since it was on a relatively small island, although it appears to have swiftly attracted far more people than one can imagine being dependent wholly on exchange for their livelihood. The arguments for a similar settlement of Greeks at Al Mina in Syria seem weak by comparison, involving, as Snodgrass has pointed out (1994: 4), the presence of fine-ware eating and drinking vessels only, which need no more indicate settlement than comparable material does when found at other Syrian sites. Nevertheless, Al Mina was clearly a trading centre to which much Greek material was brought over a long period, and it is hard to doubt that at least some of this was brought by traders from Greek home ports (cf. Snodgrass 1994: 5). As before, the pottery includes Euboean and Attic types and Cycladic imitations of them, but Rhodian and Corinthian vessels were also appearing by the end of the eighth century (Coldstream 1977: 359; see now Luke 2003).

Debates over the extent to which the evidence reflects distinctively Greek or Phoenician enterprise are beginning to seem increasingly sterile, in the light of the widespread evidence for Near Eastern artistic and technical influence in Greece, the indications that there was a Near Eastern element among the settlers on Pithecusae (Ridgway 1992: 111–18 sets out the evidence most fully; see also 1994), and the virtual certainty that the Greek alphabet

217

was devised by Greeks intimately familiar with Phoenician writing. This may even have taken place before 750 (Coldstream [1977] 2003: 406) and very plausibly outside 'old Greece'. It seems more important to note that different sites and regions responded very differently to Near Eastern influences. It is also noteworthy that only certain Greek wares appeared overseas in any quantity at all: if this does not necessarily signify that traders from the producing centres were especially active in overseas exchange, as argued most frequently for the Euboeans, it does at least suggest that these centres were those most regularly frequented by traders of whatever origin. But even here an exception must be made for Crete, for despite the large quantities of evidence for external, especially Near Eastern, contacts and influences of many kinds, Cretan pottery is rarely found outside the island, although Cretan metalwork sometimes travelled (Coldstream 1977: 288–9). The reason may simply be that Cretan pottery was not so attractive as that of other regions; the drinking vessels in particular are rather drab by comparison with Attic and Euboean skyphoi. It may also be that, being well placed on a natural route through the Mediterranean, the Cretan communities did not need to make exceptional efforts to acquire foreign goods and materials. Finally, whatever their degree of activity in overseas exchange and ultimately settlement, the Greek communities at this time were still essentially recipients of external influences, rather than exerting influence elsewhere, and would remain so for some time to come.

Bibliography

General: Dickinson (1994a: ch. 7) considers Aegean BA trade and exchange (250–6 are especially relevant to the Third Palace Period and Postpalatial Period). Cline (1994) is a valuable general survey; see also Knapp (1990, 1991). Gale (1991) contains important papers (especially those by Catling, Snodgrass), also Karageorghis and Stampolidis (1998), Laffineur and Greco (2005). For references for the Uluburun and Cape Gelidonya shipwrecks see the Chapter 2 bibliography (p. 57).

S.P. Morris (1992: 130–46) assembles the literary references to Phoenician activity in the Aegean. Whitley (2001: ch. 6) valuably discusses the topic of Near Eastern links and influences; he also makes important observations on trade (2001: 175). On Lefkandi and the Near East, Popham (1994b) is useful. Hoffman (1997) is an important survey of the whole question of Near Eastern connections, focusing on Crete.

Luke (2003), a detailed and valuable study of the Geometric material in the Near East, focusing on Al Mina, only came to my attention at the last moment; I have inserted some references in this chapter, hoping that I have not misunderstood her hypothesis.

8

RELIGION

(Figure 8.1 shows all sites mentioned in this chapter)

Introduction

Religion played a very large role in historical Greek society. It was central to the Greeks' perception of themselves as a distinct people (see Herod. 8.144) and to their various communities' expression of their identity. Up to and including the Classical period, the most monumental public buildings in every state were with very few exceptions sacred structures, especially temples, which as well as being symbols of reverence for their patron deities served to advertise the wealth of the communities that undertook their construction and, when found outside the main centres, might be used to state claims to territory (de Polignac 1995: ch. 2). Further, the fine arts were very largely deployed to produce offerings to the gods and representations of them, and all major festivals, including the pan-Hellenic athletic contests, were held in their honour. By *c.* 700 or a little later, it may be argued that many of the features of this historical Greek religion had become well established: all the leading Greek gods are referred to in the Homeric poems, in which many play prominent roles, while the more or less contemporary *Theogony* of Hesiod (see Rosen 1997: 464–73 on the chronology of the poems) presents a genealogy of the gods that was to become accepted as standard.

The question is bound to arise, did this historical religion represent a continuation from the BA past, and if so, to what extent? Alternatively, did it embody significant new developments in the EIA? The belief that there was continuity in the 'essence' of Greek religion from prehistoric to Classical times was once widespread, and has been expressed as recently as Dietrich (1986) – but this has been subjected to comprehensive criticism for its methodology and assumptions (which include, as a basic premise, the completely outdated belief that the Minoan and Mycenaean religions formed a unity) by Sourvinou-Inwood (1989). Such theories of continuity have generally involved taking an extremely optimistic view of the archaeological evidence. In contrast, both Desborough (1972: 283–4) and Coldstream

219

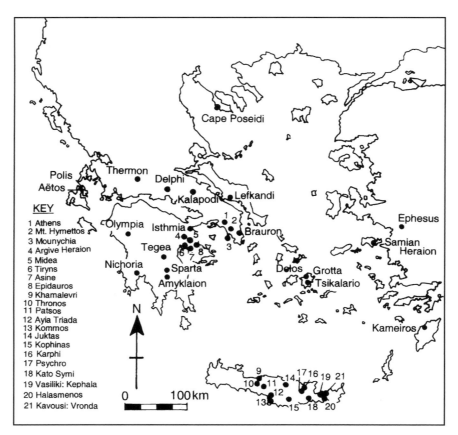

KEY

1 Athens
2 Mt. Hymettos
3 Mounychia
4 Argive Heraion
5 Midea
6 Tiryns
7 Asine
8 Epidauros
9 Khamalevri
10 Thronos
11 Patsos
12 Ayia Triada
13 Kommos
14 Juktas
15 Kophinas
16 Karphi
17 Psychro
18 Kato Symi
19 Vasiliki: Kephala
20 Halasmenos
21 Kavousi: Vronda

Figure 8.1 Postpalatial and EIA sites with significant ritual evidence.

(1977: 329) have offered extremely pessimistic assessments of the available evidence for religion in the 'Dark Age', and Burkert has also stressed the discontinuities (1985: 49–53). Although more evidence has accumulated since they wrote, it remains notably sparse prior to the eighth century. Recognising this inconvenient gap, Dietrich has tried to bridge it by arguments for a continuity of tradition, but this approach also is highly questionable, as Sourvinou-Inwood points out:

> This argument takes no account of the facts that whatever traditional beliefs and practices may have survived from earlier times were not unchanged 'fixed essences' but were affected and shaped by, and thus reshaped to fit, the changing religious framework of which they were part and which ascribed them value; and that a change in the physical framework in which cult is practised (such as the presence or

220

absence of temple) is itself a significant cultic change, which it is
methodologically illegitimate to assume was not significant . . .

(Sourvinou-Inwood 1989: 53)

As she goes on to argue, it is highly unlikely that religious features should
have remained unchanged when there were major changes in the social and
political framework within which the religion was embedded, and it is
very dangerous to assume that ancient-seeming practices must have been
inherited unchanged from the BA. I would associate myself wholeheartedly
with this approach (also argued in Morgan 1999: 369–72), which, as well as
being inherently more plausible, fits the available evidence far better. For it
is undeniable that very few significant religious sites survived from the BA
into the EIA, let alone beyond, and, as a corollary, that almost all the major
sites of historical Greek religion were new foundations of the EIA or, at the
earliest, the final stage of the BA. This is surely prima-facie evidence for
radical changes in the public practice of religion, and it provides strong
supporting evidence for the view that Greek religion underwent a constant
process of change in one aspect or another, whatever links with the past were
claimed and are in fact observable.

The continuity approach does have one positive aspect, that it sees changes
in Greek religion as largely resulting from internal processes, although it has
often incorporated the view that Ares and Dionysos were relatively late
introductions to the Greek pantheon from Thrace and Asia Minor respectively. This hypothesis is demonstrably unnecessary, now that both gods'
names have been identified in Linear B texts. But a markedly different
approach, as set out by Kirk (1990: 2–8), argues that historical Greek
religion reflects the response to a very considerable degree of Near Eastern
influence exerted over the LBA and EIA, which involved the adoption or
adaptation of many Near Eastern religious concepts and divine archetypes. I
consider this implausible for a variety of reasons, not least that the sun and
moon, which are very important focuses of cult all over the Near East, play
an insignificant role in historical Greek religion. More generally, Kirk offers
no explanation for how or why such a mass of what are presented as essentially Mesopotamian ideas was transmitted to the Aegean, when Mesopotamian religious influence is not especially marked in the religions of Syria and
Anatolia, that were closer to and undoubtedly in contact with the Aegean,
whether in the LBA or later.

It is, moreover, difficult to find any ancient parallel for such a wholesale
adoption of foreign religious ideas. On the contrary, it seems that concepts
of the attributes, functions, activities and interactions of gods were only
rarely transmitted between cultures, most often in the context of taking over
control of territories and adopting their gods (see Dickinson 1994b: 176).
Furthermore, Kirk's claim that many religious ideas and concepts of gods
and their interaction that are found in the poems of Homer and Hesiod are

of Mesopotamian origin seems to have no other basis than the supposition that, because the Mesopotamian texts in which these appear are demonstrably older than the Greek texts, the concepts must have spread from Mesopotamia to Greece. This fails to make allowances for the quite different history of literacy in the two regions, which surely makes it quite unsound methodology to suggest that a concept did not exist in Greece, simply because there is no written record of it at the relevant time. There are undoubtedly interesting parallels between the ways in which Near Eastern, especially Mesopotamian, and Greek societies imagined the nature and behaviour of the gods (see West 1997: ch. 3). But the great majority of these are features of the poetic and storytelling sphere rather than of actual cult practice.

It must be emphasised that, while Greek poets had a very important influence on the way that the gods were perceived, and their works have contributed significantly to the impression of a unified Greek religion, this is basically a poetic construct which obscures widespread local variation. In fact, Greek religion did not exist in a unified form, but rather in a great many variants that might share many features but were ultimately exclusive to particular communities (cf. Sourvinou-Inwood 1990: 295–6, 300). Such localised beliefs and practices might be expected to have the deepest roots in the past, but their history is effectively impossible to trace, for, quite apart from the major discontinuities in the archaeological record, it is clear from consideration of the textual evidence available that a great deal of public religious activity was of a kind that would be almost impossible to identify archaeologically.

For example, the religious calendars of various Athenian demes dating from the Classical period indicate the existence of a whole array of sites of public offering and sacrifice that were evidently of importance to the local community (Mikalson 1983: 68–9 counts at least thirty-five in the territory of the deme Erchia alone, and points out that these only relate to annual rites in which the deme was involved financially). Yet sites of this kind were probably not places where votives might accumulate, and had no substantial architectural features, so that barely a trace would survive archaeologically. While the Athenian demes may not provide a totally appropriate analogy for other places and times, it seems plausible that in any period we are missing evidence for a very significant proportion of public religious activity, let alone for what was done in the household. It must seem likely that those sites that can be identified were the most important of their time, but the features that they present should not be unquestioningly assumed to be typical of religious activity for the whole Aegean. Indeed, it is probable that, as in other fields, there was considerable local diversity of practice in the EIA.

The Third Palace Period and Postpalatial Period

The questions that are most easily answered, then, concern the extant evidence for the types of religious site, the practices at them, and the changes in these, which can hardly add up to a rounded picture of a religion in the absence of texts. Indeed, the earliest textual evidence, the Linear B material from the Third Palace Period, provides very little help, since it consists almost exclusively of records of offerings to a great variety of apparently divine figures. Little can be assumed about these, even where their names coincide, as a fair number do, with those of major Olympian gods (Zeus, Hera, Poseidon, Hermes, Ares, Dionysos, Artemis, and possibly Athena, which remains controversial), or of lesser divine figures whose names occur in the Homeric poems (Enyalios, Paieon (as *pa-ja-wo*), Erinys), or are of patently Greek formation (Potnia, Diwia, Iphemedeia). Although some of these names are found at two or more major sites, they are intermingled with names that are unknown later (Chadwick 1985: 194–8 gives a detailed discussion, to which much new material from Thebes can be added; cf. Dickinson 1994a: 291), and there is no basis upon which to link them with representations thought to show supernatural figures, let alone to identify their functions. The documents do, however, indicate that there were both priests and priestesses, which makes a notable contrast with the Near East where priests were normally male. This can quite plausibly be linked not only with the prominence of women in Minoan and Minoan-related ritual scenes, but with a distinctive feature of Classical Greek religion which can already be observed in the Homeric poems, that worship of gods was normally overseen by priests of the same sex as that attributed to the god.

The prominence generally accorded to Potnia and the fact that some obscure or otherwise unknown names are as widespread as the identified Olympian names provide strong indications that the religion centred on the Olympian gods was at best only incipient in the Third Palace Period. Indeed, it has been pointed out that the offerings recorded in the Linear B texts as made to certainly or apparently divine figures, consisting largely of foodstuffs, wine and olive oil, have more in common with those made to the dead than with those made to the Olympian gods in the Homeric poems (Yamagata 1995). For some time it has been argued that, while there is evidence to suggest that animal sacrifice was not unknown in the LBA and may even have been quite significant, it could not be shown to have been as central to public religion as it was in historical times, and that the form that it took and how it was portrayed seem to have changed in several ways between the BA and EIA (Marinatos 1988, comparing Minoan and Greek representations, and Bergquist 1988, comparing BA and EIA archaeological remains). In fact, Bergquist argued that the practice of burning at least part of the sacrifice on an altar as an offering to the god was an EIA innovation, potentially adopted under influence from the Near East (though Aubet

2001: 151 suggests it only became an important rite in Phoenicia at around this time).

However, convincing evidence for a form of animal sacrifice involving burning part or all of the animal has now been adduced from the Pylos palace (cattle), Methana shrine (mainly young pigs, also sheep/goat joints), and Mycenae 'Cult Centre' (including some young pigs) (Isaakidou *et al.* 2002; Hamilakis and Konsolaki 2004). Hamilakis and Konsolaki draw attention to the likely connection with feasting and the difference in setting between a monumental palace, where hundreds could have participated, and the undistinguished building at Methana, which had room for only a few (2004: 145–6). It may, then, have been quite a widespread rite, and although there are differences in detail from the characteristic form of EIA sacrifice, including the favoured types of animal, it must be considered possible that this rite continued to be practised, or at least that the memory survived and it was revived on occasion, to become increasingly important in the EIA.

The archaeological evidence for places of religious activity in the Third Palace Period is as sparse and fragmentary as the textual evidence (Dickinson 1994a: 286–93). Recent finds, such as the Methana shrine (Konsolaki-Yannopoulou 2001: 213–17 gives many details), and what seems like a house shrine whose focus was a large and elaborate clay bovid at Dhimini (Adrymi-Sismani 1994: 31, 36), do not help to identify recurrent patterns of behaviour, but rather enhance an impression of diversity. The contrast with Crete is quite marked. Here relatively many examples of definable types of cult site can be identified, although the structural setting for ritual, where it exists, is considerably less impressive than the suites of rooms in the Minoan palaces and other substantial buildings thought to have ritual/ceremonial functions.

Unsurprisingly, there is far better evidence from Crete for continuity into the EIA of types of site, symbol and votive offering than in the Mycenaean culture region. The offering of clay figurines does seem to be a common ritual practice throughout the Mycenaean cultural region (Dickinson 1994a: 287), and is well attested at Methana (where the bovid type is paramount among the animal figurines, in contrast with the actual animals used for sacrifice, a feature also seen at Minoan sites like Juktas). But figurines occur in Mycenaean funerary and settlement contexts as well as at sites that seem purely ritual, and the practice of offering them is not referred to in the textual evidence, nor reflected in the frescoes that appear to show the bringing of offerings by women in procession (the two apparent representations of figures being held show one as like a realistic doll, the other as possibly like one of the larger clay figures; Immerwahr 1990: 114, 119, 120 fig. 33). It may have been a 'popular' rather than 'official' practice – the common forms of figurine do not occur in the Mycenae 'Cult Centre', for example – but it remains unclear how far this is a useful distinction. In other respects, Mycenaean cult practice involved far fewer ritual items: there are no parallels for the Minoan 'snake tubes', tables of offering, plaques, etc., and even the 'horns of consecration' symbol only appears sporadically.

As noted in Chapter 2, it seems likely that important rituals took place in the Mycenaean palaces, but, as Albers argues (2001), they do not seem to have been temples in the sense of repositories for god images. Shrines are more likely to have played this role; but at Mycenae, at least, the 'Cult Centre' went out of use and was not replaced after the Collapse. The Post-palatial evidence is in fact strikingly diverse. At some sites older structures were partially maintained (the Ayia Irini 'temple' and Phylakopi shrines) or brought back into use after a period of abandonment (the Midea 'megaron'). At others new structures were built, like the Tiryns Lower Citadel shrines (Figure 8.2: 1), and a small rectangular structure at Kalapodi (Felsch 2001: 194), or rooms were set aside for cult within new structures (Asine House G, Room XXXII). At others again apparently open-air sites without any kind of major structure were established (the Amyklaion, perhaps founded slightly before the Collapse).

Outside Crete the evidence is still very sporadic. But in Crete, although the difficulties of establishing the local sequences in detail force deductions to be somewhat tentative, a whole variety of sites can be identified. These include buildings that can be tied in with the 'bench sanctuary' tradition, incorporating a room with one or two benches along the walls, but they may add further rooms; examples are known at Karphi, Kavousi: Vronda (Figure 8.2: 2), Vasiliki: Kephala (Eliopoulos 1998; Rehak and Younger 2001: 460–1), and Halasmenos, a site dated more precisely to middle LM IIIC (Tsipopoulou 2001). In addition to these newly established sites, old open-air sites, both high and low (e.g. the peak sanctuaries of Juktas and Kophinas, the open-air site at Kato Symi), and caves (Patsos, probably Psychro, and elsewhere) continued in use. In general, both the sites and the practices identifiable seem to continue traditions established before the Postpalatial Period, or revived at that stage (cf. Gesell 1985: ch. V; Rehak and Younger 2001: 462–3).

D'Agata (2001) presents an attractive analysis of the LM IIIC evidence which sets it in a social context. She sees the development of a common pattern in advanced LM IIIC, involving a coherent iconography, of which much can be traced into the past: recurrent items include Goddess with Upraised Arms figures, offering bowls (kalathoi) supported on 'snake tubes', and 'horns of consecration' symbols, to which Gesell (2001) adds the large plaques, evidently hung up within buildings, that are found at many sites and probably showed a symbolic scene in paint or relief (Figure 8.3: 1–4). Of the various types of site identifiable, D'Agata interprets buildings within settlements and open-air sanctuaries in or close to settlement sites as the cult centres of individual settlements, run by the local elites, but open-air rural centres as the meeting places for the communities of a whole region, organised by the elites of these communities in partnership. Some small-scale rural

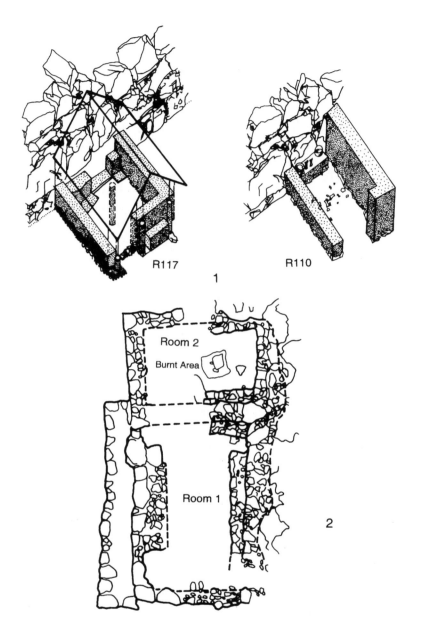

Figure 8.2 Some early shrine plans: 1 Tiryns Unterburg, shrines R117 and R110 (after Kilian 1981, 52 figs 4–5); 2 Kavousi: Vronda Building G (after Gesell *et al.* 1995, 78 fig. 3).

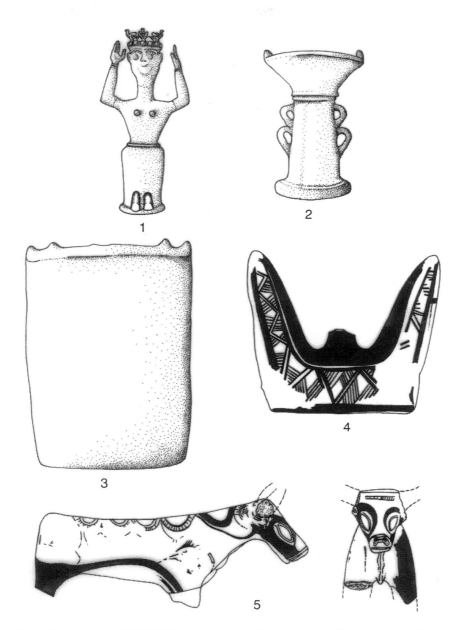

Figure 8.3 A range of LM IIIC ritual items: 1 'Goddess with Upraised Arms' (after Desborough 1972, pl. 21 left (Karphi)), 2 kalathos on 'snake tube' (after *Hesperia* 60 (1991) pl. 63e (Kavousi: Vronda)), 3 plaque (after Gesell 2001, pl. LXXXIb (Kavousi: Vronda)), 4 'horns of consecration', 5 wheelmade animal figure (both after D'Agata 1999, pl. XXXI: C 1.7 and LXI: C 3.18 (Ayia Triada)). Scale 1:8.

sites are thought to be simply holy places visited by individuals (but among these she cites Psychro, where the quality of the offerings strongly suggests elite involvement). But individual sites can display notable differences. While most seem to have only a single bench sanctuary complex, no less than five, at least three of which contain examples of the Goddess with Upraised Arms figure, have been identified at Karphi; D'Agata suggests that these reflect a situation with no central authority, so that competing groups maintain separate shrines (2001: 348–9). Again, where there is a multiple-room complex, as at Vasiliki: Kephala, this may have housed more than one cult (2001: 350; this also had 'mainland' features lacking elsewhere).

The continuation of the tradition of using clay figurines, both as divine images and as votives, provides a unifying factor and a clear link between the Third Palace and Postpalatial periods. Their evidence can sometimes be crucial in demonstrating either continued use of a site, as at Epidauros where the latest figurines have been attributed to advanced LH IIIC (Guggisberg 1996: 27–31, citing E. Peppa-Papaioannou's 1985 doctoral thesis), or its coming back into use, as at Kophinas, where there is a marked gap in datable material between LM I and IIIC. The partly wheelmade hollow animal figurines, especially cattle (intended to be bulls?), that began to be a popular type in the Third Palace Period are conspicuous at a wide range of sites in the Postpalatial Period (Zeimbekis 1998: 186; although several citations here are not closely datable or otherwise questionable, Phylakopi, Tiryns, Epidauros, and the Amyklaion are certain, apart from Cretan sites; Figure 8.3: 5). In the Tiryns shrines, a local version of the Goddess with Upraised Arms type is well represented (Figure 8.4: 1), and smaller solid Psi and bovid figurines of traditional Mycenaean types also continued to appear in the Mycenaean cultural region, both at sites and to some extent in tombs (Figure 8.4: 2, 5). But their distribution as grave-goods was considerably more restricted than before (e.g. none have been reported so far from the Achaean and Cephallenian cemeteries) and they are not always very common when they do appear, as at Perati (only seven Psis and nineteen animals). In Crete, the continuing use of a whole range of terracotta items is particularly notable, including divine images (the Goddess with Upraised Arms type), ritual items used in cult, and votives, especially animal figurines. The rich Ayia Triada group includes both hollow and solid animals, mostly cattle (even found, very rarely, in bronze) but also some horses and birds, and fantastic animals including sphinx-like creatures and human-headed bulls (D'Agata 1999a: ch. III). The bulk of this material appears to belong to the late phase of LM IIIC, and apparently sets of items were made to be used together.

The eleventh and tenth centuries

But by the end of the Postpalatial Period evidence for the dedication and even the manufacture of figurines has virtually disappeared from the Aegean

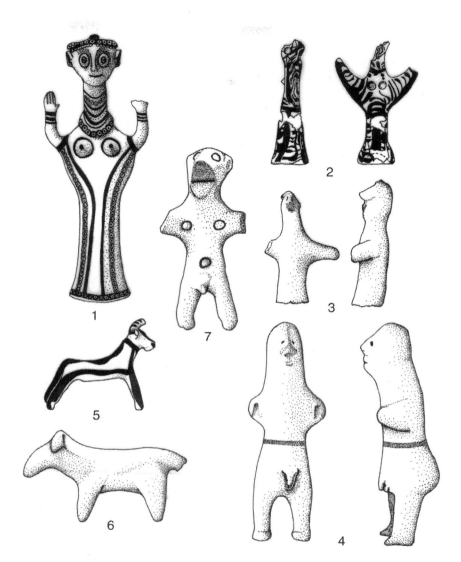

Figure 8.4 Postpalatial and EIA clay figures and figurines: 1 'Goddess with Upraised Arms'; 2 Late Psi figurine; 3 Ayia Triada human figurine, probably G (coated); 4 Olympia 'Zeus' figurine, ascribed to PG; 5 Late Linear animal figurine; 6 Olympia cattle figurine, ascribed to PG (coated); 7 Olympia human figurine, ascribed to G (1 after Kilian 1981, 54 fig. 6 (Tiryns Unterburg); 2, 5 after Renfrew 1985, 210 figs 6.1: 174, 6.29: 168 (Phylakopi); 3 after D'Agata 1999, pl. LXXX: D 2.11 (Ayia Triada); 4, 6–7 after Heilmeyer 1972, pls 28: 174, 2: 6, 27: 167 (Olympia)). Scale 1:4.

outside Crete. Here they surely continued, although figurines certainly datable in the SM and local PG phases are hard to identify (but see D'Agata 1999a: 43, 73, 88–90 for likely SM terracottas from Ayia Triada; Gesell 1985: 58 for PG), and the partly wheelmade animal type survived quite late (D'Agata 1999a: 147). This type was also common in Cyprus, and many of the sporadic examples of figurines datable to PG elsewhere belong to the same tradition, including the well-known Kerameikos stag and Lefkandi centaur (Figure 8.5). Lemos (2002: 97–100) lists the most reliably dated, including two from the Lefkandi 'Heroön' fill that may be dated to MPG. The majority come from tombs, like the incised 'dolls' from Athens and

Figure 8.5 The Lefkandi centaur, from Lefkandi: Toumba Ts 1 and 3. H. 36 cm, L. 26 cm. Courtesy of the British School at Athens.

Lefkandi (Lemos 2002: 95–6), but it is not clear what function they might have had before burial (the stag has been classified as a rhyton). Pieces of solid human-shaped and animal figurines are much rarer: the largest group comes from Olympia, where they are certainly votives but are dated on stylistic rather than stratigraphical grounds (Figure 8.4: 4, 6–7). These are much more crudely made – not in itself a proof of particularly early date (cf. Snodgrass 1971: 418) – but compare in this respect with material from Ayia Triada (e.g. Figure 8.4: 3). It may be best to see them as the products of a very localised tradition, conceivably linked to Crete. It is very hard to accept theories of continuity from the Mycenaean tradition, let alone of widespread manufacture, in the virtual absence of figurines from the quite abundant deposits at sites where there is continuity of occupation like Kalapodi, Asine and Lefkandi.

The turnover in identifiable ritual sites is another notable feature of the transition to the EIA. None of the Mycenaean sites which had survived into Postpalatial times continued into the EIA, except Ayia Irini, and the Tiryns shrine, established early in the Postpalatial Period, also went out of use. There may be a gap at some Cretan sites, such as Ayia Triada (but see D'Agata 1999a: 239), but at others (e.g. Juktas, Kophinas, Kato Symi, the Psychro cave) activity may well have been continuous, if on a diminished scale, until the clear revival in the eighth century. However, Kalapodi continued, to become the national cult centre for the Phocians, and Olympia and Isthmia were established before the end of the Postpalatial Period as major local centres that eventually became the sites of pan-Hellenic festivals. The history of the ritual site at Cape Poseidi near Mende in Chalcidice also goes back into the Postpalatial Period, and that of Thermon may well do (see further below).

Morgan sees common features at Olympia, Isthmia and Kalapodi (in the paper summarised in Morgan 1995, cf. 1999: 380, 382, 386–7). At all three the earliest material consists almost entirely of pottery, particularly drinking and eating vessels, with which ash deposits and animal bones are often associated, suggesting that a repeated act of presumably ritualised dining together was a common practice. Morgan interprets this as reflecting a deliberate decision by local magnates to establish new ritual sites and to meet at them regularly as an expression of cooperation between the local communities; such meetings would involve a joint sacrifice that provided meat for the ritual meal. The magnates and their families might also have dedicated the rare examples of bronze jewellery, a practice which is argued to have begun at an early stage (cf. Morgan 1999: 330 (Isthmia); Eder 2001: 206 (Olympia); Felsch 2001: 195 (Kalapodi)), but more emphasis would have been placed on the shared sacrifice, act of offering, and meal than on dedication. This hypothesis seems very plausible. It has the merit of placing the establishment of new cult sites firmly in the setting of social development, and foreshadows the historical emphasis on cult sites as central to community identity. But it remains rather unclear why these particular sites should have been chosen, although Morgan argues that all are on natural routeways and so could be obvious meeting places for groups of communities. It should be noted that the existence of such sites, separated from settlements and apparently used for ritual only, runs completely counter to the theory (heavily criticised in Sourvinou-Inwood 1993: 2–8) that prior to the eighth century sacred space was indeterminate.

Evidence for comparable cult practices can be gathered from a wide spread of other sites. Pits which contained pottery and/or animal bones that seem likely to be the remains of sacrifices and ritual meals can be identified at PG Asine (Sourvinou-Inwood 1993: 7), at Thronos/Kephala (ancient Sybrita) and Khamalevri in western Crete, where they represent a long-established practice traceable from early LM IIIC to late PG (D'Agata 1999b, also 2001: 353), and at the Cape Poseidi site in Chalcidice, beneath a substantial PG structure. The burnt deposits containing animal bones at Aëtos on Ithaca, over which cairns were heaped, could well represent the remains of similar ritual meals; pottery and a very few other items, including bronze pins, were associated, and the finds are linked to a cult by Coldstream (1977: 182–3). At the Amyklaion (Demakopoulou 1982), which, again, may have been a site used by several communities (Wright 1994: 65), there seems to be a break in ritual activity on the site at the end of the BA, and a marked change in deposition patterns when activity resumes, but a role as a place for communal feasting might be inferred from the prevalence of eating and drinking vessels among the votives (Morgan 1999: 383–4, 390).

The earliest EIA pottery from Mt Hymettos in Attica also consists of shapes that are drinking-related, and ash is reported, but here it is not so clear that a similar practice is being reflected, for the vessels are mainly kraters and oinochoai, and drinking vessels only become common in the G deposits. Moreover, the site is of a quite different type from the others – a hill summit. At Kommos, the earliest in a sequence of built shrines, Temple A, a small rectangular structure dated to near 1000 (Shaw 1998: 18), was surely intended for the use of the Kommos community only, but internal benches have, again, been interpreted as for communal meals. However, D'Agata points out that the open-air Piazzale dei Sacelli site at Ayia Triada is unlikely to have fulfilled this function, since there was apparently no scatter of communities in the western Mesara, but rather one large nucleated centre at Phaistos, with which the Ayia Triada site should be associated (2001: 351).

The most remarkable example of a sacrificial site at this time is the structure at Cape Poseidi, which bears witness, like Thermon Megaron B, to an urge felt in some communities to construct monumental ritual structures. The Cape Poseidi building is substantial (14.27 × 5.4 m), apparently apsidal at both ends and oriented N–S (Mazarakis Ainian 1997: 43, with fig. 27), and was established in PG times (EPG according to the excavator, but K. Wardle, pers. comm., does not feel it possible to be so precise), over a pit or pits considered to represent earlier sacrificial activity. Sacrifices continued to be made within the structure above the pit(s), resulting in the formation of an ash altar, but a scatter of PG amphora and krater sherds on stone paving around the building suggests that ceremonies also took place outside (*AR* 43 (1996–1997) 70, 46 (1999–2000) 87). The building may have been open to the sky, and was presumably a major cult centre for the community. Poseidon was clearly worshipped here by Archaic times, but a possible gap in use in the ninth century means that this cannot be unhesitatingly assumed from the beginning, although it must seem plausible. At Thermon the new excavations (most recently *AR* 45 (1998–99) 43) suggest that Megaron B, which is even larger than the Poseidi structure (21.4 × 7.3 m), may have been built at a comparable date, and ash deposits are reported, suggesting that it had a ritual function. Although it was destroyed near 800, plausible evidence for ritual features on the site is continuous until the foundation of the well-known temple of Apollo in the late seventh century (on the sequence at Thermon see Mazarakis Ainian 1997: 125–35).

Given the still relatively small number of cases, it would be unwise to assume that the practice of communal sacrifice of one or more animals, followed by burnt offering and ritual meal, had become universal, but the widespread occurrence of ash deposits and animal bones does suggest that many communities were making these acts central to public religious activity. This emphasis on the communal patently runs counter to the suggestion that rites were conducted in the houses of local magnates, even 'rulers', which has sometimes been extended to suggest that these rites were the private practices of an elite, who monopolised access to religious rituals (cf. Morris, I. 1997: 543). The sheer implausibility of the idea that the cults of major deities, or public religion in general, could be monopolised in this way has been commented upon by Parker (1996: 24). While the putative magnates surely led the rituals of sacrifice and offering and were the leading participants in ritual meals, there is no reason to suppose that more ordinary members of the community could not participate, in the major festivals of the year at least, as would be the natural expectation. It may be noted that of the two well-known accounts of sacrifice in *Odyssey* 3, that to Poseidon, taking place when Telemachus arrives at Pylos, is public, although Nestor and his family appear to preside over it: 'the people' are gathered in nine groups, each sacrificing nine bulls, which have presumably been contributed from within each group. Nestor and his household also privately sacrifice a heifer to Athena the following day, apparently outside the palace entrance; this is not a standard sacrifice, but a rather special one, described in considerable detail, in honour of her epiphany to Nestor. It may be added that the only case where it seems plausible that cult was being carried on inside a building that was *also* a dwelling place is Nichoria Unit IV-1, but it is not clear either that this was the house of the 'ruler', though it is surely an elite building, or what kind of cult was involved (*contra* Mazarakis Ainian 1997: 78–9, where it is suggested that the cult was communal; Sourvinou-Inwood 1993: 8 suggests it was domestic).

There can be no analogy in religious practice, then, with the plausible if not completely demonstrable suggestion that the observable funerary practices were the preserve of an upper social stratum. Sometimes funerary practices do seem to have been accompanied by what can be described as cult practices that arguably reflect elite behaviour. The Lefkandi 'Heroön' is not really an example of this, since its use for ritual seems to have been confined to the funeral itself, so it might seem unlikely to have served as a communal symbol, even if built by community effort (*contra* Morgan 1999: 392). But at Grotta on Naxos there is evidence of a long-established practice associated with certain graves. Here enclosures were established, apparently in LPG, over older burials sited next to the fortification wall of the abandoned BA settlement. Further burials were made in these enclosures, and a kind of ancestor cult seems to have been carried on, represented by burnt layers and pottery, including jugs which may have been used for libations. Early in the G period new enclosures were built on a higher level, no longer used for burials but only for ritual. It seems likely that this was an elite practice, designed to emphasise certain families' roots in the past, and comparable practices may be identifiable elsewhere (Mazarakis Ainian 1997: 193 suggests that rooms in a building associated with the G cemetery at Tsikalario on Naxos were used for rites connected with ancestor worship, and (87) that the oval building on the Areopagus at Athens had a comparable function). The apparently deliberate association of the burial enclosures with ancient remains may be paralleled with the positioning of the cult site at Olympia next to prehistoric tumuli. These could be examples of a potentially widespread desire to be associated with a glorious and by now effectively mythical past, which at other sites took the form of the continued or revived use of an ancient site. At Ayia Irini on Kea, parts of a very ancient building, the BA 'Temple', saw effectively continuous use; in one room a rectangular 'chapel' of probably PG date was constructed (Mazarakis Ainian 1997: 170).

The sites mentioned above are the clearest examples of ritual sites established by the end of PG. There are other plausible examples, but little can be said about most of them in comparison with those already mentioned. PG pottery is reported from later sanctuary sites at Mounychia, Brauron, Delos, and Kameiros, but this cannot be considered conclusive evidence of ritual use so early. At the Argive Heraion, where items of jewellery datable to PG have also been identified, and the Samian Heraion, where figurine fragments of possible PG date have been found, the case seems stronger (see Desborough 1972: 178 for Kameiros, 278–80 for several other sites). But it is not clear whether the Orthia and Athena Chalkioikos shrines at Sparta (Morgan 1999: 389–90) and the Athena Alea site at Tegea (Østby et al. 1994), at all of which the earliest-looking material so far reported is 'Laconian PG' or related to it, are to be traced back this far, nor if pre-eighth century material from the Polis cave on Ithaca is votive (Coldstream 1977: 184).

It may be noted that anywhere in the Aegean some of the identified sites were apparently within or close to settlements, but others were quite distant from them if not wholly separate, like the peaks and caves in Crete and Mt Hymettos in Attica. This range of variation provides a further reason for caution in making sweeping assertions that imply universal patterns of behaviour; at best, the outlines of certain common patterns seem to be emerging. But a great deal remains unknown. For example, several features among those argued in Renfrew (1985: ch. I.5), to be likely correlates for the existence of a ritual site, such as attention-focusing devices, are simply not identifiable. It seems unlikely that this is because of inadequate searches for them; more probably, they were too insubstantial to have survived.

Later developments

The perceived heterogeneity of behaviour in the tenth century can be compared with the variation in burial customs, and both may reflect the decision of local elites to choose individual ways to display their position in these areas of public activity. Heterogeneity certainly continued into the ninth century, for once established none of the sites previously mentioned seem to have gone permanently out of use, although as noted there is a possible break at Cape Poseidi, and Megaron B at Thermon was destroyed near 800 and not immediately replaced. At Kommos a new structure, Temple B, replaced Temple A *c.* 800; it was also rectangular but bigger, and contained the remarkable 'tripillar shrine', which has clear Near Eastern links (Mazarakis Ainian 1997: 230–3 gives a good summary). Several famous sites can also be shown to have come into use in the ninth century at the latest, like the Athenian Acropolis and the Academy structure, whose ritual function is clear but whose precise purpose is not (Morgan 1999: 390; it may be a site of ancestor cult rather than of hero worship). The Athena Alea site at Tegea can be no later than ninth century: animal bones are associated with all the early groups of material identified here and show traces of fire, suggesting that the rite of animal sacrifice and burnt offering, followed by a meal, was well established at this relatively remote site no later than *c.* 800 (Østby *et al.* 1994: 99, n. 46, and information from M.E. Voyatzis).

No earlier than the late tenth century, Morgan identifies a change in practice at some major centres, with emphasis being increasingly placed on the dedication of votives, including expensive types such as tripod vessels and figurines of bronze (1999: 389–92; see Figures 5.19: 1, 4 and 5.20). But these only appear at certain ritual sites. Examples are known in particular from the Athens Acropolis, the Amyklaion, Olympia, and Ayia Triada (D'Agata 1999a: 166–96; the earliest bronzes are likely to date from PG B), but at Isthmia very little metalwork of ninth-century date was found

(Morgan 1999: 393–4), and none at the Mt Hymettos and Academy sites. Also, although very largely found at ritual sites as votives, bronze figurines and even tripods can occur in other contexts, as shown by the recovery of fragments from Nichoria (*Nichoria III*: 279, 281–2). As with the emphasis on sacrifice, offering and shared meal, it is possible to argue that practices which were originally followed only at certain centres later began to spread, to become very widely established by the end of the eighth century. Votive types in terracotta, mainly animal figurines, were also coming into fashion again, although these became much more common in the eighth century (Coldstream 1977: 332–3). These votive types were apparently not designed to be exclusive to the cult at a particular site or of a particular god, so that without other indications it cannot be determined who is the receiving cult. This is symptomatic of a growing homogeneity of Greek cult practice that is perceptible in the later centuries of the EIA and even more evident in the Archaic period.

It may well be supposed that the purpose of dedicating expensive items of bronze at ritual sites was social display, and that to some extent this practice was replacing that of displaying the wealth and prominence of a family though grave-goods. But this was only one element of the process of burial, which in Attica at least also included major processions accompanying the corpse to the grave site, impressive ceremonies at the graveside, and the erection of massive vase markers over the graves of the most important dead. Thus, there may not have been quite such a wholesale transference from burial to religion as an arena for competitive display as has often been argued. Nevertheless, it is clear that public religion was attracting more and more attention, and it is not surprising that it is during the eighth century that evidence appears at several leading sites for the erection of temple structures that were clearly intended to impress either by their size or their material and features (as with the eighth-century stone structure with columns under the temple of Artemis at Ephesus). Competition may well have been increasing between the more important sites, providing a background for the explosion of Archaic temple building. Whether these early temples and shrines included buildings that had previously been the dwellings of rulers, as argued by Mazarakis Ainian (1997), is much more open to question. The theory presupposes the existence of clearly identifiable 'rulers', which is – to say the least – hard to demonstrate (see further Chapters 4 and 9). It is hard to prove that any of the early buildings cited above actually were rulers' dwellings, and while it might explain where the chief god of the community was worshipped, it offers no provision for the other gods in what was certainly a polytheistic society.

As noted in the introduction to this chapter, the Homeric poems suggest that most elements of the standard 'Olympian' religion had become established by *c.* 700, at least in the region (probably Ionia) where the poems were composed. But it remains debatable to what extent the poems, in their presentation of an accepted pantheon of gods, represent a widespread pattern of belief rather than a poetic ideal. They are most likely to be true to life in their emphasis on the centrality of animal sacrifice, followed by a burnt offering and a meal made from the sacrifice, conducted in a particular manner that was essentially the same as that of later Greek religion (as shown by the detailed descriptions in *Iliad* 2: 421–9, *Odyssey* 3: 436–63 and 12.352–65); in contrast, there are few references to the offering of goods. How this and other typical features of 'classic' Greek religious behaviour, such as the recognition of Delphi and to a lesser extent Dodona as oracular centres throughout the Greek world, the incorporation of athletic contests as an important feature of major religious festivals, and the widespread establishment of local hero cults came to develop are questions that are very important but difficult to answer. We cannot even be sure at what time the festivals that were celebrated in many states, and which in some cases have been recognised as typically 'Dorian' or 'Ionian' festivals, came to be established. But it seems hard to doubt that most of these features were developments in the EIA at the earliest, not inherited from the BA past, and although the rite of animal sacrifice may well have Mycenaean roots, it cannot yet be shown to have been central to Mycenaean public religion. These points serve as a reminder of how crucial developments in the EIA, and later, are likely to have been, in this field as in others.

Bibliography

A major text on Greek religion is Burkert (1985); though its account of the prehistoric material is now outdated, I 3.6 and 4 contain comments of value on the Mycenaean evidence and on the idea of continuity, on which see also Sourvinou-Inwood (1989). On Mycenaean sites and material in the Third Palace and Postpalatial periods, see Shelmerdine (2001: 362–72, specifically 365–6 on Tiryns, Asine, and Phylakopi), and Wright (1994) on Mycenaean religion generally. Renfrew (1985) fully publishes the Phylakopi shrines. The most recent extended study of the Linear B material is Chadwick (1985); see Rehak and Younger (2001: 457–8) for Crete.

On Cretan sites and material after the Second Palace Period, see Rehak and Younger (2001: 456–8 (LM II–IIIA), 462–3 (LM IIIB–C), 472), also Gesell (1985, ch. V), and on the LM IIIC material D'Agata (2001). For caves see Tyree (2001: 49), Watrous (1996).

Valuable comments are made on mainland Postpalatial and EIA sites and practices in Morgan (1999: on continuity 295–8, on early shrines 378–86), see also Morgan (1995), Sourvinou-Inwood (1993) and Mazarakis Ainian (1997: especially pp. 393–6). For brief general accounts of EIA Crete see D'Agata (forthcoming), Prent (forthcoming).

9

CONCLUSIONS

Preliminary comments

As has been stressed in the Introduction, the quantity of data available for use in discussing the Postpalatial Period and EIA has increased dramatically in recent years. The new data provide a much fuller background, even for the most 'dark' period, than was available before 1970. But this does not necessarily make it any easier to fulfil the 'urgent task' identified by Snodgrass, to explain why, for such a relatively long period, the people of Greece were so unambitious materially, when they had supported cultures of marked achievement earlier and would do so again ([1971] 2000: xxxii). In this concluding chapter, in what cannot avoid being a personal response to the material and its problems, I should consider whether such an explanation can be offered and whether it is possible to answer how the sustained development that brought Greece out of the 'Dark Ages' was initiated.

Of course, this is to assume that this period of recession is a real phenomenon that needs explanation. Papadopoulos has been the most vehemently opposed to the concept of a 'dark age' (1993: 194–7, also 1996a: 254–5; see also Muhly 2003), but in criticising particular features of the approach of scholars like Snodgrass, Morris and Whitley he seems to sidestep the main point. With the exception of the Lefkandi 'Heroön', there is virtually no sign of the investment of exceptional effort and resources in *anything*, whether monumental buildings, tombs, communal ritual sites, or works of craftsmanship, in the centuries upon which this book focuses (the list of rich burials datable to the mid-eleventh century cited in Muhly 2003: 23 is dominated by sites in Cyprus, which is not in the Aegean). The most plausible explanation is surely that social organisation was not developed enough to allow the mobilisation of resources on any scale. I firmly believe that it is impossible to explain this simply by suggestions that less centralised political and economic systems had been established. It represents a reality that no appeals to 'Greek tradition' can wish away.

'Greek tradition' is in any case a broken reed. It is not just that, as Whitley has pointed out in his reply to Papadopoulos, 'There simply was *no unified*

238

Greek view of the past' (italics in original)' (*JMA* 6 (1993) 226). In fact, the evidence indicates that the Greeks preserved hardly any accurate information about their past at all. It not only failed to preserve any real memory of the importance of the civilisations of the Aegean islands, including Crete, but because it consisted largely of heroic myths, foundation legends, and the like it gave a completely false impression. It cannot be emphasised enough that the account of 'old Greece' which Thucydides extrapolated from Greek tradition (I.1–13) is patently wrong for the BA, not least in its emphasis on constant instability and movement of population, and might be considered overstated in some respects even if taken to apply only to the Postpalatial Period and after.

Thus, the appeal to tradition cannot be a valid counter-argument to the testimony of archaeology. Even if population was spread so thinly as to be archaeologically undetectable outside the major centres, as implied by Papadopoulos's reference to 'a shift in the nature of occupation and in subsistence strategies in Greece in the later twelfth and eleventh centuries' (1996a: 254), this does not counter the main point, that emphasises the almost total lack of anything striking in the archaeological record over several centuries. Papadopoulos gives no clear explanation for this, but it seems inconceivable that, if there had been polities at this time that had a comparable level of organisation to their Archaic successors, they should have left so little trace. For this reason among others, suggesting that the history of Athens as a *polis* began in the Bronze Age (Papadopoulos 2003: 315) seems to base too much simply on the evidence for continuity of occupation. On the view taken in this book, then, what has been called the 'Dark Age' was, like the Collapse that brought about the conditions for its onset, a real phenomenon.

The mistake that Thucydides could not have known that he was making was to treat the only sources of information available to him, the Homeric poems and other traditional material, as reliable sources from which to extrapolate historical information. Modern scholarship has often taken a similar approach, since the discoveries of Schliemann demonstrated the possibility that there was reality behind the legends, and for many years the dominant tendency was to interpret the world of the Homeric poems as an essentially Mycenaean one. But in recent years opinion has swung markedly towards an approach that sees them as reflecting an essentially EIA setting (e.g. Bennet 1997: 511–14; Morris, I. 1997: 536–9). They have even been taken, once the fabulous element and veneer of 'heroic' magnificence have been stripped away, to present a realistic picture of life in the EIA, even as late as the period of their composition (now generally placed in the later eighth or the earlier seventh century).

I am convinced that this approach is fundamentally wrong. While there can be little doubt that the poems reflect features of the society within which and for which they were composed, it must be remembered that they are *epics* – and epic poetry by its very nature has little concern with the practical and mundane. It necessarily focuses on heroic individuals and their deeds, placing them in a setting that has a strong flavour of the supernatural, so that the fabulous element is an integral part of the story, not simply something 'bolted on' for effect. Even where apparently concerned with mundane matters, an epic cannot be a trustworthy guide to reality. For example, the descriptions of warfare that fill much of the *Iliad* mix conventions appropriate to the description of duels with what sounds more like battle between organised groups, switching between them almost at will, and the weapons and armour that the heroes carry are demonstrably a mixture of items that could never have been in use at the same time, where they are realistic at all. Again, the poems show precious items and materials in common use, but make few references to the trade by which these and the more common metals such as iron and bronze must normally have been acquired. Yet it would be foolish to deduce that there was effectively no trade in the EIA; quite simply, epic poets have little interest in trade.

Also, epics share basic storytelling devices with folktale, and this will affect all references to social arrangements. It is surely a requirement of the plot, not a reflection of any real type of society, that Telemachos should be presented in the *Odyssey* as being without effective support (cf. van Wees 1992: 291). Telemachos' isolated position would be virtually impossible in a kin-based society like that of Greece throughout the historical period; he does not even have tenants on whose support he can call, as any EIA or Archaic aristocrat surely would. Equally, there is an obvious conflict between the concept of ruling kings and of elite-dominated citizens' assemblies, like that described in *Odyssey* I, which has rules of procedure and is controlled by a herald who seems to be a public official, not the king's representative. The suggestion that features of contemporary but different societies are being conflated (Whitley 1991a: 344) seems a desperate expedient: why should the poet do this? It seems more plausible that 'kings' survive, like chariots, because the audience knew they should be there, but in neither case was the poet clear how they operated (see further below on chariots).

Overall, Morris's comment, 'the epic was not some kind of bad history. It was a poetic creation, what *some* eighth-century Greeks thought the heroic world *ought* to have been like' (Morris, I. 1997: 558), surely represents much the best approach to take. It may be apposite to cite a Homeric reference for some individual feature – the more prosaic the feature and the more the reference is part of the background, not intended to attract attention, the better – and it is certainly possible to deduce some consistency in patterns of behaviour. But it seems risky to assume that the Homeric poems give a reliable, let alone comprehensive, depiction of any single historical society (van Wees 1992 makes a strong argument for this, but even he concedes that some elements of the picture are fabulous).

The archaeological material, then, has to be considered the only truly reliable source of evidence upon which to base conclusions about the period, but, as should be evident from the preceding chapters, its interpretation is beset with problems. While an outline sketch of historical development in the Aegean during the Third Palace Period can be given, this becomes virtually impossible later. It cannot even be considered certain that the most important Postpalatial and EIA sites have all been identified, as can reasonably be suggested for the Third Palace Period. The archaeological record may still be concealing major surprises, as suggested by the remarkable finds from the Elateia cemetery, for instance.

Athens clearly was a site of considerable importance in the EIA, but the past tendency to concentrate on it in general accounts has had a distorting effect which has still not been totally eradicated. The early history of other sites that were clearly very important by the Archaic period, such as Sparta and Miletus, remains largely obscure, and the role played by Crete, so rarely referred to in Greek historical sources before the Hellenistic period, has almost certainly been totally undervalued. In contrast, at least one site of very clear significance for almost the entire period, Lefkandi, cannot even be certainly identified by its ancient name. But although Lefkandi was evidently having fruitful contacts with the Near East at a notably earlier date than Athens, and probably for this reason was the wealthier and more important of the two for a considerable period, it would be quite wrong simply to substitute Lefkandi for Athens as a focus for general accounts. When so little is known about many regions of the Aegean, it is perfectly possible that more sites like Lefkandi will be discovered, in Ionia for example, to challenge our preconceptions. Further, it should be recognised that, despite the obvious importance of the Near Eastern contacts so lavishly in evidence at Lefkandi, these relate to only one of the significant processes that were under way in the period. Morgan (1990) has drawn attention to another, the development of certain sites as ritual focuses for whole regions, particularly Olympia and later Delphi; but neither Athens nor Lefkandi became such a site, or controlled one.

It does at least seem unlikely that any new find will completely undermine the overall impressions that have been developed up to now. As Snodgrass has pointed out, even the Lefkandi 'Heroön', 'while greatly extending the picture of the aspirations of the building practices of its time . . . leaves the range of those practices largely unchanged' ([1971] 2000: xxix). There is now enough evidence from a spectrum of sites all over the Aegean to give some confidence that we have the range within which all evidence of development can be situated. It seems unlikely that any buildings or tombs of a markedly superior level of sophistication to the 'Heroön' will be identified. It must surely represent, as Snodgrass remarks, 'the very apex of the social pyramid', although it must be admitted that the existence of such an apex would not have been considered likely a generation ago.

241

The Collapse and its sequel

It has already been suggested in Chapter 2 that the Collapse need not have been an inevitable result of the nature of Aegean palace society, but that there are plausible indications that the Aegean world was experiencing economic and hence social difficulties in the thirteenth century. If it is accepted that, as argued there, the Collapse is most likely to be the result primarily of a breakdown in the internal workings of Aegean society, probably given added impetus by the deteriorating conditions in the Near East, then it follows that this society could not, or could no longer, withstand unfavourable conditions.

The drastic nature of the Collapse needs to be emphasised. The archaeological evidence for destruction and dislocation surely indicates that what happened was far more catastrophic than a simple bypassing of palatial control of trade which caused the palaces' decline into obsolescence (Sherratt 2001). Equally, Rutter's suggestion that 'the Aegean world weathered the actual palatial collapse of *c.* 1200 BC well enough' (1992: 70) surely takes far too sanguine a view. Rather, it must have been an extremely traumatic experience for the Aegean populations, for it marked the disappearance of the underlying stability that had characterised much of the LBA, during which settlements tended to continue, even if administrative centres and systems changed and polities rose and declined (admittedly, Crete had already suffered major dislocation with the effective collapse of Minoan civilisation). Following the Collapse instability set in, to persist for a very considerable time, and I do not think it an overstatement to identify instability as a major if not the primary factor in causing the relative depression and backwardness of the 'dark age'.

It seems very likely that the Collapse was in some way bound up with the increasing turmoil in the Near East. But there, although the major states collapsed or lost much of their influence, urban civilisation did not collapse. In contrast, while in many parts of the Aegean there was indeed a degree of recovery following the Collapse, as is indicated particularly by the network of substantial settlements that continued to be involved in exchange systems extending beyond the Aegean, the palace societies and the systems of exchange that they had been involved in were gone. Attempts to revive the old style may have been made at a few sites, as has been suggested for Tiryns, but there are no comparable indications in regions as important as Messenia, Boeotia and central Crete, and the overall impression is that social and political organisation everywhere reverted to simpler forms.

In the leading regions these can hardly have represented social structures inherited directly from the past. At best, they might have been analogues of the early Mycenaean principalities, for example, with the important difference that the relatively abundant funerary evidence for the Postpalatial Period gives little indication, in most parts of the Aegean, that there was a clearly defined ruling class, able to display its prominence in elaborate tombs and rich grave-goods. With occasional exceptions, those burials that are provided with impressive goods, such as Type II swords and other weapons, metal vessels, rich jewellery, seals, and exotic foreign items, and might be further singled out by receiving the rite of cremation, were placed alongside far less impressively provided burials, often in the same tombs. That the most prominent male burials were 'warrior princes' (Muhly 2003: 24–6), even 'returning heroes' who had spent some time in the Near East (Catling 1995), may be true, but they are notably rare outside certain regions, especially Achaea, and the status they apparently represent does not seem to be inherited by successors. This suggests a social hierarchy much closer to that hypothesised for later times, in which status was far more fluid, and the position of the ruling families, even of persons possessing a monarch-like status, was much less secure than has been postulated for the Third Palace Period. This may well be reflected in the searching for symbols of status detectable in the Postpalatial Period, that relied sometimes on recalling the past, sometimes on the attraction of the new and exotic, especially when it advertised connections with distant regions.

The effects of the new instability would surely have been worst in the regions once controlled by palace societies, but similar phenomena are visible all over the Aegean, except that in Crete the abandonment of old sites is balanced by the foundation of many new ones, though none are particularly large. This serves to emphasise what a profound effect the Collapse had. But we should reject, as overdramatic and overstated, theories that explain it in terms of hordes of raiders sacking every major centre or posing a sustained threat for a considerable period (as in Drews' and Nowicki's reconstructions), or of invading tribes scouring the mainland and dislodging refugee populations en masse, or of the onset of such severe conditions of drought that whole regions were depopulated (see Desborough 1972: 331 for comments on Rhys Carpenter's theory of long-term drought).

Indeed, in some mainland provinces, especially in central Greece, and in many islands it is not easy to identify signs of serious trouble, and the degree of recovery in some regions where major destructions have been certified, like the Argolid, should not be underestimated. But the general impression remains that a whole way of life, based on long-accepted patterns of behaviour, had been irreparably damaged. This is surely emphasised by the progressive abandonment of so many settlements, not merely farms and small villages but ancient and substantial centres. When the population is so evidently ready to abandon its long-established roots, something really serious must be affecting the general mentality.

As emphasised in Chapter 4, it is impossible to demonstrate from the archaeological evidence that population was dispersing over the landscape to sites so small that they normally escape detection. Admittedly, it was argued there that the lack of common diagnostic types makes it very difficult to identify EIA sites of any kind. But there really ought to be some indication, from surveys carried out as intensively as those in parts of Boeotia and Laconia, of the existence of small farmstead-like sites, and not a hint has been identified so far. It may also be noted that the numerous sites in Crete are not so small as to be easily missed in survey. It seems much more likely that population was concentrating at certain sites, perhaps also in certain regions, around which it seems necessary to imagine an unpopulated and only partially exploited hinterland. Also, it seems beyond question that the absolute level of population within the Aegean was falling. If this fall was not quite as drastic as previous studies have estimated, it is still likely to have been substantial, for only in Crete can a really considerable number of sites be identified. Some of the population of the mainland provinces worst affected by the Collapse may well have moved over the period to Crete, also to the Cyclades, Cyprus, and later the Anatolian coast. Certainly, the evidence for the relatively swift growth and decline of sites suggests considerable mobility of population, which may well have contributed indirectly to the decline in absolute numbers.

As suggested above, instability seems to be the keynote of the Postpalatial Period. This, as much as anything else, must call into question Snodgrass's concept ([1971] 2000: xxvi, cf. 385) of an underlying 'Greek' substratum of continuity, used by him to explain the cultural similarities that he identifies between the MH and EIA periods. Such parallels as may be drawn between these periods may reflect the prevalence of comparable types of society, but it would be a mistake to suppose that they represent a continuum onto which an essentially alien Mycenaean structure had been imposed. Some of the Mycenaean features that Snodgrass lists in this connection, such as the use of chamber tombs and the 'Cyclopean' fortifications, are not exotic but indigenous mainland developments, even though their ultimate sources may lie elsewhere. But there is also a major difference in character between the two periods. Though materially impoverished, the MH period gives an impression of stability, in that a great many sites, fairly evenly distributed over the mainland, were occupied for much or all of the period. Study of the pottery has also identified evidence for a substantial degree of exchange that involved many of the Aegean-facing regions. In contrast, identifiable Postpalatial and EIA sites are few outside Crete, and evidence for exchange, though real, is concentrated at a handful of clearly important sites. (For further criticisms of this theory with particular reference to the popularity of single burial, see Chapter 6, p. 183.)

It is important to note the continuing evidence for widespread overseas contacts in Postpalatial times, and to draw attention to the elaborate and varied styles of decoration deployed on some of the best pottery, which may be one sign, though hardly the most significant, of the relative self-confidence and prosperity of the communities that produced it. But it is also important not to make too much of these phenomena, all of which had disappeared or become far less evident in most parts of the Aegean by the end of the Postpalatial Period. Further, whatever the degree of evidence for contact and wealth, it seems reasonable to suggest that long-distance trade was becoming a far more hazardous business than before, and correspondingly would have less effect on the general level of prosperity.

It is hard to tie down the observable processes in close chronological terms, because good evidence for the relative chronology of the different parts of the Aegean is so sparse, but it does seem possible to perceive a general decline over the period, not merely in the evidence for overseas contacts and exchange but also in the settlement and exploitation of the land. Some substantial settlements that survived a long way into the Postpalatial Period, like Korakou and Midea, had been abandoned by its end, to remain so throughout the EIA and often in later periods. Others became shadows of their former selves, like Mycenae and Tiryns. The best explanation for this continuing decline seems to be a continuing mobility of population. One cause of this might be an increase in small-scale raiding by land and sea, in which communities might be aggressors and victims at different times. This is unlikely to have been severe enough to wipe settlements off the map; even at Koukounaries on Paros, which looks as if it may have been stormed and fired by enemies, there is evidence of continuing occupation in the neighbourhood. But the constant threat of raiders, who might be most interested in livestock and food supplies, and so willing to attack even the smallest farm, might be the basic stimulus to the gathering of population in substantial settlements that, if not completely nucleated, were at least composed of segments that were not situated at a very great distance from each other, and so able to come to each other's aid in trouble.

The return of stability

It seems clear that some kind of equilibrium was being established again around the time of the transition from the Postpalatial Period to the EIA, though there is no clearly marked dividing line between these phases at any known settlement. At Tiryns, Asine, Kalapodi, Mitrou, and many Cretan sites, especially Kavousi, buildings that can be associated with EPG material or its equivalent are founded directly upon or are closely associated with earlier features. There was still some population movement, to judge from the evidence for the founding of new settlements, deduced particularly from the discovery of PG pottery at sites on the Anatolian coast and east Aegean islands (see Cook 1975: 785–6; Lemos 2002: 211–12 summarises the now quite substantial evidence from this whole region), and the finds at Torone and Mende. These last seem to represent settlements with links to the south that must have been established early in the EIA, if not slightly before (Lemos 2002: 207). It is not clear what motivated this continuing movement, at a time when there should have been plenty of space on the mainland

245

and islands, but those who founded new settlements may, like later colonisers, have been looking for better opportunities, away from the social constraints of their home communities. Overall, stability seems to have been returning. Identified settlements that had survived this far were rarely abandoned thereafter except in Crete, but here the population may simply have been moving from remote to more conveniently situated locations (Wallace 2000: 91; cf. Watrous 1980: 282–3 on Lasithi).

It could be argued that the opening years of the EIA saw a 'new beginning'. New cemetery areas were established at many settlements, including Athens, Lefkandi, and Knossos, which were to remain in use for very long periods thereafter, if not continuously into the historical period. This suggests a reorganisation of the settlements, for which further evidence might be seen at Athens in the development of the Kerameikos as a potters' quarter. It was in this period also that new sanctuaries were established at Olympia and Isthmia, probably for use by a group of communities. Morris has argued for the emergence of a new ritual system, 'imposing order on the chaos of Submycenaean times', in which an elite which dominated, even monopolised ritual activity, represented itself in its burials as internally egalitarian, homogeneous, and inward-looking, making no reference to the past or the outside world (1997: 542–3, and 1999, ch. 6).

But there are many difficulties with this view, not least that it effectively relies on taking the Kerameikos cemetery as typical. Here, indeed, there seem to be clear-cut rules governing how a dead person should be represented in the burial ritual, though there are variations: PG children's burials may be virtually excluded from the Kerameikos, but they are found in the Agora. But such clear distinctions and marked differences from previous practice are not so easy to identify in the PG burials at Lefkandi or Argos. More generally, the absence of items advertising links with the outside world, especially the Near East, is not necessarily a striking new phenomenon, since this is far commoner than the presence of such items in earlier burials. In any case, objects of iron, made with a technology introduced from abroad, could be interpreted as advertising precisely such links.

Also, several mainland provinces have produced evidence which seems to reflect a notable degree of continuity with the past. While single burial became widely prevalent, in Phocis and Locris multiple burial in rock-cut chamber tombs continued, and here a major ritual site, Kalapodi, founded in the Postpalatial Period if not before, continued to be an important focus of ritual. Also, in Thessaly and Messenia, both in a sense peripheral regions, stone-built tombs descended from the BA tholos continued to be built and used for multiple burials. In Crete there are even more prominent signs of continuity with the BA past, visible not only in burial customs but in the survival of ritual symbols and practices (some very old), house and shrine plans, even special pottery shapes like the stirrup jar.

Indeed, in Crete it is possible to identify a truly regional culture with unique local features, though, notoriously, it is not possible to identify either an archaeological break, or any major regional differences between Cretan districts, that could be associated with the supposed intrusion of 'Dorians' and the division of the island between different peoples set out in a famous *Odyssey* passage (19.175–7). In the north Aegean too, on Thasos, and in Macedonia and Chalcidice, there are well-established 'native' cultures that have largely individual traditions in artefact types, particularly pottery and jewellery, as well as in burial customs. But elsewhere in the Aegean there is a notable degree of similarity in the material evidence from EIA sites, in favoured types of artefact, house, grave, and in the rituals and goods thought appropriate for the burial of the dead; even the differences observable in local styles of fine pottery only vary within a narrow range.

The transition from Postpalatial Period to EIA is an appropriate point at which to consider how much had survived from the BA, apart from such basic features as the Greek language and the normal range of agricultural and craft practices. Much of the material culture of this world would have seemed familiar to people of earlier generations, especially those of the Postpalatial Period. One major change that was under way by now would be the increasing use of iron, not only for weapons, tools and functional items like horse bits, but for jewellery, especially pins and rings. But this new development did not involve the introduction of a range of new types, but rather the continuation and elaboration of old ones.

The chariot seems to have survived (the horses buried in the Lefkandi 'Heroön' make best sense as chariot teams), and so, presumably, the skills required to make all parts of them, especially the spoked wheels, and to train horses to pull them. This survival may seem paradoxical, since these skills must have been highly specialised and thus represent an exception to the lack of evidence for the survival of such skills into the EIA. But it seems hard to controvert Crouwel's arguments (1992: 29–30, 52–4), and it may be noted that it had already survived the collapse of palatial civilisation to be prominent on Postpalatial pictorial pottery. The survival of the oared galley may be comparable (Wedde 1999; there is a representation not cited there on a PG krater from Dirmil – see Lemos 2002: 51), but is less surprising, given the evidence for continuing maritime activity, if on a much reduced scale, around the Aegean and between the Aegean and Near East, which surely did not involve only non-Greek ships.

But, while galleys would have had considerable practical uses, it seems likely that chariots were now being used largely for show in ceremonial and funerary processions, and for races; they are hardly ever shown in scenes of warfare on Geometric vases (Crouwel 1992: 57). The way they are presented in the *Iliad*, essentially to move heavily armed warriors around the battlefield, is one of the few ways in which a chariot can be used, especially in Greek terrain (Crouwel 1992: 54–5). But their ability to move easily and swiftly, for attack or escape, through what is sometimes presented as close-packed mêlée, seems unrealistic, though the British use of chariots as described by Julius Caesar (*De Bello Gallico* 4.33) may offer some parallels.

It has been indicated above that many settlements survived the transition to the EIA, but was there continuity not only in settlement but even in land tenure? Small (1998) has suggested that lineage units retained control of land over the transition, but this seems to underestimate the degree of disturbance associated with the Collapse and the Postpalatial Period. This might have happened in Crete, once the new settlement pattern and any accompanying reordering of land tenure and social structure had been established in the Postpalatial Period, but it is less plausible elsewhere in the Aegean, where so much of the land was apparently abandoned, though families or lineages could have survived and retained their holdings in some of the major settlements.

Overall, one might imagine that an inhabitant of a BA settlement, if magically transported to an EIA one, would not have felt totally out of place. But he or she would surely have noticed that signs of prosperity were rare, and if able to interrogate the EIA people would have perceived that social arrangements were rather different from before, and that communities did not necessarily have stable roots in the past.

The world of the Early Iron Age

The form that social structures took is a matter of particular importance, for they must have constituted the primary factor affecting the nature of economic organisation and mobilisation of resources in the EIA. This has been perceived by commentators such as Tandy (1997), but unfortunately he and others have been working with an extremely questionable model of 'Dark Age society'. Indeed, it is completely open to question whether the communities of the Aegean were all organised on similar lines. Whitley's distinction between stable and unstable settlements has been criticised in Chapter 4, but it remains perfectly possible that there were different kinds of leader, some of whom were considerably less secure in their position, because it depended on their personal qualities, than those whose position was supported by the sanctions of tradition and perceived hereditary right. Similarly, the variations in burial customs between different communities, especially the distinction between a preference for single burials and for tombs that were evidently built with the expectation of reuse, indicate that the social arrangements in these communities might have varied comparably. Such variations might well lie behind the notable differences in social arrangements that are detectable when the Greek communities emerge into something more like history in the Archaic period.

That there was everywhere some kind of division between leaders and led can be assumed. It is possible that some small-scale communities were of the type defined as egalitarian by Fried, in which there is no 'means of fixing or limiting the number of persons capable of exerting power' (1967: 33). But, on the basis of the rather scanty evidence from settlements and the more substantial material from cemeteries, it looks more likely that as a general rule each community contained a number of more prominent families, and each of these families possessed its own circle of followers and dependants. Social stratification might have continued in some way what has been hypothesised for the Third Palace Period and potentially carried over into the Postpalatial Period, a system involving a large class of dependants. On the Morris model discussed in Chapter 2, the dependent class would be the *kakoi*, not entitled to formal burial rites of the kind most easily perceptible archaeologically, which were for the *agathoi*. The latter in turn might well be divided between an 'aristocracy' and others, who might include poor relations and free tenants of the elite. One might see such a division within the *agathoi* reflected in the *Odyssey*, between the families that produced the *basileis* who court Penelope, and those other 'citizens' of Ithaca who attend the assembly but are presented as essentially spectators of the action. That distinctions of this kind existed in the EIA seems plausible, given that in Archaic Greek society there seems to have been a comparable distinction between 'aristocrats', free 'citizens', and a dependent class whose members were clearly not truly free, though they could still, unlike chattel slaves, form their own communities.

It would surely be possible within communities organised in this manner for individuals to arise who by their personal achievements and charisma established themselves in a monarch-like position. But if one is to judge from the evidence of the Toumba cemetery at Lefkandi, such a position did not usually outlive the individual: the cemetery shows a whole group of burials dating between the mid-tenth and mid-ninth centuries, that range from extremely rich to quite poor in terms of grave-goods. This suggests that those who seem to be deliberately associating themselves with the Heroön were more like a clan than a dynasty of successive 'chiefs'. Occasionally, perhaps, the position was inherited and something like a dynasty was established, which might help to account for the familiarity with the notion of a monarch displayed in the Homeric poems. But what relationship such a position had to that of the rulers of BA principalities remains a matter for speculation.

Here we encounter a theory well established in analyses of EIA society, that of the origins of the *basileus*, a term which is used in Classical Greek to signify what we would call kings, but in Homer and Hesiod, our oldest literary sources, is applied to an elite class that includes but is not limited to monarchical rulers. The theory essentially supposes that previously subordinate figures in Mycenaean society, leaders at village level, came forward as the effective rulers, each of their local community, when larger polities collapsed (cf. Bennet 1997: 521–2; but not all are convinced that the *pa₂-si-re-u* of the Linear B texts held such a position). These are the personages whom

Mazarakis Ainian has seen as controlling public religion and using their own dwellings for rites (1997: ch. V), and who have been supposed to be the 'kings' whom Thucydides identified as rulers with fixed rights and privileges in the past (I.13).

There were kings in Sparta in historical times, as there were in Macedonia and Epirus to the north. The Spartan kings' position was supposedly established at the time of the 'Dorian Invasion', and was inherited in the standard way expected of monarchs, but Sparta was effectively unique in having a dual kingship. Traditions that contain some detail suggest the existence of monarch-like figures elsewhere in the Peloponnese on the edge of the historical period if not within it. But, as Drews has shown in his critical analysis (1983: ch. II), the traditions relating to post-'heroic age' kings elsewhere are extremely scanty. Often they refer to no more than the supposed founder of a *polis* and his son, and many of the references better suit the way that the term *basileus* is used in Homer and Hesiod. Drews's theory that single monarch-like *basileis* were established as effective heads of state only at the end of the EIA raises its own problems that are not relevant here. But what he presupposes to have been the common form of political organisation before that, a loosely organised oligarchy, fits what evidence we have much better than any suggestion of single kings or chiefs, and traces of it can be perceived in the literary and other written material relating to the early Archaic period, including early poetry, fragments of law codes, and traditions like those enshrined in the *Athenaion Politeia* (*Athenian Constitution*) once attributed to Aristotle.

From the archaeological point of view, also, this would fit the evidence far better, for with the single exception of the Lefkandi 'Heroön', features that could be associated with a monarch-like figure are, quite simply, lacking. It is unwise to assume, without much more extensive excavation, that large buildings like Nichoria Units IV–1 and IV–5 were the unique 'ruler's dwellings' in their communities. Rather, the relatively abundant source of information that we do possess, the burials, suggests the existence of an elite class within which it is hard to distinguish outstanding figures, such as one would expect kings to be. Contemporary rich burials of apparently equivalent status, to judge from their grave-goods and other features of their tombs, can be found in different cemeteries, or in different tombs within the same cemetery, at major sites like Athens, Lefkandi, Knossos, and even Argos, where the traditions concerning the existence of a single *basileus* have more substance than at most centres.

Whether communities were linked in larger groupings is a question that is at present impossible to answer from the archaeological evidence alone. The later recognition by some communities that they belonged to a single *ethnos*, e.g. Ionians, Boeotians, Phocians, Arcadians, who might have a common cult centre, or that they at least formed an amphictyony using such a centre, is not something that should be assumed to derive from these still prehistoric times. There is ample evidence that these groupings were still being developed and manipulated much later, in Archaic and even Classical times (as discussed in Hall 1997). The use of a common pottery style over broad regions has no necessary significance for political organisation, particularly since close inspection often throws up evidence of significant local variations within the region of the style. But Morgan's argument that Olympia, Isthmia and Kalapodi developed as common cult centres for surrounding communities seems reasonable, although it should be noted that the communities using Olympia and Isthmia remained separate politically, not even sharing an *ethnos* name. On the whole, it seems most likely that each substantial community formed an effectively independent polity, although the biggest might have offshoot and satellite communities, and that this pattern was a major contribution of the EIA to later Greece, replacing the often much larger principalities of the Third Palace Period.

Reference to cult centres introduces the question of whether it is possible to detect much evidence for the public religion of the communities, and the answer has to be frustratingly little, outside Crete, where buildings and religious paraphernalia and symbols that seem to derive directly from LB traditions continued in use into the eleventh century, if not the tenth, and some LB ritual sites continued or were brought back into use. At Olympia, Isthmia and Kalapodi the evidence suggests ritualised feasting, probably following sacrifice, in a manner that might reflect a tradition inherited, or developed from, what has now been identified at some Mycenaean sites (Chapter 8, p. 224), but it would be unsafe to say more when the evidence is so scanty. It must seem likely that the leaders of the community conducted rites on behalf of the community, but the argument that they effectively monopolised these and conducted them in their own houses seems most implausible.

It may reasonably be hypothesised that the communities' economy was mixed farming, but beyond that it does not seem possible to go. As noted in Chapter 4, there is nothing to support the hypothesis basic to Tandy's interpretation of the later EIA economy (1997: 101–11, cf. 89), imported from anthropological models of chiefdoms, that the leading persons or families formed the centre of redistributive networks, in which their followers and dependants felt a social obligation to send them livestock and products and the leading families felt an equal obligation to redistribute these. It might be considered likely enough that the leading families not only had considerable resources derived from their own land, but may have possessed more land than they could work with their close dependants and so have leased it out. They may even have claimed, on the basis of status, that in some sense a great deal of the land 'belonged' to them, and that those using it therefore owed them some form of tithe or tax. This could apply particularly when land that had lain fallow was opened up as population grew (see Gallant 1982: 122–4, although this analysis has problems). But this has to be regarded as largely speculative. The only thing that can be said for certain is that some families were clearly able to gather sufficient surplus to exchange it in some way for relative necessities such as the common metals and also for luxuries such as gold or Near Eastern exotica, both of which could be used as symbols of status and prestige.

It cannot be emphasised too often that the need for metals meant that it was impossible for any community to be truly self-sufficient, and that some form of exchange, which would have linked the Aegean, however weakly, with a wider world, must therefore have persisted through the most depressed times. Even iron was not readily available to every community, and would therefore have to be acquired. In some cases metals may not have been acquired directly from foreign or local traders, but by exchange between communities, some of which (e.g. Lefkandi) were much more in touch with the outside world than others. To the evidence that the distribution of metals and the spread of the technology of working iron provides for intercommunal contacts can be added that from the spread of elements of pottery styles, particularly Athenian PG, which was imitated in the neighbouring mainland regions (north-east Peloponnese, Boeotia, Euboea) and across the Aegean as far as central Ionia.

All these features provide evidence for a greater degree of contact than we actually have evidence for in the shape of certainly identifiable foreign imports, whether pots or other items. These inferred patterns of contacts could have been the vehicle for the spread of intangibles such as religious beliefs and practices, and the celebration of particular festivals which gave their names to months; several of these were distinctive enough to seem typical, later, of whole groups like Ionians and Dorians. But, although it is often assumed, it cannot be demonstrated that such shared month-names and festivals reflect original unities whose history lies deep in the past from the point of view of Archaic times. When the Athenian month-name Lenaion, formed in the distinctive 'Ionian' manner, can be found in Hesiod (*Works and Days* 505), although it occurs in no later source for Boeotian communities' calendars, it does not seem wise to make such assumptions, which do not allow for the active manipulation of such features in historical times to express beliefs about the past of a community and its links with other communities.

In short, frustratingly little can be said with much certainty about the nature of social structure within the EIA communities, or their social and political links with each other, but it is possible to say something about the nature of their economy and external contacts, particularly those that relate to exchange of goods and materials. In this connection, the close link in the eleventh to tenth centuries between evidence for an exceptional degree of wealth, as indicated by grave-goods, and evidence for contacts with the Near East cannot be ignored. Lefkandi is the obvious example, although Knossos also provides notable evidence. But it must be admitted that this applies mainly to the southern Aegean, for the graves of Elateia, Vergina and Thasos are rich in bronze and iron but show no comparable evidence of Near Eastern links.

The question of whether, in the evidently fruitful connection between Lefkandi and the Near East, Euboeans or Phoenicians were the leaders has been discussed inconclusively in Chapter 7. As noted there, the Greeks' need for raw materials has been thought the prime mover by Coldstream, but the evidence for a 'special relationship' between Euboea (principally Lefkandi?) and Phoenicia (principally Tyre?) might point in the opposite direction. The extraordinary honours paid to the couple buried in the Lefkandi 'Heroön' might even suggest that the 'hero' was instrumental in forging this link. The basis of the link on the Lefkandi side could have been the special knowledge of the north Aegean suggested by the distribution of certain types of pottery (Chapter 7, pp. 207–8). This knowledge could allow the Euboeans to collect valuable materials like metals in the north, that they could then pass on to Cypriots and Phoenicians who came into the Aegean as far as Lefkandi, or even take to the Near East themselves. But, as so often, this is admittedly rather speculative.

In the tenth century Attic PG pottery spread increasingly widely in the Aegean, but it may reasonably be questioned whether this was the result of Attic enterprise. The fact that some of the finest Attic PG known comes from Lefkandi graves might well be taken to imply that it was acquired in Attica and distributed by Euboean ships. Certainly, taken as a whole the evidence suggests that ships based in Euboea and the Near East are most likely to have been active in exchange within the Aegean and beyond in the tenth century, but that in this respect Euboea was exceptional. In general, if Aegean communities produce evidence of overseas contacts at this time, it more probably reflects visits from outside rather than the activity of any of their own citizens. But whether, as Morris has argued, the prevailing ethos was inward-turned and isolationist at this period is another matter. The wide distribution of Attic and Euboean PG might seem to point the other way, and it should not be forgotten that our knowledge of many parts of the Aegean region in the tenth century remains extremely patchy.

The beginnings of sustained development

The continuing prominence of Lefkandi in the ninth century, when the Euboean style of pottery had a dominating influence in the north Aegean and northern Cyclades, and is found in some quantity in Cyprus and Phoenicia, suggests that the 'special relationship' referred to above endured. But other regions were finally coming to the fore. Athens, in particular, now starts to show evidence of valuable external contacts. Again, one might speculate whether Athens' (probable) control of the silver source at Laurion was the main attraction to Near Easterners, as it might have been to Euboeans earlier.

But it is possible that the increasingly stable conditions in the Aegean, which would contribute to population growth and prosperity, played a considerable role in encouraging Near Eastern exchange activity generally. Certainly, there are many indications that long-distance exchange links had a crucial role to play in the revival of the Aegean.

It is also likely that increasing population and prosperity would have stimulated a greater degree of organisation in many communities and the development of a more established hierarchy. Graves such as the rich female cremations datable to the mid-ninth century at Athens suggest the establishment of a definable aristocracy, which was increasingly demonstrating its superior status by more elaborate funerary rites and grave-goods, and the marking of graves with increasingly large decorated vases. But it is not easy to identify comparable phenomena elsewhere. Sometimes this is because the evidence is quite simply lacking – the Lefkandi cemeteries go out of use around 825 – but they are still absent where they might be expected, as in the leading regions of the Peloponnese.

By the end of the ninth century, the features considered typical of the 'dark age' had largely disappeared, and during the eighth century various phenomena suggesting the development of a common 'Greek' consciousness can be identified. The tendency of all regions to produce fine pottery that derived its style and at least some of its shapes, sometimes at one remove, from a single source – the pottery of Athens – surely suggests a world that had become much more closely bound together, and the absence of such a local style in inland Macedonia may be considered one indication that it was not becoming part of the Greek world in the way that some coastal communities like Torone were. But much more significant are the features that can be identified in the field of religious ritual. These are particularly the widespread production and use of comparable types of votive offering, especially the most expensive, bronze tripods and figurines, and the following of a particular style of sacrifice in ritual practice, while a shrine building was increasingly often being built to house the image or symbol of the deity and probably the most valuable offerings (again, these features are effectively lacking in inland Macedonia). The ability of certain religious centres, especially Olympia and Delphi, to attract offerings that came from different parts of Greece is another sign that the Aegean world was coming to recognise a common interest in certain religious centres.

But in terms of funerary ritual there were still notable divergences between different parts of Greece, and the switch among the elites from expenditure on family funerals to expenditure on religious offerings was by no means universal, as the rich offerings in eighth-century graves at Argos and Knossos demonstrate. This suggests that there may have been continuing substantial differences in social structure between different communities. Also, the artefacts produced were not everywhere of identical types, though they largely belonged to the same very widespread classes. Thus, long pins and fibulae were produced as major items of costume jewellery everywhere, and figurines of particular types, especially the horse, standing male (originally a warrior, often a horse-leader) and standing female, were produced at several different centres on the mainland (but not apparently in Euboea) and also in Crete, while tripods seem to be the most elaborate and presumably the most valued items universally, suiting Homeric references. In the remoter parts of the Aegean region the range of types produced was more limited, the types themselves less elaborate, and precious materials were very rare, if we can judge by what has survived. Still, the prodigality in the use of metal would have astonished the populations of the same regions only a few generations earlier.

These phenomena demonstrate that the period of very limited resources had ended and that the standards of Aegean-based craftsmanship were improving greatly. It is really not of great significance whether the new techniques that can be seen particularly in the metalwork of the eighth century were introduced by immigrant craftsmen from the Near East, or were learned in some way by native craftsmen, since in either case it was Aegean-based 'Greek' craftsmen who would carry them on and improve them. They show clearly that skill in working metal, in particular, was constantly improving from this time, although the most remarkable finds are very localised in their distribution, such as the bronze 'shields' and openwork stands from Crete and the gold headbands from Athens and Eretria. It is significant that many of the most elaborate items are personal adornments and come from elite graves, for this is a reminder of how much the concerns and desires of the elite drove development in this area. Yet the most elaborate of all in terms of size and quantity of metal used, the tripods and stands, were almost entirely used in the ritual sphere, and in that respect represent the beginning of the Greek tradition of expenditure on public religion, which is also detectable in the eighth-century tendency to make religious buildings larger or otherwise more impressive in appearance.

Final comments

Is it possible to explain why the 'dark age' lasted so long? The relatively low population and the probably rather unstructured nature of social organisation, both of which probably reflect the fundamental instability continually referred to above, would not be conducive to the regular production of surpluses, without which lasting prosperity cannot be established. Instability will also have had a very inhibiting effect on the long-distance exchange contacts with the Near East on which conspicuous prosperity had been built in the LBA. But it is not easy to demonstrate that continuing or renewed links of this kind formed an absolutely essential stimulus for the lifting of the 'darkness'. For evidence for such links is confined to a very few sites in the eleventh, tenth and ninth centuries, and how far the prosperity that they can be connected with was disseminated secondarily to other sites remains unclear, although Athens in particular may have benefited through its links with Lefkandi.

Much must have been owed to solid but unspectacular internal progress in the regions which, as pointed out elsewhere (Dickinson 1994a: 297), seem to have a natural capacity to develop sophisticated and relatively wealthy societies, if circumstances are reasonably favourable. The precise mechanism is not clear, but it surely reflects an ability to produce commodities that can be marketed in bulk, for if no valuable raw material like a metal source is controlled, there can be no other source of wealth than the produce of the land and what can be made from it. The shifting of focus to different regions and different patterns of interconnection that seems to have resulted from the collapse of the BA civilisations may have resulted in a freeing of energies and so have been ultimately beneficial. Here, Snodgrass's comment on the need for greater stress on the positive aspects of choices made by the Aegean population has relevance ([1971] 2000: xxxii). But regions that had frequently been in the lead before the EIA, such as Boeotia and the more fertile parts of the Peloponnese, seem to lag behind in development. Possibly this reflects the degree to which the revival of prosperity was due to the actions of certain adventurous members of local elites, originally Cypriots and Phoenicians rather than Greeks in all probability, who seized favourable opportunities to establish long-distance contacts – for behind all the processes that we see evidence for in archaeology, there lie eventually the decisions of individuals. Their success, it may be hypothesised, encouraged more general exploration and establishment of more extensive connections over time. Archaeology cannot usually recover history at this level, although the occupants of the Lefkandi 'Heroön' may be just such individuals, but special circumstances are likely to lie behind the startling prominence of Lefkandi, for instance, as behind that of Mycenae before it, for neither had obvious natural advantages. Answers of this kind may seem unsatisfactorily speculative and old-fashioned, but they may be the best available.

It still seems reasonable to follow Snodgrass, Coldstream and Morris in arguing that the pace of development really began to quicken in the eighth century. But Whitley is surely right to lay emphasis on the re-establishment of stability earlier, a process which had clearly taken place in most regions by the end of the tenth century, although new settlements might be founded later. But at that time there is less evidence for interconnection between the Aegean communities, let alone between the Aegean and the wider world, than becomes evident in the eighth century. With further increases in knowledge, it may prove possible to push back the beginnings of really substantial development over a wide area of the Aegean before 800, but there is little support for such a view in the current state of the evidence.

Is it possible to detect the familiar outlines of Archaic and Classical Greece already in the EIA? Obviously there is much that is familiar. Religious and ritual practices that would be familiar to later Greeks were already becoming current. There is good reason to believe from the iconographic evidence that the specific form of ritual female mourning for the dead, shown in representations from the eighth century onwards, had LBA roots, and it may well be that a particular style of chariot racing, probably reserved for ritual occasions like festivals and funerals, also derived from the LBA (Rystedt 1999). To judge from the evidence of the Homeric poems, by the eighth century the gods in whose honour rites were celebrated were coming to be widely recognised, and many famous cult sites were already well established and prestigious. But the custom of providing the gods with cult buildings built of stone had only established itself at a few sites by 700, and stone sculpture appeared later still. Alphabetic writing, originally put to personal uses, notably religious dedications, was on the most widely held view only beginning to be developed.

Social arrangements may for a long time have been similar to what can be dimly perceived as typical of Archaic times, but there was much still to come. Homeric heroes did not recline to eat, as became typical for elite males in Archaic times, but sat on stools, and they ate roasted or grilled meat (Murray 1993: 81), not the fish that, as clearly demonstrated in Davidson (1997: ch. 1), was the luxury food by Classical times, at least at Athens and other leading cities. Indeed, the whole symposium style of meal and drinking party, closely associated with the elite, clearly reflects a level of influence from the Near East exercised at a later date (Chapter 7, p. 199). Furthermore, the 'centre of gravity' in Greece may still not have been where it was later, when the mainland powers were clearly the leaders. The archaeological evidence from Crete shows how rich and cosmopolitan its communities were right through the eighth century and beyond, but they played very little part in the affairs of Greece in the later Archaic and Classical periods.

On an overall view of the transition from LBA to EIA it must seem that, despite the evidence for various forms of continuity mentioned above, the changes in the most prominent archaeological features are more striking. An analogy could be found in the tradition encapsulated in the Homeric poems. Although this undoubtedly has its source in the LBA, it probably went through a whole series of transformations to produce the final blend, in which very little that is genuinely BA survived. Similarly, the communities of the Aegean were probably in the process of creating new social identities and institutions for themselves throughout the EIA, and continued to do so in the Archaic period. In the course of this they evolved much of what we think of as typically Greek that was not there in the LBA. The EIA, then, saw recognisable advances towards the Greece of later times, but many very significant developments were still to come.

Finally, the outstanding problem in interpreting the EIA deserves mention, a lack of information which may never be fully remedied. We can hope for more evidence from important regions which were to be highly important in the Archaic period, like Laconia on the mainland and the islands and coasts of the east Aegean, but it must be admitted that not just in these regions but everywhere there must have been more people than we can find evidence for even in intensive surveys, just as there were in Archaic times. This in particular brings out the limitations of archaeological evidence, our only trustworthy source of information for the period. The Aegean EIA, then, will probably always remain somewhat mysterious.

Bibliography

Whitley (2001: ch. 5) is a recent and valuable survey of the period, with useful comments on social structure and its relationship to the Homeric picture (89–90, 97–8).

The question of the specifically EIA component of the Homeric poems and its significance is considered in more detail in Dickinson (1986), Morris (1986) and Sherratt (1990); cf. also Morris, I. (1997: 557–9), and Van Wees (1992) who makes many useful comments on the consistency and level of realism of the Homeric picture of society.

GLOSSARY

Amphictyony   A confederation of communities sharing the control of a common shrine.

Amphora   A large jar with two handles, placed horizontally or vertically.

Amphoriskos   A small amphora.

Aryballos   A narrow-necked juglet.

Bird vase   A vase whose shape has some resemblance to a bird.

Carnelian   An opaque red or brown semi-precious stone.

Chalcedony   A semi-precious form of quartz.

Chamber tomb   A room-like tomb hollowed out in rock, variously shaped.

Cist   A generally rectangular tomb lined and covered with stone slabs.

Dinos   A handleless round-bodied shape on a raised foot.

Dromos   An open entrance way into a chamber or tholos tomb, cut down from the surface.

Faience   An opaque glassy substance.

Fibula   A brooch.

Flask   A flattened circular shape with mouth and two handles at the top.

Hydria   A water jar, with one vertical handle from lip to shoulder and two horizontal handles on the belly.

Kalathos   A handleless shallow bowl with wide flaring mouth.

Kantharos   A drinking vessel with two vertical handles from belly to lip, often raised.

Koinē   A common style diffused over a wide area.

Krater   A large mixing bowl, often on a raised foot, with two horizontal handles on the body.

Kylix   A high-stemmed drinking vessel with two handles from belly to lip.

Larnax   A clay coffin, normally chest-shaped.

Lekythos   A small narrow-necked flask with one vertical handle.

Oinochoe   A jug with trefoil-shaped lip.

Peplos   A blanket-like robe, pinned at the shoulders.

Pisé   A style of building in which the wall is moulded from stiff earth or clay.

Pithos   A large, open-mouthed, thick-walled storage vessel of coarse fabric.

259

Pyxis   A small circular or straight-sided box shape, usually with a lid.

Repoussé   A technique of decorating sheet metal with hammer and punches.

Rhyton   Any perforated vessel thought to be used for libation.

Ring-vase   A vase shaped like a ring, with a neck and handle at the top.

Skyphos   A drinking vessel with two horizontal handles.

Sphinx   A human-faced lion, often winged.

Steatite   A term long used in Aegean archaeology that actually signifies serpentine, a soft stone, in almost all cases.

Stirrup jar   A closed jar with a false spout at the top, supporting two handles (the stirrup) and a narrow spout on the shoulder.

Tholos   A stone-built tomb of circular plan, rising into a vaulted dome.

Waster   A misfired piece of pottery, often vitrified.

BIBLIOGRAPHY

This is not intended to be a comprehensive bibliography of the subject, but to list those sources which I have cited, together with some basic sources for major sites. Reports of excavations in *AD*, *AR* and *BCH* Chroniques have only been listed if they provide considerable detail or form a major article; otherwise, they, and some single citations of articles and reviews, are referred to in the text by periodical year number and page reference. Some major excavation reports are cited so frequently that they have been given abbreviations, as shown below, where the most significant references concerned with major sites are grouped separately, before the main bibliography. General studies and those particularly concerned with chronology have also been listed separately.

As in Dickinson (1994a), I have harmonised the spelling of names and the initials given for various authors where these are cited differently in different sources.

Major general studies of relevance to the period

Boardman, J.B. (1999) *The Greeks overseas* (fourth edition), London: Thames and Hudson.

Coldstream, J.N. (1977) *Geometric Greece*, London: Benn (reissued with supplementary chapter 2003, London: Routledge).

Cullen, T. (ed.) (2001) *Aegean prehistory: a review*, Boston: Archaeological Institute of America.

Desborough, V.R. (1964) *The last Mycenaeans and their successors. An archaeological survey c. 1200–c. 1000* BC, Oxford: Clarendon Press.

—— (1972) *The Greek dark ages*, London: Benn.

Finley, M.I. (1977) *The world of Odysseus*, London: Chatto & Windus.

Lemos, I.S. (2002) *The Protogeometric Aegean. The archaeology of the late eleventh and tenth centuries* BC, Oxford: Oxford University Press.

Morgan, C. (1990) *Athletes and oracles. The transformation of Olympia and Delphi in the eighth century* BC, Cambridge: Cambridge University Press.

Morris, I. (1987) *Burial and ancient society. The rise of the Greek city-state*, Cambridge: Cambridge University Press.

Morris, I. (1997) 'Homer and the Iron Age', in Morris and Powell 1997, ch. 24.

—— (1999) *Archaeology as cultural history: words and things in Iron Age Greece*, Malden, Mass. and Oxford: Blackwell.

—— and Powell, B. (eds) (1997) *A new companion to Homer*, Leiden: Brill.

Morris, S.P. (1992) *Daidalos and the origins of Greek art*, Princeton: Princeton University Press.

Murray, O. (1993) *Early Greece* (second edition), London: Fontana.

Osborne, R. (1996) *Greece in the making 1200–479* BC, London: Routledge.

Sandars, N.K. (1978, second edition 1985) *The Sea Peoples. Warriors of the ancient Mediterranean 1250–1150* BC, London: Thames & Hudson.

Snodgrass, A.M. (1971, reissued with new foreword 2000) *The Dark Age of Greece. An archaeological survey of the eleventh to the eighth centuries* BC, Edinburgh: Edinburgh University Press.

—— (1980a) *Archaic Greece. The age of experiment*, London: Dent.

Sparkes, B.A. (ed.) (1998) *Greek civilization*, Oxford: Blackwell.

Tandy, D.W. (1997) *Warriors into traders. The power of the market in early Greece*, Berkeley and Los Angeles: University of California Press.

Thomas, C.G. and Conant, C. (1999) *Citadel to City-State. The transformation of Greece, 1200–700* BCE, Bloomington: Indiana University Press.

Vanschoonwinkel, J. (1991) *L'Egée et la Mediterranée orientale à la fin du deuxième millénaire*, Providence, R.I. and Louvain-la-Neuve: Art and Archaeology Publications.

Ward, W.A. and Joukowsky, M.S. (eds) (1992) *The crisis years: the 12th century* BC *from beyond the Danube to the Tigris*, Dubuque: Kendall/Hunt.

Whitley, J. (1991a) *Style and society in Dark Age Greece. The changing face of a pre-literate society 1100–700* BC, Cambridge: Cambridge University Press.

—— (2001) *The archaeology of ancient Greece*, Cambridge: Cambridge University Press.

Chronology

Deger-Jalkotzy, S. (1999) 'Elateia and problems of pottery chronology', in Dakoronia and Papakonstantinou 1999, 195–202.

—— and Zavadil, M. (eds) (2003) *LH IIIC Chronology and Synchronisms*, Vienna: Österreichischen Akademie der Wissenschaften.

Forsberg, S. (1995) *Near Eastern destruction datings as sources for Greek and Near Eastern Iron Age chronology*, Uppsala: University of Uppsala.

Furumark, A. (1972) *Mycenaean pottery II. Chronology*, Stockholm: Svenska Institutet i Athens.

Hallager, E. and Hallager B.P. (eds) (1997) *Late Minoan III pottery. Chronology and terminology*, Aarhus: Danish Institute at Athens.

Hannestad, L. (1996) 'Absolute chronology: Greece and the Near East *c.* 1000–600 BC', in Randsborg 1996, 39–49.

Jacob-Felsch, M. (1988) 'Compass-drawn concentric circles in vase painting: a problem in relative chronology at the end of the Bronze Age', in French and Wardle 1988, 193–9.

Manning, S.W. and Weninger, B. (1992) 'A light in the dark: archaeological wiggle matching and the absolute chronology of the close of the Aegean Late Bronze Age', *Antiquity* 66: 636–63.

Morris, I. (1996) 'The absolute chronology of the Greek colonies in Sicily', in Randsborg 1996, 51–9.

Newton, M., Wardle, K.A. and Kuniholm, P.I. (2003) 'Dendrochronology and radiocarbon determinations from Assiros and the beginning of the Greek Iron Age', *To Αρχαιολογικό Έργο στη Μακεδονία καί στη Θράκη* 17: 173–90.

Nijboer, A.J., van der Plicht, J., Bietti Sestieri, A.M. and De Santis, A. (2001) 'A high chronology for the Early Iron Age in central Italy', *Palaeohistoria* 41/42: 163–76.

Papadopoulos, J.K. (1998) 'From Macedonia to Sardinia: problems of Iron Age Aegean chronology and assumptions of Greek maritime primacy', in M.S. Balmuth and R.H. Tykot (eds), *Sardinian and Aegean chronology. Towards the resolution of relative and absolute dating in the Mediterranean*, Oxford: Oxbow, 363–9.

Randsborg, K. (ed.) (1996) *Absolute chronology: archaeological Europe 2500–500* BC (*Acta Archaeologica* 67), Copenhagen: Munksgaard.

Wardle, K.A., Kuniholm, P.I., Newton, M. and Kromer, B. (2004) 'Old trees, new dates, and the Trojan War', http://artsweb.bham.ac.uk/aha/kaw/troy.htm.

Warren, P.M. and Hankey, V. (1989) *Aegean Bronze Age chronology*, Bristol: Bristol Classical Press.

Yasur-Landau, A. (2003) 'The absolute chronology of the Late Helladic IIIC period: a view from the Levant', in Deger-Jalkotzy and Zavadil 2003, 235–44.

Some major sites

Argos

Courbin, P. (1974) *Tombes géométriques d'Argos I (1952–1958)*, Paris: Vrin.

Deshayes, J. (1966) *Argos. Les fouilles de la Deiras*, Paris: Vrin.

Hägg, R. (1974) *Die Gräber der Argolis in submykenischer, protogeometrischer und geometrischer Zeit. I: Lage und Form der Gräber* (*Boreas* 4.1), Uppsala: University of Uppsala.

Asine

Dietz, S. (1982) *Asine II. Results of the excavations east of the acropolis 1970–1974 Fasc. 1: general stratigraphical analysis and architectural remains*, Stockholm: Åström.

Frizell, B.S. (1986) *Asine II, Fasc. 3. The Late and Final Mycenaean periods*, Stockholm: Swedish Institute in Athens.

Wells, B. (1976) *Asine II, Fasc. 4. The Protogeometric Period, Part 1: the tombs*, Stockholm: Swedish Institute in Athens.

—— (1983a) *Asine II, Fasc. 4. The Protogeometric Period, Part 2: an analysis of the settlement*, Stockholm: Swedish Institute in Athens.

—— (1983b) *Asine II, Fasc. 4. The Protogeometric Period, Part 3: catalogue of pottery and other artefacts*, Stockholm: Swedish Institute in Athens.

BIBLIOGRAPHY

Athens

(the material from Athens also receives major discussion in
all general books cited above)

Kraiker, W. and Kübler, K. (1939) *Kerameikos 1. Die Nekropolen des 12. bis 10. Jahrhunderts*, Berlin: de Gruyter.

Krause, G. (1975) *Untersuchungen zu den ältesten Nekropolen am Eridanos in Athen*, Hamburg: Helmut Busche Verlag.

Kübler, K. (1943) *Kerameikos 4. Neufunde aus der Nekropole des 11. und 10. Jahrhunderts*, Berlin: de Gruyter.

——(1954) *Kerameikos 5. Die Nekropolen des 10. bis 8. Jahrhunderts*, Berlin: de Gruyter.

——(1964) 'Zu der Nekropole des 10.–8. Jahrhunderts in Kerameikos', *AA* 1964: 145–79.

Mountjoy, P.-A. (1988) (with a contribution by V. Hankey) 'LH IIIC Late versus Submycenaean. The Kerameikos Pompeion cemetery reviewed', *JDAI* 103: 1–37.

Müller-Karpe, H. (1962) 'Die Metallbeigaben der früheisenzeitlichen Kerameikos-Gräber', *JDAI* 77: 59–129.

Papadopoulos, J. (2003) *Ceramicus Redivivus. The Early Iron Age potters' field in the area of the Classical Athenian Agora, Hesperia* Supplement 31, Princeton: American School of Classical Studies at Athens.

Elateia-Alonaki

Alram-Stern, E. (1999) 'The Mycenaean figurines of Elateia', in Dakoronia and Papakonstantinou 1999, 215–22.

Dakoronia, Ph. (2003) 'Elateia in central Greece: excavations and finds', Mycenaean Seminar, Institute of Classical Studies, London, 19 March 2003.

Dakoronia, Ph., Deger-Jalkotzy, S. and Sakellariou, A. (1996) *Die Siegel aus der Nekropole von Elateia-Alonaki (Corpus der minoischen und mykenischen Siegel* V: Supplement 2), Berlin: Mann.

Deger-Jalkotzy, S. (2003) 'Elateia in central Greece: Mycenaean and Early Iron Age history of the site', Mycenaean Seminar, Institute of Classical Studies, London, 19 March 2003.

—— with Dakoronia, Ph. (1990) 'Elateia (Phokis) und die frühe Geschichte der Griechen: Ein österreichisch-griechisches Grabungsprojekt', *Anzeiger der phil.-hist. Klasse der Österreichischen Akademie der Wissenschaften* 127: 77–86.

Kalapodi

Kalapodi I = Felsch, R.S.C. (ed.) (1996) *Kalapodi. Ergebnisse der Ausgrabungen im Heiligtum der Artemis und des Apollon von Hyampolis in der antiken Phokis. Bd I*, Mainz: von Zabern.

Felsch, R.C.S. (1987) (ed.) 'Kalapodi. Bericht über die Grabungen im Heiligtum der Artemis Elaphebolos und des Apollon von Hyampolis 1978–1982', *AA* 1987: 1–99.

——(2001) 'Opferhandlungen des Alltagslebens im Heiligtum der Artemis Elaphebolos von Hyampolis in den Phasen SH IIIC – Spätgeometrisch', in Laffineur and Hägg 2001, 193–9.

Jacob-Felsch, M. (cited as Felsch-Jacob, M.) (1987) 'Bericht zur spätmykenisch und submykenisch Keramik', in Felsch 1987, 26–35.

Jacob-Felsch, M. (1996) 'Die spätmykenische bis frühprotogeometrische Keramik' in *Kalapodi I*: 1–213.

Nitsche, A. (1987) 'Protogeometrische und subprotogeometrische Keramik aus der Heiligtum bei Kalapodi', in Felsch 1987, 35–49.

Kavousi

Coulson, W.D.E. (1998) 'The Early Iron Age on the Kastro at Kavousi in East Crete', in Cavanagh and Curtis 1998, 40–4.

—— Haggis, D.C., Mook, M.S. and Tobin, J. (1997) 'Excavations on the Kastro at Kavousi. An architectural overview', *Hesperia* 66: 515–90.

Day, L.P., Coulson, W.D.E. and Gesell, G.C. (1986) 'Kavousi, 1983–1984: the settlement at Vronda', *Hesperia* 55: 355–87.

Gesell, G.C., Day, L.P. and Coulson, W.D.E. (1995) 'Excavations at Kavousi, Crete, 1989 and 1990', *Hesperia* 64: 67–120.

Haggis, D.C. (1993) 'Intensive survey, traditional settlement patterns, and Dark Age Crete: the case of Early Iron Age Kavousi', *JMA* 6: 131–74.

—— (1996) 'Archaeological survey at Kavousi, East Crete. Preliminary report', *Hesperia* 65: 373–432.

Klippel, W.E. and Snyder, L.M. (1991) 'Dark Age fauna from Kavousi, Crete. The vertebrates from the 1987 and 1988 excavations', *Hesperia* 60: 179–86.

Mook, M.S. (1998) 'Early Iron Age domestic architecture: the Northwest Building on the Kastro at Kavousi', in Cavanagh and Curtis 1998, 45–57.

—— and Coulson, W.D.E. (1997) 'Late Minoan IIIC pottery from the Kastro at Kavousi', in Hallager and Hallager 1997, 337–65.

Snyder, L.M. and Klippel, W.E. (2000) 'Dark Age subsistence at the Kastro site, east Crete: exploring subsistence change and continuity during the Late Bronze Age–Early Iron Age transition', in Vaughan and Coulson 2000, 65–83.

Knossos

NorthCem = Coldstream, J.N. and Catling, H.W. (eds) (1996) *Knossos North Cemetery. Early Greek tombs*, London: British School at Athens.

Brock, J.K. (1957) *Fortetsa: early Greek tombs near Knossos*, Cambridge: British School at Athens.

Coldstream, J.N. (2000) 'Evans's Greek finds: the early Greek town of Knossos and its encroachment on the borders of the Minoan palace', *BSA* 95: 259–99.

Hood, M.S.F. and Coldstream, J.N. (1968) 'A Late Minoan tomb at Ayios Joannis near Knossos', *BSA* 63: 205–18.

Warren, P.M. (1983) 'Knossos: Stratigraphical Museum excavations, 1978–82. Part II', *AR* 29: 63–87.

BIBLIOGRAPHY

Lefkandi

Lefkandi I = Popham, M.R., Sackett, L.H. and Themelis, P.G. (eds) (1979 plates, 1980 text) *Lefkandi I. The Iron Age settlement; the cemeteries*, London: Thames & Hudson.

Lefkandi II,1 = Catling, R.W.V. and Lemos, I.S. (1990) (edited by M.R. Popham, P.G. Calligas and L.H. Sackett) *Lefkandi II. The Protogeometric building at Toumba, Part 1: the pottery*. London: Thames & Hudson.

Lefkandi II,2 = Popham, M.R., Calligas, P.G. and Sackett, L.H. (eds) (1993) *Lefkandi II. The Protogeometric building at Toumba. Part 2: the excavation, architecture and finds*, London: British School of Archaeology at Athens.

Lefkandi III = Popham, M.R. (1996), with Lemos, I.S. *Lefkandi III, plates. The Early Iron Age cemetery at Toumba, The excavations of 1981 to 1994*, London: British School of Archaeology at Athens.

Catling, H.W. (1985) 'The arrangement of some grave goods in the Dark Age cemeteries of Lefkandi', *BSA* 80: 19–23.

Musgrave, J.H. and Popham, M. (1991) 'The Late Helladic IIIC intramural burials at Lefkandi, Euboea', *BSA* 86: 273–96.

Pakkanen, J. and Pakkanen, P. (2000) 'The Toumba building at Lefkandi: some methodological reflections on its plan and function', *BSA* 95: 239–52.

Popham, M.R., Calligas, P.G. and Sackett, L.H. (1989) 'Further excavations of the Toumba cemetery at Lefkandi, 1984 and 1986, a preliminary report', *AR* 35: 117–29.

—— and Lemos, I.S. (1995) 'A Euboean warrior trader', *OJA* 14: 151–7.

—— and Sackett, L.H. (1968) *Excavations at Lefkandi, Euboea 1964–66*, London: Thames & Hudson.

—— , Touloupa, E. and Sackett, L.H. (1982a) 'The hero of Lefkandi', *Antiquity* 56: 169–74.

—— (1982b) 'Further excavation of the Toumba cemetery at Lefkandi, 1981', *BSA* 77: 213–48.

Nichoria

Nichoria I = Rapp, G., Jr. and Aschenbrenner, S.E. (eds) (1978) *Excavations at Nichoria in southwest Greece Volume I*, Minneapolis: University of Minnesota Press.

Nichoria II = McDonald, W.A. and Wilkie, N.C. (eds) (1992) *Excavations at Nichoria in southwest Greece Volume II. The Bronze Age occupation*, Minneapolis: Minnesota University Press.

Nichoria III = McDonald, W.A, Coulson, W.D.E. and Rosser, J. (eds) (1983) *Excavations at Nichoria in southwest Greece Volume III. Dark Age and Byzantine occupation*, Minneapolis: Minnesota University Press.

Fågerström, K. (1988a) 'Finds, function and plan: a contribution to the interpretation of Iron Age Nichoria in Messenia', *OpAth* 17: 33–50.

Mancz, E.A. (1989) 'An examination of changing patterns of animal-husbandry of the Late Bronze and Dark Ages of Nichoria in the southwestern Peloponnese' (PhD thesis, University of Minnesota), Ann Arbor: University Microfilms International.

Mazarakis Ainian, A. (1992) 'Nichoria in the south-west Peloponnese: Units IV–1 and IV–5 reconsidered', *OpAth* 19: 75–84.

General bibliography

Adrymi-Sismani, V. (1994) Ἡ μυκηναική πόλη στο Διμήνι', in Νεότερα Δεδομένα των ερευνών για την Αρχαία Ιωλκό, 17–44, Volos: Dimos Volou.

Akurgal, E. (1983) *Alt-Smyrna: Wohnschichten und Athenatempel*, Ankara: Türk Tarih Kurumu Basimevı.

Albers, G. (2001) 'Rethinking Mycenaean sanctuaries', in Laffineur and Hägg 2001, 131–41.

Alcock, S.E. and Osborne, R. (eds) (1994) *Placing the gods. Sanctuaries and space in ancient Greece*, Oxford: Oxford University Press.

Andreou, S., Fotiadis, M. and Kotsakis, K. (2001) 'The Neolithic and Bronze Age of northern Greece', in Cullen 2001, ch. V.

Antonaccio, C.M. (1994) 'Placing the past: the Bronze Age in the cultic topography of early Greece', in Alcock and Osborne 1994, ch. 4.

Åström, P. (1989) 'Trade in the Late Cypriot Bronze Age', in E.J. Peltenburg (ed.), *Early Society in Cyprus*, Edinburgh: Edinburgh University Press, 202–8.

Aubet, M.G. (2001) *The Phoenicians and the West. Politics, colonies and trade* (second edition), Cambridge: Cambridge University Press.

Backe-Forsberg, Y., Risberg, C. and Bassiakos,Y. (2000–1) 'Metal-working at Asine. Report on the remains of iron production from the Barbouna area and the area east of the acropolis', *OpAth* 25–6: 25–34.

Bakhuizen, S.C. (1976) *Chalcis-in-Euboea. Iron and Chalcidians Abroad*, Leiden: Brill.

Barber, E.J.W. (1991) *Prehistoric textiles*, Princeton: Princeton University Press.

Bass, G.F. (1991) 'Evidence of trade from Bronze Age shipwrecks', in Gale 1991, 69–82.

—— (1999) 'The hull and anchor of the Cape Gelidonya wreck', in Betancourt *et al.* 1999, 21–3.

Batziou-Efstathiou, A. (1999) 'Το νεκροταφείο της Νέας Ιωνίας (Βόλου) κατά τη μετάβαση από την ΥΕ ΙΙΙΓ στην ΠΓ εποχή', in Dakoronia and Papakonstantinou 1999, 117–30.

Bennet, J. (1997) 'Homer and the Bronze Age' in Morris and Powell 1997, ch. 23.

Benzi, M. (1988) 'Rhodes in the Late Helladic IIIC period', in French and Wardle 1988, 253–62.

—— (2001) 'LH IIIC Late Mycenaean refugees at Punta Meliso, Apulia', in Karageorghis and Morris 2001, 233–40.

Bergquist, B. (1988) 'The archaeology of sacrifice: Minoan–Mycenaean versus Greek', in Hägg *et al.* 1988, 21–34.

Bernal, M. (1987, 1991) *Black Athena: the Afro-Asiatic roots of Classical civilisation, Volumes I, II*. New Brunswick: Rutgers University Press.

Betancourt, P.P. (1976) 'The end of the Greek Bronze Age', *Antiquity* 50: 40–7.

——, Karageorghis, V., Laffineur, R. and Niemeier, W.-D. (eds) (1999) *MELETEMATA. Studies in Aegean archaeology presented to Malcolm H. Wiener as he enters his 65th year*, Liège: University of Liège, and Austin: University of Texas.

Bikai, P.M. (1978) *The pottery of Tyre*, Warminster: Aris & Phillips.

Bintliff, J.L., Howard, P. and Snodgrass, A.M. (1999) 'The hidden landscape of prehistoric Greece', *JMA* 12: 139–68.

Boardman, J. (1998) *Early Greek vase painting*, London: Thames & Hudson.

Borgna, E. (2003) 'Regional settlement patterns, exchange systems and sources of power in Crete at the end of the Late Bronze Age: establishing a connection', *SMEA* 45/2: 153–83.

—— and Cassola Guida, P. (2005) 'Some observations on the nature and modes of exchange between Italy and the Aegean in the late Mycenaean period', given in Laffineur and Greco 2005, 497–505.

Bound, M. (1991) 'The Giglio wreck', *Enalia* Supplement 1, Athens.

Bouzek, J. (1994) 'Late Bronze Age Greece and the Balkans: a review of the present picture', *BSA* 89: 217–34.

Branigan, K. (ed.) (1998) *Cemetery and society in the Aegean Bronze Age*, Sheffield: Sheffield Academic Press.

Brouskari, M. (1980) 'A Dark Age Cemetery in Erechtheion Street, Athens', *BSA* 75: 13–31.

Bryce, T. (1998) *The Kingdom of the Hittites*, Oxford: Oxford University Press.

Bryson, R.A., Lamb, H.H. and Donley, D.R. (1974) 'Drought and the decline of Mycenae', *Antiquity* 48: 46–50.

Buckland, P.C., Dugmore, A.J. and Edwards, K.J. (1997) 'Bronze Age myths? Volcanic activity and human response in the Mediterranean and North Atlantic region', *Antiquity* 71: 587–93.

Burkert, W. (1985) *Greek religion*, Oxford: Blackwell.

—— (1992) *The orientalizing revolution: Near Eastern influence on Greek culture in the early archaic age*, Cambridge, Mass.: Harvard University Press.

Carington-Smith, J. (1983) 'The evidence for spinning and weaving', in *Nichoria III*: 287–91.

Carpenter, Rhys (1966) *Discontinuities in Greek civilization*, Cambridge: Cambridge University Press.

Carter, J. (1972) 'The beginnings of narrative art in the Greek Geometric period', *BSA* 67: 235–58.

Carter, J.B. (1998) 'Egyptian bronze jugs from Crete and Lefkandi', *JHS* 118: 172–7.

—— and Morris, S.P. (eds) (1995) *The ages of Homer*, Austin: University of Texas Press.

Cartledge, P. (1979) *Sparta and Lakonia. A regional history 1300–362* BC, London: Routledge & Kegan Paul.

Catling, H.W. (1968) 'Late Minoan vases and bronzes in Oxford', *BSA* 63: 89–131.

—— (1994) 'Cyprus in the 11th century BC – an end or a beginning?', in Karageorghis 1994: 133–40.

—— (1995) 'Heroes returned? Subminoan burials from Crete', in Carter and Morris 1995, 123–36.

Catling, R.W.V. (1996) 'A tenth-century trademark from Lefkandi', in D. Evely, I.S. Lemos and S. Sherratt, (eds) (1996) *Minotaur and Centaur. Studies in the archaeology of Crete and Euboea presented to Mervyn Popham*, Oxford: Tempus Reparatum, 126–32.

—— (1998a) 'Exports of Attic Protogeometric pottery and their identification by non-analytical means', *BSA* 93: 365–78.

—— (1998b) 'The typology of the Protogeometric and Subprotogeometric pottery from Troia and its Aegean context', *Studia Troica* 8: 151–87.

—— and Jones, R.E. (1989) 'Protogeometric vases from Amorgos in the Museum of the British School', *BSA* 84: 177–85.

Cavanagh, W. (1998) 'Innovation, conservatism and variation in Mycenaean funerary ritual', in Branigan 1998, 103–14.

—— and Curtis, M. (eds) (1998) *Post-Minoan Crete*. London: British School at Athens.

—— and Mee, C. (1998) *A private place: death in prehistoric Greece*, Jonsered: Åström.

Chadwick, J. (1976a) *The Mycenaean World*, Cambridge: Cambridge University Press.

—— (1976b) 'Who were the Dorians?', *La Parola del Passato* 31: 103–17.

—— (1985) 'What do we know about Mycenaean religion?', in A. Morpurgo Davies and Y. Duhoux (eds) *Linear B: a 1984 survey*, Louvain-la-Neuve: Institut de Linguistique de Louvain.

Cherry, J. (1988) 'Pastoralism and the role of animals in pre- and protohistoric economies of the Aegean', in C.R. Whittaker (ed.) *Pastoral economies in Classical antiquity* (*ProcCamPhilSoc* Supplement 14), 6–34.

Christou, D. (1998) 'Cremations in the western necropolis of Amathus', in Karageorghis and Stampolidis 1998, 207–15.

Cline, E. (1994) *Sailing the wine-dark sea: international trade and the Late Bronze Age Aegean*, Oxford: British Archaeological Reports.

—— (1995) ' "My brother, my son": rulership and trade between the LBA Aegean, Egypt and the Near East', in Rehak 1995, 143–50.

Coldstream, J.N. (1968) *Greek Geometric pottery*, London: Methuen.

—— (1984) 'A Protogeometric Nature goddess from Knossos', *BICS* 31: 93–104.

—— (1988) 'Early Greek pottery in Tyre and Cyprus: some preliminary comparisons', *RDAC* 1988, Part 2: 35–44.

—— (1998a) 'Crete and the Dodecanese: alternative Eastern approaches to the Greek world during the Geometric period', in Karageorghis and Stampolidis 1998, 255–62.

—— (1998b) 'The first exchanges between Euboeans and Phoenicians: who took the initiative?', in Gitin *et al.* 1998, 353–60.

—— (1998c) *Light from Cyprus on the Greek 'Dark Age'?* (Nineteenth J.L. Myres Memorial Lecture), Oxford: Leopard's Head Press.

Cook, J.M. (1975) 'Greek settlement in the eastern Aegean and Asia Minor', *CAH* II: 2, ch. XXXVIII, Cambridge: Cambridge University Press.

Coulson, W.D.E. (1985) 'The Dark Age pottery of Sparta', *BSA* 80: 29–84.

—— (1986) *The Dark Age pottery of Messenia*, Göteborg: Åström.

—— (1991) 'The "Protogeometric" from Polis reconsidered', *BSA* 86: 43–64.

—— and Tsipopoulou, M. (1994) 'Preliminary investigations at Halasmenos, Crete, 1992–1993', *Aegean Archaeology* 1: 65–97.

Courbin, P. (1993) 'Fragments d'amphores Protogéometriques à Bassit (Syrie)', *Hesperia* 62: 95–113.

Crielaard, J.P. (1998) 'Surfing on the Mediterranean web: Cypriot long-distance communication during the eleventh and tenth centuries BC', in Karageorghis and Stampolidis 1998, 187–204.

Crouwel, J.H. (1992) *Chariots and other wheeled vehicles in Iron Age Greece*, Amsterdam: Allard Pierson.

Cucuzza, N. (1998) 'Geometric Phaistos: a survey', in Cavanagh and Curtis 1998, 62–8.

Cunliffe, B. (ed.) (1994) *The Oxford illustrated prehistory of Europe*, Oxford: Oxford University Press.

D'Agata, A.L. (1999a) *Haghia Triada II. Statuine minoiche e post-minoiche dai vecchi scavi di Haghia Triada (Creta)*, Padua: Italian School of Archaeology in Athens.

—— (1999b) 'Defining a pattern of continuity during the Dark Age in central-western Crete: ceramic evidence from the settlement of Thronos/Kephala (ancient Sybrita)', *SMEA* 41: 181–218.

—— (2001) 'Religion, society and ethnicity on Crete at the end of the Late Bronze Age. The contextual framework of LM IIIC cult activities', in Laffineur and Hägg 2001, 345–54.

—— (forthcoming) 'The cult activity on Crete in the Early Dark Age. Changes, continuities, and the development of a Greek cult system', paper given in Lemos and Deger-Jalkotzy 2003.

——, Goren, Y., Mommsen, H., Schwedt, A. and Yasur-Landau, A. (2005) 'Imported pottery of LH IIIC style from Israel. Style, Provenance, and Chronology,' in Laffineur and Greco 2005, 371–9.

Dakoronia, Ph. and Papakonstantinou, M.-Ph. (eds) (1999) *Η περιφέρεια του μυκηναϊκού κόσμου. Α΄ Διεθνές διεπιστημονικό συμπόσιο, Λαμία 1994*, Lamia: Ministry of State – T.A.P.A., 14th Ephorate of Prehistoric and Classical Antiquities.

Dakouri-Hild, A. (2001) 'The House of Kadmos in Mycenaean Thebes reconsidered: architecture, chronology, and context', *BSA* 96: 81–122.

Davidson, D. and Tasker, C. (1982) 'Geomorphological evolution during the late Holocene', in C. Renfrew and M. Wagstaff (eds), *An island polity. The archaeology of exploitation on Melos*, London: Thames & Hudson, 82–94.

Davidson, J. (1997) *Courtesans and fishcakes, the consuming passions of Classical Athens*, London: HarperCollins.

Davies, J.K. (1984) 'The reliability of the oral tradition', in L. Foxhall and J.K. Davies (eds) *The Trojan War. Its historicity and context*, Bristol: Bristol Classical Press, 87–110.

Davis, J.L., Alcock, S.E., Bennet, J., Lolos, Y.G. and Shelmerdine, C.W. (1997) 'The Pylos Regional Archaeological Project Part I: overview and the archaeological survey', *Hesperia* 66: 391–494.

de Fidio, P. (2001) 'Centralization and its limits in the Mycenaean palatial system', in Voutsaki and Killen 2001, ch. I.

Deger-Jalkotzy, S. (1995) 'Mykenische Herrschaftformen ohne Paläste und die griechische Polis', in Laffineur and Niemeier 1995, 367–77.

—— (1996) 'On the negative aspects of the Mycenaean palace system', in E. de Miro, L. Godart and A. Sacconi (eds), *Atti e memorie del secondo congresso internazionale di micenologia*, Rome: Gruppo editoriale internazionale, 715–28.

—— (1998) *'The Last Mycenaeans and their Successors* updated', in Gitin *et al.* 1998, 114–28.

—— (forthcoming) 'Late Mycenaean warrior tombs', paper given in Lemos and Deger-Jalkotzy 2003.

Demakopoulou, K. (1982) 'Το Μυκηναικό ιερό στό Αμυκλαίο καί η ΥΕ ΙΙΙΓ περίοδος στη Λακωνία', PhD. thesis, Athens.

—— (1995) 'Mycenaean citadels: recent excavations on the acropolis of Midea in the Argolid', *BICS* 40: 151–61.

—— (2003) 'The pottery from the destruction layers at Midea: Late Helladic III

B2 late or transitional Late Helladic III B2/Late Helladic III C Early?', in Deger-Jalkotzy and Zavadil 2003, 77–92.

——, Divari-Valakou, N. and Schallin, A.-L. (2003) 'Excavations in Midea 2002', *OpAth* 28: 8–28.

De Polignac, F. (1995) *Cults, territory and the origin of the Greek city-state*, Chicago: Chicago University Press.

Desborough, V.R. (1952) *Protogeometric pottery*, Oxford: Clarendon Press.

Dickinson, O. (1977) *The origins of Mycenaean civilisation*, Göteborg: Åström.

—— (1983) 'Cist graves and chamber tombs', *BSA* 78: 55–67.

—— (1986) 'Homer, the poet of the Dark Age', *Greece and Rome* 33: 20–37.

—— (1994a) *The Aegean Bronze Age*, Cambridge: Cambridge University Press.

—— (1994b) 'Comments on a popular model of Minoan religion', *Oxford Journal of Archaeology* 13: 173–84.

—— (1999) 'Robert Drews's theories about the nature of warfare in the Late Bronze Age', in Laffineur 1999, 21–7.

Dietrich, B.C. (1986) *Tradition in Greek religion*, Berlin and New York: de Gruyter.

Dimaki, S. (1999) 'Νεκροταφείο Ελατείας: Περιδέραια από στεατίτη', in Dakoronia and Papakonstantinou 1999, 203–14.

Donder, H. (1999) 'Pin-types of the Late Helladic and the Early Iron Age in North and Central Greece', in Dakoronia and Papakonstantinou 1999, 91–8.

Donlan, W. (1997) 'The Homeric economy', in Morris and Powell 1997, ch. 28.

Doumas, C. (1992) *The wall-paintings of Thera*, Athens: Thera Foundation.

Drerup, H. (1969) *Griechische Baukunst in Geometrischer Zeit, Archaeologia Homerica Kapitel O*, Göttingen: Vandenhoeck & Ruprecht.

Drews, R. (1979) 'Argos and Argives in the *Iliad*', *Classical Philology* 74: 111–35.

—— (1983) *Basileus: the evidence for kingship in Geometric Greece*, New Haven: Yale University Press.

—— (1988) *The coming of the Greeks: Indo-European conquests in the Aegean and the Near East*, Princeton: Princeton University Press.

—— (1993) *The end of the Bronze Age: changes in warfare and the catastrophe ca. 1200* BC, Princeton: Princeton University Press.

—— (2000) 'Medinet Habu: oxcarts, ships, and migration theories', *Journal of Near Eastern Studies* 59: 161–90.

Eder, B. (1998) *Argolis Lakonien Messenien. Vom Ende der mykenischen Palastzeit bis zur Einwanderung der Dorier*, Vienna: Verlag der Österreichischen Akademie der Wissenschaften.

—— (1999) *Die Submykenischen und Protogeometrischen Gräber von Elis*, Athens: Austrian Archaeological Institute.

—— (2001) 'Continuity of Bronze Age cult at Olympia? The evidence of the Late Bronze Age and Early Iron Age pottery', in Laffineur and Hägg 2001, 201–9.

—— (2003) 'Patterns of contact and communication between the regions south and north of the Corinthian Gulf in LH IIIC', in Kyparissi-Apostolika and Papakonstantinou 2003, 37–54.

—— and Jung, R. (2005) 'On the character of social relations between Greece and Italy in the 12th/11th century BC', in Laffineur and Greco 2005, 485–95.

Eiteljorg, H., II (1980) 'The fast wheel, the multiple brush compass and Athens as the home of the Protogeometric style', *AJA* 84: 445–52.

Eliopoulos, T. (1998) 'A preliminary report on the discovery of a temple complex of the Dark Ages at Kephala Vasilikis', in Karageorghis and Stampolidis 1998, 301–13.

Fågerström, K. (1988b) *Greek Iron Age architecture: development through changing times*, Göteborg: Åström.

Feuer, B. (1983) *The northern Mycenaean border in Thessaly*, Oxford: British Archaeological Reports.

Forbes, H. (1995) 'The identification of pastoralist sites within the context of estate-based agriculture in ancient Greece: beyond the "transhumance versus agro-pastoralism" debate', *BSA* 90: 325–38.

Foxhall, L. (1995) 'Bronze to Iron: agricultural systems and political structures in Late Bronze Age and Early Iron Age Greece', *BSA* 90: 239–50.

—— (1998) 'The Greek countryside', in Sparkes 1998, ch. 6.

French, E.B. (1999) 'The post-palatial levels at Mycenae: an up-date', *BICS* 43: 222–3.

—— and Wardle, K.A. (eds) (1988) *Problems in Greek Prehistory*, Bristol: Bristol Classical Press.

Fried, M.H. (1967) *The evolution of political society: An essay in political anthropology*, New York: Random.

Galaty, M.L. and Parkinson, W.A. (eds) (1999) *Rethinking Mycenaean palaces. New interpretations of an old idea*, Los Angeles: Cotsen Institute of Archaeology, University of California, Los Angeles, Monograph 41.

Gale, N.H. (1979) 'Some aspects of lead and silver mining in the Aegean', in *Miscellanea Graeca 2: Technological Studies 1979*, 9–60, Ghent: Belgian Archaeological Mission in Greece.

—— (ed.) (1991) *Bronze Age Trade in the Aegean*, Göteborg: Åström.

Gallant, T.W. (1982) 'Agricultural systems, land tenure, and the reforms of Solon', *BSA* 77: 111–24.

Georganas, I. (2000) 'Early Iron Age tholos tombs in Thessaly (*c.* 1100–700 BC)', *Mediterranean Archaeology* 13: 47–54.

—— (2002) 'Constructing identities in Early Iron Age Thessaly: the case of the Halos tumuli', *OJA* 21: 289–98.

Gesell, G.C. (1985) *Town, palace, and house cult in Minoan Crete*, Göteborg: Åström.

—— (2001) 'The function of the plaque in the shrine of the goddess with up-raised hands' in Laffineur and Hägg 2001, 253–8.

Gillis, C. (1997) 'The smith in the Late Bronze Age – state employee, independent artisan, or both?', Laffineur and Betancourt 1997, 505–13.

Gilmour, G. (1993) 'Aegean sanctuaries in the Levant in the Late Bronze Age', *BSA* 88: 125–34.

Gitin, S., Mazar, A. and Stern, E. (eds) (1998) *Mediterranean Peoples in transition, thirteenth to early tenth centuries BCE*, Jerusalem: Israel Exploration Society.

Guggisberg, M.A. (1996) *Frühgriechische Tierkeramik*, Mainz: von Zabern.

Gurney, O. (1990) *The Hittites*, Harmondsworth: Penguin.

Hägg, R., Marinatos, N. and Nordquist, G. (eds) (1988) *Early Greek cult practice*, Stockholm: Swedish Institute in Athens.

Haggis, D.C. (1999) 'Some problems in defining Dark Age society in the Aegean', in Betancourt *et al.* 1999, 303–8.

—— (2000) 'Settlement patterns and social structure in the Dark Age Aegean', conference paper at Wardle 2000.

—— (2001) 'A Dark Age settlement pattern in east Crete, and a reassessment of the definition of refuge settlements', in Karageorghis and Morris 2001, 41–59.

—— and Nowicki, K. (1993) 'Khalasmeno and Katalimata: two Early Iron Age settlements in Monastiraki, East Crete', *Hesperia* 62: 303–37.

Hall, J.M. (1997) *Ethnic identity in Greek antiquity*, Cambridge: Cambridge University Press.

Halstead, P.H. (1992) 'The Mycenaean palatial economy: making the most of the gaps in the evidence', *ProcCamPhilSoc* 38: 57–86.

—— (1999a) 'Surplus and share-croppers: the grain production strategies of Mycenaean palaces', in Betancourt *et al.* 1999, 319–26.

—— (1999b) 'Towards a model of Mycenaean palatial mobilization', in Galaty and Parkinson 1999, 35–41.

—— (1999c) 'Mycenaean agriculture: the nature of palatial intervention', *BICS* 43: 211–12.

—— (2001) 'Mycenaean wheat, flax and sheep: palatial intervention in farming and its implications for rural society', in Voutsaki and Killen 2001, ch. IV.

Hamilakis, Y. and Konsolaki, E. (2004) 'Pigs for the gods: burnt animal sacrifices as embodied rituals at a Mycenaean sanctuary', *OJA* 23: 135–51.

Hammond, N.G.L. (1932) 'Prehistoric Epirus and the Dorian invasion', *BSA* 32: 131–79.

—— (1975) 'The literary tradition for the migrations', *CAH* II: 2, ch. XXXVI(b), Cambridge: Cambridge University Press.

Hansen, J.M. (2000) 'Palaeoethnobotany and palaeodiet in the Aegean region: notes on legume toxicity and related pathologies', in Vaughan and Coulson 2000, 13–27.

Harding, A.F. (1984) *The Mycenaeans and Europe*, London: Academic Press.

—— (2000) 'Weapons, warfare and deposition practices in south-east Europe, 1200–800 BC: cultural transformations at the beginning of the first millennium BC from the Alps (almost) to Anatolia', opening conference lecture at Wardle 2000.

Haskell, H. (2003) 'Region to region export of transport stirrup jars from LM IIIA2/B Crete', paper given at the conference 'Ariadne's Threads', Italian School of Archaeology, Athens, 5 April 2003.

Hawkins, D. (1998) 'Tarkasnawa king of Mira, "Tarkondemos", Boğazköy sealings and Karabel', *AS* 48: 1–31.

Hayden, B.J. (1987) 'Crete in transition: LM IIIA-B architecture, a preliminary study', *SMEA* 26: 199–233.

Heilmeyer, W.D. (1972) *Frühe Olympische Tonfiguren (Olympische Forschungen* 7), Berlin: de Gruyter.

—— (1979) *Frühe Olympische Bronzefiguren: die Tiervotive (Olympische Forschungen* 12), Berlin: de Gruyter.

Heltzer, M. (1988) 'Trade relations between Ugarit and Crete', *Minos* 23: 7–13.

Higgins, R.A. (1969) 'Early Greek jewellery', *BSA* 64: 143–53.

—— (1980) *Greek and Roman Jewellery* (second edition), London: Methuen.

Hoffman, G. (1997) *Imports and immigrants. Near Eastern contacts with Iron Age Crete*, Ann Arbor: University of Michigan Press.

Hooker, J.T. (1976) *Mycenaean Greece*, London: Routledge & Kegan Paul.

—— (1982) 'The end of Pylos and the Linear B evidence', *SMEA* 23: 209–17.

Hope Simpson, R. (2003) 'The Dodecanese and the Ahhiyawa question', *BSA* 98: 203–37.

Houby-Nielsen, S.H. (1995) ' "Burial language" in Archaic and Classical Kerameikos', *Proceedings of the Danish Institute at Athens* 1: 129–91.

Hughes Brock, H. (1999) 'Mycenaean beads, gender and social contexts', *OJA* 18: 277–96.

Iakovidis, S.E. (1969) *Περάτη: το νεκροταφείον*, Athens: Archaeological Society.

—— (1977) 'On the use of Mycenaean "buttons" ', *BSA* 72: 113–19.

—— (1980) *Excavations of the necropolis of Perati*, Los Angeles: Institute of Archaeology, University of California.

—— (1998) *ΓΛΑΣ II. Η ανασκαφή 1981–1991*, Athens: Archaeological Society.

Immerwahr, S.A. (1990) *Aegean painting in the Bronze Age*, Philadelphia: Pennsylvania State University Press.

Isaakidou, V., Halstead, P., Davis, J. and Stocker, S. (2002) 'Burnt animal sacrifice at the Mycenaean "Palace of Nestor", Pylos', *Antiquity* 76: 86–92.

Jacobsthal, P. (1956) *Greek pins and their connexions with Europe and Asia*, Oxford: Clarendon Press.

Jameson, M.H., Runnels, C.N. and van Andel, T. (1994) *A Greek countryside: the Southern Argolid from prehistory to the present day*, Stanford: Stanford University Press.

Jones, W. (1999) 'The archaeology and economy of Homeric gift exchange', *OpAth* 24: 9–24.

Kanta, A. (1980) *The Late Minoan III period in Crete. A survey of sites, pottery and their distribution*, Göteborg: Åström.

—— and Karetsou, A. (1998) 'From Arkadhes to Rhytion. Interactions of an isolated area of Crete with the Aegean and the east Mediterranean', in Karageorghis and Stampolidis 1998, 159–73.

—— and Stampolidis, N.C. (2001) 'Orné (ΑΙΠΥ) in the context of the defensive settlements of the end of the Bronze Age', in Karageorghis and Morris 2001, 95–113.

Karageorghis, V. (1982) 'Metallurgy in Cyprus during the 11th century BC', in Muhly *et al.* 1982, 297–301.

—— (ed.) (1994) *Proceedings of the international symposium 'Cyprus in the 11th century BC'*, Nicosia: Department of Antiquities of Cyprus.

—— (2001) 'Patterns of fortified settlements in the Aegean and Cyprus c. 1200 BC', in Karageorghis and Morris 2001, 1–12.

—— and Demas, M. (1988) *Excavations at Maa-Palaeokastro 1979–1986*, Nicosia: Department of Antiquities of Cyprus.

—— and Morris, C. (eds) (2001) *Defensive settlements of the Aegean and the eastern Mediterranean after c. 1200 BC*, Nicosia: Trinity College, Dublin and the Anastasios G. Leventis Foundation.

—— and Stampolidis, N.C. (eds) (1998) *Proceedings of the international symposium 'Eastern Mediterranean: Cyprus–Dodecanese–Crete 16th–6th cent. BC'*, Athens: University of Crete and the A.G. Leventis Foundation.

Kayafa, M. (2000) 'From Bronze Age to Iron Age: alloy making and its implications in mainland Greece and offshore Aegean islands', conference paper given at Wardle 2000.

Kilian, K. (1981) 'Zeugnisse mykenische Kultausübung in Tiryns' in R. Hägg and

N. Marinatos (eds), *Sanctuaries and cults in the Aegean Bronze Age*, Stockholm: Swedish Institute in Athens, 49–58.

—— (1985) 'Violinbogenfibeln und Blattbügelfibeln des griechischer Festlandes aus mykenischer Zeit', *PZ* 60: 145–203.

—— (1988) 'Mycenaeans up to date, trends and changes in recent research', in French and Wardle 1988, 115–52.

Kilian-Dirlmeier (1980) 'Bemerkungen zu den Fingerringen mit Spiralenden', *Jahrbuch des römisch-germanischen Zentralmuseums, Mainz* 27: 249–69.

—— (1984) *Nadeln der frühhelladischen bis archaischen Zeit von der Peloponnes (Prähistoriche Bronzefunde XIII, 8)*, Munich: Beck.

—— (1993) *Die Schwerter in Griechenland (ausserhalb der Peloponnes), Bulgarien und Albanien (Prähistoriche Bronzefunde IV, 12)*, Stuttgart: Steiner.

Killebrew, A.E. (2000) 'Aegean-style early Philistine pottery in Canaan during the Iron I age: a stylistic analysis of Mycenaean IIIC:1b pottery and its associated wares', in Oren 2000, 233–53.

Killen, J.T. (1996) 'Administering a Mycenaean kingdom: some taxing problems', *BICS* 41: 147–8.

—— (2001) 'Some thoughts on *ta-ra-si-ja*', in Voutsaki and Killen 2001, ch. XI.

Kirk, G.S. (1975) 'The Homeric poems as history', *CAH* II: 2, ch. XXXIX(b), Cambridge: Cambridge University Press.

—— (1990) *The Iliad: a Commentary*, Vol. II, Cambridge: Cambridge University Press.

Kling, B. (1989) *Mycenaean IIIC:1b and related pottery in Cyprus*, Göteborg: Åström.

—— (2000) 'Mycenaean IIIC:1b and related pottery in Cyprus: comments on the current state of research', in Oren 2000, 281–95.

Knapp, A.B. (1990) 'Ethnicity, entrepreneurship, and exchange: Mediterranean inter-island relationships in the Late Bronze Age', *BSA* 85: 115–53.

—— (1991) 'Spice, drugs, grain and grog: organic goods in Bronze Age East Mediterranean trade', in Gale 1991, 21–68.

Konsolaki-Yannopoulou, E. (2001) 'New evidence for the practice of libations in the Aegean Bronze Age', in Laffineur and Hägg 2001, 213–20.

Koukouli-Chrysanthaki, Ch. (1992) *Προϊστορική Θάσος: τα νεκροταφεία του οικισμού Καστρί*, Athens: Dimosievmata tou Arkhaiologikou Deltiou.

Krzyszkowska, O. (2005) *Aegean seals. An introduction*, London: Institute of Classical Studies, University of London.

Kuniholm, P. (1990) 'Archaeological evidence and non-evidence for climatic change', *Philosophical Transactions of the Royal Society of London* A330: 645–55.

Kurtz, D.C. and Boardman, J. (1971) *Greek burial customs*, London: Thames & Hudson.

Kyparissi-Apostolika, N. and Papakonstantinou, M. (2003) *The periphery of the Mycenaean world. 2nd international interdisciplinary colloquium, Lamia 1999. Proceedings*, Athens: Ministry of Culture, 14th Ephorate of Prehistoric and Classical Antiquities.

Laffineur, R. (ed.) (1987) *THANATOS. Les coutûmes funéraires en Egée à l'Age du Bronze*, Liège: University of Liège.

—— (ed.) (1999) *POLEMOS. Le contexte du guerrier en Egée à l'Age du Bronze*, Liège: University of Liège.

—— and Betancourt, P.P. (eds) (1997) *TEXNH. Craftsmen, craftswomen and craftsmanship in the Aegean Bronze Age*, Liège: University of Liège.

——— and Greco, E. (2005) *EMPORIA. Aegeans in the Central and Eastern Mediterranean*, Liège: University of Liège.

——— and Hägg, R. (eds) (2001) *POTNIA. Deities and religion in the Aegean Bronze Age*, Brussels: University of Liège.

——— and Niemeier, W.-D. (eds) (1995) *POLITEIA. Society and state in the Bronze Age Aegean*, Liège: University of Liège.

———, Galanaki, I., Tomas, H. and Galanakis, I. (2005) (conveners) 'Between the Aegean and Baltic seas: prehistory across borders', conference organised by the Department of Archaeology, University of Zagreb, April 2005.

Lambrinoudakis, V.K. (1988) 'Veneration of ancestors in Geometric Naxos', in Hägg *et al.* 1988, 235–46.

Langdon, S. (ed.) (1997) *New light on a dark age: exploring the culture of Geometric Greece*, Columbia and London: University of Missouri Press.

Lemos, I.S. (1994) 'Birds revisited', in Karageorghis 1994, 229–37.

——— (1998) 'Euboea and its Aegean koine', in M. Bats and B. d'Agostino (eds) *Euboica. L'Eubea e la presenza euboica in Calcidica e in Occidente*, Naples: Centre Jean Bérard, 45–58.

——— (2003) 'Lefkandi and Athens: a tale of two cities', paper delivered at Lemos and Deger-Jalkotzy 2003.

——— and Deger-Jalkotzy, S. (2003) (conveners) 'From *Wanax* to *Basileus*', Third A.G. Leventis Conference, Edinburgh, January 2003.

Lewartowski, K. (1995) 'Mycenaean social structure: a view from simple graves', in Laffineur and Niemeier 1995, 103–14.

——— (2000) *Late Helladic simple graves. A study of Mycenaean burial customs*, Oxford: British Archaeological Reports.

Littauer, M.A. and Crouwel, J.H. (1996) 'Robert Drews and the role of chariotry in Bronze Age Greece', *OJA* 15: 297–305.

Loader, N.C. (1995) 'Mycenaean fortifications: defining Cyclopean and a consideration of building practices', *BICS* 40: 254.

——— (1998) *Building in cyclopean masonry, with special reference to the Mycenaean fortifications of mainland Greece*, Jonsered: Åström.

Lorimer, H.L. (1950) *Homer and the monuments*, London: Macmillan.

Luke, J. (2003) *Ports of trade, Al Mina, and Greek Geometric pottery in the Levant*, Oxford: British Archaeological Reports, International Series 1100.

Macqueen, J.G. (1986) *The Hittites and their contemporaries in Asia Minor*, London: Thames & Hudson.

Maran, J. (2001) 'Political and religious aspects of architectural change on the Upper Citadel of Tiryns. The case of Building T', in Laffineur and Hägg 2001, 113–22.

——— (2002) 'Tiryns town after the fall of the palace: some new insights', Mycenaean Seminar, Institute of Classical Studies, London, 13 February 2002.

——— (2004) 'The spreading of objects and ideas in the Late Bronze Age Eastern Mediterranean: two case studies from the Argolid of the 13th and 12th centuries BC', *Bulletin of the American Schools of Oriental Research* 336: 11–30.

Marinatos, N. (1988) 'The imagery of sacrifice: Minoan and Greek', in Hägg *et al.* 1988, 9–20.

——— and Hägg, R. (eds) (1993) *Greek sanctuaries: new approaches*, London: Routledge.

Markoe, G. (1998) 'The Phoenicians on Crete: transit trade and the search for ores', in Karageorghis and Stampolidis 1998, 233–40.

Matthäus, H. (1980) *Die Bronzegefässe der kretisch-mykenisch Kultur (Prähistoriche Bronzefunde II, 1)*, Munich: Beck.

—— (1988) 'Heirloom or tradition? Bronze stands of the second and first millennium BC in Cyprus, Greece and Italy', in French and Wardle 1988, 285–300.

—— (1998) 'Cyprus and Crete in the early first millennium BC. A synopsis with special reference to new finds from the Idaean Cave of Zeus', in Karageorghis and Stampolidis 1998, 127–56.

Mazarakis Ainian, A. (1997) *From rulers' dwellings to temples. Architecture, religion and society in Early Iron Age Greece (1100–700 BC)*, Jonsered: Åström.

McDonald, W.A. and Rapp, G.R., Jr. (eds) (1972) *The Minnesota Messenia Expedition: reconstructing a Bronze Age regional environment*, Minneapolis: Minnesota University Press.

Mee, C.B. (1998) 'Gender bias in Mycenaean mortuary practices', in Branigan 1998, 165–70.

—— and Cavanagh, W. (1984) 'Mycenaean tombs as evidence for social and political organisation', *OJA* 3: 45–64.

—— and Forbes, H. (eds) (1997) *A rough and rocky place: the landscape and settlement history of the Methana peninsula, Greece*, Liverpool: Liverpool University Press.

Meriç, R. and Mountjoy, P.A. (2002) 'Mycenaean pottery from Bademgediği Tepe (Puranda) in Ionia: a preliminary report', *Istanbuler Mitteilungen* 52: 79–98.

Mikalson, J.D. (1983) *Athenian popular religion*, Chapel Hill: University of North Carolina Press.

Mommsen, H., Hertel, D. and Mountjoy, P.-A. (2001) 'Neutron activation analysis of the pottery from Troy in the Berlin Schliemann Collection', *AA*: 169–211.

Moody, J. (2003) 'Unravelling the threads: environmental change in Late Bronze III', paper given at the conference 'Ariadne's Threads', Italian School of Archaeology, Athens, 5 April 2003.

Moran, W.L. (1992) *The Amarna letters*, Baltimore and London: Johns Hopkins University Press.

Morgan, C. (1995) 'From palace to polis? Religious developments on the Greek mainland during the Late Bronze/Early Iron Age transition', *BICS* 40: 250.

—— (1999) *Isthmia Volume VIII. The Late Bronze Age settlement and Early Iron Age sanctuary*, Princeton: American School of Classical Studies at Athens.

Morris, I. (1986) 'The use and abuse of Homer', *Classical Antiquity* 5: 81–138.

Morris, S.P. (1997) 'Homer and the Near East', in Morris and Powell 1997, ch. 26.

Mountjoy, P.A. (1986) *Mycenaean decorated pottery, a guide to identification*, Göteborg: Åström.

—— (1993) *Mycenaean pottery, an introduction*, Oxford: Oxford University Committee for Archaeology.

—— (1995) 'Thorikos mine no. 3: the Mycenaean pottery', *BSA* 90: 195–227.

—— (1997) 'The destruction of the palace at Pylos reconsidered', *BSA* 92: 109–37.

—— (1998) 'The east Aegean–west Anatolian interface in the Late Bronze Age: Mycenaeans and the kingdom of Ahhiyawa', *AS* 48: 33–67.

—— (1999) *Regional Mycenaean decorated pottery*, Rahden: Leidorf.

Muhly, J.D. (1992) 'The crisis years in the Mediterranean world: transition or cultural disintegration?', in Ward and Joukowsky 1992, 10–26.

—— (1999) 'The Phoenicians in the Aegean', in Betancourt *et al.* 1999, 517–26.

—— (2003) 'Greece and Anatolia in the Early Iron Age: the archaeological evidence and the literary tradition', in W.G. Dever and S. Gitin (eds), *Symbiosis, symbolism, and the power of the past. Canaan, ancient Israel and their neighbors from the Late Bronze Age through Roman Palestina*, Winona Lake: Eisenbrauns, 23–35.

——, Maddin, R. and Karageorghis, V. (eds) (1982) *Early Metallurgy in Cyprus 4000–500* BC, Nicosia: Pierides Foundation.

—— , Maddin, R., Stech, T. and Özgen, E. (1985) 'Iron in Anatolia and the nature of the Hittite iron industry', *AS* 35: 567–84.

Musgrave, J.H. (1990) 'Dust and damn'd oblivion: a study of cremation in ancient Greece', *BSA* 85: 271–99.

Naumann, U. (1976) *Subminoische und protogeometrische Bronzeplastik auf Kreta, Mitteilungen der Deutschen archäologischen Instituts: athenische Abteilung*, Beiheft 6.

Negbi, O. (1988) 'Levantine elements in the sacred architecture of the Aegean', *BSA* 83: 339–57.

Niemeier, W.D. (1998) 'The Mycenaeans in western Anatolia and the problem of the origins of the Sea Peoples', in Gitin *et al.* 1998, 17–65.

Niklasson-Sönnerby, K. (1987) 'Late Cypriot III shaft graves: burial customs of the last phase of the Bronze Age', in Laffineur 1987, 219–25.

Nowicki, K. (1996) 'Arvi Fortetsa and Loutraki Kandilioro: two refugee settlements in Crete', *BSA* 91: 253–85.

—— (2000) *Defensible Sites in Crete c. 1200–800* BC (*LM IIIB/IIIC through Early Geometric*), Liège: University of Liège.

—— (2001) 'Sea-Raiders and refugees: problems of defensible sites in Crete ca.1200 BC,' in Karageorghis and Morris 2001, 23–40.

Nur, A. and Cline, E.H. (2000) 'Poseidon's horses: plate tectonics and earthquake storms in the Late Bronze Age in the Aegean and eastern Mediterranean', *Journal of Archaeological Science* 27: 43–63.

Oren, E.D. (ed.) (2000) *The Sea Peoples and their world: a reassessment*, Philadelphia: University of Pennsylvania.

Osborne, R. (1997) 'Early Greek colonization? The nature of Greek settlement in the West', in N. Fisher and H. van Wees (eds), *Archaic Greece: new approaches and new evidence*, London: Duckworth, 251–69.

Østby, E., Luce, J.-M., Nordquist, G.C., Tarditi, C. and Voyatzis, M.E. (1994) 'The sanctuary of Athena Alea at Tegea: first preliminary report (1990–1992)', *OpAth* 20: 89–141.

Pakkanen, P. (2001) 'The relationship between continuity and change in Dark Age Greek religion', *OpAth* 25–6 (2000–01): 71–88.

Palaima, T.G. (1988) 'The development of the Mycenaean writing system', *Minos* Supplement 10: 269–342.

—— (1995) 'The last days of the Pylos polity', in Laffineur and Niemeier 1995, 623–37.

Papadimitriou, A. (1998) 'Η οικιστική εξέλιξη της Τίρυνθας μετά τη Μυκηναϊκή εποχή. Τα αρχαιολογικά ευρήματα και η ιστορική ερμηνεία τους', in A. Pariente and G. Touchais (eds), *Argos et l'Argolide. Topographie et urbanisme*, Paris: Boccard, 117–30.

Papadopoulos, J.K. (1993) 'To kill a cemetery: the Athenian Kerameikos and the Early Iron Age in the Aegean', *JMA* 6: 175–206.

—— (1994) 'Early Iron Age potters' marks in the Aegean', *Hesperia* 63: 437–507.

—— (1996a) 'Dark Age Greece', in B.M. Fagan (ed.), *The Oxford companion to archaeology*, Oxford: Oxford University Press, 253–5.

—— (1996b) 'Euboeans in Macedonia? A closer look', *OJA* 15: 151–83.

—— (1997) 'Phantom Euboians', *JMA* 10: 191–219.

——, Vedder, J.F. and Schreiber, T. (1998) 'Drawing circles: experimental archaeology and the pivoted multiple brush', *AJA* 102: 507–29.

Papadopoulos, Th. (1999) 'Warrior-Graves in Achaean Mycenaean Cemeteries', in Laffineur 1999, 268–74.

Papazoglou-Manioudaki, L. (1994) 'A Mycenaean warrior's tomb at Krini near Patras', *BSA* 89: 171–200.

Parker, R. (1996) *Athenian religion: a history*, Oxford: Clarendon Press.

Pennas, C., Vichos, Y. and Agouridis, C. (2000–01) 'The Point Iria wreck (1994) I. The completion of the excavation. II. The pottery, by Y.G. Lolos', *Enalia* Annual V (2000–01): 30–44.

Photos-Jones, E. and Ellis Jones, J. (1994) 'The building and industrial remains at Agrileza, Laurion (fourth century BC) and their contributions to the workings at the site', *BSA* 89: 307–58.

Pickles, S. and Peltenburg, E. (1998) 'Metallurgy, society and the Bronze/Iron transition in the east Mediterranean and the Near East', *RDAC* 1998: 67–100.

Pieridou, A. (1973) *Ο πρωτογεωμετρικός ρυθμός εν Κύπρωι*, Athens: Archaeological Society.

Piggott, S. (1965) *Ancient Europe*, Edinburgh: Edinburgh University Press.

Piteros, Chr. I. (2001) 'Τάφοι και τεφροδόχα αγγεία τυμβού της ΥΕΙΙΙΓ στο Άργος', in Stampolidis 2001, 99–120.

Popham, M.R. (1967) 'Late Minoan pottery, a summary', *BSA* 62: 337–51.

—— (1994a) 'The collapse of Aegean civilization at the end of the Late Bronze Age', in Cunliffe 1994, ch. 8.

—— (1994b) 'Precolonization: early Greek contact with the East', in Tsetskhladze and de Angelis 1994, ch. 2.

—— and Milburn, E. (1971), 'The Late Helladic IIIC pottery of Lefkandi: a summary', *BSA* 66: 333–52.

Prent, M. (forthcoming) *Cretan Sanctuaries and Cults. Continuity and Change from the Late Minoan IIIC to the Archaic Period*, Leiden: Brill.

Pulak, C. (1998) 'The Uluburun shipwreck: an overview', *IJNA* 27: 188–224.

Purcell, N. (1990) 'Mobility and the *polis*', in O. Murray and S. Price (eds), *The Greek city from Homer to Alexander*, Oxford: Clarendon Press, 29–58.

Rackham, O. and Moody, J. (1996) *The making of the Cretan Landscape*, Manchester: Manchester University Press.

Raftopoulou, S. (1997) 'Τάφοι της εποχής του σιδήρου στη Σπάρτη', in *Acts of the V International Congress of Peloponnesian Studies*, Athens: Society of Peloponnesian Studies, 273–80.

—— (1998) 'New finds from Sparta', in W.G. Cavanagh and S.E.C. Walker (eds), *Sparta in Laconia*, London: British School at Athens, 125–40.

Reber, K. (1991) *Untersuchungen zur handgemachte Keramik Griechenlands in der submykenischen, protogeometrischen und der geometrischen Zeit*, Jonsered: Åström.

Reclus, E. (1875) *Nouvelle géographie universelle. Volume I. L'Europe méridionale*, Paris: Hachette.

Redford, D.B. (2000) 'Egypt and western Asia in the late New Kingdom: an overview', in Oren 2000, 1–20.

Rehak, P. (ed.) (1995) *The role of the ruler in the prehistoric Aegean*, Liège: University of Liège.

Rehak, P. and Younger, J.G. (2001) 'Neopalatial, Final Palatial, and Postpalatial Crete', in Cullen 2001, ch. VII.

Renfrew, C. (1972) *The emergence of civilization: the Cyclades and the Aegean in the third millennium* B.C., London: Methuen.

—— (1985) *The archaeology of cult. The sanctuary at Phylakopi*, London: British School at Athens.

—— (1989) *Archaeology and language*, Harmondsworth: Penguin.

Ridgway, D. (1992) *The first Western Greeks*, Cambridge: Cambridge University Press.

—— (1994) 'Phoenicians and Greeks in the West: a view from Pithekoussai', in Tsetskhladze and de Angelis 1994, ch. 3.

—— (1997) 'Nestor's Cup and the Etruscans', *OJA* 16: 325–44.

Rosen, R. (1997) 'Homer and Hesiod', in Morris and Powell 1997, ch. 21.

Runnels, C. (1982) 'Flaked-stone artefacts in Greece during the historical period', *JFA* 9: 363–73.

Rutter, J.B. (1974) 'The Late Helladic IIIB and IIIC periods at Korakou and Gonia', Ph.D. thesis, University of Pennsylvania.

—— (1978) 'A plea for the abandonment of the term "Submycenaean" ', *Temple University Aegean Symposium* 3: 58–65.

—— (1990) 'Some comments on interpreting the dark-surfaced handmade burnished pottery of the 13th and 12th century BC Aegean', *JMA* 3: 29–49.

—— (1992) 'Cultural novelties in the post-palatial Aegean world: indices of vitality or decline?', in Ward and Joukowsky 1992, 61–78.

Rystedt, E. (1999) 'No words, only pictures. Iconography in the transition between the Bronze Age and the Iron Age in Greece', *OpAth* 24: 89–98.

Sacconi, A. (1999) 'Les tablettes de Pylos et la guerre', in Laffineur 1999, 361–5.

Sackett, L.H., Hankey, V., Howell, R.J., Jacobsen, T.W. and Popham, M.R. (1966) 'Prehistoric Euboea: contributions toward a survey', *BSA* 61: 33–112.

Sandars, N.K. (1964) 'The last Mycenaeans and the European Late Bronze Age', *Antiquity* 38: 258–62.

Sapouna-Sakellaraki, E. (1997) 'A Geometric electrum band from a tomb on Skyros', in O. Palagia (ed.) *Greek Offerings*, Oxford: Oxbow, 35–42.

Sauerwein, F. (1998) 'The physical background', in Sparkes 1998, ch.1.

Schweitzer, B. (1971) *Greek Geometric Art*, London: Phaidon.

Shaw, J.W. (1995) 'Two three-holed stone anchors from Kommos, Crete: their context, type and origin', *IJNA* 24: 279–91.

—— (1998) 'Kommos in southern Crete: an Aegean barometer for East–West interconnections', in Karageorghis and Stampolidis 1998, 13–27.

Shelmerdine, C.W. (1985) *The perfume industry of Mycenaean Pylos*, Göteborg: Åström.

—— (1987) 'Architectural change and economic decline at Pylos', *Minos* 20–22: 557–68.

—— (1999) 'Pylian polemics: the latest evidence on military matters', in Laffineur 1999, 403–8.

—— (2001) 'The palatial Bronze Age of the southern and central Greek mainland', in Cullen 2001, ch. VI.

Sherratt, E.S. (1982) 'Patterns of contact: manufacture and distribution of Mycenaean pottery', in J.G.P. Best and N.M.W. de Vries (eds), *Interaction and acculturation in the Mediterranean*, Amsterdam: Grüner, 179–95.

—— (1985) 'The development of Late Helladic IIIC', *BICS* 32: 161.

—— (1990) ' "Reading the texts": archaeology and the Homeric question', *Antiquity* 64: 807–24.

—— (1992) 'Immigration and archaeology: some indirect reflections', in P. Åström (ed.), *Acta Cypria Volume I*, Jonsered: Åström, 316–47.

—— (1993) 'Daidalic inventions: the Hellenization of art and the art of Hellenization' (review of Morris 1992), *Antiquity* 67: 915–18.

—— (1994) 'Commerce, iron and ideology: metallurgical innovation in 12th–11th century Cyprus', in Karageorghis 1994, 59–106.

—— (2000) 'Circulation of metals and the end of the Bronze Age in the Eastern Mediterranean', in C.F. Pare (ed.), *Metals make the world go round. The supply and circulation of metals in Bronze Age Europe*, Oxford: Oxbow, 82–98.

—— (2001) 'Potemkin palaces and route-based economies', in Voutsaki and Killen 2001, ch. XIV.

—— (2002) 'Visible writing: questions of script and identity in Early Iron Age Greece and Cyprus', *OJA* 22: 225–42.

—— and Crouwel, J. (1987) 'Mycenaean pottery from Cilicia in Oxford', *OJA* 6: 325–52.

Shrimpton, G. (1987) 'Regional drought and the economic decline of Mycenae', *Echos du monde classique/Classical Views* 6: 137–77.

Silberman, N.A. (1998) 'The Sea Peoples, the Victorians and us: modern social ideology and changing archaeological interpretations of the Late Bronze Age collapse', in Gitin *et al.* 1998, 268–75.

Sipsie-Eschbach, M. (1991) *Protogeometrische Keramik aus Iolkos*, Berlin: Volker Spiess.

Sloan, R.E. and Duncan, M.A. (1978) 'Zooarchaeology of Nichoria', in *Nichoria I*, ch. 6.

Small, D.B. (1997) 'Can we move forward? Comments on the current debate over Handmade Burnished Ware', *JMA* 10: 223–8.

—— (1998) 'Surviving the collapse: the oikos and structural continuity between Late Bronze Age and later Greece', in Gitin *et al.* 1998, 283–92.

Smithson, E.L. (1968) 'The tomb of a rich Athenian lady circa 850 BC', *Hesperia* 37: 77–116.

Snodgrass, A.M. (1964) *Early Greek armour and weapons*, Edinburgh: Edinburgh University Press.

—— (1974) 'An historical Homeric society?', *JHS* 94: 114–25.

—— (1980b) 'Iron and early metallurgy in the Mediterranean', in Wertime and Muhly 1980, ch. 10.

—— (1984) Review of *Nichoria III*, *Antiquity* 58: 152–3.

—— (1986) 'Interaction by design: the Greek city state', in C. Renfrew and J.F. Cherry (eds), *Peer polity interaction and socio-political change*, Cambridge: Cambridge University Press, 47–58.

—— (1987) *An archaeology of Greece: the present state and future scope of the discipline*, Berkeley: University of California Press.

—— (1991) 'Bronze Age exchange: a minimalist position', in Gale 1991, 15–20.

—— (1994) 'The nature and standing of the early western colonies', in Tsetskhladze and de Angelis 1994, ch. 1.

Sourvinou-Inwood, C. (1989) Review of Dietrich 1986, *CR* 39: 51–8.

—— (1990) 'What is polis religion?', in O. Murray and S. Price (eds), *The Greek city from Homer to Alexander*, Oxford: Clarendon Press, ch. 12.

—— (1993) 'Early sanctuaries, the eighth century and ritual space. Fragments of a discourse', in Marinatos and Hägg 1993, 1–17.

Stampolidis, N.C. (1998) 'Imports and agalmata: the Eleutherna experience', in Karageorghis and Stampolidis 1998, 175–85.

—— (ed.) (2001) *Καύσεις στην εποχή του Χαλκού και την πρωιμή εποχή του Σιδήρου*, Athens: University of Crete ΚΒ ΕΠΚΑ [and] Mesogeiaki Archaeological Society.

Steel, L. (1998) 'The social impact of Mycenaean imported pottery in Cyprus', *BSA* 93: 285–96.

Stiebing, W.H. (1980) 'The end of the Mycenaean Age', *Biblical Archeologist* 43: 7–21.

Stos-Gale, Z.A. (1998) 'The role of Kythnos and other Cycladic islands in the origins of Early Minoan metallurgy', in L.G. Mendoni and A. Mazarakis Ainian (eds), *Kea – Kythnos: history and archaeology*, Athens: Research Centre for Greek and Roman Antiquity, 717–35.

—— and Macdonald, C.F. (1991) 'Sources of metals and trade in the Bronze Age Aegean', in Gale 1991, 249–88.

—— Kayafa, M. and Gale, N.H. (1999) 'The origin of metals from the Bronze Age site of Nichoria', *OpAth* 24: 99–120.

Styrenius, C.-G. (1967) *Submycenaean studies. Examination of finds from mainland Greece with a chapter on Attic Protogeometric graves*, Lund: Swedish Institute in Athens.

Tainter, J. (1988) *The collapse of complex societies*, Cambridge: Cambridge University Press.

Taylour, W.D. (1981) *Well-built Mycenae, fascicule 1. The excavations*, Warminster: Aris & Phillips.

Thomas, C.G. (1970) 'Mycenaean hegemony? A reconsideration', *JHS* 90: 184–92.

Thomas, R. (1989) *Oral tradition and written record in Classical Athens*, Cambridge: Cambridge University Press.

Tsetskhladze, G.R. and de Angelis, F. (eds) (1994) *The archaeology of Greek colonization. Essays dedicated to Sir John Boardman*, Oxford: Oxford University Committee for Archaeology.

Tsipopoulou, M. (2001) 'A new Late Minoan IIIC shrine at Halasmenos, East Crete', in Laffineur and Hägg 2001, 99–101.

Tyree, E.L. (2001) 'Diachronic changes in Minoan cave cult', in Laffineur and Hägg 2001, 39–50.

Van Andel, T. and Runnels, C.N. (1987) *Beyond the acropolis: a rural Greek past*, Stanford: Stanford University Press.

Vandenabeele, F. (1987) 'L'influence égéenne dans les coûtumes funéraires chypriotes', in Laffineur 1987, 227–34.

Van Wees, H. (1988) 'Kings in combat: battle and heroes in the *Iliad*', *CQ* 38: 1–24.

—— (1992) *Status warriors. War, violence and society in Homer and history*, Amsterdam: Gieben.

—— (2000) 'The development of the hoplite phalanx. Iconography and reality in the seventh century', in H. van Wees (ed.), *War and Violence in Ancient Greece*, Swansea: Duckworth and Classical Press of Wales, 125–66.

Vatin, C. (1969) *Médéon de Phocide: rapport provisoire*, Paris: Boccard.

Vaughan, S.J. and Coulson W.D.E. (eds) (2000) *Palaeodiet in the Aegean*, Oxford: Oxbow Books.

Ventris, M. and Chadwick, J. (1956, second edition 1973) *Documents in Mycenaean Greek*, Cambridge: Cambridge University Press.

Verlinden, C. (1984) *Les statuettes anthropomorphes crétoises en bronze et en plomb du IIIe millènaire au VIIe siècle av. J.C.*, Providence, R.I.: Brown University, Center for Old World Archaeology and Art.

Vlachopoulos, A. (1998) 'Naxos and the Cyclades in the Late Helladic IIIC period', *BICS* 42: 237–8.

Vokotopoulos, L. (1998) 'Κάτω Κάστελλας, *Λενικά. Δυο οχυρές θέσεις της Ζάκρου*', *Κρητική Εστία* 6: 237–70.

Voutsaki, S. (1993) 'Society and culture in the Mycenaean world: an analysis of mortuary practices in the Argolid, Thessaly and the Dodecanese', PhD thesis, University of Cambridge.

—— (1995) 'Social and political processes in the Mycenaean Argolid: the evidence from the mortuary practices', in Laffineur and Niemeier 1995, 55–66.

—— (2001) 'Economic control, power and prestige in the Mycenaean world: the archaeological evidence', in Voutsaki and Killen 2001, ch. XIII.

—— and Killen, J. (eds) (2001) *Economy and Politics in the Mycenaean palace states*, Cambridge: Cambridge Philological Society.

Voyatzis, M.E. (1997) 'Illuminating the "Dark Age": an examination of the Early Iron Age pottery from Tegea', *AJA* 101: 349–50.

Walberg, G. (1998a) 'The excavations of the Midea megaron', *BICS* 42: 214–15.

—— (1998b) *Excavations on the acropolis of Midea, Vol. I:1. The excavations on the Lower Terraces 1985–1991*, Stockholm: Swedish Institute in Athens.

Waldbaum, J.C. (1980) 'The first archaeological appearance of iron and the transition to the Iron Age', in Wertime and Muhly 1980, ch. 3.

—— (1982) 'Bimetallic objects from the eastern Mediterranean and the question of the dissemination of iron', in Muhly *et al.* 1982, 325–47.

—— (1987) 'Copper, iron, tin, wood: the start of the Iron Age in the eastern Mediterranean' (summary), *AJA* 83: 285.

Wallace, S.A. (2000) 'Case studies of settlement change in Early Iron Age Crete', *Aegean Archaeology* 4: 61–99.

—— (2003a) 'The changing role of herding in the Early Iron Age of Crete: some implications of settlement shift for economy', *AJA* 107: 601–27.

—— (2003b) 'The perpetuated past: re-use or continuity in material culture and structuring of identity in Early Iron Age Crete', *BSA* 98: 251–77.

Walloe, L. (1999) 'Was the disruption of the Mycenean world caused by repeated epidemics of bubonic plague?', *OpAth* 24: 121–6.

Wardle, K.A. (1980) 'Excavations at Assiros, 1975–9', *BSA* 75: 229–67.

—— (1994) 'The palace civilizations of Minoan Crete and Mycenaean Greece 2000–1200 BC', in Cunliffe 1994, ch. 6.

—— (2000) (convener) 'Lighten our darkness: cultural transformations at the beginning of the first millennium BC – from the Alps to Anatolia', conference organised by the University of Birmingham and the British School at Athens, January 2000.

—— and Wardle, D. (2003) 'Prehistoric Thermon: pottery of the Late Bronze Age and Early Iron Age', in Kyparissi-Apostolika and Papakonstantinou 2003, 147–56.

Watrous, L.V. (1980) 'J.D.S. Pendlebury's excavations in the plain of Lasithi. The Iron Age sites', *BSA* 75: 269–83.

—— (1982) *Lasithi, a history of settlement on a highland plain in Crete, Hesperia* Supplement 18, Princeton: American School of Classical Studies at Athens.

—— (1996) *The cave sanctuary of Zeus at Psychro. A study of extra-urban sanctuaries in Minoan and Early Iron Age Crete*, Liège: University of Liège.

Wedde, M. (1999) 'War at sea: the Mycenaean and Early Iron Age oared galley', in Laffineur 1999, 465–76.

Wertime, T.A. (1983) 'The furnace versus the goat: the pyrotechnological industries and Mediterranean deforestation in antiquity', *JFA* 10: 445–52.

Wertime, T.A. and Muhly, J.D. (eds) (1980) *The coming of the age of iron*, New Haven and London: Yale University Press.

West, M.L. (1997) *The east face of Helicon: West Asiatic elements in Greek poetry and myth*, Oxford: Clarendon Press.

Whitelaw, T. (2001) 'Reading between the tablets: assessing Mycenaean palatial involvement in ceramic production and consumption', in Voutsaki and Killen 2001, ch. V.

Whitley, J. (1991b) 'Social diversity in Dark Age Greece', *BSA* 86: 341–65.

—— (2002) 'Objects with attitude: biographical facts and fallacies in the study of Late Bronze Age and Early Iron Age warrior graves', *CAJ* 12: 218–32.

Wright, J.C. (1994) 'The spatial configuration of belief: the archaeology of Mycenaean religion', in Alcock and Osborne 1994, ch. 3.

Wrigley, E.A. (1969) *Population and history*, London: Weidenfeld & Nicolson.

Xenaki-Sakellariou, A. (1985) *Οι θαλαμώτοι τάφοι των Μυκηνών ανασκαφής Χρ. Τσούντα*, Paris: Boccard.

Yalçın, Ü. (1999) 'Early iron metallurgy in Anatolia', *AS* 49: 177–87.

Yamagata, N. (1995) 'Ritual offerings in Homer and in Linear B', *SMEA* 35: 57–68.

Yasur-Landau, A. (2003) 'Why can't we find the origin of the Philistines? In search of the source of a peripheral Aegean culture', in Kyparissi-Apostolika and Papakonstantinou 2003, 587–98.

Zangger, E. (1994) 'Landscape changes around Tiryns during the Bronze Age', *AJA* 98: 189–212.

—— Timpson, M.E., Yazvenko, S.B., Kuhnke, F. and Knauss, J. (1997) 'The Pylos Regional Archaeological Project Part II: landscape evolution and site preservation', *Hesperia* 66: 549–641.

Zeimbekis, M. (1998) 'The typological forms and functions of animal figures from Minoan peak sanctuaries with special reference to Juktas and Kophinas', PhD thesis, University of Bristol.

INDEX

(Terms that appear very frequently, such as Aegean, Mycenaean, chronological terms (e.g. ninth century), and stylistic designations (e.g. PG) have not been listed, as too numerous and generally insignificant)

285

Made in United States
Orlando, FL
31 January 2022

14261397R00174